D0919865

# BEYOND ALL FRONTS

# Beyond All Fronts

*A Bystander's Notes
on This Thirty Years War*

by

MAX JORDAN

PROVIDENCE HEIGHTS
ALLISON PARK, PA.

*"For our wrestling is not against flesh and
blood, but against principalities and powers,
against the rulers of the world of this darkness,
against the spirits of wickedness in high
places."*

*Sixth Chapter of Ephesians.*

THE BRUCE PUBLISHING COMPANY
*Milwaukee*

This book is produced in full accord with the Government rules and regulations for the conservation of paper and other essential materials.

Copyright, 1944
The Bruce Publishing Company
Printed in the United States of America

For
Mother and Marianne
who suffered
and waited
and never gave up

# PROLOGUE

*T*HESE *pages are dedicated to the memory of the men and women who gave their lives in the most heroic of battles, on a field that stretches beyond all fronts, across all border lines — the battlefield of the European "Underground."*

*To all of them this book is dedicated in reverence — to the fearless patriots of Poland and Belgium — to the intrepid Czechs — to the indomitable new Vikings of Norway — to the dogged, unbending Danes and Dutch — to the fighting Maquis of France — to the undaunted guerillas of Greece and Yugoslavia — to the persecuted Christians and Jews who endured pain and grief in a measure that will arouse compassion to the end of time.*

*It is also dedicated to the "Underground" in the lands that first became victims of tyranny in this age of darkness — to the martyrs of freedom in Italy, Germany, and Austria. Their names, too, deserve to be inscribed on the roster of the brave.*

*The story of one, of just one, of these martyrs of whom we have heard so little up to now will be a part of this book — the story of Carl Goerdeler. The nazis claim to have executed him on September 11, 1944, linking him to a plot in which he had no part.*

*Once our armies of liberation have ripped apart the last barbed wire fences of totalitarian abomination many such tales will unfold themselves. They will not fit into preconceived patterns, but they will make the picture complete. The epic of the "Underground" will ultimately involve both friend and foe.*

*Then we will realize that long before Gestapo heels tramped savagely all over an enslaved continent, over soil drenched with innocent blood, long before Lidice and Majdanek, the despots had used their own people as guinea pigs to try out the monstrosities which soon they were to inflict a hundredfold on the nations they set out to crush.*

*While misguided appeasers were still doing business with Hitler, these early champions of the resistance movement faced their oppressors almost single-handed, suffering mental and physical agonies in torture chambers and concentration camps. They were humiliated, abased, disgraced, outlawed, beaten to death, garroted, beheaded — but never broken, never defeated.*

*Along with the heroes of Warsaw, the Maquis, and all the others who helped pave the road to victory — and let us hope to a better world — we should remember the Goerdelers and their kin. If we do, we will, perhaps, this time plan the peace a little more wisely, a little more humanely, a little more stably. Then the sacrifices of all the "undergrounds" will not have been in vain, and the peace may be won — beyond all fronts!*

# INTRODUCTION

THIS book is to serve two purposes.

In the first place, I hope that in making the readers fully aware of the inter-relation between World Wars I and II it will encourage them to seek the causes behind the causes of World War II.

And I trust that in sharing with me some of the experiences I have had in these two wars, my readers will find, as I have found, that there is always light where there is darkness. In the Psalmist's words: "Even the night is as the day to the Lord."

As for the first scope, I do not believe we can appreciate sufficiently the causes and implications of the present conflict unless we understand that it really started back in 1914 and has been going on ever since.

The peace of 1919 was but a truce. Although it lasted two decades, there was no abatement of hate. The war went on all the while with undiminished bitterness. The only difference was in weapons — now they were politics and economics, then they were guns and shells. Finally, after the "test wars" of Spain and Ethiopia, the powers of hell broke loose again. There had never been peace.

If in charting a river from the estuary to the source we were to stop half way, we could hardly describe its whole course. Likewise, to locate its origins and to understand its full meaning, the stream of blood and tears which has engulfed this generation must be charted not only up to 1933 when the evil flood of naziism entered the European watershed, but back to 1918, or even 1914, and as much further as may be necessary if a well-rounded, rather than a limited perspective of the whole tragedy is to be gained.

In telling the story of this thirty years war as I have observed it, my incidental, though not secondary, purpose will come to light. I can sum it up in the words of Oliver Cromwell, who said at one time, while addressing a group of people who would not see eye to eye with him: "I beseech you, in the bowels of Christ, think it possible you may be mistaken!"

I must say that the older I grew — and I am near the fifty mark now where true wisdom is said to begin! — the humbler I became. Often I would find issues clearly defined, but battle fronts seemed to cut through all party lines and all boundaries. In this war, too, we have a clear issue, but its protagonists are in both belligerent camps, and in both we encounter forces making for selfishness and oppression.

I do not think we can expect real progress in bringing the world to sanity unless we accept the basic fact that human nature is immutable in its potentials, for good and for bad, and that irrespective of creed, color, or nationality, it is the same everywhere throughout the ages. Because we are all human we are greatly in need of God's mercy. Only in the spiritual brotherhood of humanity can there be real peace, and the Lord has no step-children.

\* \* \*

Soon Europe will have another armistice. Whether this time it will lead to a real peace is the question this book attempts to raise with as much emphasis as the writer is able to command.

These past thirty years do not leave much room for optimism. The record is certainly not one of which to be proud. Looking back we can see how the tragedy of this war could have been averted. For their failure to prevent it, all nations share in the blame, though not all in the same degree, and many by omission rather than by commission.

Too little and too late is the theme which runs through the whole cruelly cacophonous gamut of the two world conflicts. Too little the courage, too late applied when the rudder might have been thrown to a course of sanity, into placid waters and away from menacing clouds. Too little the understanding, too late asserted, of the dreadful reserves in the dark arsenals of the human race where the explosives of cold hate and exacerbated prejudice are piled up for our destruction. Too little cooperation of the forces of charity and justice because everybody distrusted everybody else. Too late the realization that only the solidarity of civilized nations maintained by a spirit of give and take can prevent relapses into jungle and caveman eras where everyone looks out only for himself and no one wants to be his brother's keeper.

The whole world now pays a heavy price for the errors of the past. Only after tremendous sacrifices can we hope once more to shut the gate of war. To have kept it shut would have been child's play, had the lovers of peace but closed the ranks before it was thrust open by brutes and bullies. There will always be war-mongers. It is for us to keep them in check.

Despite the dreams of technologists it would be folly to expect a golden age of universal harmony and bliss, simply because a great deal of planning is being done and helicopters may replace the family car. Plans are made by human beings and they must be applied to human beings. Their value is bound to be relative. The millennium is not around the corner, no matter what idealistic and superficial reformers may say. When the war is behind us, this world will be pretty much the same as before with all its aptitudes for better or for worse. Humanity is not fashioned to raise its head above the clouds by its own strength. Whether we stand on our heads or on our feet, we remain the same creatures, frail and limited in our understanding.

*  *  *

A few of my associates will come in for due praise in this book. Many others should have been mentioned. Very warm thanks I owe in particular to my friend, Dr. George N. Shuster, President of Hunter College, and to Miss Jennie Hirsch, of Rutherford, N. J., for valuable advice. To Mrs. Marie H. Doyle, of New York and to Dom William Michael Ducey, O.S.B., I am grateful for painstaking editorial assistance. I also wish to express my appreciation to the newspaper, magazine, and book publishers who allowed me to quote so liberally from the writings of their authors, editors, and correspondents.

In conclusion, may I add that there is no fiction in this book. However, in some instances, and for the sake of those concerned, I have found it necessary to conceal the true identity of names and places, to reverse the chronological order, and to incorporate oral reports in the form of letters.

In telling of my experiences and observations, I hope I have succeeded in bringing to light a few lessons of the past — dispassionately.

M. J.

Orienta Point
Mamaroneck, N. Y.
November 5, 1944

# CONTENTS

Page

PROLOGUE . . . . . . . . . . . . vii
INTRODUCTION . . . . . . . . . . . ix

## PART I

## TRAGIC PRELUDE

CHAPTER
1. Precarious Democracy . . . . . . . . 3
2. "America Is Better Off" . . . . . . 22
3. The Brown Earthquake . . . . . . . 29
4. "An Expensive Experiment" . . . . . . 42
5. The Down-Hill Race . . . . . . . 53

## PART II

## GERMANY ENSLAVED

6. Cataracts of Evil . . . . . . . . 69
7. Blitzkrieg at Home . . . . . . . . 81
8. Collapse of the Intellect . . . . . . 94
9. Appeasement Is Born . . . . . . . 113
10. The Anti-Christ . . . . . . . . 123
11. The Gruesome Hoax . . . . . . . 135
12. Defiance Wins . . . . . . . . . 144
13. A People Blindfolded . . . . . . . 164

## PART III

## THE HOLOCAUST

14. The Second Victim . . . . . . . . 183
15. A Shaky Axis . . . . . . . . . 198
16. The Folly of Munich . . . . . . . 212

xiii

# CONTENTS

CHAPTER     Page

17. Black-Out of Peace . . . . . . . . 226
18. There Were Two Fronts . . . . . . 240
19. The Norway Coup . . . . . . . . 256
20. Avalanche in the West . . . . . . 276
21. The Inside Angle . . . . . . . . 282
22. None Could Escape . . . . . . . . 296

PART IV

## TWILIGHT OF THE GODS

23. Why So Helpless? . . . . . . . . 311
24. The Lights Are Out . . . . . . . 313
25. Let's Not Ape Them . . . . . . . 317
26. "Now I Have Seen . . ." . . . . . 319
27. Satan's Passport . . . . . . . . 321
28. Poor People . . . . . . . . . . 325
29. The Way Is Charity . . . . . . . 327
30. Which War Next? . . . . . . . . 329
31. Beyond All Fronts . . . . . . . . 334

PART V

## PRIMER OF PEACE

32. The Great Challenge . . . . . . . 341
33. The Only Answer . . . . . . . . 350
34. The Crossroads — This Time . . . . 356
Epilogue . . . . . . . . . . . . 360
Appendix I: Lessons of the Past . . . . . 363
Appendix II: The Part for the Whole . . . . 366
Appendix III: Prussians and Germans . . . . 371
Appendix IV: Patterns for Tomorrow . . . . 373
Appendix V: "And So We Resolve Again" —
      by David Lawrence . . . . . 379

# PART I
## TRAGIC PRELUDE

*"We have our share of responsibility for the
nazi phenomenon."
(Sir Norman Angell, "For What We Fight,"
New York, Harper Bros., 1939, p. 3.)*

# PART I.
## TRAGIC PRELUDE

"We have our share of responsibility for the

# Chapter 1

## PRECARIOUS DEMOCRACY

THE GERMAN newspaperman with whom I was dining on September 14, 1930, in Bombay, British India, excused himself in the middle of the meal to put through a telephone call.

"I must keep in touch with our news agency," he explained. "This is election night, you know. I want them to give me a ring as soon as results come in from Berlin."

Results did come in later in the evening. My friend emerged pale and nervous from the hotel's telephone booth. I had known him in Washington and when we started our conversation that night, he was anxious to hear all about his friends in America. But now he was evidently not at ease.

"One hundred and seven Reichstag seats for the nazis," he reported when he returned to our table. "Five million votes for Hitler out of thirty-five million cast. It's a landslide!"

I did not immediately fathom the import of the news. Europe seemed far away. Since leaving Washington in the Spring of 1930 my interest had been focused on problems of Asia and Australasia. For several months I had traveled all over the Pacific area, and I had just been telling my dinner partner of my impressions.

To me it seemed that the age of colonial expansion was fast drawing to a close. Industrialization was beginning to cause the same reaction among the masses of China, Japan, and Malaya which it had caused in Europe before the last war. The spirit of adventure and conquest of the great explorers had opened up immense territories to European enterprise. Mighty empires had been built with bravery and endurance, but greed and selfishness were motive powers of equal force.

Nations are not unlike individuals. They often fail to realize the responsibility involved in ownership until they lose what

3

they have not deserved to possess. Although the pattern of
the past is spread out before our eyes, every generation, like
every individual apparently must go through the same basic
cycle of experience. Amidst the powerful stream of historical
destiny human nature never changes. Progress does not follow
a straight, vertical line. There are relapses into the horizontal
plane more frequently than we like to admit.

"Is not this German election a case in point?" said my
Bombay friend, again taking up the conversation. "For almost
ten years I have seen this coming. Europe is like a sick old
man. The peace treaties of 1919 did not cure him. The formulas of Versailles were inadequate. The war is still on. I fear
it will grow worse."

Soon I left the Orient. Coming up from Egypt and Pales-
tine, I crossed Turkey and the Balkans. Budapest was my first
stop in Central Europe. Then came Vienna; not much later
Berlin.

I had been away six years and it was difficult to settle down
again in this city which had always impressed me as stimulating and breezy, but also as overgrown and bare of the patina
of tradition. During the four years I had spent there after the
war I had longed for warmer climes; warmer physically, but
also warmer in human qualities — such as the German south.

My parents had come from Wuerttemberg and there were
both Austrian and French ancestors in the family. My dear
mother who was a convinced idealist, always yearned for the
good and the true, no matter where it could be found. As a
young girl, reading about it, she had visualized Italy as the
fulfillment of her dreams. Certain that she would go there
some day, she learned Italian. My father too, had been gifted
with wanderlust. As a young chemist, soon after finishing
college, he secured a job in Florence. Returning home, he
found his bride-to-be of one mind with him, and they set out
for the Riviera on their wedding trip. Mother's dowry was
just sufficient to buy a pharmacy in San Remo, so they decided
to settle down amidst the orange groves. I could not have
wished for a more attractive birthplace.

Soon my father became connected with the Eastman Kodak
Company — which gave me the first inkling of fabulous America — and opened branches for them in various cities of Italy

and Switzerland. Thus from my boyhood on I became a
traveler. My father would take the family along to Venice, to
Interlaken, to St. Moritz, and once in a while we would all
pay a little vacation visit to grandmother in Stuttgart. Ours
were genuinely democratic Swabian traditions, and seeing so
much of the world in my carefree youth, I soon became confirmed in them myself. Mother was pleased by it. In our
formative years she never missed an opportunity to instill, in
my younger brother and myself, an appreciation of tolerance
and international understanding.

Having attended school in three different countries, by the
time I reached my teens, I was able to carry on in French,
German, Italian and sundry dialects. To me the world was
vast and beautiful and intriguing. In Italy I had learned of
Mazzini and Garibaldi, of the poets and thinkers who paved
the way for a national revival based on the conviction that all
men are equal before their Creator. In Switzerland I was imbued with ideals of political freedom as upheld throughout
the heroic history of that country. So it was natural that at the
age of seventeen I joined the German youth movement enthusiastically when in 1912 we had moved to Stuttgart, capital
of Wuerttemberg, because my father, not having been too fortunate with his foreign business, wanted to establish new contacts in his old home town.

There were two factions at the Stuttgart High School to
which I was transferred — those who favored the youth movement, and those who were opposed to it. The opponents
reveled in flag-waving, and thought our group was much too
rebellious. But we "rebels" rather gloried in the feeling of
being martyrs for the cause of freedom. Forming "underground cells," and furtively passing around mimeographed
blueprints to reform society, we debated ardently all the time
on how to free the world of stuffy militarists and sabre-rattling
jingos.

I remember how on "Kaiser's birthday" I ran into trouble.
There were glittering parades with brass-bands galore, and
goose-stepping much too rigid to suit me.

"All nonsense," I remarked to a classmate disrespectfully.
"Just a show for the 'All-highest!'"

The boy was more patriotic than I had ever been. He re-

ported me to the principal, and I was given a moral spanking.
"If it happens again," said the professor sternly, "I will have
to report you to the police, for this is lese majesty!"

The war of 1914–1918 did not succeed in blotting out German pre-war liberalism. The youth movement was kept alive.
Those who were part of it could not forget the lofty idealism which had spurred it on. Only temporarily their hopes
were drowned in the turmoil of a disastrous war.

For half a century explosive issues had been smouldering
under the surface of Europe's body politic which was torn
asunder by alliances and coalitions, all in arms one against the
other. Secret diplomacy helped to set up military systems that
eventually were bound to clash.

Today in the books of history we find that by and large,
governments absorbed by fear, were caught by surprise in the
sudden tide, confused by the cross-purposes of power-politics
and overwhelmed by the emotional forces suddenly unleashed
in all camps. None of the rulers really wanted war, but everyone played with fire, fanning the flame regardless of the interests of the common people. From the German angle it had
seemed as though the country was being "encircled," the victim of a huge plot. The Berlin propagandists put this thought
across so cleverly that the German rank and file became convinced they had to fight a defensive war.

The younger people had no choice. They took their government's orders, donned uniforms and marched to the fronts.
Soon they were being mowed down by the thousands. Only
after the first reverses on the Marne did the survivors stop to
think. Back home pan-German agitators seized the opportunity
to reveal their true motives of conquest and annexation, but
the democratic groups took issue with them. In the midst of
the battles, the home front split.

At that time, the press had relative freedom, and there was
a parliament to give vent to complaints. The Kaiser could be
held to account. Budgets had to be approved by the representatives of the people, who by 1917 were becoming increasingly
hesitant to back the war-lords. Unlike twenty years later, under
Hitler, the political party organizations remained intact. Labor
was still a factor that could not be ignored, and even amongst

the more gullible university youth, patriotic catch-phrases did not crush independent thinking altogether.

Soon the popular enthusiasm for what had first appeared as a just war began to wane. There was outspoken criticism of the government. Few could understand why the peace move of Pope Benedict XV had been disregarded. Easy victory was not at hand, and the British blockade was so effective that the people suffered cruelly. In the second winter of the war, while I was attending Frankfort University as a student of philosophy, turnips were the staple food. Workers and their families were without enough to eat. Housewives were grumbling. The military was exacting the last energies of the people, and there was a limit to their endurance. When the collapse came, Germany's dead numbered almost two million, while her casualties were nearly 65 per cent of the total mobilization.

The people were not to blame for the defeat. They had undergone the privations and sufferings of four long years. Neither was a lack of fighting spirit the cause of the German surrender. The power-drunk military had aimed wide of the mark, and underestimated their opponents. They pretended that "the Americans could neither fly nor swim," and in their quest of "total" victory brazenly refused every opportunity for an honorable peace.

By the time the German fronts in France began to crack, Bulgaria, Turkey and Austria had capitulated. Mutinies in the German navy increased. The people had had enough. They knew the outlook was hopeless. They were not interested in conquests. The soldiers wanted to return home, the sooner the better, while those at home could not wait to be delivered from the military grip, to be free again to lead their own lives. When General Ludendorff informed the Kaiser, on August 8, 1918 that "the war must be ended," the masses were near the point of exhaustion, weary of fighting, distrustful of their leaders.

The revolution of 1918 was violent only in spots. Throughout the land people were glad the war was over. With the Kaiser a fugitive, the nation's liberal elements immediately set out to revive the nobler traditions of the past, traditions which the younger generation had upheld with such brave determination, although many of them had been slaughtered on the battlefields. Their spirit, which was the spirit of the pre-war youth movement, the spirit of democracy, still survived. It was at the same time the spirit of the Weimar republic, the spirit of a new and better Germany which gave hope and courage for the future.

After graduation from Jena University — happily, I had received my Ph.D. diploma at the hands of the venerable Rudolf Eucken, the pace-maker of modern idealistic thought and former Harvard exchange professor — I returned to Stuttgart to prepare for an academic career. The city had long been a center of democracy. I knew Robert Bosch, the self-made industrialist, one of the foremost pioneers of social reform in pre-war Europe. He had gathered a group of men around him who were utterly opposed to militarism in every shape and form. Throughout the state, traditions of freedom were vigorously upheld even in the midst of the war.

On the eve of the revolution, November 8, 1918, Otto Weltin, an engineer of the Bosch group, had asked me to dinner at his home which nestled in the hills overlooking the lovely town.

"The socialists will be marching along Koenig Street in the morning," he said.

"But the military have guns mounted all around the city," I observed.

"They won't shoot," answered Weltin coolly. "They know their time is up."

The next morning the workers marched down the main street unmolested. They gathered on the Schlossplatz, listened to some speeches, sang the *Internationale,* and went home for lunch. Some skirmishes flared up in the suburbs, mostly between communists and socialists, but soon quiet was restored.

In other parts of the country, in Berlin, Kiel, and the industrial districts trouble was more severe, but the issue lay between radicals and moderates. The few who hoped the Kaiser would come back were too frightened to open their mouths. I went around with my Stuttgart friends to address mass meetings, and to organize democratic action groups. Grandma was shocked:

"You may get in the papers," she warned me with a shudder. And I did!

It was the call of freedom that now rang out unimpeded. All of us in the democratic movement felt we were torch-bearers of a new age. We knew that once the military yoke was thrown off, the nation would assert itself. For the first time in years it had won the right to speak freely. Because the people wanted it, democracy finally won out.

Few remember today that powerful impulse, the strength of which was demonstrated on January 19, 1919. By votes freely given, the people elected 358 Reichstag deputies supporting the new democratic order as against 34 openly hostile to it. Twenty out of the twenty-five millions of ballots cast in the subsequent election of June 8, 1920 were in support of the democratic regime.

Certainly, these twenty million voters were not all camouflaged, potential nazis! So little of the militaristic spirit was alive in them that even twelve years later, at the presidential election in April, 1932, Hitler polled no more than 36.8 per cent of the popular vote in spite of the many circumstances in his favor. About a year later, and shortly after his accession to power, he had only 142 out of a total of 477 Reichstag members under his immediate control, not counting the 81 communist and 26 socialist deputies whom he had put in jail.

However, the young democracy which emerged from the country's defeat in 1918 was struggling precariously. Progressive elements were making an almost superhuman effort to consolidate the new regime, but they were fighting against heavy odds.

After the collapse, while desperation engulfed the country, the defeated military, the privileged land-owner class, and the heavy industry magnates who had been the sponsors of all-out conquest, chose to escape responsibility by hiding in what the democratic press aptly called "their rat holes." The opportunity to tell the people the full truth about the causes and consequences of the war was unique, but the democratic leaders, in mistaken patriotism, missed it. Their lack of determination made it possible for the reactionary forces to gather new strength. Friedrich Ebert, Joseph Wirth, and Walter Rathenau

were among those at the helm of the republic. They represented a non-militaristic and peace-minded Germany. The
politicians who had caused a national disaster by their reckless
policies would have none of it.

The Weimar regime had barely come to life when the deposed chieftains of the old order concocted the legend of a
"stab in the back of the German fighting front." The democratic elements were said to have committed high treason
while victory for the Kaiser's armies was almost within grasp.
The warlords and the steel barons could not bear the thought
of losing their prerogatives. They dreamed of a revival of the
"old glories" of the Reich, and hoped to punish the "traitors"
of the Fatherland, the "marxists" and the "peace-mongers"
when the tide would turn again. By hiding arms and training
"home guards" they were preparing secretly for that day of
reckoning and revenge. Fretting under the humiliation of
defeat they had to find an alibi.

The vicious opposition of this unscrupulous camarilla of
vested interests, which scoffed at the parliamentary system and
laughed at those who believed in the rights and the dignity of
all men, to whom democracy was a sham and contrary to
Germanic conceptions, made life miserable for the new
leaders. The balky forces of the old order were holding forth
stubbornly against the new rulers who were striving in all
sincerity to revert to the traditions of 1849, when after Napoleon's downfall, the national assembly at St. Paul's Cathedral
in Frankfort adopted black, red and gold as the colors of a
united Germany.

I met quite a few of these men and women who were instru-
mental in inculcating a new idealism into the nation. At Weimar, in 1919, they had framed a constitution shaped after the
model of Philadelphia. They were sons and daughters of the
people who had come up from the ranks. All were motivated
by a high sense of civic responsibility, and by a passionate de-
votion to the ideal of social justice.

Through seven turbulent years Friedrich Ebert, first chief
executive of the young republic, struggled valiantly. During
that whole period the Hugenbergs, the Ludendorffs, the Thyssens never missed an opportunity to "smear" him. To the
landed aristocracy of the East, to the military — with a few

notable exceptions — and to the steel barons, Ebert was "just a saddler," a workman who had climbed the political ladder, wholly unworthy of being the Kaiser's successor.

Ebert did pretty well under the circumstances. He was a typical member of the social democratic party which had been so tame that the more radical socialists established themselves as an independent unit. When the republic came to life in 1918, the extremists, at first, gained almost complete control. Communistic tendencies were strong and Germany might easily have gone to pieces in the throes of radicalism.

It was this internecine warfare among the labor groups which provided the first excuse for the military adventurers to force their way back into the picture. After the chaotic days of 1918 the "red peril" was a dreaded reality throughout Central Europe. The experiences in Munich and Budapest particularly, where communist fanatics had ruled during blood-stained intervals of civil war, had left their mark. Under the pretext that they were indispensable in suppressing leftist uprisings, the future hitlerites banded together, forming "free corps" and "brigades" which were to become the forerunners of counter-revolution. Blindly the extremists of the left played into the hands of their deadliest foes, by sabotaging the democratic government.

The victors did not appreciate the severity of the struggle behind this German factionalism. They were inclined to conceive of it as a bluff, not realizing that the moderates who had come out on top in Berlin were hard pressed by domestic enemies on the right and on the left, and badly in need of support.

* * *

The necessity of making a living had caused me to be sidetracked in my academic ambitions. Early in 1920, after a trip to Italy on behalf of a press feature syndicate, I joined the staff of the *Berliner Tageblatt,* one of the leading German newspapers the nazis were later to suppress because of its militant democratic spirit. I had been one of its contributors ever since my college days, and I felt proud that Theodor Wolff, one of the great editors of our times, was now my boss. When he let me write my first editorial, and use my own by-line I thought I had established my fame for posterity!

Berlin, in those years, was a strange place to me. It was a city, heterogenous in its social structure and yet fascinatingly dynamic. Berliners are known for their sense of humor, but the official world was austere, and academic life, centered around the university and various colleges, rather rigid. After the revolution great intellectual activity was manifest, and people were taking themselves much too seriously.

In the governmental press conferences some of us younger men openly spoke our mind. There was no Gestapo to arrest us, and I enjoyed the word battles immensely. Wolfgang Kapp's ill-fated attempt to overthrow the democratic regime had been thwarted by a general strike of labor, and we newspaper people were vigorously denouncing the would-be-tyrants, in the very building which was to become Goebbels' headquarters.

In my spare hours I carried on at the university. Philosophy of religion was my favorite field. One of the teachers who impressed me deeply was Romano Guardini, an Italian whose parents had emigrated to Silesia. He had gone to German schools, and become a priest and educator. Upholding high ethical standards and wielding a tremendous influence for good, he played a leading part in the youth movement from its very inception. His sincerity and zeal won the hearts of the younger generation.

After the war Guardini was asked to take over a chair at Berlin University — an unprecedented move for this high seat of predominantly Protestant learning, but indicative of the attitude of post-war Germany toward Catholicism. The young intelligentsia crowded Guardini's classroom. This sincere thinker, with his ascetic features, was to them a living embodiment of Roman tradition and Germanic learning. His message was inspired from the depths of Christian faith. Its fervor shone like a beacon-light in the midst of political chaos.

Many were badly in need of such guidance, for it was not easy to reconcile the professed intentions of the new leaders with the realities of defeat. French and British military control commissions were sitting in Berlin. The Kaiser was gone, and the colors of democracy were flying over his castle, but Germany's former enemies still insisted on the letter of the treaties of peace.

Was Germany really bent on evading her obligations? Poincaré and Maginot and Tardieu and all the other die-hard nationalists in Paris were convinced of it while the Berlin government insisted that the treaty had been imposed under duress and that many of its stipulations could not be lived up to, no matter how good their intentions were.

The first serious difficulties arose when the French claimed that German coal deliveries due under the terms of Versailles were in arrears. Both the American observer, Roland W. Boyden, and the British representatives in the Reparations Commission opposed the use of force. Nevertheless, France decided on January 11, 1923 to apply "sanctions."

French troops, 100,000 of them, including African contingents, entered the Ruhr region and parts of the Rhineland, occupying all the mines and such important centers as Essen, Duisburg, Gelsenkirchen and Karlsruhe. Serious disorders and bloodshed occurred in various towns. Pope Pius XI urged the French to moderate their course, but he was rebuked. Thousands of people were driven from their homes. Prison sentences were meted out wholesale by French military courts. Newspapers were suppressed.

Mine owners were arrested and court-martialed because they refused deliveries, in compliance with the orders of the Berlin government. "Passive resistance" had been decreed and a wave of genuine patriotism swept the country. The Cuno cabinet, which preceded Stresemann's, found itself supported by a united home front, from the extreme right to the extreme left. The workers went on strike against the French. Rail traffic and river navigation stopped.

In those days Leo Schlageter, a retired young army officer, blew up a railway track between Duesseldorf and Duisburg in order to hamper French movements. He was caught and executed and the nazis, who later on were to denounce as saboteurs the patriots in Norway and Czechoslovakia and France, raised him to the rank of a martyr of freedom. There were to be Schlageters by the thousands among Hitler's victims.

*     *     *

During the French occupation of the Ruhr district, German

democracy suffered a severe blow. The cause of extreme nationalism could not have been served more effectively by its German adherents than by Poincaré and his army. The army was withdrawn in the late Fall of 1923, but a few weeks afterwards Hitler was able to stage his abortive Munich *putsch*.

While the nazi storm was brewing I made my rounds of Embassies and Legations as a diplomatic correspondent, attended press conferences, and looked in on Reichstag sessions, scanning the political horizon all along for an honest-to-goodness "scoop."

One dreary Saturday afternoon in the Spring of 1922, what seemed a minor item came across my desk. George Tchitcherin, Soviet Foreign Minister had arrived in Berlin. He was on his way to Genoa where he was to attend an international diplomatic conference, the first one since the Bolshevik revolution at which Russia was to be represented.

I called the big hotels and found that Tchitcherin had registered at the Esplanade. Whether the week-end had caught my competitors off guard, or the name had not been familiar to them, I do not know. But the next day I had my front-page scoop consisting of an exclusive interview with the Soviet official, who was the first one in five years to cross the Russian border and to re-establish contact with the western world.

Tchitcherin was easy to approach. He received me without much ado and told me all I wanted to know. Here, then, was one of those Bolsheviks that was depicted with long whiskers and high boots in newspaper cartoons! But Tchitcherin was an aristocrat of old lineage, one who moved with perfect ease in that bourgeois atmosphere which his government considered the embodiment of all evil. Instead of saluting me with a clenched fist, as I had almost expected he would, he offered me a cigarette. So I "went to town" and applied the technique of "Information, please!" without any further restraint.

The statements I obtained were important in that they gave notice that Soviet Russia had no intention of remaining in splendid isolation behind her borders, but insisted on having her share in the councils of the world. The interview was the forerunner of the Rapallo agreement, which shortly afterwards was signed by German and Russian representatives. It came as a bomb-shell to the other governments because it established

Germany's determination to regain her own initiative in the international field.

Monday morning I had a call from Karl von Wiegand, chief of the Hearst editorial staff in Europe. He wanted me to have tea with him that afternoon. For a young reporter this was quite a distinction, as Wiegand's reputation had been sky-high ever since his great journalistic "firsts" in the last war, when through his brilliant interviews with the great and near-great he revealed their minds to the world.

Wiegand was impressed by my scoop and wanted to have a look at me. It was the beginning of a real friendship — and the preliminary to an important turning point of my life.

"Let's keep in touch from now on," said Wiegand. "Once in a while we might do some trading."

First, I was just a "tipster" to Karl, but soon our contacts became fairly regular, and he appointed me as his full-time assistant. One of my first assignments in the new job was to report the trial of Hitler.

I went to Munich for the trial. In the Bavarian capital, Ludendorff, the future "Fuehrer's" fellow conspirator, was out on bail. I called on him at his home in a suburban community of Munich. There was nothing martial about him any longer. He wore a tweed suit and short breeches. While we sat talking in the parlor, a huge police dog rested at his feet.

The former quartermaster general was full of scorn for those in power. To me it seemed as though he had all the pent up bitterness of a man unable to take a defeat. He was to a large extent responsible for Germany's undoing in 1918, but would not admit it, not even to himself. His rancor carried him away, making him lose all sense of proportion. No other explanation could be offered for his decision to associate himself with Hitler in staging a humbug march through the streets of Munich, a march which ended in a miserable collapse. Sixteen nazis were killed, an event glorified into national importance, later on, by the hitlerites.

"I will be acquitted," Ludendorff told me defiantly.

"But how about Hitler?"

Ludendorff made a gesture as though that were of no interest.

"He'll look out for himself."

And abruptly he added:

"You can tell them over there (he meant America) that I am not giving up. I will fight to my last breath!"

It seems almost incredible that all that mockery in the Munich courtroom was staged on a wrong premise: The reactionaries accused the democratic government of weakness in dealing with disorders caused by communist rebels who had set up independent governments in Saxony and Thuringia, and had staged serious riots in Hamburg. A red army stood in the Ruhr, and a separatist movement was gaining momentum in the Rhineland. Ludendorff, Hitler, and their Bavarian followers pretended they had to save the country from the "reds," but before they were even organized, the Berlin authorities had successfully squelched the revolts.

As a Hearst correspondent I sat on the front bench of the courtroom in the heavily guarded Bavarian war college when Hitler was asked to state his case. The date was February 26, 1924, nine years before his advent to power. The future dictator wore a black cutaway and striped trousers. The iron cross was his only decoration. There were no "heils" in those days, but the nazi leader thundered with a self-assurance that was almost visionary, pleading for what he frankly termed a "ruthless, brutal fascism."

Apparently, the court agreed with him that fascism was the proper treatment for Germany's ills, for they sentenced him to what amounted to a pleasant vacation in the fortress of Landsberg on the Lech, affording him all the leisure to write (or rather sketch, for the actual writing was not his) *Mein Kampf,* and to plot his cruel revolution.

\*    \*    \*

There was only one hope to stave the rising tide of nationalism that was a *rapprochement,* a closer cooperation between France and Germany. I remember how I discussed this with Gustav Stresemann at a dinner party not long after Hitler's Munich coup.

The stout, jovial foreign minister who was then guiding German destinies had formerly been of nationalistic convictions himself, but the lesson of the war had not been lost on him and his views had broadened by experience.

"Remember," said Stresemann, in a pleasant vein, "that Goethe, Germany's greatest poet, scoffed at Napoleon and denounced his dreams of world domination. To me Goethe is the symbol of the true Germany, the Germany of literary, artistic and scientific achievement which must make its contribution to human progress."

"But why," I objected, "has this true Germany such a hard time in asserting itself within its own borders? Why is it that the trouble-makers so frequently gain the upper hand?"

The question seemed to elicit a deep response in Stresemann, and quickly he retorted:

"Because we and the French have not yet found a way to maintain the proper balance in our relationship! As long as we quarrel it will always be to the trouble-makers' profit — in both camps."

"Will the quarrels ever end?" I asked.

"I know what you mean, and you remind me of Jules Cambon, the French ambassador. When he left Berlin at the outbreak of the last war, Cambon said that there will be an armed conflict between France and Germany every forty or fifty years because in that period the generation which has witnessed the horrors of the last war will have passed away."

"So far, events have borne him out, haven't they?"

"So far, yes. But why should it always be so? I disagree with the calamity-howlers. I see no reason for periodically recurring bloodshed. My hope is for a lasting peace in the spirit of Goethe's *Weltbuergertum,* of a citizenry of the world which may some day lead to a united Europe, to a new comity of nations upholding their cultural rather than their military traditions."

About a year later Briand and Stresemann met in Locarno, idyllic sea-side resort on the shore of *Lago Maggiore.* Together, aboard the vessel "Orange Blossom," they solemnly initialled the treaties which were to open a new era of peace. Here was a supreme effort to reconcile the dynamism of restless Germany with the determination of France to leave unchanged at least the frame-work of the Versailles treaty.

But the differences between the two countries were too profound to be bridged by mere rhapsodies. They were rooted in their social structures. The natural self-sufficiency of the French people and the expansive tendencies of the Germans clamoring for *Lebensraum* found expression in an instinctive antagonism. Basically, it was a question of centripetalism against centrifugalism. Ever since Germany had attained national unity in 1871, her population had been on the increase. That of France, for decades, had remained quite stationary. Other European countries doubled their population figures while France maintained an almost constant level of forty million. During that whole period both England and Germany were forced to develop their home industries and to push their export trade vigorously. Beyond territorial expansion there was no other means to provide employment for their growing populations.

Efforts to bridge the gap and to find a way out of the dismal maze of national prejudices had been made incessantly. While economic cooperation between France and Germany, for a time, was quite successful, distrust of Germany's political ambitions halted all truly comprehensive efforts. Thus, despite frequent good-will moves of farseeing leaders in both countries, the pessimism of Jules Cambon seemed distressingly justified.

Stresemann died before he could accomplish his mission. He died of a broken heart on October 3, 1929. His own party, and the intransigent nationalists, had doggedly opposed his "pacifism." His very patriotism was questioned, because he was a good European. On the other hand, the French never seemed to believe that he was sincere. After the failures of the postwar conferences of Spa, San Remo, Cannes, and Genoa, the meeting of Locarno had been the first one where victors and vanquished dealt as equals with each other. But the "Tories" in Paris as well as in Berlin laughed at the Locarno treaties. They obstructed both Briand's and Stresemann's moves which were planned with the hope of burying the hatchet between the two countries. Recalcitrant "die-hards" on both sides of the fence were stronger than the friends of peace. Soon Locarno was a dream of the past. Resentment grew. The two camps no longer even made an attempt to speak the same language.

Wiegand had foreseen it all.

"Don't put too much stock in the panegyrics of the politicians," he warned me. "They all must cater to popular favor, but in the end it's the impact of economic pressure which

determines their moves. It will be so in the case of Franco-German relations, too."

A practical demonstration of this theory was soon to be provided. I was now earning a dollar salary. It meant my promotion to the rank of a millionaire in paper marks. As a newspaperman I had first had an income of 150 Marks a month, but they multiplied to some 300 millions, three years later when monetary inflation was at its peak. It was a vortex of figures suddenly turning a whole nation topsy-turvy. When you have to pay a million-odd for an ordinary street-car token or a newspaper, and five million for a ham sandwich, all sense of stability is upset, and the trouble-makers have a carnival.

In those days Americans in Germany had to be careful not to be caught in the downward plunge of the Mark. They did their best to hold on to their dollars and to leave the billions to the Reichsbank, but it was often enough a catch-as-catch-can proposition between morning and afternoon hours. Whoever did not have the proper hunch was bound to be a loser in the whirl of millions of paper notes. The scramble was really maddening when in the course of one year the dollar exchange rate rose from 8350 to 4.2 trillion Reich Marks. All sense of monetary value was lost. Savings, mortgages, bank accounts and capital stock investments were wiped out like get-rich-quick gold mine shares.

In the midst of this sudden feast of billions and trillions everything seemed within reach — provided one had dollars. I myself was nurturing high hopes. Distrusting the banks, I bought a portable miniature safe with a battery alarm. In it rested my precious savings — 76 dollars! By the time I had a hundred, I thought I could retire. When the battery failed to function, and someone broke into my desk and almost stole the hidden treasure, I knew something of the worries of a nabob!

Toward the end of 1923 a halt was finally called, and the brakes were put on by the creation of new currency. There was no longer much to be salvaged. Millions of modest fortunes had gone overboard. The big fellows had made huge profits, but the middle-class people, the small land-owners, the retired annuity holders and life insurance beneficiaries were all suddenly landed on the steps of the poor-house. Later on the

speculators who had purchased large real estate holdings and business interests for a song in paper Marks were forced by law to surrender at least part of their profits, but the large majority of the people who were depending on reserves and savings, found that the damage was irreparable.

It was at this juncture that Hitler won his first popular following. Revolutions always grow out of discontent. For the nazis, the task of staging one was made relatively easy. The deadly foes of democracy at home, and the Poincarés, Tardieus, and Lavals did a splendid job of playing into their hands.

When General Dawes finally stepped into the picture as a sort of good-will emissary he told the creditor governments that rough kicks won't make a mule walk faster. Good financial doctor that he was, "Hell'n Maria" Dawes in 1924 prescribed a five-year period of rest for the German patient. It was quite an experience at the time to see him sit quietly in front of a fireplace in his Berlin hotel, smoking his famous underslung pipe and discussing reparations as though he was taking part in a round-table forum of his home-town university. The very fact that he had come to Europe, about a year after the Ruhr incident, was a tonic for the German people. He was a new hope on a troubled horizon.

The road from debt-collector Poincaré to Doctor Dawes had been tedious and thorny. Now the treaty executors could no longer refuse to face unpleasant realities, but they did so all too slowly. While reparation loans began to pour into Germany from the United States, and German international trade showed some signs of recovery, many Germans remained resentful over what to them seemed a deliberate attempt to enslave their country with "reparation chains," and at the same time refuse it equal status in the markets of the world. When caravans of brown-shirted nazi riff-raff began driving through the streets, shouting their violent "Germany, wake up!" it was obvious that the country was approaching the zero hour.

German democracy was now facing the death struggle. While the liberals were on the defensive, the nationalists gained ground rapidly. Dr. Heinrich Bruening was Chancellor and Germany's man of destiny. In 1923 I had met him for the first time, at a gathering in the home of Romano Guardini

who continued to rally some of the best minds of the country around him. Bruening was then a modest young man connected with the Christian Trade Unions. He sat as a quiet observer, speaking only a few words himself, while listening intently to our discussions on liturgy and apologetics.

When he was appointed Chancellor of the Reich by Marshal von Hindenburg, the unassuming Doctor, whom a foreign diplomat had once described as "a mixture of a Cardinal and a Prussian officer," was forty-five years old. He tried to steer a safe middle course in a raging sea of popular discontent, but his success or failure depended largely on the backing he could secure from the victor governments.

In a moral sense, his strongest support came from America where public opinion advocated fair play; Americans do not believe in hitting a fellow when he is down. At the same time it was plain enough that the reparation creditors were determined to drive at least as hard a bargain with Germany as Uncle Sam was driving with them. The infant German Republic, struggling precariously, its steps still halting after twelve uncertain and vexatious years, seemed destined never to grow up.

## Chapter 2

## "AMERICA IS BETTER OFF"

I HAD bought a fresh battery for my portable strong-box, so there was no reason to worry. My savings had miraculously risen to 154 dollars, a sum that would easily have bought a suburban residence, house and lot and everything, at the height of the inflation! Then something happened.

"How would you like to go to New York?" the boss asked me one bright spring morning in 1924.

"New-new-new York?" I stammered.

"Yes," said Wiegand. "We are planning to set up a service for Europe and need a man in New York to handle it. I think you are just the fellow for that."

In May that year I set sail for the new world.

My first day in New York was a thrill beyond all anticipation. The skyscrapers. The subways. The Great White Way. I felt like another Columbus, discovering everything from double-rich chocolate milk-shakes to Roxy's follies. It seemed a spree of a thousand and one wonders. The Wall Street district, the Hudson river boats, and Coney Island! But then life started in earnest.

I had my desk in the Pulitzer Building, on City Hall square. The tickers clattered day and night. I had to be on duty late hours and never got to bed before two or three in the morning. It meant midnight lunches and rides in jammed trolleys. The din of traffic was exasperating, and the summer heat seemed fierce to the unaccustomed newcomer. The big city was to me like a huge moloch devouring souls of people, holding them tightly in his feverish grip.

Aside from the heat and the noise, however, there were a good many things I liked. For instance, I liked to see night workers ordering ham and eggs, a luxury never dreamed of by their comrades in Europe. I liked the informality of the people, the way they met, the way they dispensed with useless frills in social intercourse. Men didn't have to tip their hats to one another. There were no titles. Nearly everyone was plain Mister or Doc or Judge rather than a Herr Inspektor or a Cavaliere. And best of all, it seemed as though all Europe and his wife had settled on the banks of the Hudson and the East River. There was no reason to feel lonely.

Mulberry Street was like Naples. Papa Moneta was running his restaurant just as he used to back home. Boy! Was his spaghetti good! And despite prohibition, every assortment of Chianti and Castelli wines could be had. At the Brevoort the French cuisine was as palatable as Escargot's in Paris, the waiters just as courteous. And Luchow's served pig knuckles and sauerkraut with a stein of beer, according to the best Hofbrau standards.

So this was America. At least, America in New York, Little America, the melting-pot. Reason enough for the greenhorn to feel thoroughly at home. "Chuck" Miller, Mr. Hearsts' cable editor — the Lord bless his memory — got a great kick out of my initiation. In between rewrites he would take me to the drug-store downstairs.

"Have a soda, buddy," he used to say. "Can't be American without a soda. Two chocolate sodas! That's the boy. Yes, sir."

And then he would tell me of the wife and the kids. Soon he took me out to his home in Jersey for a week-end. Everything was new to me. The way everyone drove his own car. The relishes at dinner. Oh, yes, and particularly the apple pie a la mode! Why had no one in Europe thought of that dish?

"Have another piece," Miller urged me on. "Mother's made this one special today so you can see what home-cooking is like. Yes, sir."

He always said: "Yes, sir." Everything in life was "okay" with him. He was a rotund, heavily-built gentleman, with a pleasant twinkle in his eyes, and a winning smile. Typically American, I thought. Optimistic, a go-getter and a straight-shooter.

"Yes, sir," he insisted. "This is the land of plenty. You'll like it here, young feller. You just wait."

I saw no reason why I shouldn't like it. But I had to see
more of Uncle Sam's domain before I made up my mind
whether I really liked it. One Sunday in September I ventured
to Washington. I find it difficult to recall my sensations. Everything, now obvious and commonplace, was then fresh, exciting like spring. The friendly negro porter on the train. The
revolving chairs in the club car. The free ice-water service. The
news-boy selling candy and gum.

Those were the bagatelles. But then I stopped over in Philadelphia and saw Independence Hall. The bell that rang out
freedom. Benjamin Franklin's grave. The home of Betsy Ross.
America began to reveal itself.

In Washington I felt at home immediately. What a relief
it seemed after hectic life in the big city to walk along tree-
lined streets again! To have a public park almost in every
block! To hear the birds singing in the morning!

Indian summer on the Potomac! I sat on a Jackson Square
bench feeding peanuts to the squirrels. No longer was I homesick for Europe. People were so friendly, like my very own. I
looked across the street in the direction of the White House.
The simplicity of the building was fascinating. So simple and
yet so dignified, symbolic of America's strength.

Would I ever see that place inside, I wondered. And the
President? It seemed a far-fetched dream for one accustomed
to European formalities. But why not try to find out?

I walked over to the White House executive wing. There
were guards, but they paid little attention to the passers-by.
At the main entrance an attendant came up to me.

"Can I help you?"

"Yes, please," I said somewhat timidly. "Could I look at the
President's office, sometime when he is not in? You see . . ."

"Oh, you want an appointment?"

"No, no, just a look at the office, so I can write a story."

"Newspaperman, eh?"

"Yes, sir."

"Come on in."

A minute later I was sitting in the office of the Secretary
to the White House. The incumbent at the time was Bascom
C. Slemp.

"You want to see the President?" he asked.

I was almost scared. How could he think I'd be that bold!

"Why, Mr. Secretary, I had no idea, I don't know. Is it possible?"

"Of course. Just wait a minute."

Did he take me for a politician? I had properly identified myself and shown him my credentials. Now I was afraid I'd be thrown out. Perhaps he had gone to call a detective. Did he think I was a crank? Imagine me asking to see the President! It was preposterous. No such thing could ever have happened in Europe. I wondered if I had not better do a vanishing act while Slemp was out of sight.

But there he was.

"Come right in!"

I looked up. The door into the adjoining room had been opened, and there was the President of the United States behind his desk. Slemp introduced me.

"Sit down," said the President. "How long have you been over here?"

Those were quiet times, with no threats of war, no armament races, no dictators around. Still, Mr. Coolidge was a busy man, and here I was chatting with him for a full half hour about my travels and what things were like in the Europe I had left behind. It all was as informal and natural as though the President had been my good friend for years.

"Well," he said at the close of a statement on the domestic situation which proved most enlightening, "I was glad to see you. Hope you'll like it here. Good-bye."

I walked out of the room, and again found myself in Mr. Slemp's outer office. He was not in and I waited. After a while he returned.

"Everything all right?"

"Thank you, Mr. Secretary. I certainly appreciate . . ."

"That's okay. Of course, you know the President must not be quoted. Call again; 'bye."

What a cold shower! Here I had landed an exclusive interview with the President of the United States, but had to keep my mouth shut!

It was a revealing experience just the same, one that determined my path for years to come. "I hope you'll like it here," the President had said. I did indeed, and have liked it ever since. Liked it? Loved it!

\*   \*   \*

"You must get into the country," urged Hugh Wilson, then chief of the Division of Current Information at the State Department, who was to become the last American Ambassador to Germany before the outbreak of World War II. "The East alone is not America. Go West, young man!"

I was in no particular hurry. The welcome in the capital had been so cordial that I decided to linger on and settle down, to become a real Washingtonian. There just did not seem to be any problems. All doors were open. I went to the press conferences, to Capitol Hill, to the Press Club. The stranger was accepted as though he had been a native son. At first I was the most puzzled man in town.

"Why," I said to a fellow correspondent at a White House press conference, "you all stand there facing the President of the United States with your hands in your pockets!"

"Why not?"

"But he is the President!"

"Sure, I voted for him!"

There was the spirit of America! There was man's freedom in action. The citizen had the innate consciousness of his natural dignity. No one felt like a "subject." Equal rights were a living thing, taken for granted, a birthright not to be questioned. Democracy! Something happened inside of me.

Hugh Wilson's advice had been good. I went West soon, in a flivver, and managed to visit almost every State in the Union, interviewing people, all kinds of people, all of them revealing America, the soul of America which is so gloriously free and unspoiled.

By this time my former paper in Berlin had appointed me its Washington correspondent, giving me all sorts of roving assignments on the side. It was a great opportunity to learn by seeing for myself. I saw the beauty of the land, and the people at work and experienced their kindness, their overpowering sense of humor, their hospitality.

Soon I felt thoroughly at home in America, cozily at home and as much at ease as in the land of my birth. I acquired the various slangs and local habits wherever I went. Never were distinctions made between the host and the stranger. Friendships were cemented with an ease and sincerity that made the heart beat faster. Human relations were of a straightness, directness, and simplicity unknown in hapless, torn, divided Europe. Truly, Goethe was right when he said: "America, you are better off!"

I experienced my Americanization as a real conquest. Every step was an adventure. Though at first I had felt I could never adapt myself, to live an American life the American way, I slowly fell into line, acquired the habits of my new surroundings, and happily submerged myself in a crowd I found congenial, whose colloquialisms I began to use with zest, whose mannerisms became my own.

America made it easy for me to become an American. I was taken into the family, as it were, generously and without prejudice. Eventually, the grant of citizenship was but the seal on a pact which had existed for a long time as far as I was concerned. America had adopted me before I adopted her. It was a pact of love before it became a pact of law, and my oath of allegiance to the Stars and Stripes was at the same time a pledge of gratitude.

When I started on my trip to the Far East, in 1930, I was worried. I had dropped the contacts with the Hearst organization long ago, and now Theodor Wolff thought of transferring me to Rome. I had once applied for that post, but things had changed. Now there were American opportunities which tempted me much more. I had become a contributor to various magazines and feature syndicates. Also, radio loomed on the horizon. NBC had moved in across the hall from my office in the National Press Building in Washington, and their men would occasionally ask me questions when there were European angles to be considered in their work. Photography had become quite a hobby of mine, and I had sold pictures to the agencies after my trips to Central and South America, trips which had helped to round out my knowledge of Western Hemisphere relations.

Before leaving Washington I "sewed up" as many of these

contacts as I could. It was quite like the habit of travelers in Rome who toss pennies into the pool of the Trevi Fountain. It is supposed to help bring them back! When my boat left San Francisco harbor, Hawaii-bound, I felt like throwing all my cash behind the Golden Gate, to assure a safe return to my adopted country.

# Chapter 3

# THE BROWN EARTHQUAKE

IN WASHINGTON I had had my first contacts with the
National Broadcasting Company as far back as 1928. Three
years later, by the time I had arrived in Berlin on my trip
around the world, John Elwood, then in charge of the company's foreign relations and now its general manager in San
Francisco, decided to look over the European field.

"Transatlantic broadcasting," he said, when we met, "is just
about to emerge from the experimental stage. It will grow
fast from now on. We must be prepared for it."

It sounded tempting and I made up my mind to implement
Elwood's words. Soon an opportunity arose to show what
I could do.

Jacob Gould Schurman, United States Ambassador to Germany, had helped raise sizable funds for a new building at
Heidelberg University, his former alma mater. American
alumni contributed generously. There, I thought, was a suitable subject for a transatlantic hookup. I went to the no-longer-
so-romantic city to arrange a special broadcast of the ceremonies dedicating the modernistic annex.

Naturally, the feeling toward the United States among
faculty and student body was most pleasant. America seemed
the one true friend taking a real interest in battered Germany;
and every one of the thousands of American visitors crowding
the popular hostelries in town was greeted as a harbinger of
a new and happier era.

There was always a great deal to attract tourists on the banks
of the Neckar River. Inspiring musicals were held amidst the
courtyard ruins of Heidelberg castle which had been burned
to ashes by the French armies in the 17th century. And, of
course, there was the huge wine cask in the castle's vault

which, despite its fifty thousand gallons capacity, the court jester Perkeo was said to have emptied to the last drop, in the course of fifteen years!

Perkeo's emulators were no longer to be found. Floret-fencing, scar-faced, beer-drinking university students leading a carefree life were a thing of the past. The once famed fraternities were dwindling rapidly. Most people were experiencing too hard a time making a living to have much patience with money-squandering, happy-go-lucky youngsters engaged in duels and banquets. Nor was there anyone who could afford the amenities of a student prince.

I drove up to Frankfort to catch the night train to Berlin. Homey villages lined the beautiful landscape in the Neckar valley. A monastery bell rang the Angelus and the farmers in the fields bowed their heads, absorbed in silent prayer. I stopped at a wayside inn for a bite.

"Oh yes," said the young woman, depositing a stack of huge pretzels on my table, before pouring in my glass some of the light wine of the region, "The boys still come out this way from Heidelberg. On the boats, you know."

"So it's still Old Heidelberg?"

"No, not quite," she replied nostalgically. "It'll never be Old Heidelberg again. . . . Never! We are a poor people now."

\*    \*    \*

In Berlin, Bruening stood firm in the midst of a raging political storm.

"A government must have the courage of unpopularity," he used to say. But the combined federal, state and municipal budgets showed a shortage of half a billion dollars, a gigantic sum at that time. Over and over, Bruening told his diplomatic friends that there are no arguments against hunger.

One out of every four Germans, including dependents, was unemployed. Half of the sixteen million wage-earners in the country were paid the equivalent of twenty-four dollars a month. Thirty millions had incomes of less than forty-eight dollars a month; only about three million people were earning more than that.

The British and the Americans understood, but other foreign observers would not listen. Bruening told them the truth. He was a fanatic about truth and insisted on facing cold facts. He could feel the impatience of the young people of his country who while seeking outlets for their energies refused to share in the responsibilities of the past. The older people had almost given up hope, the middle-aged, who were in the saddle, still hoped that somehow, sometime a miracle would occur. But the youth had only one real hope — to revolt against the immediate past.

Wasn't it David Lloyd George who had warned at Versailles that no stipulations would last which were meant to be enforced beyond the living generation?

I joined a club in Berlin which had become headquarters of the political younger set professing democratic ideals. Its main backer was Robert Bosch, the Stuttgart industrialist.

At lunch time one would meet a goodly cross section of the capital's progressive element in the main lobby of the comfortable building Robert Bosch had acquired, and a newspaperman could pick up the talk of the town. Friday was the regular day when some of my friends at the club would foregather in a corner of their own, with coffee and smokes. We called it the Friday Circle; and rarely did I miss it.

As a rule, conversation centered around the problems of the day. Often opinions differed, but everybody had something to offer, and it was worth-while to get the viewpoint of people in various walks of life. There was Werner Pratt, for instance, the gaudy stage manager whose briefcase was always bulging with dramatic scripts; and Wolfgang Hart, the former Reichstag member and editor who knew everybody and everything; and Otto Weltin, the Robert Bosch engineer who had been transferred up north from the Lake Constance region and simply loathed the big city and its turmoil; and Walter Kegel the legal adviser of the oil industry who was a confirmed Berliner and liked to deliver chamber-of-commerce talk on the slightest provocation. The variety in the group was indeed stimulating.

Perhaps the most articulate of these men was Karl Nord, a former New York shipping agent, now back with his home firm. His American experiences added to his prestige in the Circle, so everyone listened patiently when he sailed off on one of his favorite arguments. I vividly remember the one he got

into when general interest was focused on Bruening's efforts
to stabilize the budget.

"It's overpopulation," he insisted, "that's causing all this
trouble. In America I have seen what it means to have wide
open spaces in which to settle."

"But space alone is not sufficient," I objected. "It must be
space that is livable as well."

"I know, I know," Nord nodded impatiently. "But in America, at least there's a prospect, an opportunity! What have we
got? Fifty years ago the German population was only 23
millions. In ten years it more than doubled, and it rose to some
67 millions before the war. In spite of the losses we have
suffered, we are on the same level again today."

"Is not Belgium even worse off?" I asked. "And what about
Italy, or Czechoslovakia? They all have their population problems. Yet, they seem to manage."

"After a fashion! Belgium, of course, has valuable colonies
while we have none. Formerly, emigration helped to relieve
the pressure at home. Now bars are raised in most of the
overseas countries, and where immigrants still can get in, only
farmers with working capital, willing and able-bodied enough
to venture into the tropical wilderness of such countries as
Brazil and Paraguay, are considered acceptable. Why increase
the number of sheep-ranchers or cotton-growers or rubber-
planters so long as there is agrarian overproduction the globe
over?"

Otto Weltin could not refrain from throwing in his bit.

"What about our domains in the East?" he burst forth,
"Why holler about the loss of colonies when we don't even
seem to be able to tell the Junkers where to get off?"

Nord must have expected this for he came right back at
Weltin.

"The East? Why, you ought to know that even if all the
large estates were parcelled out, probably not more than, say,
fifty thousand new settlers could be taken care of, and then
only at a considerable expense to the tax-payer."

"You mean to say that there are no swamps to be reclaimed,
and that we could not improve our agricultural methods?"

"Of course, we could, but what has that to do with Pomerania and East Prussia? Do you realize that they represent only one-third of one per cent of German farm land? Why, all that has been done under the rural settlement laws is tremendous! The reclamation work, too, is of a scope that I think is admirable. But where is the money to carry on?"

Nord knew his facts although much depended on their interpretation. He had read his editorials carefully, but only those to which he subscribed. No one could blame him, for it was really beyond the ordinary mortal to distinguish propaganda from legitimate reporting in the acrimonious outpourings of the newspapers. I remembered how Wiegand after brooding over them for hours often had thrown them all into the waste-basket.

"Newspapers without news!" he used to say in disgust.

"But there are editorials," I would suggest.

"You can have them!"

Now I was up against the same problem. I hesitated to invite speakers for NBC. Those who amounted to something were so one-sided in their views that no useful purpose could be served by airing their views in America.

Dr. Hjalmar Schacht, for instance, the wily banker never forgave me that I had dared to delete a couple of sentences from his address, an address crammed with bias and venom.

Pacing the floor from one end of his office to the other, he kept shouting at me.

"I won't stand for it! Either I say what I please, or I won't go on at all! It's up to you!"

I had to call for help. Ira Nelson Morris, former American Minister to Sweden, happened to be in town and he knew Schacht well. He came to my rescue and finally persuaded his explosive friend to give in.

Party lines were severely drawn in every field. People belonging to the "right" were not on speaking terms with those on the "left." The reporter of, say, the "Deutsche Zeitung," would not even think of asking his colleague of the "Tageblatt" for a match! Who was right and who was wrong amongst all these jumpy, high-tensioned "politicians" no one could decide.

But everybody seemed to agree on one element of the situa-

PROVIDENCE HEIGHTS

ALLISON PARK, PA.

tion, and that was unemployment. There could be no doubt that the grumbling mass of dole-seekers was the main source of the all-pervading unrest.

The army had been a reservoir of German man-power before the war, but the Versailles treaty reduced it from 800,000 to 100,000. There were thousands of refugees from Alsace Lorraine, from Poland and various territories conquered by the victors, and thousands of Germans expelled as enemies from their homes overseas. Most of their properties were confiscated during the war and were never returned to them. Accordingly, the strain on the home labor market was tremendous. There were just not enough jobs. Employment agencies were frantic, the unemployed grew rapidly in number, especially after pensions, insurances and savings had been wiped out by the inflationary process. A whole army of unskilled laborers added to the embittered and menacing new proletariat — easy prey for agitators and demagogues.

During that first winter of discontent which I spent in a seething Germany it became constantly more evident that the nazis were gaining ground. Stresemann's death had marked the beginning of a downward trend. The masses were despondent.

Hitler did not make the empty stomach the primary issue of his campaigning. Going about the job systematically, he and his fellow stump orators went from town to town, from hamlet to hamlet, appealing to the pride of the people. Weren't things going from bad to worse? Wasn't the Versailles treaty responsible for the mounting national debt and the growing tax burden? What were the democratic rulers doing about it? Talking, talking, talking, while people starved! But Germans were too proud to stand for this mess much longer! They had a sense of national dignity and would assert themselves! "Germany, wake up!"

This battle-cry resounded through the length and breadth of the country. Bavarian mountain folk were no less responsive than the farmers of the Black Forest, the Rhenish vineyard workers, or the miners in the Ruhr district. Among the young people in particular, enthusiasm was aroused by irresponsible agitators. The tide was rising fast. I could see it wherever I went, in the big cities and in hidden-away mountain resorts.

Swastika flags began to appear in greater number. It was all stage-managed, but somehow the people were struck by the novelty of this crude campaign. Many welcomed the opportunity to shout with the nazis, even if their ideas seemed abstruse, because shouting was the only way to express disapproval of things as they were. There were plenty of rowdies, adventurers and people who could not adjust themselves socially, only too willing to hop on the band-wagon, to wear a brown shirt and heavy boots and to strut about with an air of importance. But there were also a good many respectable citizens to whom hitlerism appeared as a light in the darkness.

The class of those dispossessed by the war, the ex-army officers who had been deprived of uniforms, rank and decorations; members of the aristocracy stripped of their former privileges and public prominence; disgruntled beneficiaries of the defunct monarchies; and particularly the many middle-class families whose modest fortunes, pensions, or insurance policies had been swept away by the monetary inflation — for all these people, Hitler meant a new hope. True, it was a vague, unspecified hope, irrational and even fool-hardy, but it was a hope nevertheless, at which an overwhelmed people clutched frantically.

Hitler's personal grudge was but an expression of the bitterness of the whole German nation whose nerves were cracking under the postwar ordeal. Hitler released all this disgruntled feeling, all this disillusionment by stirring up the national pride of the people, by recalling proud traditions of the past, and by painting in darkest colors the humiliating plight of the present. It was natural that so many of the young people should protest instinctively, like Hamlet, against the "cursed spite that they were born to set it right."

Hitler had issued a manifesto in the fall of 1930 which said in part: "With lies the armistice was brought about! With lies our people were induced to accept the dictates of London and Paris! With lies Germany was made to sign the so-called peace treaty of Versailles! With lies our people were led into subscribing to the Dawes reparation plan and the Locarno treaties!" It was the language a despairing people understood.

At the very same time Joseph Wirth, then Minister of the Interior, warned the world: "Statesmen of all nations should consider whether the time has not come to re-examine the problems of the German people within the scope of a great, all-embracing economic conference." But France answered by raising her annual military budget to the staggering total of almost half a billion dollars, and like another King Midas she kept on storing up gold reserves although actually threatened by gold inflation in her "embarrassment of riches!"*

\* \* \*

In the Spring of 1931, Dr. Julius Curtius, Bruening's Minister of Foreign Affairs, hard pressed by domestic critics who wanted action rather than diplomatic notes, returned to Berlin one morning from a mysterious trip to Vienna. An announcement immediately issued from the Wilhelmstrasse that the minister had agreed with his friends in the Austrian capital on the desirability of an Austro-German customs union which was to pave the way for similar arrangements between Germany and the countries of southeastern Europe. *Mitteleuropa* was to be revived as a preliminary to the fulfillment of Briand's dream of a "U.S.E.," a United States of Europe, a Pan-European Union after Count Coudenhove-Calergi's pattern. Even more important at the time seemed the prospect of opening south-eastern markets, with the potential buying power of over 160 million people.

Had Herr Curtius been too daring? Probably so. Sensing trouble, France vetoed the plan a few hours after it was announced. The German move was timid, incoherent and carried out clumsily. Yet, it represented Berlin's second attempt since the end of the war — the first one having been the Rapallo agreement with Russia — to make an independent move in the foreign field. Had it succeeded it might have taken some of the wind out of Hitler's sails. But the French did not like the idea of Germany acting on her own, and they feared that a customs union would be but an *Anschluss* in disguise. Once more the static and the dynamic forces clashed, and the former won — to their detriment. Curtius had to bury his brainchild just as sheepishly as he had brought it to light. To Hitler his defeat was but another proof of the hopelessness of "appeasement."

* Cf. Appendix I.

"We're at the end of our rope," was Otto Weltin's comment at the Friday Circle. "We might have known that we would burn our fingers."

"To please Hitler," nodded Werner Pratt, "we tried to stand on our own feet again, but we didn't get very far. They've slapped us down all right."

"If you read the French papers," Weltin went on, "you'd think we are living merrily at our creditors' expense. They blame Bruening for spending too much money for social security."

"Apparently our five million unemployed mean nothing to them," Karl Nord said bitterly.

"What is your answer to the problem?" I asked.

"Increased production which would mean increased employment! But how can there be increased production when there are no markets?"

"No markets?"

"That's what I said. Our exports are being choked up by twelve thousand miles of customs borders on the continent — not to mention the tariff walls put up by Uncle Sam. How can we buy the raw materials we need to keep our industries going, if sufficient proceeds are not forthcoming from exports?"

"But look at the loans that were raised in America! Until recently German bond issues sold like hot cakes in New York."

"That's no solution. Borrowed money led to a shortlived boom which did us no good. Easy cash was easily spent and often enough on futile projects. Reparations absorbed a considerable share of it anyway!"

Discussions such as these could be heard all over Germany when men familiar with the facts got together, and the press was full of them. The rank and file of the people did not understand the whys and hows, but they felt the pinch of an economy which was getting tighter all the time, with prices spiraling upwards.

Visitors from overseas who wanted to size up the situation for themselves were frequent in Berlin. When "Roxy," and Jimmy Walker arrived, I was to arrange for them to go on the air. Both spoke enthusiastically of what they had seen in Germany, and of the hospitality extended to them.

Roxy was amazed.

"Why," he said after he had been quartered in a luxurious hotel suite, "this country shows what a defeat can do! It spurs you on and lifts you up. Positively, it's amazing how fast they have recovered."

Others were more skeptical. Oswald Garrison Villard, for instance, then the editor of the New York *Nation,* was concerned with what rightly appeared to him as a growing tide of radicalism amongst the German masses.

"I saw Bruening this morning," he told me, "and I am going to London next week. I will call on my old friend Ramsay MacDonald and urge him to get together with the Chancellor. He must know that Bruening is sincere and deserves every support in his efforts to keep the German nation on the road to sanity."

Villard was a good ambassador in that he had a real understanding of German problems. Unlike so many chance visitors he had been acquainting himself with conditions in Germany for many years. He spoke the language and knew people in key positions. His heart was with the democratic forces who had come to power after the war and he saw clearly that they were imperiled by the systematic onslaught of the old vested interests, which had never really called retreat even though beaten in 1918.

Since then Europe had gone quite a long way on the path of disillusionment. The five-year debt holiday which had been prescribed by "Doctor" Dawes finally had led to the adoption of the Young plan for reparations. It took the "experts," who had assembled in Paris, four months of juggling with figures until at last the German debt had been fixed anew at approximately 8.8 billion dollars — quite a reduction from the fantastic original assessment of thirty-one and one half billions, equivalent to fifty thousand tons of gold! However, there was more than just one catch to the scheme.

"You know," remarked Villard while we were talking of how the crisis had come about, "it all reminds me of the famous concession our government once made with reference to the cost of the Allied armies of occupation in the Rhineland. Do you remember?"

I did not.

"Well," Villard went on, "a ten per cent share of the whole bill was supposed to go to America, but one of our officers who was figuring coldly said: 'How much is ten per cent of zero?'"

"Zero is right," I agreed. "I guess now the zero level is more real even than it was at the time of the Rhineland occupation."

"Whether it is real in cold figures or not is a moot question," said Villard. "National destinies cannot be determined in terms of dollars and cents. After all, the Young Plan, too, had only one purpose: to provide a breathing spell. A transaction such as the one recommended by the Young committee, involving the payment of several dozen annuities of about half a billion dollars each is too much even for bankers to figure out."

"It's the compound interest that always got me!" I interrupted. "To ordinary mortals it's a sort of kabala anyway."

"Of course," Villard laughed. "But in this instance it proves a helpful device in saving everybody's face for awhile and in keeping the world guessing."

Villard made a full report to MacDonald of what he had seen in Germany. He convinced his British friend that an extraordinary effort was needed to break the deadlock. The essential thing, to him, was preventing a collapse of the German economy. Failing this chaotic forces were bound to break out all over the continent.

When he returned to Berlin, Villard was exultant.

"It's done!" he told me. "MacDonald has invited Bruening to England."

It was to be a week-end in Chequers, the British Prime Minister's country estate, and it might well have been a turning point. For the first time since Versailles, England stretched out a hand of friendship to Germany at the very stage when European society was beset by imminent dangers. At last, someone seemed to have a heart!

But how could France be won over to a policy of common sense? Her Maginots and Tardieus did not think much of a better understanding between victors and vanquished. The Austro-German move had meant fresh grist to their mill. The friends of reconciliation in Paris had almost been silenced. Locarno and Thoiry were forgotten. Briand had been defeated

in the presidential elections and was struggling to keep politically alive. And above all, France distrusted England since
the reparation meeting at the Hague. She didn't like the idea
of the appointment at Chequers which seemingly had been
arranged behind her back, and she was in utter disagreement
with MacDonald regarding the treatment of Germany.

The news leaked out prematurely. MacDonald had only
thought of a friendly chat with Bruening. If the first personal
contact with the German Chancellor turned out to be promis-
ing, it was to be followed by a joint meeting with the French
at a later date. But apparently strong forces in the London
Foreign Office who opposed MacDonald and worked hand
in hand with the Paris irreconcilables were determined to
throw a monkey wrench into the scheme.

On Easter morning the London *Times* suddenly came out
with a story of the plan, adding that Briand had also been
invited. It was a bomb-shell! MacDonald had no intention of
inviting Briand at that stage. The immediate effect was the
postponement of the Chequers party till after the May meeting of the League of Nations council in Geneva which was
expected to torpedo the Austro-German agreement.

Anglo-French antagonism now became fully evident. In
Geneva it was decided to pass the buck to the World Court,
but before it had even spoken, on May 16, 1931, the Austrian
Minister in Paris was handed a French ultimatum whereby
his country was offered financial assistance provided it was
willing to "solemnly renounce every combination, be it of an
economic or political nature, to change the international status
of Austria." Vienna's reply was "no." A few hours after this
negative answer had been dispatched to Paris, the Bank of
England put a twenty-one million dollar credit at the disposal
of the Austrian "Kreditanstalt."

A crash was thus prevented, but the gap between Paris and
London widened considerably. The domestic situation in England was critical. The coalition government was struggling to
balance the budget. Labor was restive. The world began to lose
confidence in Britain's credit. Had it not been for Washington
stepping in with a quarter billion dollar credit to support the
Bank of England, the French attack upon the British gold
reserve would have been serious. There were unemployment

riots in London, Manchester, and Glasgow, and minor disorders occurred even in the Navy. But France had the whip hand and she meant business. Having caused a "run" on Austria's and Germany's gold reserves, she eventually forced England off the gold standard. Hard pressed on all sides, Germany and Austria at last had to renounce the pact.

From now on calamities poured thick and fast over all Europe. Instead of facing them, governments everywhere shunned the burning issues.

"If the wolf howls outside your house, just keep the doors shut, pretend not to hear him," Villard remarked caustically. "But the wolf is there just the same, and your beauty sleep won't be too comfortable!"

Elections were forthcoming in France, in Germany, in England and in the United States. Politicians were praying that for a while at least, troubles would somehow take care of themselves. Montague Norman, perennial governor of the Bank of England, went to Washington to describe the European picture to Secretary of the Treasury Andrew W. Mellon. His close personal contact with Germany's Doctor Schacht made him an ideal interpreter. England by now was thoroughly alarmed. A German collapse might mean a collapse of all Europe. Mr. Norman said so in Washington, but Mr. Mellon's reply was that there was nothing he could do.

Even the least educated German learned to read Reichsbank statements in those days. The financial page of the newspapers was no longer scanned by only stockbrokers and investors. Discount rates and gold reserves were popular topics for discussion in public cafés and around the family dinner tables. The "flight from the Mark" became a mass phenomenon once more. People of all walks of life again completely lost confidence in their national currency. Everybody tried to hoard dollars and other foreign currency while the majority, the millions who had nothing to hoard rallied in growing numbers behind radical party banners. "Steel helmet" and nazi parades became every day occurrences. Old imperial flags were defiantly displayed beside the swastika and the trouble-makers were riding the crest of a resurgent wave of despair.

# Chapter 4

## "AN EXPENSIVE EXPERIMENT"

IN ENGLAND, too, the rising shadows of unemployment cast deep gloom over the Isles. In the United States the number of jobless now reached the six million mark. The world total was twenty million. So long as business sagged and purchasing power was declining rapidly everywhere no improvement could be expected. In 1930 Germany had spent three billion marks for unemployment doles alone. The financial liquidation of the war required another four billions, two of which went for reparations and one for the service of private foreign loans which were absorbed largely for the same purpose. That meant seven billion marks, or approximately 1.7 billion dollars per annum above ordinary budget needs.

Hitler used these figures profitably for his agitation. Had not former Chancellor Joseph Wirth produced the captivating slogan "First bread — then reparations"? Had not Germany already paid fifteen billion dollars on account of her treaty obligations? (Of course, that figure included the value of German private property confiscated under the terms of Versailles, deliveries in kind on the reparations account and actual cash contributions such as the two and one half billion dollars paid under the Dawes plan.) And still the creditors were not satisfied? Still they insisted Germany was evading her obligations?

Paris remained adamant. The French would not consider reparation concessions to Germany as long as the Washington administration would not hear of war debt concessions to them. Washington, in turn, was in no mood to forgive as long as France was spending ten times as much on armaments as she paid Uncle Sam on her war debt.

Bruening finally left for Chequers, the first week of June. On the eve of his departure he had issued a decree burdening the German taxpayer with an additional 400 million dollars. It was the last straw. The next day Senator Borah, after consulting with the White House, gave out a statement saying that "to grind the German working people into unspeakable misery would be a calamity the evil consequences of which, to say nothing of its inhumanity, no tongue can properly express."

Former Ambassador Alanson B. Houghton was no less emphatic when he stated in the course of a commencement address at the Carnegie Institute of Technology in Pittsburgh that "we cannot expect a prosperous Europe, or, for that matter, a prosperous United States, if Germany is in economic and financial distress and nearing the point of collapse. . . . To impoverish the German people, to convince them that for the next sixty years they will be held to the letter of a bond whose justice they deny, and that we regard them as moral outlaws, may prove an expensive experiment."

At last the ball started rolling. President Hoover summoned Ambassador Frederick M. Sackett from Berlin, General Dawes from London, Ambassador Hugh Gibson from Brussels. Bruening's emergency decrees had shown the world that Germany was on the brink of disaster. The drastic cuts in her federal budget, principally at the expense of social security, and the further reduction of civil service salaries caused violent protest among the masses, but there simply was no other way of proving to the whole world that the country was being squeezed dry.

Bruening was on his way back from Chequers when Sackett arrived in Bremen again. There they met and went on to Berlin together on the same train. In the meantime Mr. Mellon had gone to London. He saw the dark clouds gathering on the horizon. The Reichsbank had suffered severe "runs." As a result, the gold cover of the German currency had been lowered below the legal limit. Every nineteenth German citizen now depended on public support or charity. Mr. Mellon communicated his observations directly to President Hoover. It would have been folly to remain indifferent to such violent storm signals.

Soon events were moving at a breath-taking pace. Hurried conferences were held at the White House. On June 20, 1931, the "Hoover moratorium" was suddenly proposed to an astonished world: "Postponement during one year of all payments on inter-governmental debts, reparations and relief debts, both principal and interest — subject to confirmation by Congress."

It was like a fast express stopping at the edge of an abyss. Once more a breathing spell had been gained. But Paris pulled a sour face, like a man saying that there are only two opinions: "One is mine, and the other is wrong."

No doubt France had reasons to be stubborn. Looking across her borders, she could see the tide of hate constantly rising in Germany. It was a hate born of desperation and suffering, a hate against France in particular, whom the nazis blamed for it all. The hitlerites didn't believe in negotiations. They, rather, were in a mood for banging diplomatic conference tables with their fists, of slamming the door in the face of the Geneva League, and of telling the whole world to go hang. No wonder the French were nervous.

Had they but realized at this time that there were in Berlin men of good will anxiously waiting for a friendly gesture. Had they but heeded those who were counseling moderation!

In glancing through my notes, I find that I wrote on June 14, six days before the Hoover moratorium was announced: "France cannot see the other fellow's viewpoint. With an obstinacy which is perfectly astonishing she clings to a vision of the world as though it had not changed since 1918. May she not awaken some day, to a terrible reality."

That was in 1931 — almost ten years to the day before Hitler's triumph in Compiègne!

The debt holiday, of course, meant more than just the prevention of a collapse. It meant the breakdown of the whole artificial structure of postwar intergovernmental debts. For years creditors and debtors had argued reparations pro and con. The simple truth was that reparations could not be paid without upsetting trade balances all over the globe, and without causing a social revolution in Germany.

Hoover's moratorium came too late to stop hitlerism. Instead of subjecting the patient to a major operation, only a sleeping powder was prescribed. Soon it was found that the pains were too fierce to be assuaged by a mere palliative.

Paul Claudel, the French poet, at that time ambassador to Washington, found the right words when he proposed a toast after the acceptance of Hoover's moratorium "to the pause between a crisis and a catastrophe."

About a month after Mr. Hoover's announcement, and through the strenuous efforts of Secretary of State Henry L. Stimson, who had journeyed specially to Paris, France finally agreed to a meeting of the seven Powers in London. Her spokesman was Pierre Laval, then premier of France, the same Laval who became Hitler's partner in 1941. In 1931 he refused even the slightest concession to Bruening.

*     *     *

All through that turbulent summer, radiograms from NBC in New York became more frequent. There were odds and ends to look after, but radio was growing too fast to make this just a part-time job. By fall I had made my plans. John Elwood accepted my suggestion to talk things over at headquarters.

I soon came to terms with NBC, and was appointed as the company's continental European representative. It was an ideal assignment: to work for American interests as an emissary between the two continents, always close to both through the radio, and with frequent opportunities to visit back and forth.

Toward the end of the year, after I had been "broken in" by my new associates, I started out from New York, feeling like a pioneer under Uncle Sam's banner.

"There is a front-page of the air," John Elwood had told me before I bade him good-bye, "and we need headlines on it twenty-four hours a day. Go and get some!"

It was a novel kind of a job and I was not so sure I could succeed. Cesar Saerchinger, now well known as a commentator in New York, was pitching for Columbia in London and a powerful rival he was — widely experienced on the Continent, a newspaperman of exceptional merit, and a musician to boot. I could see that my new job was not going to be a sinecure.

There was no limit to one's opportunity. Radiowise, Europe was almost virgin territory. Although broadcasting organizations were in existence in most countries, they could not easily provide for specific American requirements. We had to start from scratch for our own needs.

Germany was a pivotal point, and the contacts there mattered a lot, but at that time, fortunately, it was not so much politics that I had to look after. The cultural exchange was more important and it was a pleasant task to arrange broadcasts from such places as Oberammergau and Bayreuth.

But Germany was not my only hunting ground. Italy, my native land, and Austria, the land of my father's ancestors, engaged my interest no less intensely. And there were the Scandinavian countries and Poland, Switzerland, and Holland. Czechoslovakia, Hungary and the Balkans, the whole Near East and vast, mysterious Russia. They all had to be explored as potential sources of radio copy.

Soon regular schedules of programs began to evolve, relayed from the European centers of art and culture straight to the air lanes of the United States. It was a pioneering job, full of adventure and excitement, a real challenge to one's imagination and enterprise. I loved it; and for a while, at least, almost forgot about Europe's ills and trepidations.

A prize "catch" in those early days of adventurous broadcasting was the first flight into the stratosphere. The story of how Professor Auguste Piccard, the Swiss savant, became a radio performer had a prelude almost as exciting as the flight itself.

I was attending a broadcasters' meeting at Montreux when I heard that my friendly rival, Cesar Saerchinger, had suddenly stolen away, bound for Bucharest on the Orient Express — via the southern route. Immediately I caught another flyer, Rumania-bound — via the northern route!

King Carol, who was to become an unhappy refugee in Mexico, had been a bone of contention between us for some weeks. Cesar must have been tipped off that the time was ripe to "land" His Majesty for a broadcast. As far as I was concerned, he was not going to get away with it, but when I arrived in Bucharest it was found that through some misunderstanding the king had been booked with both of us — an unpardonable crime according to the ancient and honorable laws of scooping!

Days went by. New York was getting impatient. One night my telephone rang.

"New York calling!"

The night porter almost awakened the king's bodyguard in his excitement, for never before had there been a private telephone call to Bucharest from faraway America. The next morning the whole hotel knew that the man in Room 316 had been talking transatlantic. It was embarrassing to be so conspicuous, particularly because Saerchinger's spies got wind of it immediately and went about wondering what I was up to.

At noon the next day I had just returned from another appointment to bring additional pressure to bear on the king when Saerchinger rushed into the lobby shouting:

"It's off — all is off!"

"What happened?"

"The king's left," Cesar sighed, letting himself drop exhausted into one of the huge leather chairs which adorned the pretentious bar.

It was true. The king had become tired of us and solved the problem by packing his bags and going off on a trip.

I was glad when we got to Switzerland. While in Rumania, I had been worrying about the stratosphere and Professor Piccard all along. The day I had left Montreux I had just reached him by long-distance telephone in Brussels. Now that King Carol was out of the way, I meant to beat friend Cesar to that spectacular "first" of a stratosphere broadcast.

Soon the balloon was ready in Zurich. I was on hand when Piccard arrived from Belgium; and one early morning the telephone rang me out of bed again.

"I'll be off in an hour," announced Piccard, the novel Columbus.

Everything was ready and presently our party started out, with a cargo of radio gadgets too numerous to mention.

The balloon ascended in due time, with Professor Piccard waving a farewell from what looked for all the world like a clothes basket attached to a miniature whirlwind. We set off in pursuit, for our object was to get a broadcast immediately after the landing. Over mountain roads through the dawning hours went the caravan, speeding toward St. Moritz. We had reached the outskirts of Sargans when a railroad worker stopped us and pointed excitedly up at the bright blue sky already radiant with sunlight.

"There's the balloon!" he shouted. "See — right up there!"

And sure enough, twenty thousand feet or so above our

heads there was a plainly discernible white speck. Was it really Piccard's gondola?

Our experts set to work unraveling their assorted mechanisms. They finally arrived at the conclusion that our friend the railroad worker had been blessed with an eagle eye. Yet it seemed most extraordinary that the white speck did not move. We stared at it, we studied it scientifically, for two or three hours, but it never gave an indication of movement. Had Professor Piccard decided to establish a new record for stability? We began to grow restless. Then it gradually dawned on us that what we saw above was one of the most ancient of all stratosphere devices — nothing less than the planet Venus, the morning star! It was up there brilliantly defying us and the sun. We bowed our heads in shame.

Professor Piccard had long since crossed the Alps, coming down at Desenzano on Lake Garda. Taking the curves of mountain passes as if they were bends in a Jersey road, we sped thither. When we reached Desenzano, the professor had already gone to bed, but on the next afternoon he supplied us with the first personal description of his experiences in what Francis Thompson, the poet, once called "the long savannahs of the blue." It was a magnificent broadcast, telling of that first plunge into regions with which a swift-moving future generation may some day be as familiar as we are now with railroad tracks or auto highways.

*  *  *

The year 1932 came with ominous forebodings. For the fifth time bankers met in Basel and Berlin to investigate Germany's capacity to pay. Bruening was losing out. Starving people cannot be fed on promises and forlorn hopes indefinitely. Again there was talk of an extended moratorium on German payments. The bankers who had sold bonds at high interest rates, to trusting American investors, were unwilling to admit defeat. Their stake was three billion dollars — certainly no trifle!

One by one the European countries associated with the Sterling block were caught in the deluge of currency depreciation. Tariffs were increased, imports reduced. The depression was deepening. Bruening banned all public political gatherings. The socialistic "Reichsbanner" groups, displaying the colors of black, red, and gold, were reorganized to fight the "inner foe." New emergency decrees caused a further drop in living standards. Bankruptcies and receiverships were growing alarmingly frequent. Finally Bruening cut the Gordian knot by issuing the flat statement that no further reparation payments could be expected from Germany.

The experts at Basel were in agreement with him. Privately, they admitted Germany's inability to pay. But the politicians in France behaved as though they were blind and deaf. England was too weak to take a stand, her own currency being constantly exposed to French gold attacks. As for the United States, no concessions could come from Washington as long as Paris was unwilling to drive an easier bargain with Germany.

It was the same old story, the same permanently vicious circle. Hitler had only to sit tight. The longer the confusion lasted the more confident he could be of reaching his goal.

In the spring of 1932 I went to Geneva. The disarmament conference was about to be opened. Quartered in fashionable hotels, delegates of all nations set out to devise ways and means of reducing their armies. It all seemed so simple. After all, the best method of disarmament was to disarm, but none of the delegates, except the Germans, who had little to lose, were prepared to consider so radical a procedure. The Kellogg Pact renouncing war as an instrument of national policy had been adopted by forty-five nations, and yet the annual armament bill of this peace-time world was five billion dollars. Five million men were under arms and twenty million were trained as reserves.

It was a cold winter. The famous *bise* wind blew down from the mountains, but the delegates didn't care. For three weeks they engaged in rather academic discussions, attending dozens of meetings and listening to endless speeches. Then they adjourned. In the Hall of the Reformation no reformer's spirit came to life. The pressure of public opinion seemed to have no effect. Peace groups, religious organizations, and women's unions poured petitions upon the conference. Mass meetings for peace were held in the city practically every day. The organizers took this business of disarming seriously, and for a while it seemed as though the delegates, too, were paying attention to them. They could not wholly ignore the will of the masses, but they all had their own pet schemes, and the other fellow's ideas would not do.

Every delegation was profuse in expressing a sincere desire for international cooperation, but the real issues were dodged and politics was uppermost in the politicians' minds. To some, disarmament meant recognition of the *status quo* in Europe; to others, the sacrifice of sacred national interests. To one group of nations "security" signified the maintenance of a preponderant position of military power, to the other the recognition of a new international order devoid of military sanctions.

What a hide-and-seek game it was! We tried to reflect it in our broadcasts to America, but it was quite a job to nail the speakers down, to induce them to say anything specific at all. When it was Dr. Bruening's turn, he found it difficult to pronounce the English word "unanimity."

"The word is so rarely used," he remarked pregnantly.

Indeed, it was still *homo homini lupus*. Whenever a delegate spoke, all those not sharing his views were figuratively plugging their ears so they might not be contaminated by dissenting opinions. The whole misery of the European body politic, all its ailments, wounds and aches, all its sins and failures and shortcomings, were laid open in the limelight of a relentless world-wide publicity. What could the diplomats do? They had been poor diagnosticians before, and they had not learned by experience.

NBC's commentator in Geneva was William Hard — and none better was ever heard on the American air. At breakfast one morning Bill pointed to a Washington dispatch in a Paris newspaper, quoting Senator Borah as having stated that unless a recognition of the freedom of the seas was arrived at he was willing to predict "that nations will engage in competitive armament building, with nothing in the future, perhaps, except a tremendous burden of taxation for the American people and another cataclysm such as that of 1914."

"Borah is right," said Bill, "but here is the answer."

According to the same paper, Viscount Lee, of Fareham, ex-First Lord of the British Admiralty, had remarked on naval parity:

"We might as well insist on parity of umbrellas between London and California!"

When the Japanese delegate, Ambassador Tsuneo Matsudeira, went on the air for NBC, he pleaded for the abolition of air raids. The very same day Japanese planes razed the Woosung forts, and mercilessly bombed Chinese territory. It was difficult not to wax satirical, with the League Council struggling over its prerogatives to stop a war, and the Disarmament Conference trying to devise new sanctions against an aggressor nation.

Dr. Edward Benes, then Czechoslovakia's foreign minister, performed a great service for his colleagues when, addressing a plenary session, he quoted these words of his compatriot, the philosopher and educator, Johann Amos Comenius, spoken to the peace congress of Breda some 250 years ago:

"Therefore, you ambassadors of peace, if you are fully to deserve your name, bear in mind not only the plans of mankind, but also the plans of God; consider not only what your kings demand of you, but also what the King of Kings demands of you, and take as your goal not war, but peace; and therefore remember that your negotiations must be conducted in tranquillity, without anger; in frankness, without deceit; in openness of heart, without treachery. Then you will win the approval of your kings and your peoples, if peace, the glorious work of God, so prosper in your hands that hence-forward the people shall dwell in a peaceable habitation, and in sure dwellings, and in quiet resting places."

Dr. Bruening echoed these inspiring sentiments when he said in his broadcast to America that "the will to peace, to a just and true peace which is one of the Christian commandments, is the essential and primordial condition which every nation must bring to this conference."

After struggling for weeks to report the conference fairly, Bill Hard and I reached the conclusion that it was all a sham.

One evening we were dining at the Bavaria restaurant across the Rhone River, the meeting place of press and diplomacy which Derso and Kelen, the Hungarian cartoonists, had adorned with wall sketches of celebrities. In the League's heyday, such political stars as Briand, Stresemann, and Austin Chamberlain could be seen in the cozy corners of this popular tavern, hobnobbing with reporters over a dish of *choukroute* and a bottle of Dole, the ruby-colored vintage of the Canton Valais that rivals the best Bordeaux brand.

That evening, Giulio Gallarati, an Italian member of the League Secretariat, was just coming in. We all knew him well for he was in charge of newspaper and radio credentials.

"Giulio!" Bill Hard called to him. "Sit down with us."

"In just a moment," said Gallarati.

He went over to another table and talked to a group of Italian correspondents for a while. When he finally joined us, he was in a serious mood.

"They are all excited about the statement Maginot, the French minister of war, made in Paris this morning," he explained.

"What was it?" I asked.

"Simply that not all nations can be placed on the same footing."

"It means that the conference is wrecked, doesn't it?" asked Bill Hard.

Gallarati smiled.

"Won't you give it another day?"

"Well," replied Bill, "maybe till tomorrow morning! But we might as well pack up and go home."

On the way back to the hotel Bill and I stopped on the bridge. It was a clear night, with the moon reflecting its bright face in the darkness of the slumbering lake. The white swans near the Rousseau Isle were asleep, their necks tucked under their wings. Nature was breathing peace.

"Could this not be the ideal background for disarmament?" Bill reflected.

"Yet," he continued, "everybody makes it entirely a business of armies and navies, of soldiers and guns. No one thinks of the moral aspects of the problem. How can there be peace without surrender, without a sacrifice of national pride?"

For two more years, diplomats kept the conference going in a half moribund state. Then Hitler quit the League. Another two years, and the nazis began rearming. Eight years after Maginot's cynical challenge his country was again at war, entrenched behind a line of defense bearing his name, which in effect proved but a push-over for a victorious German army.

# Chapter 5

## THE DOWN-HILL RACE

THE vision, in the days of Locarno, of a "silver lining on the horizon" had not materialized. When Bruening returned to Berlin from Geneva, a tinge of hopelessness again enveloped German public opinion.

For a short stretch I had ridden on the same train with the Doctor and had tried to convince him that he should broadcast to America once more. Finally I pinned him down and introduced Bill Hard, who was to be his interviewer on the air.

We both could see that Bruening was worried. His smile was sad. Somehow it was difficult to believe that he was a government leader. He looked much more like a scholar of distinction than like a man of the world accustomed to battle with politicians. Perhaps he was too deep a thinker to be a man of action in emergencies. Too often he hesitated, too often he was pondering when prompt and decisive measures were imperative. But to his friends who were trying to urge him on he always replied:

"You don't understand."

Men of his caliber find this wicked world hard to cope with.

Returning to his desk empty-handed, Bruening was faced with new intrigues. His right-wing enemies had torpedoed his plans in Geneva. Spreading rumors that he was about to resign, they undermined his prestige the very moment when he should have been certain of the wholehearted backing of the nation. Now the demagogues had fresh arguments against him.

"Another failure!" shouted the nazis. "How much longer will this kowtowing go on?"

Evidently the agitation was planned to bring about a panic. Capital began rolling out of the country at an appalling pace. Even small investors opened bank accounts in neutral countries. A wave of bankruptcies set in. A large insurance concern in Frankfort was the first to break down. Other firms, with branches all over the country, followed.

Politicians everywhere lacked the courage to tell the truth to the people, the full truth that hurt, and certainly not the truth which might have impaired their own chances of re-election. As for the governments, they were no less human, and hated to admit mistakes. The wizards of high finance, the would-be experts and economic theorists who tried to force the flow of water uphill, were at their wits' end.

In the meantime rumblings from nazi mass meetings grew steadily stronger and louder. The moderates in Germany, the "appeasers," were fast losing out. Spellbinders and rabble-rousers were rapidly gaining ground. An increasing number of Germans in all walks of life began to tire, to use Hitler's words, of being kicked around and getting nowhere. What were they profiting by the endless deliberations at Geneva or by platonic pronouncements of American bankers? Was that the kind of internationalism the democratic leaders preached? A fine mess they were embroiled in! How much more preferable would be a goodly portion of nationalistic selfishness! Arguments such as these struck a responsive chord amongst people who were disillusioned and hopeless.

Only impartial outsiders could hope to cool tempers of those who were in the midst of such a strain. Frederick M. Sackett, American ambassador to Germany, was one of them.

I frequently went to see him at the embassy which then was located in quiet Bendlerstrasse, just half a block away from the German War Department. The building had formerly been a private mansion. There was a small garden in the rear, which furnished a restful view from the ambassador's windows.

Having just returned from Geneva, I thought Mr. Sackett might be interested in some of my observations. I called friendly Tyler Ogletree, who had held the office of personal aide to many ambassadors, and asked for an appointment.

"Come right over," said Ogletree, "the ambassador is having a walk in the garden. I am sure he'll be glad to see you."

I found Sackett exploring his flower beds. It was springtime, not long before Easter.

This quiet Kentuckian was not easily thrown off balance. As a businessman, he looked at the issues of a troubled world soberly. When he first arrived in Germany he knew little of the country and did not speak the language. He even had difficulty reading it. Yet, he worked hard to become acquainted with the people and their problems. He traveled widely, visited large and small towns, studying things carefully — all by himself.

Germany had been fortunate, ever since the end of the war, with the men Washington picked for the Berlin post. First had come Alanson B. Houghton, a truly eminent statesman who broke the ice and built a bridge of better understanding — a real ambassador of peace. He was followed by Dr. Schurman, of whom I have spoken before, a scholarly type of man with a profound knowledge of the country he was accredited to. But Mr. Sackett undoubtedly arrived at the most critical period. Bruening held him in high esteem and took him into his confidence more intimately than any other foreign diplomat.

"To us in America," Sackett remarked casually while still checking on his gardener and enjoying the first sunshine after a long period of gray, dull Berlin winter weather — "to many Americans the issues all Europe is worrying about are so remote. Sometimes I wish I could take our whole Congress from Washington to Berlin so they could see for themselves."

"Would it do any good?" I asked.

"Perhaps not. On the other hand, the people over here are loath to acknowledge that our problems at home are just as close to us as theirs are to them, and reparations aren't the worst headache we have."

I remember many details of that conversation. How Sackett recalled the statement in the annual report of Albert Wiggin, then chairman of the Chase National Bank, strongly urging a reduction of interallied debts; and the fourth inauguration speech of Albert C. Ritchie of Maryland when the governor insisted that "we will not prosper if the countries of Europe are prostrate"; and the warning of Edward N. Hurley, former member of the World War Foreign Debts Commission, that "it is questionable whether the world will pull out of its economic rut until such time as our country takes the initiative by some constructive international move"; and the address of

Dr. Nicholas Murray Butler, president of Columbia University, before the Chicago League of Nations Association which contained the challenging sentences: "What use is it to take in millions of cash in Washington if billions of value are flying out of the windows of the farm houses, the workmen's dwellings, the industrial, commercial, and financial establishments of the land? What shall it profit a nation to collect war debts in cash and to lose twenty times their amount in industry and trade?"

"You see," Sackett concluded, "many of our leaders know exactly what is at stake, but does the nation as a whole?"

Clearly everything depended on Bruening's success or failure.

At least they thought so at the Friday Circle. Over the luncheon table they were debating Bruening's policy of systematic deflation; and Hans Melk, meticulous public relations chief of the "Dresdner Bank," whose Jewish wife eventually was to be the cause of his dismissal from a lucrative job, once the nazis had moved in, was the most vociferous in his complaints.

"I've had two salary cuts now in three months," he reported.

Karl Nord, the ex-New Yorker, did not see eye to eye with him.

"What good does it do to gripe? Would you rather have inflation again? Bruening has no choice as long as the creditor countries pretend that we are evading our obligations."

"But aren't we?" insisted Melk. "Rather than cut salaries, we might as well pare down the budget of the military."

"And leave the country without defense?"

"We aren't going to wage a war, are we?"

"Not that I know of. However, the nations of Europe aren't all sheep and lambs, and so long as the others don't disarm, do you think we alone should go on the assumption that wolves don't bite?"

"Gentlemen," I interjected, "you are sailing straight into a red-hot argument. I heard all the pros and cons in Geneva last week. But what about reparations? I see where Hitler has just delivered another speech denouncing the Young Plan. Is he going to make this the theme of his campaign?"

"Certainly," Melk interrupted. "It is a 'natural' for him. Walter Funk, who seems to be Schacht's rival in the nazi camp, has an editorial in his paper this morning saying that you cannot milk the cow and get a steak out of its ribs at the same time!"

"He means reparations, of course," explained Nord, who was a stickler.

"No, the bovines!" Melk went on, sarcastically and unperturbed. "Let me read you from this clipping. Funk makes the point that you cannot take a cripple's crutch away and then force him to dance the rumba! I don't care for the man, but here he is talking of the artificial curtailment of German exports our creditors want to bring about. You must admit he's got something there."

"It's a simple alternative," Nord concluded. "Either we pay reparations in cash and go broke, or we pay them in kind, underselling our competitors in the world markets, and they'll be down on us for 'dumping.' It's always hard to please everybody."

"Especially when you have nazis around the house!" Weltin burst forth. "I tell you, reasonable people could settle this issue reasonably. But these rabble-rousers will ride it to death until they've got what they really want."

"What do you think they want?"

"War, of course, a war of revenge!"

"Oh, you are an alarmist! No one wants war."

It was time for me to leave.

"Let me tell you fellows," I said on my way to the door, "what I heard the Archbishop of York explain at a Cathedral service in Geneva the other day: 'It is not a question,' he said, 'of who lit the match in 1914, but of who had strewn the ground with gunpowder.' If we don't watch our step, all of us, a spark may well unleash the furies again. There is plenty of gunpowder around."

Few were such pessimists as to think of another war. The postwar disturbances, the communist uprisings, the Kapp *putsch,* the monetary inflation, and all the other troubles were still too vivid in everybody's memory. Somehow, that last war was not quite over yet.

"I cannot make ends meet any longer," one of the girls in Broadcasting House told me frankly. "I have a mother to support, and the cost of living is going up while salaries are going down, but the boss just laughs at me if I only mention a raise."

A young engineer was standing by.

"What's the use," he asked. "Here I am trying to do a decent job and keep a little money for a rainy day, but I don't seem to get anywhere. All I save, and more, is taxed away. For reparations, they say, all for reparations! What is that to me? I wish I could go to America."

"That's the way my boy friend talks," the blond miss nodded. "We can hardly afford a movie any longer. It's no fun having dates and no money! Let's all go to America!"

Had I only encouraged the people I knew personally, to emigrate, I could have filled both the Normandie and the Queen Mary, plus a few Zeppelins!

There was no use arguing. The rank and file did not care why and how the difficulties had arisen. What did they know of the intricacies of currency control and foreign exchange? What did they care about war debts? A new lease on life was all they wanted, and Bruening kept telling them this was the time to retrench, to make sacrifices, to give up things, if their country were to get back on its feet. He had no mirage to hold before them.

"Overtaxed bodies politic and economic are liable to suffer nervous breakdowns just as easily as human beings," he remarked to a friend one day. "The latter land in hospitals, the former are left to rebel."

\*       \*       \*

Came the presidental election of April 10, 1932. For the second time Hindenburg won. At the almost biblical age of eighty-four he was re-elected for another seven-year term which, fortunately for the old man, he did not live through. He had never aspired to public office. As a soldier he had not been particularly interested in politics. In 1925, after the death of Ebert, the Weimar Republic's first head, the presidency had been forced upon him. The nationalistic groups had chosen him as their standard-bearer at the instance of Ludendorff, the marshal's hothead war companion, the great loser of the battles of 1918. The marshal would much rather have remained in retirement, enjoying the quiet atmosphere of his

Hanover home, but he was finally prevailed upon to make the sacrifice for what he believed to be "the interest of the Fatherland."

The democratic parties in Germany had good reason to distrust Hindenburg. They were only too well aware of his testimony before a Reichstag committee of inquiry into the causes of the defeat, when he supported the preposterous legend that Germany's army had been "stabbed in the back" by defeatists at home. In reality, the refusal of the military and their clans to consider an honorable peace, and their insistence on fighting "to the last German," had brought disaster to a worn out and half-starved nation.

All this the democratic groups had not forgotten. To them, Hindenburg's election and the defeat of Wilhelm Marx, the Catholic candidate who stood for peace and international amity, and opposed exaggerated nationalism and militarism, meant a serious and disheartening setback. But after Hindenburg had taken over his new office, both his supporters and his opponents had to revise their opinions.

My first indirect contact with the old marshal was through a broadcast which had been made available for relay abroad. When he finally faced the microphone which had been set up in his office at the Wilhelmstrasse, no one was allowed to be present except his secretary. The man who was an almost mythical figure to his own people put on his glasses and stuck carefully to the manuscript. Microphones were not familiar to him. He was more accustomed to giving orders than to orating, but he did pretty well. From the heart of a distressed and chaotic Germany he spoke in a deep, rough-sounding voice of typically Prussian and military timbre.

I am afraid the aged man did not relish the event. It had taken a great deal of persuasion for him to go on the air, and some listeners thought they had heard him say *Gott sei Dank!* at the close of his remarks!

During his initial term of office Hindenburg had been strictly nonpartisan. For the first time in his life he watched government operate from inside. Now problems were brought home to him with which, as a soldier, he had never dealt. He became actively interested in the task, and though he had taken it on reluctantly, he found the job of president almost rejuvenating. In his sixty-odd years of public service he had not once felt the need of taking the waters of Karlsbad or Gastein. Now he had his daily walk in the park of his official residence, went hunting once in a while, and led a regular life.

Hindenburg's influence could well have been on the side of common sense and moderation, had his erstwhile friends and supporters been willing to play ball. They had no such intention and were incensed when it turned out that their idol, seemingly, was falling in line with the majority.

"They prefer a fire-eater," said Karl Nord at the Friday Circle. "Now that Hindenburg sticks to Bruening, they want none of him any longer."

"That's just their conception of loyalty," agreed Otto Weltin. "As they used to say in the old days, 'I'll let the king be an absolute ruler, if he will only do what I want!'"

"But is not Hindenburg perhaps the last bulwark between order and chaos?" I wondered.

"I wish he were," replied Weltin. "The old man is in a difficult position. His own cronies are old-line monarchists of the militant Prussian type. At heart he is one of them himself. They make him feel miserable right now by insinuating that he is conniving with the 'reds' and the Catholics."

"If he had to make a choice," Karl Nord concurred, "he would drop Bruening like a hot potato, and the general staff which has plotted against the republic all these years, would give the Doctor the coup de grâce!"

When the time came for the 1932 presidential election, Hindenburg found himself in an awkward position. While his own crowd was now backing Hitler, he emerged as the candidate of the democratic-socialist-Catholic coalition. It was as though the cards had been turned, and the old man did not like it.

Hitler was beaten, but he pulled double the vote he had obtained at the Reichstag election eighteen months before. Numerically, his party had now become the most powerful. The emotional impulse of nazi preachings definitely began to appear as a major factor in German politics.

This election was the German electorate's reply to the dallying of the experts — a manifestation of deep resentment. The masses vented their feelings by turning to the demagogues who promised a new day, if only they were raised to power.*

Half of the German voters were now in a mood of open defiance. They had abandoned hope for a peaceful revision of the Versailles treaty and for the restoration of normal economic conditions by parliamentary and diplomatic means. They were no longer willing to listen to appeals to reason.

The anti-democratic moles were hard at work. General Kurt von Schleicher, with the aid of Franz von Papen and Hindenburg's own son and aid-de-camp, Oskar, was plotting to overthrow Bruening. Again it was a question of taking the wind out of Hitler's sails. None of the big landowners and high financiers really wanted the rabble-rouser to win the race. To them he was far too "red." They were afraid of the masses he had goaded into a frenzy. Bruening, they told the old president, was powerless to handle the situation. Was not his own Catholic Center party depending on socialist support? Was not the struggle between Hitler and Bruening growing more bitter all the time? Something had to be done before it was too late. Bruening had to go.

The showdown was precipitated by an edict of Bruening's secretary of war, General Wilhelm Groener, suddenly banning the nazi storm troopers. A hue and cry went up from the hitlerites! Schleicher and his friends became alarmed. How could they stem the brown flood? They finally notified Groener that he no longer enjoyed the confidence of the army. Groener had to resign. A fortnight later Bruening's whole government collapsed. The intrigues of his foes had succeeded. Bruening requested the dissolution of the Reichstag that the people might express their views in a national election. Hindenburg refused.

With Bruening's resignation on May 30, 1932, Europe's last hope for peace was buried. The last barrier between a precarious order and uncontrollable chaos had broken down.

The months which followed, up to Hitler's conquest of all Germany, were like a downhill race into bottomless space. Two last-minute attempts were made to stop it, but it was

---

* "All unhappy and oppressed nations will run after any able adventurer who promises to deliver them," said George Bernard Shaw in an 88th birthday interview with the Associated Press. And he continued: "Our business, therefore, is not to make any nation unhappy or oppress it. If we had not oppressed Germany after 1918, there would have been no Hitler."

too late. Neither Papen, who had reaped Bruening's harvest when he obtained a belated agreement at Lausanne to scale Germany's remaining reparation debt down to 714 million dollars, nor Schleicher, who succeeded him for a brief interval, could build domestic levees fast enough, once the floodgates had been opened. Each remained chancellor only as long as it pleased Hitler.

When Papen dared face the issue by calling a national election, Hitler won again. This time he bagged 230 out of 600 Reichstag seats. But Papen refused to give up and dissolved the Reichstag once more. For the fifth time in one year the German people were called upon to express their preference for parties and party creeds. Call it democracy, or parliamentary government, but the actual will of the people becomes inarticulate when distorted by the mere moods of the hour. Excluding municipal elections, there had been no less than forty-five federal and state elections in Germany in the course of six years. And now another one!

This last free election of the German republic, on November 6, 1932, was a turbulent event. Over a three-day period, like thousands of others, I had to walk a considerable distance to reach my Berlin office, as the transportation workers had gone on strike against the Papen clique. Subways, streetcars, and bus services stopped completely. The feeling of the masses was deeply aroused against the nazis. Their votes brought an unexpected setback to Hitler. He lost thirty-four of the Reichstag seats he had previously won. This meant that only one third of the voters were for him — one third in the last free election Germany has had since 1932! Only one third in spite of all the misery, and all the agitation!

But Papen's position remained insecure. He was caught between two fires. By now the parties on the extreme left as well as those on the extreme right were against him. Playing both ends against the middle did not work any longer. The growling mass of "underdogs" was up in arms against the "top dogs." Hitler had no trouble undermining Papen. On November 17 the dapper colonel resigned.

After Papen it was Schleicher's turn, but only for eight weeks. His spasmodic days of government were filled with bitter feuds and with shameful juggling of political fortunes. On

January 28, 1933, Schleicher, too, was forced out. His was a tragic end indeed for he had made an honest effort to placate the riotous sea of popular passion. When it was evident that this last government of the Weimar Republic could not rally sufficient support, Papen appeared on the scene once more.

On January 4, 1933, a fateful meeting took place between Hitler, Papen, and Baron von Schroeder at the latter's residence in Cologne. Schroeder was a banker representing powerful interests of the Rhine and Ruhr industries. The Voegelers, the Springorums, the Thyssens, all the magnates of heavy industry, had been plugging for Papen. They opposed Schleicher, whom they considered too social minded. They were decidedly antisocialistic, antiunion, antidemocratic, and for this reason had strong misgivings lest Hitler himself turn out to be too "red." Papen did a yeoman job to convince them of the contrary. He was Hitler's first "appeaser," who felt that the wild man could somehow be tamed, and he made good temporarily by representing Hitler to the leaders of industry as the "savior from bolshevism," as the man who knew how to "handle" the masses, with bombast, parades, and the right ballyhoo.

Fearing for their possessions, anxious to maintain their privileges, the steel barons made a pact with the devil. They thought they were fooling Hitler, but Hitler jolly well fooled them. And the German people, despairing, starving, bewildered, and helpless, were caught in the trap almost unawares. Presaging the catastrophe, Theodor Wolff, the great editor, wrote in his *Berliner Tageblatt* on January 15, 1933: "We are now in a dark tunnel — if the mountain doesn't collapse, we will find the way out again." A fortnight later the mountain did collapse. Adolf Hitler rose to power.

In spite of the fact that over two thirds of the electorate had expressed themselves as against the nazis; in spite of the deep distrust which the nationalist groups entertained against them; in spite of the definite prospect of alleviation of Germany's debt burdens under the agreement of Lausanne; in spite of the promise finally exacted from the allied powers to grant equal status to Germany in the matter of armaments — in spite of all this the plotters of the Papen group succeeded in forcing the self-styled "Fuehrer" upon a confused nation torn by strife, weakened by long mental suffering, and emaciated by years of a cruel struggle for mere physical existence.*

Hugenberg, the "tory" newspaper and movie magnate; Seldte, the swaggering exponent of the ex-combatants; Blomberg, the obtuse career general; and Neurath, the indolent royalist, moved with Papen into a cabinet headed by Hitler. All thought he would only be a figurehead amenable to their whims. Instead they were easy bait for Hitler. When he ascended the "throne" of the Third Reich, he knew that thousands of Trojan horses would be taken inside the walls of the weak, dilapidated republic, thousands of quislings who for years had played his game while giving lip service to the democratic governments, thousands of adventurers and profiteers who were willing to "heil" him, if it only served their selfish interests. He also knew that there were millions of citizens unenlightened and lazy enough to resign themselves to a leadership such as his. He had only to provide sufficient emotional stir, brass bands, flag waving, and grandiloquence, to make these millions forget freedom and justice. He knew that the masses could be led and misled, for twenty years of war and revolution and economic chaos had eaten into the very foundations of the German nation.

Three years later Hitler said in one of his speeches: "The world need not think that the German people have rebelled simply because a certain man, Adolf Hitler, stands at its head; no, if I were not here, another would have come sooner or later."

In a sense this was exactly what *The New Statesman and Nation* of London had stated editorially after the tragedy of

---

* How in the light of these facts there can still be those who insist that Hitler was made head of the Reich by constitutional and democratic means is hard to understand. The statement recurs in a recent *New York Times* dispatch from London (July 29, 1944) which maintains that "with the full concurrence of the German people, the Weimar republic was dissolved into the nazi Reich," and the writer adds that this happened in spite of the "lenient peace" of Versailles. He might well have referred to the *New York Times* editorial of July 13, 1942, which said that "Hitler came into power as much by a series of governmental accidents and coups as by popular demand!" And he might have consulted the book by Professor Thomas A. Bailey of Stanford University, *Woodrow Wilson and the Lost Peace* (Macmillan, 1944) to satisfy himself that to a Germany made safe for democracy its death warrant was handed at Versailles with a treaty incorporating a war-guilt clause, impossible reparation bills, confiscation of colonies, etc. "The victor," concludes Professor Bailey, "can have vengeance, or he may have peace, but he cannot have both."

January 30, 1933, the greatest of our times: "When the history of the last twelve years comes to be written, we shall see that the central tragedy has been the failure to make use of the pacific mood of postwar Germany. For years after the war Germany was not only disarmed but she did not want to re-arm. The Hohenzollerns, the Junkers, the whole paraphernalia of Prussian militarism, were utterly discredited, and if the Allies had made a different use of their victory, the endless chain of Franco-German hostility would have been broken."

Whom the Gods would destroy, they first make mad, says a Latin proverb; and we might add, that some are stricken blind. To the postwar period in Europe the proverb can well be applied. The blindness of statesmen, the selfishness of all nations, led to another holocaust of humanity.*

---

* Cf. Appendix I.

# PART II

# GERMANY ENSLAVED

"*The people always have some champion whom they set over them and nurse into greatness. This and no other is the root from which a tyranny springs; when he first appears above ground he is a protector. In the early days of his career he is full of smiles and he salutes everyone he meets — he is to be called a tyrant, who is making promises in public and also in private; liberating debtors and distributing land to the people and his followers, and wanting to be so kind and good to everyone! But when he has disposed of foreign enemies by conquest or treaty, and there is nothing to fear from them, then he is always stirring up some war or other, in order that the people may require a leader. He has another object, which is that they may be impoverished by payment of taxes and thus compelled to devote themselves to their daily wants and therefore less likely to conspire against him. And if any of them are suspected by him of having notions of freedom and of resistance to his authority, he will have a good pretext for destroying them by placing them at the mercy of the enemy; and for all these reasons the tyrant must always be getting up a war.*"

(*Plato, "Republic."*)

# Chapter 6

## CATARACTS OF EVIL

THE only nazi I had known back in 1932 was "Putzi" Hanfstaengel, who was a sort of liaison officer for Hitler with the American press and radio. E. F. Sedgwick Hanfstaengel was his full name. His American mother was the daughter of General William Heine of the Fifth Army of the Potomac. Putzi had been a freshman at Harvard and had rowed on the Varsity crews in 1909 before returning to Germany. In Munich he met the future "Fuehrer" who admired his virtuosity on the piano. His house became one of the early nazi headquarters. Putzi was said to have saved Hitler's life one day when a mob of outraged citizens was after him. Had Putzi kept out of it, the whole course of history might have been altered. After the nazi "blood purge," he repented and eventually became a refugee in Canada.

I pounced on Putzi at the Kaiserhof Hotel in Berlin some months before Hitler's rise to power. He did not notice me at first, for he seemed carried away to the seventh heaven by the orchestra that was playing in the lobby.

I started the conversation. "They are good, aren't they? Should we put them on the air?"

"I wish you would!" Putzi echoed absentmindedly.

"Perhaps we will, but right now we're after your boss."

"Not a chance."

"Why not? He'd make news."

"I know, but you fellows haven't got anything to offer."

"Offer? He doesn't expect to be paid, does he?"

"Well . . ." Putzi hesitated. "You know what I mean. For some charity, of course, such as the storm trooper pension fund."

"We are not paying for political speeches."

"Beautiful music, isn't it?" was all the further information I could elicit.

It meant, cold cash, or no Hitler. Besides, the Bruening government would not have given permission for a broadcast by the rabble-rouser. Putzi suggested a way out of this difficulty on a later occasion.

"We could go to Luxemburg, or Monaco, or some such place, you know," he hinted the next time I saw him. Since we remained adamant on the cash involved, that scheme, too, had to be dropped.

When Hitler became Chancellor of the Reich, it was a different story, and the program manager phoned from New York to say that we should get Adolf on the air.

I had just set up headquarters in Basel, Switzerland. It had become essential to operate from a neutral territory in order to maintain full mobility. The historic border city, romantically perched on the slopes of the Rhine and strategically situated on one of Europe's most traveled crossroads, was an ideal vantage point for our purposes. To be assigned to this post meant securing a grandstand seat at the European drama which was fast reaching its climax.

When the news came that the nazi avalanche had struck, people stood on Basel's street-corners reading the "extras" and rubbing their eyes. I picked up a copy. That moment I felt the hopes of a century had collapsed. It was like a ghastly nightmare, exasperating because it made no sense, revolting because of the brutality of the change, seemingly unavoidable, chaotic, and cruel.

I took the night express to Berlin, arriving the day after the brown earthquake. Life in the city had not changed. It was like a landscape after a storm, with deep, dark clouds overhanging the horizon, and threatening further outbursts, but for the moment people were glad that they had somehow weathered the first shock.

To the rank and file the change of regime had come as a complete surprise. Few were aware of the stubborn dogmatism of revolutionary doctrinarians such as Rosenberg and Goebbels. Few realized that the materialistic nazi creed of "blood and soil" meant a fanatical emphasis on the body over the soul.

At the same time there were many among the younger generation as well as among the unthinking masses who were just in
the right mood to listen to promises entailing the destruction
of "capitalistic tyranny," the elimination of Jewish competitors
and the unquestioned rule of the supposedly superior "Aryan"
race.

At the club, my friends did not know very much. It had all
come about with dramatic suddenness, and it was difficult
to get the facts. A hush-up atmosphere seemed to permeate
public life. Hearsay was plentiful, and most of it distressing.
Unfamiliar faces began to appear in government offices, mostly
appointees from nazi ranks. There was much saluting in the
Hitler manner. Many did it awkwardly.

A wild scramble for political safety was in full progress
everywhere. I remember one man in Berlin who for some
time had held a semiofficial position. A few weeks before the
change of regime he had said to me:

"Aren't we cowards? Here we see it coming. It's unavoidable. Hitler will win. And yet I cannot bring myself to join
his ranks. Something tells me I should not. I know Hitler is
on the wrong track, but if he comes out on top, where will
I be?"

The fellow joined up with the nazis the day Hitler moved
into the Wilhelmstrasse. He was a latecomer, a *Maerzge-
fallener,* as they called them, one who "fell in March," who
had made up his mind just a trifle late when it was no longer
risky to bet on the nazi horse. He was one of thousands.
Men and women of the last hour, frantically rushing to
save their skins, their jobs, the livelihood of their families,
swelled the total of Hitler's legions. Although some were
weak of character, or confused by campaign oratory, many
more were simply dead tired and discouraged after years of
futile struggle, years of war and revolution, of unemployment
and depression. Also, many were frankly disgusted by the
corruption of public morals which had set in after the devastating period of monetary inflation. They thought that the
degenerating influences which had crept into the life of the
nation could be eliminated quickly, if someone would only
use an *"eisernen Besen,"* an iron broom.

"Why did you vote for Hitler?" I asked a well-to-do businessman who had been a believer in popular government all his
life. "How could you?"

"Why," he replied wearily, "I felt we had to have a change
— that's all."

A change — but a change for what? Most people did not
know. Most did not care. Hitler promised everybody everything, like Louisiana's Huey Long who had promised to
make "every man a King." He promised capital that labor
would be crushed; he promised labor the social revolution.
To the middle class he promised revaluation of their de-
preciated properties, to the farmers, higher prices. And to the
nation as a whole he promised the tearing-up of the treaty of
Versailles and a shining army and navy, parades and pageants
and a paradise on earth — if they would only vote for him, the
great wizard and leader of leaders! Now the time had come
to pay up.

After checking in at my hotel I went to see Kurt Rathke,
the program manager at Broadcasting House.

"Heil Hitler!" he greeted me.

"What?"

I was completely taken aback. Never before had Rathke
professed nazi sympathies, but now he wore the party button
on his lapel, "the birdie," as the people nicknamed it.

"You, too, Brutus?" I was about to say; but I held my
tongue.

"You need not be surprised," Rathke explained coldly.
"We've been getting ready for this, you know. I have been
a member of the party under an assumed name for some
time."

"But you drew a salary from a corporation controlled by a
democratic government, didn't you?"

"That's got nothing to do with it. Hitler is the government
now, isn't he?"

Just in case Hitler should win, thousands had held their
"insurance" secretly for years. Had he lost, all these water-on-
both-shoulders people would never have disclosed their underground affiliations. Now they could come out into the open and
throw off the mask. They had aided and abetted hitlerism
under cover, as a matter of self-protection. Now they were in

the saddle, with prospects of higher income and promotion.

"Is Hitler to go on the air?" I asked, struggling to conceal my disgust.

"We expect so," said Rathke. "Better stand by. I'll give you a ring as soon as I know."

Hitler did not want to broadcast. He was accustomed to mass meetings, not to the microphone, and shied away from it. It took some persuading before he finally made up his mind. I got the promised call the following afternoon.

"Come right over to the Chancery," Rathke phoned breathlessly. "Hitler is going on half an hour from now."

I rushed a wire off to New York and dashed for a taxi. Rathke was waiting. We went upstairs. Rudolf Hess, tall, quiet, then still Hitler's deputy as party leader, stood in the reception room, not knowing what to do with himself, and seemingly lost in the sudden governmental glory. After Rathke had introduced me to Hess, I asked if Hitler would agree to have his talk relayed to America.

"The Fuehrer cannot be disturbed," Hess ruled abruptly.

That very moment Dr. Hjalmar Schacht walked into the room. Barely a year before he and I had tiffed, so I could expect but little help from him. Concentrating on Hess again, I managed at last to get him into a corner.

"You surely want the world to listen to this speech, don't you?" I coaxed.

Hess blew up, impatiently.

"It's going to be a German speech. It makes no sense putting it on for those abroad."

"I could translate it."

"There is no copy available. The Fuehrer speaks from notes."

"That's all right. I'll just interpolate the English, sentence after sentence, while I listen."

"No one can do that. How could you render the proper meaning so quickly!"

Hess meant what he said. He could not conceive of anyone tackling the shrieks and shouts of the boss except in mute admiration.

"How about Dr. Schacht checking up on me while I do it?" I suggested.

Hess stared at me. I was rather persistent, wasn't I?

"Well," he said finally, "you'd better talk to Schacht about that. I haven't time now."

At that moment Hitler walked into the room, dressed in a blue lounge suit. Hess could not help presenting me, and we shook hands.

..*"Guten Tag!"* Hitler muttered.

He looked ill at ease. His movements were awkward and I noticed a gleam in his eyes which I did not like. There was nothing fascinating or startling about his appearance. The man who was to set the world aflame struck me as a dull, below-average person. Most of my acquaintances who had had an opportunity to observe him shared this impression although they admitted that Hitler certainly knew how to captivate crowds with the violence of his language. Later on when his harsh metallic voice came barking over the air all too frequently, many listeners would turn off their radios with repugnance.

To witness Hitler's first broadcast was no glamorous experience. I had met Papen in that same room, a few weeks before while putting him on the air. Papen was a discerning host and invited the radiomen to share a bottle of wine after we had finished the job. Hitler was in no such hospitable mood. He looked somber and unfriendly and his speech was commonplace.

Talking of the "terrible heritage" he claimed he was taking over, he modestly described his as "the heaviest task assigned to a German statesman since time immemorial." I looked at Schacht who stood there impassive. Could all this nonsense be taken seriously?

"German people!" Hitler shouted into the microphone, gesticulating hectically. "Give me four years' time and then judge!"

It was not necessary to wait four years to conclude that with this maniac in charge, the nation's ruin was a certainty. A magnified Pied Piper, he played the tune which plunged a whole people into chaos.

After Hitler had finished, he walked out of the room. He did not even say good-bye to his attendants. The broadcast had been carried to America without further objections and as no one paid any attention to me any longer, I could now give a brief English summary of the "Fuehrer's" revelations to the world. After that first attempt the Hitler speeches we took were far fewer than the ones we didn't.

* * *

The memorable "triangular" voyage of the airship "Graf Zeppelin" to Brazil and Chicago in 1933 had been planned when only few people were expecting the nazi calamity, and aviation was not going to stop because of Hitler. So there was no point in canceling the arrangements I had made with Dr. Kurt Eckener, the skipper, for broadcasts during the flight.

The crew of the airship included many honest-to-goodness nazis, naïvely sincere men, misled, confused Hitler addicts who looked up to the "Fuehrer" as to a savior. Among themselves they used the nazi salute, but they never tried it on Eckener. The huge swastikas painted on the ship's fins were a deep humiliation to the sturdy mariner. When I talked to him alone, I could sense how he felt, but he thought little could be accomplished by public remonstration.

"How is it all going to end?" I asked him the day after we had started from Friedrichshafen, when German territory was safely behind us. A shrug of the shoulder was his only answer. The old man puffed at his pipe and looked into the endless spaces of the sky and water ahead of him as though he were steering his ship into an inscrutable eternity full of ill forebodings. Late at night he used to stand in the Commander's gondola all by himself, like a rock in a stormy sea, silent, grim, unshakable.

The crew respected and obeyed him, but they knew he was of another breed. They instinctively felt that he belonged to an age from which they were trying to break away. They had faith, an unreflecting, sentimental faith in the alluring promises of the blustering new leader who was now on his way up. They wanted a hope, a fresh confidence in their national destiny. They wanted it so badly that they let themselves be completely taken in by the noisy boastings of the usurpers.

Three years later, on a trip of the "Hindenburg" which took up where the "Graf" had left off, the number of politically blind among the crew was still appallingly large. A Mass said by Father Paul Schulte, priest and missionary aviator, was an important event of that journey. It was the first time that a divine service was conducted on an airship and the holy function was favored by perfect weather. When the priest lifted the chalice for consecration it reflected the gleam of a glorious sun over the wide blue expanse of the ocean. To me it was an unforgettable experience to have been acolyte on such an occasion, but no less impressive was the reverent attendance of the crew which even then did not seem to be remotely aware of the anti-Christian bias of nazi preachings.

Our broadcasts from aboard the great airships were successful, in 1936 as well as in 1933. During the first trip, it was an exciting moment when, after testing with New York for days, the cheerful voice of ever-alert William Burke Miller, manager later on of NBC's Public Service Department, suddenly came clear through the ether from Radio City, to engage in the first two-way conversation publicly broadcast in radio history between an airship aflight and the mainland.

I was so excited that while reading the verses a fellow passenger had written to commemorate the event, quite unconsciously I began to sing; and a tenor solo (or was it baritone?) from a maestro until then — and since — unknown to the world of music was relayed to a vast unseen audience. A little later congratulations which, I suspect, were mildly ironical, began to arrive from headquarters.

"You must admit," remarked the young nazi engineer who had been in charge of the radio tests, "that this is a great accomplishment for Germany."

"It is an accomplishment all right," I conceded, "but have you forgotten Marconi and the Wright Brothers? All nations contribute their share to the progress of civilization."

"But this," he insisted ecstatically, "this could not have happened without Hitler!"

I gave up.

\* \* \*

When I got back to Berlin a few weeks later, I had occasion to explore further this phenomenon of a mass mind fitted into a single groove, and the mob hysteria whipped up by means of a mammoth propaganda organization.

The city had just been through another one of those huge affairs in the sports stadium which Goebbels staged at regular intervals, to provide distraction. I knew a young worker who had attended. While telling me about it, he expressed his scorn.

"Bluffers!" he sneered.

"But didn't you fellows all join in the cheering?" I asked.

"Why, of course," he admitted. "What else could we do?"

"Kept quiet!"

"With a dozen snoopers in our group? Do you realize that not to cheer means the concentration camp? Besides, you know how it is when the brass bands strike up martial tunes, and the searchlights are turned on, and there is a parade with all the regalia! Somehow, everybody is taken in by the show. And so was I. But then I went home and told my wife what fakes those brass-hats are!"

And, as for good measure, he added:

"All the fellows in my plant, with very few exceptions, think exactly as I do."

How did it happen that these wage-earners, most of them socialists of a moderate brand, were completely subdued by the nazi whip? How could they be stripped so suddenly of the democratic rights they had valiantly fought for during the postwar period? Disunity of the labor ranks is only one of the answers.

Hitler himself, upon taking hold of the government, had asserted in an official proclamation, that he had come "to lead the German people to liberty." Through his Secretary of the Interior, Wilhelm Frick, he gave the assurance that "the new government seeks to live in peace and friendship with all the world." The nazi press promised the millennium "after the democratic mismanagement of fourteen years."

"Let the country sit in judgment," orated Hitler. "Let them crucify me, if at the end of four years we have not succeeded!"

And again: "I have been represented as making blood-thirsty, firebrand speeches, but I never have! Anybody who has seen war as I have seen it, knows what a tremendous waste of effort and strength it is. We can only guess what the results of another war would be, and nobody wants peace more than I do."

Far too many were willing to trust these promises. Worn

out by long years of suffering, discouraged and tired, the
working men, too, felt they had no choice. They did not
sense the dreadful portent of Hitler's threat of "a merciless
war on spiritual, political, and cultural nihilism," but a few
days later when all civil liberties were crushed, they knew
they had been caught in a trap.

The politicians were taken by surprise, no less than the
workers, but they tried to stall and gain time, to reorganize
their squadrons. When Hitler asked for a one year recess
of the Reichstag, the Catholic Center Party raised the simple
question whether the new government meant to respect the
Constitution. Hitler's answer was to send the Reichstag home
to clear the way for a national election managed by his own
machine.

A wave of terrorism swept the country. Anti-nazi meetings
were banned. Socialists and members of the democratic parties
were wantonly arrested. Brown-shirted bullies who had been
outlaws only a few days before, became "auxiliary police."

Still the rank and file of the German people did not
realize what the whole business was about. They wondered
and pondered. Hitler now denied having ever been a "firebrand." Yet, a few months before he had threatened that
"heads would roll." And what about the violence of his
campaign methods? Had not his gangs been engaged in
street brawls and strong-arm methods throughout the country?

The perennial optimists sought to dispel such misgivings.
Things would change, they insisted. The madmen would cool
down. And there was still Hindenburg, and Papen, and
Hugenberg to see to it that the wild fellows were kept under
control. After all, the nazis seemed to be patriots. Had they
not gained power by seemingly legal means? There were
rumors of backstage intrigues, but no one knew anything for
certain. Perhaps the nazis really meant well. They wanted
Germany to get back on her feet economically and to grow
strong and respected again in the family of nations. With that
no one could quarrel.

Most of these befuddled people wanted so much to believe.
They refused instinctively to be disappointed again. A Berlin
school teacher whom I had known for some time came to
see me one afternoon, just to ask whether I thought Hitler

meant what he said. Her name was Irma and she belonged to the landed gentry of the East, which meant that her family was nationalistic to the marrow. Irma herself had not quite fallen in line with the family tradition and did some thinking of her own. Nevertheless she had never entertained any sympathy for the democratic regime and felt rather relieved when "better people" such as Barons and Generals took over the reins again.

"Of course," she said smiling, and she looked attractive in her simple dress, and her big wondering eyes revealed a sincere heart, "Of course, I'd rather have Papen than Hitler."

"Why?" I retorted. "With Hitler you know at least where you stand."

"Oh, but Papen is a gentleman."

"You really think so? And you doubt that Hitler is one, do you?"

That was an embarrassing question.

"Well, after all, he is rather new, isn't he?"

"Should that not recommend him in a way?" I pursued.

"Perhaps. But why do these nazis destroy so much of the past?"

"What, for instance?"

"For instance, our old flag, and our imperial emblems. My brother says that we may have to get used to 'socialism' in national socialism and he doesn't like it."

"How are things in your school?" I inquired.

She laughed.

"All upside down!"

"How?"

"Well, you see, the children can't get used to the Heil Hitler and I have to scold them when they don't use it, but then they catch me, when I forget to use it myself!"

"Would you say that the children like it?"

"They don't know. They are too little. It's just that Jewish girl in our class that's causing us some worry."

"How do the other kids behave?"

"Fine. They are nice to her, but shy. They hear all this talk about the Jews. It's pitiful, you know."

"It's pitiful, too, that everybody seems to stand for it."

"But that isn't so!"

"Not in your school?"

Irma became all excited.

"In no school! I know what the other teachers tell me. This whole Jewish thing is not taken seriously. It just can't last!"

"And you still think that Hitler is sincere?"

"Well, I don't know. Everybody is so confused. Some of the things Hitler does I like, and others I don't like at all. Neither does my older brother. The younger one says everything will turn out all right, and, after all, if only our country gets back on its feet, nothing else will matter. In the beginning, you can't help some *Schoenheitsfehler,* some minor blemishes, I suppose. It's so great a change. If I had to choose, I'd certainly prefer the nazis to the communists."

"Is that what your brother tells you?"

"Yes, and I think so, too."

"Then you should really support Hitler, shouldn't you?"

"Maybe I should, but something tells me that there is a catch. You see, he's got too much red in his flag. My brother says that's only temporary and that Hindenburg will have it changed soon. Do you think he will?"

No, I did not think so, and I felt sorry for Irma, for she and her brother were like the many other wishful thinkers who had a rude awakening in store for them. They had been brought up in accordance with the old rugged standards, were ignorant of the world beyond their narrow fences and were now caught utterly unprepared by the bravado of upstarts whom their kind had cultivated and supported, only to be outsmarted in the end. If there was any fault on the part of these people, it was mainly their incredible stupidity.

# Chapter 7

# BLITZKRIEG AT HOME

LESS than a week after Hitler's triumphant entry into the Wilhelmstrasse Chancery, a decree "for the protection of the German nation" was issued in Berlin, completely gagging the press, prohibiting newspapers from attacking the government, making appeals for labor strikes a criminal offense, and banning foreign publications which carried even a hint of criticism of the nazi regime. At the same time authority was given to suppress public meetings "when danger to the public security must be feared, disobedience to the laws or to measures of the government or its officers is invited, or prominent officials are defied" — a provision broad enough to stifle all opposition.

The Hitler press, of course, remained free to vilify its opponents, to distort the news without fear of contradiction and to intimidate all those who dared to disagree with the infallible "Fuehrer." Catholic papers which were bold enough to publish a party manifesto protesting the dissolution of the Reichstag and condemning "every policy that leaves the path of law and justice" were promptly banned for three days.

A climax was reached on February 28th, 1933. For almost five weeks an election campaign of unprecedented violence had been in progress. Only the nazis had had complete freedom of speech. All other parties were at a disadvantage. "Emergency decrees" restricted them from saying what they thought was essential. Many of their speakers were jailed. Ordinary electioneering was made impossible. But despite these precautions there were millions unconvinced by Hitler's promises, millions who did not trust him. Something had to be done to swing that election.

It was not enough to threaten the voters by assigning storm troopers to police duty. It was not enough to make these perpetrators of mass assaults on peaceful citizens, the instruments of public order. It was not enough to have opposition newspapers muzzled, and to give every freedom to the nazi press to disparage their foes. It was not enough to raid communist headquarters in Berlin and to "discover" as though by prearrangement that the "reds" were about to start a violent revolution. Goebbels and his boys had their field day slandering to the core those who were not nazis. The attacked were defenseless. Anything they might say could be construed as "endangering the security of the state." Still, it was plain that the majority of the people were not behind Hitler.*

The Reichstag fire was to save the day. Less than a week before the election Berliners woke up one morning to find that flames and smoke had destroyed the glass-ceilinged assembly chamber and eaten through the cupola of the huge building during the night.

When the news reached me in the early morning, I rushed to the scene. A puzzled crowd was being held back by the police.

"I hope Adolf took out good insurance!" I overheard a newsboy whispering to his pal in true Berlin slang.

"I bet you," was his answer, "Hermann will get a fireman's medal!"

The fire engines had not even reached the blazing structure when nazi police started wholesale arrests of communists. Before dawn most of their leaders were taken into custody. Thousands more were arrested in the days that followed, thrown into concentration camps, beaten, tortured, and killed in Gestapo jails, and their families exposed to unspeakable indignities. Offices were raided, literature and other belongings confiscated. All constitutional guarantees of private property, freedom of the press and assembly, personal liberty, secrecy of postal communications, and even autonomous state rights were abolished.

Hitler had started his war against the German people. His

---

* Wm. Philip Simms, editorial writer of the Scripps-Howard newspapers was fully justified in saying in his column (January 30, 1943) that "to believe all [the pre-Hitler] anti-nazis suddenly turned pro-nazi the moment the Chaplin-mustached megalomaniac supplanted von Hindenburg is to be naïve. . . . It is quite clear that millions of Germans do not love Hitler; to protest, however, meant the concentration camp."

first stroke was against the communists. Others were to
follow.

"No hurry!" said Goebbels. "We'll get to all of them."

And, indeed, they did get to all of them, first at home, and
then all over the world.

\* \* \*

The day after the fire Hitler, Papen, and Hugenberg went
on the air together with lesser nazi lights to decry the "Bolshevist peril." At last "the night of long knives," which Hitler
had forecast for some time, was here. The fire provided the
pretext for crushing all legitimate opposition on the eve of
the national election. A reign of terror had begun.

There were wholesale arrests without warrants. Some sixty
thousand brown-shirted storm troopers armed with guns and
rubber truncheons were turned loose. People began to tell
stories of gruesome happenings in storm trooper dungeons.
There were spots in Berlin and other cities no one dared
go near any longer. Fearful crying and shrieking was heard
in these neighborhoods. Patrol-wagons had been seen carrying
away blood-stained victims. Fear gripped the minds of a whole
nation that bolshevism, either red or brown, had really gained
a foot-hold in the country.

Election day, March 4th, was a holiday filled with sunshine.
No disturbances occurred. On Unter den Linden members of
the nationalist "Steel Helmet" organization marched proudly
as though they were trying to emphasize that besides the
Brown Shirts, they too, were in the picture. All kinds of nazi
doggerel were sold in public places.

The night before, the whole country had been ablaze with
bonfires. Torch-light parades had been staged in the smallest
villages. Brass bands were blaring. Five weeks of ruthless
terrorism and unprecedented propaganda had put across the
slogan "For Hindenburg and Hitler!" The voters were made
to believe that by casting their ballots against the democratic
parties they were serving the best interests of the country.
Hindenburg's name was freely used to shield every breach
of the law and to denounce as unpatriotic anyone disagreeing
with Hitler. The simple-minded were impressed by the claim
that a "day of liberation" had come, that a new era was being
ushered in, one of endless bliss under the sway of the swastika.

The opposition having been completely muzzled, it was a "one-way" election. Dissenters were strictly *verboten*. Only nazi candidates were given time on the air. Blatantly the nazis announced that they would stay in power, no matter what the result of the election might be. However, there was no doubt about the outcome. What with all the non-nazi leaders silenced and the complete domination of the press by nazi censors, a landslide victory for Hitler seemed assured.

It was the eighth national election since the adoption of the Weimar Constitution in 1919. Some 200,000 nazi party bosses were candidates for government offices of all kinds, and they triumphed (the very day President Roosevelt was inaugurated in Washington). But their triumph was a Pyrrhic victory.

In spite of brutal intimidation of the voters, of incredible election clownery, big-stick methods, and every conceivable roorback, the nazis did not succeed in winning more than 44 per cent of the voters — some 17 million ballots out of a total of 39! In the Prussian Diet election held on the same day their share was even smaller, that is, 43 per cent of the total vote cast. Despite all the repressive measures, 56 per cent of the voters still were not convinced of the desirability of nazi blessings.

In the Reichstag, the nazis now held 288 and the Nationalists 52 seats, out of a total of 647. Only by including the Nationalist party vote of some three million did Hitler succeed in controlling 52 per cent of the Reichstag membership.

At the Friday Circle these results were the subject of lively debate.

"It's really a defeat for the nazis," Otto Weltin concluded his analysis, "especially when you think of all the tampering they must have done with the ballots."

"Has there been any evidence of that?" I asked.

"You babe-in-the-woods!" laughed Werner Pratt.

"Plenty," Weltin continued. "Let's not talk about it. The Gestapo has long-distance ears, you know!"

"The democratic parties," said Pratt, changing the subject, "have not made such a bad showing at all when we keep in mind the terrific handicaps they labored under. Why, back in 1919, when the Reichstag had only 430 members, they won 283 seats, the radical socialists and communists jointly 82, and the reactionaries 65. We've slipped, of course, but everything considered, far less than might have been expected."

"Right," agreed Weltin. "It's amazing. After these years of constant setbacks for the republican regime, in spite of mass unemployment and all the troubles in connection with the execution of the peace treaties, and notwithstanding the incredible boondogling of our politicians, and the whole nazi mess, in spite of it all, the enemies of democracy haven't won yet!"

"That is, if you can depend on the rules of the game being observed," I cautioned. "Who tells you that Hitler will abide by them and recognize a parliamentary majority?"

"He won't," admitted Weltin. "Incidentally, where is Herzberg today?"

Dr. Nathan Herzberg, an old member of the Circle, a retired judge beloved by all of us had not attended the Friday sessions for some time.

"He's gone," said Hans Melk.

"Gone? Where to?"

"Holland. He thought he'd better beat the nazis to it."

We all remained silent for a while. Then Melk spoke with a strange melancholy in his voice.

"He is the first one. There'll be more. . . ."

\* \* \*

Hitler himself must have been aware of his failure to win over a majority of the German people. His mouthpiece, the *Voelkischer Beobachter* came out with a significant front-page editorial two days after the election.

"Hitler does not mean to establish a tyranny in Germany," it said, "as is still believed by many who have been deceived."

It was an interesting statement in the light of subsequent events, but even more so because of the implied admission that "many" were full of doubts regarding the real intentions of the nazi regime.

After that last relatively legal election Hitler might still have had a chance to set things straight. He could have succeeded, had he been honest in his intentions. The weary people were even prepared to condone some of the more disturbing nazi habits, hoping that many of the "rough edges" might be smoothed out in due course, once Hitler had assumed power and shouldered the responsibilities of government. They forgot that they had opened the gates of government to the nation's lunatic fringe, and were now under the rule of the mob's lowest dregs.

The day after the election, orders came from Berlin to seize the "Free Cities" of Hamburg, Bremen, and Luebeck. Storm troopers lined up in front of the historic city halls. Nazi commissars moved in. It was Hamburg's turn first. Bremen and Luebeck were taken over the next day. These proud, ancient centers of trade and commerce, of culture and learning, cities praised for their international-mindedness, and envied for their world-wide contacts, were now like deposed queens. Narrow-minded fanatics, "small fry" which the aristocratic upper class found hard to swallow, took over control. Likewise, nazi overlords were appointed as administrators of the states of Bavaria, Saxony, Württemberg, and Baden.

Now that the restraint imposed by an election campaign seemed no longer essential, the nazis came out into the open more boldly every day. Self-appointed posses began to picket Jewish stores in Berlin. Goebbels' own newspaper, *Der Angriff,* stated bluntly that the nazi "hatred of the Jews is not a passing fancy, for the Jews brought international capitalism and they also brought marxism" — a pliable argument that could be fitted into any pattern of thinking. At the same time Goering maintained that "the life and properties of Jewish citizens pursuing loyal conduct toward the government would be guaranteed by the law." Hitler himself was even more specific when he proclaimed, in Munich, on March 13th: "Our will is not to coerce anybody, but to guarantee the highest measure of ideal freedom by raising the German nation to the status of equality."

Evidently, the new rulers were out to fool the people on a gigantic scale. Their basic premise was a brazen identification of country and nazism. Whoever was not with Hitler was branded "un-German," a traitor to his country. The nazi party membership had only been one and a half million when Hitler came to power, yet these one and one half million, many of whom were just turn-coats, claimed to be the only real patriots. Anyone daring enough to object, faced social ostracism, beatings, concentration camp confinement, or worse.

Public officials who had come into office following the change of regime in 1918, also those of the Jewish race and those not considered loyal to the new regime were summarily dismissed, and deprived of their pensions. Nazi office-seekers were at hand to replace them. Men with criminal records, such as Count Helldorf and Edmund Heines, in Potsdam and Breslau respectively, were made chiefs of police. Indeed, Hitler's first *Blitzkrieg* was the one against the German people themselves.

However, Hitler's Reichstag majority remained meager. A two thirds' vote was required to change the constitution. The nazis controlled only 340 votes while at least 376 were required. The Catholic Center and the Bavarian Catholic party were in a quandary. Hitler's claim that he was out to destroy "marxism" and was not thinking of violence against anyone else, made an impression on some of their constituents. At the same time theirs had been only a six per cent share of the popular vote, and religious leaders were still hoping that once in power, the nazis would be amenable to reason. Had not Hitler himself made binding promises to respect the rights of the churches?

As for the ruling caste of the army, it shared the illusion of the nationalist groups that nazism was but a sort of catalytic agent, that the hitlerites could be kept in bounds, and that their patriotic fervor could be used to good advantage to promote rearmament and a new policy of the iron fist. They had reason to be hopeful, for in the course of seven weeks the brown avalanche had uprooted the last vestiges of what the military called "democratic balderdash."

Was it because democracy in Germany was an unnatural product of the defeat in 1918; or merely that it was too decent, too naïve, too disorganized, to face so unscrupulous and callous a foe? Was it the hesitancy of its leaders, or the blindness of the victors that caused its downfall?

There was one man who had anticipated events. That man was Bruening. He who had stood at the head so long, "taking it" patiently from all sides, had disappeared from the public eye. To him many were still looking for guidance and advice, but he was aware of the overwhelming strength of the sudden impact and preferred to keep his counsel until it was sought.

He had found a hide-out in St. Hedwig's Hospital, in the heart of Berlin. Although he was not a patient, the good Sisters watched over him and visitors were allowed only by personal introduction and after a careful check-up.

"I suppose there is a good reason for it," the kindly Doctor told me when I first saw him in the dark parlor adjacent to his bedroom. "Over there, they are keeping an eye on me!"

"Over there" meant across the street, where the nazis had set up a spy nest, just for him, Bruening explained.

"They have hired a room exactly opposite mine and watch me day and night, to see who calls on me, and to get a clue as to what I may be up to. I guess they must be scared of me!"

Bruening was a son of the West and fond of choice wines. He also liked his smoke although the house physician had warned him that his heart condition would not permit too many cigars.

"My friends send me such good brands," he smiled, "that it's hard to resist. What would you like? A Johannisberger, or a Niersteiner Domtal?"

Those who really knew him were unable to understand how the opposition could ever have conceived of this man as a sinister plotter. Bruening had too much of an academic mind, and was too sincere a patriot ever to think of himself. The hesitancy and cautiousness for which he was criticized sprang from his intimate knowledge of the problems he was dealing with. Knowing the many sides of every question he frequently was slow to act, and his unscrupulous opponents knew how to take advantage of this quality.

"They have won out for the present," Bruening commented bitterly. "They won't in the long run though."

"Why," I asked, "could you not have grabbed the nazi bull by the horns and simply have had Hitler and his gang arrested?"

"I know," Bruening replied. "That's what everybody is saying now. Why didn't we? As though it had been as simple as that! The nazi movement was not a cause. It was a result, a consequence. Eliminating the symptoms rather than the causes would have meant nothing."

"But would it not have strengthened your position at home and abroad and helped you to gain time at least?"

"While conditions remained what they were? I doubt it. You know that I was not alone in my views. Men like Sackett and Keynes and Andrew McFaydean* were in full agreement with us that a major operation was required to stave off disaster. The evil growth that has now developed could have been stopped, had all the governments agreed to act when there was still time to act. We did our part. There was nothing else we could have done."

"Suppose you had prevailed on Hindenburg to call a national assembly. Would that not have helped in stealing Hitler's thunder?"

"It might have. But who would have dared suggest such a thing after the fiasco of the Austrian customs union plan? A national assembly could easily have decided to restore the monarchy. You can imagine what a hue and cry the world would have raised!"

"Particularly," I suggested, "since you were constantly reproached for having abandoned the conciliatory policies of some of your predecessors."

Bruening smiled wryly.

"I think you know the answer yourself. We went to the very limit in our efforts to bring about a working agreement with our creditors. Remember how I traveled to Paris, to London, to Geneva, to meet our partners more than half way. But for every statesman who depends on popular backing there is a limit. He can go only as far as the innate sense of self-preservation of the people will permit. Governments aren't miracle workers, and crowns totter when the crowds are howling!"

"They indeed totter right now," I agreed. "But what is in store?"

Bruening did not answer. He looked at me, puffing at his cigar, as though he meant to imply that I should have known better and not asked a question for which there was no answer.

"Have you seen Father Herbert recently?" he asked after a moment of thoughtful silence.

No, I had not. This priest who had been a close friend of

* Cf. Appendix I.

Bruening's for many years and had taught at one of the
major universities, had held a determined stand against nazi
ideas. No doubt, he was on Hitler's blacklist.

"I wish you'd go and see him. He ought to be careful.
Many brave men are now in danger."

"And you yourself?"

The Doctor had stepped up to the window. Across the
street the Gestapo men were watching him. Quietly he turned
to me again.

"Our lives are in God's hands."

I saw Bruening several times during that interval. He worked
incessantly in an attempt to soften the shock of the sudden
change that had occurred, consulting with his friends, advising
diplomatic representatives, trying to forestall greater damage
than had already been done. The public knew nothing of all
this. It was too great a risk for the average citizen to go near
the former Chancellor. New rulers were basking in the limelight of success. Those out of power were forgotten. Scurry-
ing for shelter, as many as could afford it catered to the good
will of the men who had taken over.

Virtually overnight the people had been deprived of their
birthright. Their fate had been sealed on the backstairs of
feudal clubs. Traitors to the nation were in the saddle, acclaimed as liberators, heroes and leaders of a new age by their
own appointees and by a misled minority of blind adherents.
Why should anyone listen to Bruening now, when he had not
been listened to even before his downfall?

Skillful nazi propaganda helped to make the transition easy.
Both the "red" and the "black" parties were depicted as the
bad boys. "They," Hitler asserted, "caused the Reich to suffer
constant humiliation." Now the Reich was coming into a new
glorified life. The republican flag of black, red, and gold was
abolished and the old colors of black, white, and red were
reinstated. Once more national honor was identified with a
gleaming sword. "May our army ever remain the symbol and
pride of the nation," said Hindenburg after the imperial war
flag had been restored officially.

Hitler's partners did not realize that he was leaving them
their trinkets to play with up to the time when he would be
strong enough to lay down his own law for everybody.

Dapper Vice-Chancellor von Papen ventured to say in a Breslau speech that "we don't want an almighty state destroying all liberty and creating subjects without any will of their own." Three days later Heinrich Himmler, executioner and hangman extraordinary, announced the establishment of the first concentration camp, at Dachau, Bavaria. There could be no "petty scruples," said Heinrich. At Zweibruecken in the Palatinate the monument erected to the memory of Ebert, Erzberger, and Rathenau was demolished by nazi hoodlums, who went unpunished. Even the proud "Steel Helmet" men who had thought they could get the better of the Hitlerites were shoved out of the way and eventually dispersed by their erstwhile brown-shirted "friends." Their presidential candidate, Colonel Duesterberg, was found to be only "a three quarter Aryan," and so was disqualified for public office, according to nazi standards.

No wonder the university fraternities, mainstays of conservative German society, began to grow restless. "Saxoborussia," a swank fraternity at Heidelberg, was dissolved because the members held a beer session instead of listening to a Hitler speech on the air, and a few days later had daringly discussed the question of whether the great "Fuehrer" ate asparagus with his fingers, or with a fork!

Many an incident occurred to denote the real trend of things which the appeasers of the Papen-Hugenberg-Thyssen brand had meant to ignore. In Munich two members of the Bavarian government were seized in their homes and forced to go to police headquarters in their night clothes.

"That's all right," said Goering the next morning. "Didn't they take away our brown shirts? Don't let them howl now because we make them walk in their night shirts."

With shirts as political issues to keep one's shirt on was quite a problem!

In Essen, Heinrich Hirtsiefer, former Prussian Minister of Public Welfare, was forced to march down the city's main street with a placard around his neck denouncing him as an extortioner — without offering any proof. Manfred von Killinger, a notorious murderer, was appointed commissar for the state of Saxony. Some of his associates who had been given life sentences under the Weimar regime were set free. (Kil-

linger himself became nazi envoy to Rumania later on and
is reported to have committed suicide when Bucharest capitulated to the Russian army.)

At the same time innocent people such as the whole editorial
staff of the leading Centrist organ in the Rhineland, the
*Koelnische Volkszeitung,* were taken into "protective custody"
which simply meant jailed without warrant or trial.

In spite of all this, amidst a wave of Roman holidays, the
"Day of Potsdam" was staged on March 21st, to celebrate
Hitler's inauguration as Chancellor. Church bells, impressive
divine services, goldbraided uniforms and martial parades
created the impression among the masses that the nation was
seeing a new dawn. Reverently, Hitler bowed over old Hindenburg's hand, for the benefit of the newsreels.

Irma had phoned me excitedly that she would be in Potsdam. A friend of the "Steel Helmets" had obtained a ticket for
her to attend the function in the Garrison Church.

"Aren't you going?" she asked.

"No, thank you," I replied, "But give me a ring when it's
all over. I'd like to have your impression."

What a sad contrast it was! Pageants and merriment on the
one hand, and mass arrests on the other. Those who pointed
at Himmler's dungeons and at the brutal suppression of
civil liberties got no answer. Too many were intent on saving
their necks. Too many spines were weak.

"You know," reported Irma, when she got back, "I was
amazed."

"At what? The weak spines?"

"Aw, stop kidding! I mean at Hindenburg."

"What did he do?"

"Why, he didn't give the Hitler salute, never even stretched
out his arm!"

"Good for him," I applauded.

But Irma was disappointed and bewildered. Her idols
seemed to be at odds.

To the end of his days, the old man refused to perform
the arm-stretching motion. He was unhappy about his heir
apparent.

Shortly after the Potsdam affair, the Weimar democracy was
solemnly buried. With a vote of 441 to 94 the Reichstag signed

its own death sentence, by adopting an "enabling act" which gave dictatorial powers to Hitler for a four year period. Only 44 per cent of the people had voted for Hitler, and most of them under duress and false pretenses. Yet sixty-eight per cent of their representatives in the Reichstag now subscribed to their own political suicide. The Catholic Center Party, under Monsignor Ludwig Kaas's leadership but against Bruening's advice, acquiesced with a bad conscience. Only Otto Wels of the Socialists spoke up bravely. The republic was successfully torpedoed when Hitler, rebutting Wels, shouted "Do you want peace or war?" thus flinging a challenge at the elected body of the nation which robbed of all its prerogatives, and stripped of all its powers, had no longer any choice but that of surrender.

# Chapter 8

## THE COLLAPSE OF THE INTELLECT

AT BERLIN'S Broadcasting House gloom reigned among the old-timers. Walter Schaefer, the chief engineer, had found a note on his desk saying that his services were no longer wanted. He was Jewish, one of the foremost pioneers in radio. Both he and his wife were reported gassed in their kitchen a few hours later. Schaefer's former superiors, broadcasting executives of unimpeachable moral character, such as Kurt Magnus, Hans Giesecke, and Karl Flesch, were taken to a concentration camp shortly afterward and treated like common criminals. The preposterous charges brought against these men in the nazi press, such as squandering of public funds and corruption, were never corroborated. They had to be released without trial — but without any public apology.

The quislings among the radio people who had secretly belonged to the nazi party all along were rather embarrassed about it.

"You are lucky not to be with those at the camp," I remarked to one of the engineers who had worked with his deposed chief for years.

"Well," he replied cynically, "some get it this time, some others may get it some other time. It's the ups and downs of life, you know."

He was among the many now experiencing their ups, and it was amazing to see how quickly they fell in line. Political rivals were fired without much ado and new people came in who knew nothing of the radio business. Political "pull" was all that counted, and Hitler reigned supreme from the executive offices down to the boiler room.

In the early days the people found it difficult to get used to the new form of greeting, but saying "Hello" meant losing your job. Some would try to get away with a mumbled

"Heil'tler," but it worked only on rare occasions and implied the risk of a black mark in your personnel file. Heiling became perfunctory.

A secretary would call the linen room, and the linen room would respond:

"Heil Hitler! Linen Room."

"Heil Hitler," the secretary would order. "Send two cakes of soap to room 603. Heil Hitler!"

"Right away. Heil Hitler!"

Soon, "no soap" will be flung at anyone even mentioning the accursed name, but ten years ago you were making yourself dangerously conspicuous, if you stuck to the customary *Guten Morgen!* or *Guten Tag!* or *Guten Abend!* In the long run, of course, Hitler-heiling became so commonplace that people no longer attached any meaning to it.

"How can you stand it?" I asked one of the old-timers, a radio program manager who had been retained because he could not be dispensed with.

"I don't stand it," was his reply. "I endure it. Don't forget I've got five children below their teens, and my wife is ill. If I quit, I cannot find another job. It's cruel, but I have no choice."

One of his colleagues had quit. His wife was Jewish, so there was no use even trying to compromise. He knew he would get the ax sooner or later. He searched several months for employment, but without success. Finally England granted him a safe haven.

"No matter what work I find," he said, "I'll do it, if I can only be a free man, if only my wife can keep her chin up instead of being humiliated and mentally tortured as she is now."

Behind the scenes a struggle was going on: the "moderates" versus the "radicals." Goering spoke a few weeks after Hitler's triumph.

"You can never make a country great," he bellowed, "if within its borders you oppress and exploit part of the people." Was he sincere, or just putting up a front? Evidently, the brown-shirts were proving uncomfortable companions for the Papen group. The country was uneasy. People went about in sullen moods, fearful of things to come.

The Jews were wondering whether they should disregard what nazi chieftains preferred to call "local incidents." Hans Priwin, of the Executive Committee of German Jews, broadcast to America. I told him not to pull his punches, but his friends felt nothing could be gained by striking blows publicly. They, too, hoped for compromise, for appeasement, and Priwin, as their spokesman, pleaded with American listeners not to give credit to reports which made the outlook appear desperate. Like most of the non-Jews, he and his friends were still hoping that the brown flood might recede, but those who could afford it, followed Dr. Herzberg's trail and began moving to friendlier climes.

On Hitler's birthday, April 20th, millions wore artificial Edelweiss, the "Fuehrer's" favorite floral decoration, on their lapels as a tribute to him. The Edelweiss, of all flowers! The symbol of purity and loftiness as the mascot of an inhuman tyrant! Tons of birthday gifts arrived at the Chancery—bronzes, carvings, cakes, canaries, flowers. The papers carried profuse editorials comparing Adolf to Bismarck and Frederick the Great. Only Goebbels spoke somewhat out of turn: "When once the history of the nazi movement is written, Hitler's defeats more than his victories will be praised." It sounded ambiguously reasonable, almost like arousing hope in the camp of the crushed opposition!

Then, on April 27th, the Gestapo, "Secret State Police," was formally established, sinister machinery of civil war, instrument for the mass enslavement of a whole nation, and later on of almost a whole continent. But the biggest stroke came on May 2nd, after the spectacular first mass-celebration of "May Day" which Hitler cleverly took away from the socialist workers international, converting it into a pageant of his own, to fool and confuse labor at home.

The stupefied workers had just returned to their benches when storm troopers swooped down on all free trade union offices and arrested the leaders who had not escaped in time. Rudolf Ley, known drunkard and loan shark, took charge of a total membership of more than four million workers. Labor banks were seized, all trade union publications stopped. The whole German labor movement was throttled. A "Labor Front" organization of national scope and colossal proportions absorbed the former unions, streamlining and regimenting them. Within this framework "Strength through Joy," with forced membership, was set up as a special unit, providing entertainment and sports and summer cruises in place of the right of free bargaining which labor had enjoyed under the republic.

Irma was one of the first beneficiaries of Herr Ley's tender solicitudes.

"I'll be on the Madeira trip," she phoned joyfully. "Now I know Hitler is sincere!"

She had not been told that the excursion boats built for "Strength through Joy" soon were to become troop transports, with her older brother one of the passengers — not to Madeira, but to his grave in the African desert.

The "national socialist" Adolf Hitler took all socialism away from a helpless, emaciated, distraught people. Soon they were systematically catalogued and finger-printed. At the same time wages went down, overtime without pay was enforced and there was a constant stream of compulsory collections for the benefit of the party, no one knowing where the money went. The dazzled, befuddled workers had only one right left to them: to shout, salute, and parade. It simply meant "grin and bear it all, or else — "

The new rulers had a way of forcing all these changes down the throats of the people by a clever sugar-coating of the bitter pills. Thus, some of the more gullible workers were greatly impressed by having their bosses march in line with them on May Day celebrations, or to find the mail-boxes all over town painted in flaming red, in place of the customary yellow. These and similar trifles were meager substitutes indeed for the freedom of which the people had been robbed, but it took some time before the whole great piece of deceit was brought home to them.

Among the middle classes the disposition to make the best of things was even more evident. Hitler's bombasts were pleasing to many, as long as they themselves did not have to foot the bills. Proudly the Dance Teachers Association of the Reich, the Berlin fish market, and similar politically enlightened groups proclaimed full adherence to the "Fuehrer"! Other enthusiasts asked for permission (which was refused) to christen their girl babies "Hitlerina," while even tennis clubs such as "Red-White" in fashionable Berlin struck names of Jewish members from their lists. Because his cook had bought lamb chops from a Jewish butcher, the rector of Bonn University was forced to resign. Innumerable instances of this kind made it plain that political myopia was widespread.

However, a good many eyes were again opened the day of the book-burning, May 10, 1933, when the very intellectual foundations of a once proud nation were exposed to the deadly attack of a yelling mob. Two days before, dueling had been resumed in Heidelberg. At last the old-style fraternities had regained the privilege of landing scars on each other's cheeks. Hitler was entirely in favor of that brutal sport. As far as he was concerned, the more brutal, the better. The more fencing, the more efficient soldiery. Under the republican government dueling had been banned, but the nazis restored the custom because to their way of thinking it was apt to develop "manly virtues."

As for the book-burning, the youngsters were not really aware of what they were doing on that day of mass stupidity when their ill-conceived college-boy fervor was directed against "degenerating literature," as it had been represented to them by Goebbels' agitators. They started collections, some of them not quite spontaneously, in public and circulation libraries, digging up books they had been told were obnoxious. A truly amazing blacklist of 160 authors including names such as Jack London and Upton Sinclair, Karl Marx, Albert Einstein, and Helen Keller, had been prepared and some 25,000 volumes labeled as "un-German" were finally piled up on the square in front of Berlin's university. At midnight a huge bonfire was staged in the presence of a crowd of 40,000 people who stood in drizzling rain for hours. Hegel, one of the fathers of totalitarian philosophies, looked down upon them from his monument. One wondered what he would have thought of the childish performance.

True, this was not the first book-burning in history. Confucius' disciples in China once burned what to them were "immoral books." Supposedly "heretical" volumes went to ashes in Spanish autos-da-fé. Martin Luther sent a copy of the code of the Roman Canon Law up in flames, and during the

German War of Liberation against Napoleon, students had often thrown the works of "reactionary" writers into the fire. In each instance the purpose was symbolical. This time, too, it was more the motive than the deed itself which counted, and it did not matter so much which books were burned. Not all of them deserved to be kept for posterity, but many were an expression of the spirit of freedom, though sometimes ill-conceived, which was now being outlawed in the name of a pretended national rebirth.

The reaction of the people at large was one of embarrassment. Long after the book-burning in Berlin which was followed by a few minor, similar performances in other cities I noticed copies of the condemned works in private homes. Most book-lovers refused to part with them, even if it meant the risk of being accused of "pro-Jewish" sympathies.

One of my friends simply re-shuffled his library.

"On my shelves," he explained beaming, "I've set up a foreground defense! Goethe, Shakespeare, Dante, and all the others not yet on the nazi index, are lined up conspicuously right in front. Behind them, in the second row, carefully hidden, I keep the 'outlaws,' Thomas Mann, Franz Werfel, and the rest of them. I am sure Shakespeare and Goethe won't mind serving as camouflage for their younger emulants!"

The burning of the books was symptomatic. It showed the nazis were determined to weed out what they considered alien influences. Nietzsche (whom they misinterpreted to suit their own purposes), Gobineau and Sorel, the French protagonists of racialism and totalitarianism, and Houston Stewart Chamberlain, the British convert to doctrines of Germanic superiority, were to be elevated to the altars of state idolatry. Writers, artists, composers, or scholars, actually or seemingly out of tune with Hitler's perverted ideas of culture were to be banned. Every vestige of the era which had had its inception with the rise of German democracy was to be destroyed.

The nazi prophets did not realize that by burning the books of living authors they also burned, by implication, and at least for themselves, bridges connecting with the nation's past, with the realm of Clemens Brentano and Herder, of Wieland and Theodor Storm, of the Grimm brothers and

Duerer, of Schopenhauer and Kant, of Leibniz and Lessing.
None of them could ever have achieved greatness, had they
not enjoyed intellectual and spiritual freedom.

One of the bards the hitlerites had claimed as their own
was Stefan George, but this truly eminent poet left Germany
in ill-concealed disgust after Goebbels had praised him as the
spiritual leader of the nazi revolution. Stefan George was
horrified by the vulgarities of a plebeian regime which was
to remove Felix Mendelssohn from the concert halls and
to discontinue the presentation of Schiller's "William Tell"
on German stages.

"You should have seen the crowds!" Werner Pratt, my
friend of the theatrical world, told me at the Friday Circle.
"'William Tell' was sold out whenever we put it on. The
people never tired watching the legendary hero challenge the
Austrian overlord, Gessler, with his 'braggart spirit of
freedom!'"

"I wonder what they are going to do with Schiller's 'Don
Carlos,'" I asked.

"Oh, that's next on the list!" Pratt announced. "Imagine
Don Carlos shouting night after night: 'Sire, give us freedom
of thought!' Yesterday we had it on, and the crowds just
went wild applauding! No, Sir. Joe Goebbels won't stand for
it much longer. He cannot possibly tolerate Schiller, who to
him must appear positively subversive!"

Sure enough a week later, "Don Carlos," too, was cancelled
on all the listings while the nation looked on horrified.

Men like Goebbels — who himself had failed as a dramatic
writer — claimed that the nazis were merely fighting destructive and negatively dissective influences which had manifested themselves in the writings of certain postwar authors, or
the "soulless" intellectualism of the exponents of marxian
historic materialism. They failed to explain their antagonism to
such great minds as Walter Hasenclever and Hermann Suder-
mann, to Leo Weissmantel and Hermann Hesse, to Ricarda
Huch, Gertrud von le Fort, Ruth Schaumann, and many
others of the same rank, who could not possibly be labeled as
"destructive" or unpatriotic. There could be no question of the
creative genius of artists such as Kaethe Kollwitz or composers
such as Max Reger. But the nazis were determined to use

the convenient excuse of "demo-liberalism," which they had
borrowed from the fascists of Italy. The principle of *l'art pour
l'art,* art for art's sake, did not fit into their conception of a
new "heroic" age which was to discard all that was not
utilitarian in the sense of promoting a policy of narrow
nationalism.

Goebbels' real reasons were avowedly selfish. The literary
romanticism of a Franz Avenarius, the pioneer editor, the spiritual quest of philosophers such as Rudolf Eucken or Leopold
Ziegler or Franz Husserl, the religious fervor and depth of
men like Ernst Troeltsch, and Romano Guardini, the crusad-
ing spirit of priests like Karl Sonnenschein in the field of social
reform, and even the historical insight of Oswald Spengler —
all this, innovators proclaiming the "Aryan" blood and the
Germanic soil as the measure of all things, could not condone
unbridled. If creative minds could not be fitted into the Pro-
crustean bed of bigoted nazi doctrines, they were dismissed
as unessential to the nation's well-being, along with all that
was considered "foreign."

Gestapo snooping in public and scientific libraries, the
proscription of literary classics such as Heinrich Heine's
"Lorelei" — formerly one of the most popular German songs,
but now carried in nazi textbooks with the sheepish note:
"author unknown!" — and a fanatical application of so-called
Aryan standards in all fields of literary and artistic endeavor
were but phases of a general onslaught against what Goebbels
had termed the "intellectual beast." But quite a few Germans
were little impressed. After all, Goethe had said too many
things denouncing nationalism, and Schiller had praised freedom eloquently enough.

As for higher education, Hitler had plainly professed in
*Mein Kampf* that "the youthful brain must not be burdened
with subjects, ninety per cent of which it does not need and
therefore forgets again." In the first, unexpurgated edition of
that book, he had proclaimed as the sole purpose of education
to "burn into the heart and brain of the youth an instinctive
sense of race." And he had added: "Education must be so
arranged that the young person leaving school is not half
pacifist, democrat, or what have you, but a complete German.
For the girls, the greatest importance is to be attached to the

development of the body and only after that to the requirements of the mind and finally (sic!) of the soul."

Educators came across such sentences only after it was too
late to do something about them. By the time they woke up,
the crack-pots and half-baked pseudo-scientists had gained
control. Now the sciences as well as the humanities had been
banned from the *universitas litterarum*.

Dr. Ernst Kriegk, elected first rector, or president, of the
university of Heidelberg, under Hitler, announced arrogantly
that "the epoch of pure reason, of objective and free science
is at an end," that "general education as such and the uni-
versality of high culture will melt away together with the
outworn idea of humanity." And he meant what he said.
From then on, classes were opened with Hitler "heiling" on
the part of professors as well as students. Faculty members
not belonging to the imaginary Aryan race were dismissed.
Those adhering to political groups on the nazi blacklist fared
no better. At least two thousand German scholars were deprived of their professorships and pensions as "politically un-
reliable," as in the case of Hermann Oncken, the Berlin
historian.

Many did not wait until they were thrown out. For instance,
Fritz Haber, the great chemist, of his own accord, left the
country he had served so unselfishly in World War I. He
reached Switzerland with a broken heart and died shortly
afterwards. Others, torn between the natural love for their
home-land and their responsibility as teachers of youth, kept
quiet trying to save their jobs for the sake of their families.
They hoped, like so many others, that the madmen would soon
become the victims of ridicule and disrepute. They did not
realize that totalitarianism is total, that it wants total politics,
total war, and total education, that it is not satisfied just to rule,
that it claims wholly the body and the soul.

It was clear from the start that nazism would admit no
compromise. Bernhard Rust, a former public school teacher
who in pre-Hitler days had lost his teaching job because of an
unbalanced mind, and had never obtained an academic degree,
was appointed Federal Secretary of Education. He announced
officially that it was "the task of the German universities to
put scientific research into the closest possible relationship with

the political requirements of the nation," and in servile submission, the presidents of all the Prussian colleges immediately came out with a statement thanking him for his "clear
directives!"

To apply Herr Rust's new principles, compulsory training
camps for faculties and student bodies alike were set up by
Hitler's lieutenants in the typical nazi style. The training consisted in marching and parading, and in singing crude storm
trooper songs. The main purpose was to create what the nazis
liked to call the national community, or in other words, the
leveling down of all people to their own intellectual standards.
In these camps which were organized on the pattern of
military barracks, professors of medicine, law and philosophy,
mathematicians and historians, anthropologists and astron-
omers, theologians and physicists had to goose-step and attend
lectures delivered by young nazi guards entrusted with the
teaching of what they called *Weltanschauung*.

Imagine these men of learning forced to listen to the
diatribes of Goebbels, to Rosenbergian teachings of race and
soil, to boss Streicher's anti-semitic tirades! And this over
periods of between four and six weeks. The students generally
had their own camps. The large majority of them were bored
to death. The time spent in camp was lost for studies. It
meant an unpalatable intellectual diet of hitlerian hocus-pocus
forced upon unwilling, yet helpless victims. They simply
were not admitted to examinations unless they had a stamp
of good behavior applied to their worksheet by some minor
brownshirted nazi moron to whom *Mein Kampf* was the
Bible and the whole truth.

One of the professors of Berlin university told me of these
experiences.

"How do your students take it?" I asked him.

"Well," explained my friend, a man of unquestionable
integrity, "It's like this: When I enter the classroom, they all
stretch out their arms and shout Heil Hitler! Of course, I must
do the same. We go through these motions once more after
class is over. Then I retire to my private office, and the students
come to see me individually to ask for advice and to execrate
everything under the sun that's nazi!"

"Isn't this going to cause twisted characters, with the coming generation growing up in an atmosphere of insincerity and mental crookedness?"

"I am afraid so."

The professor asked me to come to his house the following Sunday.

"Just drop in for a chat, if you have time," he said.

His house was in Nikolassee, one of those garden suburbs of Berlin amidst an infinity of lakes and woods that was restful to the soul no less than to the eye. Commuting distance was only half an hour, but it made a great deal of difference in atmosphere. You could not escape nazi intrusion entirely, for the swastika dominated every landscape. However, here in the country it was easier to ignore it than in the city where it overwhelmed you with ostentatious insistence.

The professor — let me call him Kraus to protect his identity as he may still be alive — was working in his study when I arrived. His wife, an attractive lady of about thirty, the "nordic" type, with a radiant personality, was enjoying the sun in an easy chair on the lawn. Soon we were on our favorite subject, again.

"Have a brandy?" asked the professor after we had gathered for coffee in the library.

"Thank you," I replied, "I'd like to, but finish your argument."

"What's the use?" he resumed. "We've been arguing long enough, and it doesn't get us anywhere. Perhaps it's the Faustian instinct in the German race. I don't know. This nation is infected with a blight of restlessness. Now it's breaking loose again. I thought it was all settled in 1918, but the old gang is having a heyday once more. Challenging the world! Reverting to pagan ideas! Glorifying the sword! You'd think we were thrown back to the Nibelungen era of constant strife and bloodshed, picking fights right and left, bragging about our own valor!"

"You wouldn't say that the whole nation is like that," interrupted his wife.

"Too many of them to suit me at any rate!" growled the professor. "And the trouble-makers won't have peace. They live on strife and bravado and drag us all from one disaster to another."

"In the academic world," I said, "the flagwavers seem to be particularly numerous. Isn't it strange that educated men should fall so easily for the catch-phrases of politicians?"

"It doesn't surprise me. So many of them are specialists removed from the realities of the political world. They are the ones that Hitler can use. Take that man, Professor Ulrich Kahrstedt, of Goettingen, for instance, who said the other day that 'we don't engage in research for its own sake, or to discover abstract laws, but to sharpen the implements of the German people in their competition with other nations.' Or Professor Philip Lenard, the Nobel Prize winner of Heidelberg who proclaimed that 'science is racially bound and a result of blood.' Eugen Fischer, the anthropologist, Martin Heidegger, the philosopher, Wilhelm Pinder, the art historian, they've all betrayed their calling by falling in line with the nazis."

"Not all though," objected Frau Kraus. "Not all . . ."

"No," the professor conceded. "Not all, but those who did go astray and let themselves be tempted by the vainglories of this corrupted world were like traitors in this nation's citadel of truth and virtue."

Frau Kraus was right. Not all had betrayed their calling. In the early stages brave men stood up to protest. Max Planck, winner of the Nobel Prize for Physics (of that Nobel Prize which Germans could no longer receive because Hitler feared the racial and political impartiality of the Stockholm governing body), was one of them. When Hitler heard of his protest against the removal of scholars on "racial" grounds, he replied coldly: "If dismissing Jewish professors means the end of German science, well, then let's do without science for a few years."

If without science, why not without law? Alfred Rosenberg, the author of *The Myth of the Twentieth Century*, a sort of nazi super-primer, had stated bluntly that "nazism knows no equality of human beings, no right in itself, no object except a German nation of strong men." Wilhelm Stapel, another nazi theorist, went even farther by saying that "right is determined by the Fuehrer." Why, then, study law? The Hitler youth organ, *Wille and Macht,* had admitted that in its view, "the struggle of life has no bearing on good and evil," that it has "its own dynamics which we feel in our own blood." All of which amounted to doing away with moral principles, and with the independent search for truth. It meant indeed putting out the light of the intellect.

What could parents such as the Kraus's do when facing the ruins of all the civilized values of which they had been so proud? Their children had no choice. One mother whose husband was a lawyer, and who herself had been anxious for her children to get a college education, told me the story simply.

"My two boys," she said, "are about to enroll at the university; but they don't know what to do. If they don't join the nazi groups, they'll be at a disadvantage from the start. It would be held against them, no matter how proficient they are in their studies. Yet, they can't stand all that Hitler nonsense. As for my daughter, she is now at the nazi girls' camp, which is compulsory. I don't know what they'll do to her. These children are taken away from us as though they were no concern of their fathers and mothers."

The nazis were at work like termites, silently, persistently and in the dark, with the connivance of the resurgent squirarchy and their middle-class kin. They could not understand why their new gospel was being received with considerable misgivings by so many whom they had considered natural partisans — or victims. The book-burning had fallen flat and that failure was indicative of a trend which did not fit into the Hitler strait jacket. The German people still seemed to want freedom. Despite Goebbels' blatant claims of national unity under the "Fuehrer," there were apparently too many independent minds who insisted on doing their own thinking. Against them, Goebbels concentrated his main drive, soon after he had been appointed "Minister of Propaganda."

Even before that date the nazi broom had swept through theatres and concert halls: Fritz Busch was ousted as Dresden opera conductor in the midst of a "Rigoletto" performance, and Bruno Walter and Otto Klemperer were banned outright. The home of Lion Feuchtwanger was raided during his absence. "German art temples must be purged," announced Goebbels and cancelled Max Reinhardt's contracts. Rudolf Serkin, the pianist, was put on the blacklist.

Again, brave men protested. Thomas Mann resigned from the authors' league, and Adolf Busch refused to participate in the Brahms centennial celebration. Oswald Spengler whom the nazis had thought they could count among their mainstays declined the coveted chair of history once occupied by the famous Karl Lamprecht at Leipzig university. Max Liebermann, eighty-five-year-old dean of German painters, resigned from the Prussian Academy of Arts, after Ludwig Justi, head of the Berlin National Gallery and Max Friedlaender, of the Emperor Frederick Art Museum in Berlin, both world renowned experts in their fields, had been wantonly dismissed under the provisions of the "Aryan" decree.

Fritz Kreisler, the Austrian master of the violin, announced that he would not play in Germany "until it is established beyond peradventure of doubt that all my colleagues in the musical world, irrespective of nationality, race, or creed, are not only tolerated, but actually welcomed." Karl Muck, seventy-five-year-old veteran conductor of the Hamburg Philharmonic, resigned in protest against racial discriminations although he was not of the Jewish race himself. Actor Albert Bassermann gave up his membership in the National Theatre Guild after his wife had been banned from the stage as "non-Aryan." It all served to draw the line between misguided zealots and men of culture, but it did not alter the zealots' course.

From now on the nazi index of forbidden books was rigidly enforced. Bookstores were no longer allowed to display the works of banned authors. Anyone still daring enough to ask for them was told they were "sold out," and publishers were refused permission to prepare new editions. Some booksellers soon became "doubled-faced dealers." They displayed nazi literature profusely in the front-windows, keeping all other books in the rear of their stores for those who came inside to do the actual buying. Doc Goebbels must soon have realized that the "intellectual beasts" did not take to swastika books, but, of course, the readers' protest was a silent one.

Books dealing with subjects as remote as possible from the nazi atmosphere were the most popular, as shown by the official book-trade statistics. People would buy books on travel, and arts, on physics, but they wanted nothing of *Mein Kampf,* or Rosenberg's "Myth." Hitler's book was rarely bought anyway, for every newly married couple was given a free copy of it at the government's expense, and to the ample profit of the author.

A bookdealer in Berlin told me one day that he had completely run out of heavy historical novels dealing with a happier past. He was now busier than ever because his customers were actually book-starved. There was a lively quest for truth in the midst of the intellectual chaos Hitler had brought about. People wanted to know for themselves, find out for themselves.

"If authors were only free to speak their minds," said my dealer friend, taking a moment for a chat, "we could probably sell books as never before."

"But you are doing a land-office business as it is, aren't you?" I objected.

"Surely, but that's not what I mean. You see, what the people buy right now, in a sense, is escapist literature, books that they buy because they cannot get the ones they really want, the ones telling them the truth about the nazis."

"What books do they buy?"

"Oh, you'd be surprised. A heavy volume on metaphysics is just out of print. Five thousand copies of it were sold. Then, take *Das Herz ist Wach,* the romantic love story which swept this country, soon after Hitler's advent to power, almost as completely as *Gone With the Wind* did America, from what the trade papers tell me. But, of course, popular editions just can't be reprinted. No pulp is allotted for books which the nazi propaganda department does not see fit to promote. It's simple enough to put the screws on publishers in that way."

The good man was right. I knew of an author who had finished a manuscript on the racial problem. It was a scientific book, with no direct reference to anti-semitism, but the author's conclusions were clearly not in keeping with Hitler concepts, so he never found a publisher. Periodicals, too, which were not in tune with nazi ideas were simply forced out of business under the pretext that newsprint was not available although there was always an ample supply for nazi publications.

In the field of religion particularly, it was easy enough to use the "squeeze" device. Soon, even Christian catechisms were among the victims, and bans eventually extended to whole volumes of encyclopedias.

Once the German press had been a faithful mirror of German life. Now, with a law making all newspapermen a kind of public servant, establishing the death penalty for supposedly "treasonable" articles and imposing "licenses" on all editors, little dependable information could be obtained from the dailies and periodicals. Why should the German people want to know anything anyway? Politics, maintained Goebbels, was no business of the hoi polloi. They had to be satisfied with the crumbs, dropped from regimented news desks, thoroughly predigested and properly colored so as to shape that uniform public opinion which is to the perennial liking of every dictator.

When Ehm Welk, the editor of the popular Berlin weekly *Gruene Post* dared protest against such deadly streamlining, he was summarily confined to a concentration camp for three months, and silenced once and for all. Soon scores of newspapers and magazines died an inglorious death and a whole generation of German newspapermen, democrats, socialists, and liberals of all brands, Catholics and Protestants as well as Jews, were banned from their homeland, victims of organized intolerance.

Soon after Joseph Goebbels had moved to his sumptuous offices on the Wilhelmsplatz, as propaganda ringmaster extraordinary, one great name after another in German journalism disappeared.* Through his "chambers," each a clearinghouse with compulsory membership, "the Doctor," as Berliners called him, controlled everything and everybody in the field of literature, the press, the radio, the stage, the graphic arts, and the motion pictures.

Goebbels reigned supreme and all intellectual activities came under his none too benevolent wing. No one could write, or paint, or act, or sing, without the Master having had the

---

* The most tragic case was that of Theodor Wolff, famed editor of the *Berliner Tageblatt*. For years prior to Hitler's access to power he had waged a persistent campaign against the nazis. Wolff escaped to France in 1933, but the Gestapo caught up with him ten years later, and he died from brutal ill-treatment in a concentration camp — a true martyr for the cause of the freedom of the press.

final word, and without going through the blood test, back to parents' parents.

Only those willing to pay tribute to the great Mogul, day in and day out and to live by his commandments without grumbling, were granted the privilege to burn incense at Herr Goebbels' feet. If a writer or newspaperman or radio reporter or movie actor was caught sinning against the nazi dogmas in any shape or form, he or she was deprived of the press or "culture" chamber membership without mercy. That meant almost a death sentence, because then their writings could not be accepted by any editor in the country, no radio station would have dared put them on the air, no stage or motion picture studio would even consider them.

For Hitler and his chieftains it was profitable enough to drive rival papers out of business as ultimately only the nazi-owned and nazi-controlled press remained.* It was as uni-form as though coming off an assembly line, a vehicle of mass distortion almost without parallel in the history of journalism, but circulation was promoted just the same with the ruthless means typical of the nazi machine. Civil service employees were informed bluntly that paid subscriptions to Hitler's own paper, the screamingly yellow *Voelkischer Beobachter,* might help their career. No advertiser could afford to refuse orders to this and other mouthpieces of the regime, if he wished to stand in well with the big bosses. Official announcements were given only to papers in good standing with the powers that be, which in turn meant that many readers found it essential to their very livelihood to buy them.

The result of it all was a total confusion of the public mind and its complete isolation from all dissenting opinion. Since the importation of such foreign newspapers, magazines, and books as were on the nazi black list had become a felony, newspapers from Switzerland, Holland, Austria, and Sweden not yet under ban were instantly sold out at all news-stands. People would pay almost any price for a copy of the "approved" foreign dailies which, although judiciously edited, still carried considerably more complete and more unbiased

---

*On June 4, 1943, the Goebbels weekly *Das Reich* reported that only 1400 of the 24,000 daily newspapers in Germany remained in existence with two-thirds of this remnant now owned by nazi publishers.

reports than those published under Herr Goebbels' supervision. Later on, after virtually all foreign publications had been excluded from German territory, those Germans who could afford it, traveled across the borders "to read up." It was a dangerous sport, for Gestapo eyes were everywhere, and many a homecoming tourist found himself questioned by secret agents about "subversive reading abroad."

Franz Ritter, a Berlin newspaperman I had known in pre-Hitler days showed up at my home in Basel one day.

"How did you manage to get an exit visa?" I asked.

"T.B.," he explained coldly. "Doctor's orders."

"I am so sorry."

"It's okay," he mumbled. "I'm glad I'm done for. What's the use of living in such misery? I am going to Arosa. Hope they won't cure me."

While he was up in the mountains I sent him reading matter to bring him up to date. He devoured volumes of stuff avidly, starved for the truth as he was. The doctors had a hard time urging him to get enough sleep. All he wanted to do was to read, read, all about Hitler, all that Heiden and Olden and the other chroniclers of nazi infamies had to say about the *Verfuehrer,* the "misleader," as he called him.

"The truth," he wrote me in a letter. "At last the truth! Oh, what fools so many of us were to fall for Goebbels' lies! If they only knew! If we could only tell them! Make them wake up! With a crusade of truth! But no one dares. There is no concerted action. There is no faith to move these mountains of falsehood!"

Ritter died in his self-imposed exile. He made no effort to get well. "We have never had a patient," the physician in charge told me at the funeral, "who was less anxious to live."

Of course, the darkness was not quite as complete as Ritter thought. In spite of the cordon of censorship, a fair amount of news still trickled into Germany, although not enough to ease the lot of people of intelligence and common sense who felt as if they were confined behind mental prison walls. One of my friends in Berlin, a newspaper executive, summed up this experience when I went to see him several months after Hitler had taken over. He sat behind his desk exhausted.

"Are you sick?" I asked him.

"Sick?" he replied, "yes, I am sick — morally."

I was shocked.

"My goodness," I said, "what happened?"

"Nothing," he answered in a toneless voice. "You won't understand. You can't understand what it means to be wrapped in lies all day long, day in, day out."

This man, too, died shortly afterwards. He died from worry, from shame. There were legions of his kind. The swastika ruled like an octopus, penetrating into the innermost sanctum of every individual. But behind the Gestapo barbed wire and the sealed borders, the silent battle went on, the battle in millions of hearts against the subhuman barbarism of a government unworthy of that name.

# Chapter 9

## APPEASEMENT IS BORN

"IT WON'T last."

"They'll hit a snag before long."

"It's not all as bad as it looks."

Opinions such as these were expressed far and wide by wishful thinkers who thought they had the right slant on the nazi cataclysm. I was one of them myself. I just could not believe that it was more than a ghastly nightmare. In Copenhagen, in the summer of 1933, I was discussing the situation with Dr. Herzberg, first refugee of the Friday Circle. He had arrived in Denmark safely some weeks before and had written to me in Switzerland suggesting that we get together.

"I thought you were in Holland," I said when I phoned to make the appointment.

"Why should I put them on the right track?" he laughed.

Now he told me the story. Quietly he had packed up one morning, after leaving his properties with a Danish friend in Berlin, who in turn was able to transfer them across the border without trouble. Then he took the ferry at Warnemuende, carrying only an overnight bag and pretending to be just an ordinary tourist.

"It was at night," he expanded the tale while tempting courses of an opulent Danish meal were being served at the Tivoli, to the tunes of an excellent orchestra, "but I did not go to sleep. I stood on deck watching the sea, and it was like the awakening of freedom. With sunrise the seagulls were circling over the boat, and though their shrieks were not melodious, they sounded like sweet music to me, harbingers of a land of liberty which was to become my new home."

"You'll go back to Berlin when it's over, won't you?" I asked.

"Go back? What do you think? I won't live to see the end of this mess."

Herzberg was a man of about fifty-five, healthy, a widower who had led an active life, an inveterate cigar smoker who had never been inside a doctor's office. What was he talking about?

"Why," I retorted. "You don't expect to pass out so soon, do you?"

He roared with bitter laughter.

"Neither will the nazis, you hopeless optimist!"

"But they can't last!"

"Why not? You watch them! Everything is in their favor."

"The people aren't. I know that."

"The people have nothing to say. They'll be told what to do, and if they don't behave, Hitler will use the whip."

"I think you are utterly wrong. You've been away from home too long. You don't know how the people really feel now that they've had a taste of hitlerism."

"What they feel makes no difference. Hitler has the power, and he'll use it."

"Then there'll be a revolution."

"With what?"

"The army will rebel against these upstarts."

"They will, eh? Let's wait and see."

Herzberg lighted his after-dinner cigar.

"Hitler fooled most everybody," he concluded. "He'll fool the world, too. He won't let go without a terrific struggle. Remember what Goebbels said the day these madmen were let inside the Berlin gates? 'We've burned all bridges behind us,' he bragged. 'While we go into this government alive, they won't take us out of it except as corpses.' And he was dead serious about it, too. We can't have peace until this thing has run its course. It must destroy itself, but a great many innocent people will go down at the same time."

I was unable to agree with Herzberg entirely. The German people had been deceived with ensnaring words, swallowing in small doses a poison which was camouflaged with nationalistic, racialistic, and socialistic slogans. The right-wing elements particularly, and others too, had fallen for Goebbels' claim that the nation would be "regenerated," that bolshevism would be destroyed. But outside Germany the facts were better

known. Surely the big powers would not let Hitler get away
with his braggadocio. They would know how to deal with
him.

"Good-bye," said Herzberg, "I'll bet you dollars to dough-
nuts that this *dance macabre* will lead to war. The nazis will
first enslave Germany and then they'll set out to enslave the
whole world."

Was Hitler aware of these suspicions? In a Reichstag speech
on May 17, 1933, he professed his will to maintain peace.
Nothing, he insisted, was further from his thoughts than war.
He would not think of using force! "The outbreak of such
madness would necessarily lead to the collapse of the present
social and political order." It sounded all right for home consumption, and the press abroad was making headlines of it.

Back in Switzerland, to breathe some fresh air after the
harrowing weeks in Berlin, I was asked many questions. Dr.
Joseph Wirth, the former Chancellor, was in Berne on a visit.
He, too, had foreseen trouble and gone over the border. Otto
Braun, former Prussian socialist premier had taken refuge in
Ascona, on Lake Major. One after another of the better known
figures of the Weimar republic whom the Gestapo had not
caught, had slipped into neutral countries. Himmler was staging a real man-hunt, with all legal guarantees abrogated under
emergency decrees, and most of my old friends were being
dispersed to the four corners of the earth.

"What do you hear?" Wirth asked me.

He who was the very impersonation of the democratic idea,
a man who had fought the early battles against Hitler bravely,
now was ailing and getting old though he was by no means
broken in spirit. In his heart he kept the flame of freedom
alive, and a brave fighter he has remained all through this
war.

I told Dr. Wirth the bad news I knew. Paul Loebe, his
friend and former speaker of the Reichstag, and Fritz Ebert,
son of the late president, confined to concentration camps. A
man in Hamburg sentenced to fifteen months in jail because
he had shouted "Down with the nazis!" in a café. Two
workers in Braunschweig given three months because they
had failed to stretch out their arms while the nazi anthem was
being played by a band. Some fifteen year old boys jailed in

Leipzig for having caused minor damage in a Hitler Youth home. A memorial tablet unveiled to the assassins of Walter Rathenau, the great Jewish industrialist who had been in Wirth's cabinet — murderers glorified as national heroes!

"And all this is being tolerated by the men who have associated themselves with Hitler," Wirth remarked sadly. "Criminals are let loose upon the nation and men like Hugenberg and Neurath and all the other 'respectables' keep silent, condoning the evil that is done, making themselves co-responsible for it — in the name of patriotism! What a farce!"

"What do you think could be done?" I asked.

Wirth did not hesitate.

"Arouse the world! Urge the governments to act!" he answered. "Isn't it incredible that the same statesmen in Paris and London who for years went hysterical, if a German turnverein only marched down a village street, should suddenly become so conciliatory? They had only scorn for us when our groups were in power, when democratic governments pleaded for help and understanding. Now some of these leaders may well ponder whether it wouldn't have been better to play ball with the Weimar Republic."

And bitterly he added:

"Of course, we were only a democracy! Now Hitler bangs the table with his fist and delivers fiery harangues, and it is as though the world had lost its speech."

"Did you see what Philip Scheidemann, the first Chancellor of the Weimar Republic, said in Prague?" I interrupted.

"I certainly did. That the adventurers should be paralyzed immediately! He is right. But no one does anything about it. It's more expedient to be 'realistic,' I guess, and to compromise supinely with the very men who threaten the peace of Europe."

Most German refugees were of one mind with Wirth. And their friends in Germany who still had means of communicating with them were equally incensed. Wirth told me of some of these men whom the nazis had driven out of office and who were now facing a last-ditch fight.

"Not one sign of encouragement is given them," he said.

As a matter of fact, it was hard to explain why on the one hand Lord Hailsham, British Secretary of War, should invoke the sanctions provided in the Versailles treaty, in case Germany attempted to rearm, while on the other hand a sector of the British press was patting Hitler on the back. Wirth pulled some clippings out of his pocket. The sturdy man was trembling with indignation.

"There! Look at these! 'Hitler has done great things not only for Germany, but for all Europe,' says Lord Lloyd in the *Sunday Express* of May 21. And Lloyd George in his Barmouth speech asserts publicly that communism might flood Germany, if foreign powers were to intervene. What nonsense! Think of how after the Reichstag fire a few storm troopers put all the communist leaders in jail! The conscience of the world ought to be aroused over what's going on in Himmler's concentration camps. Yet, as the official German news agency reported gleefully on July 10, Lord Rothermere proclaims in his *Daily Mail* that 'there are no nazi atrocities, only a few, exceptional acts of violence!' How does he know? I tell you, it means paralyzing the meager remnants of German democracy rather than paralyzing the adventurers."

Had not the London opinions appeared in print, who would have believed there could be such blindness? In Berlin ten thousand social-democratic workers had taken part in an anti-nazi mass meeting. The German Federal Press Association had mustered enough courage to protest against the limitations of their freedom. Some courts had even granted appeals of newspapers which the nazis had suppressed, and Bavarian Premier Heinrich Held flatly ordered publication of a particularly vicious nazi sheet in Bayreuth to be stopped. Democracy was not dead. It was struggling, but it found no support abroad. No salvage operations were even attempted. It was as though Hitler was going to win out not so much by his own strength as by the weakness of his opponents.

"Insiders" reported that talking to the "Fuehrer" was like "spending an hour with a hurricane." Those near him were scared of his fits and rantings. Would the trick work in the field of diplomacy as well?

Abroad, more was known of conditions in Germany than in Germany itself. The German people were kept in the dark, torn between conflicting emotions, hopelessly perplexed by the constant torrent of oratory which kept pouring down upon them from government sources, to the exclusion of all dissenting views. There were high-sounding words which appealed even to skeptics. Protection from subversive elements! Leveling out class distinctions! At the same time nazi teachings sounded harsh to many ears: authoritarian control, self-denial, strong-arm methods to enforce the nation's order and unity, intolerance! And no chivalry, no charity! But was not this a transition period? Was it not better to forego individual liberties temporarily, if it helped to find a way out of chaos, despair and national humiliation?

Hitler claimed he knew the way. Many disliked him and his methods, but many were inclined to make a distinction between the leader and his partners. Surely, he would not tolerate excesses, indefinitely. As a matter of fact, he would stop them right now, if he only knew of them. Given time, things would calm down, perhaps.

Alfred Hugenberg, the newspaper magnate, who together with Papen had been chiefly responsible for Bruening's dismissal and Hitler's seizure of power, was certainly not one of these dreamers and dupes. He lost all hope of taming the wild men and resigned from his post as minister of economic affairs after only five months in office. Another conservative of the old school, Reichstag deputy Ernst Oberfohren, in desperation committed suicide. Little wonder that the nationalist and monarchist groups were thoroughly bewildered. The "veto power" Hindenburg had entrusted to Papen when Hitler was appointed Chancellor did not seem to work!

The big powers were in an even more serious dither. Ramsay MacDonald had addressed the House of Commons on March 23, 1933, stating that there was "not the slightest reason for the smaller countries to be apprehensive." Winston Churchill ironically replied that these were "comfortable words" but he was not backed by the majority, who wished to see things through rosy glasses rather than face cold, unpleasant facts.

Pessimists were quite prepared for a declaration of war when Hitler addressed the Reichstag on that 17th of May, but he did nothing of the sort. Though he protested against perpetuating what he called Germany's "disqualification," he accepted President Roosevelt's proposal of a non-aggression treaty and fully endorsed Ramsay MacDonald's disarmament plan. It was a mild speech. Had the leopard changed its spots? Was this but a smoke-screen? Many wondered, and yet, on the New York Stock Exchange German bond quotations improved, and an optimistic mood found reflection in London political quarters, where the *Spectator* referred to the speech as "the one of a new Hitler."

Inside Germany the people looked on in amazement. Foreign ambassadors addressed Adolf Hitler as "Your Excellency." Arthur Henderson arrived in Berlin to negotiate with the "Fuehrer" on disarmament. Reparations were not even mentioned. Suddenly the same statesmen who had found so much fault with the pre-nazi governments of Germany seemed quite unnerved. Like so many of Hitler's halfhearted associates they seemed to feel that after all, Hindenburg was still President, and that with Baron Konstantin von Neurath, the old-school diplomat and routine official of conservative observance, in charge of foreign relations, reckless experimenting was not to be anticipated.

Had Hitler pursued his initial course of seeming moderation, had he seriously meant to put down the delirious advocates of a "second revolution" in his own camp, and to eliminate at least the worst of their wild abuses, the world would have been more than willing to meet him half way. The statesmen of Europe had a real scare when the swastika flag was hoisted in Berlin. Some of them had been bothered by a bad conscience and were seeking ways and means to make amends for past mistakes. Readily they would have overlooked the uncouth features of hitlerism, if there had not been so many of them. Only too gladly would they now have granted concessions to a Bruening, had he still been in power. It was too late for all that. One could only try to gain time and steer clear of further trouble.

What it all amounted to was tacitly to keep hands off a messy situation. This was exactly what Hitler needed. When no one was looking, he would strike a new blow. Noticing the fair weather all about him, he decided to strike quickly, crushing all political parties in the Reich, outside of his own. It was the knock-out for the Weimar democracy, and it proved that the "Fuehrer" knew how to blow hot as well as cold, as circumstances required.

In those days "underground Europe" was born. It was born in Germany, when at the risk of capital punishment, the first anti-nazi leaflets were printed and distributed in secret Berlin hideouts. It had its first baptism of fire in the Gestapo executions of brave German men and women who from the very beginning of nazi terrorism had maintained their convictions, had refused to compromise with the forces of evil. Anyone provided with "safe" introductions could gain access to the resistance forces, who were keeping the flame of freedom alive. Thousands of civil service officials, political leaders, editors, artists, and workers whom Hitler had deprived of their jobs were receptive enough to suggestions of revolt. A good many businessmen too, were willing to cooperate. But there was the constant threat of Gestapo repression, the fear of secret tribunals, the sense of insecurity caused by the destruction of all constitutional guarantees.

There was the widow of the Frankfort engineer, for instance, who lost her husband in the last war, and a son in this one. In her own small way she never ceased her missionary work, pluckily using the charming *Gruessgott!* in public, instead of "heiling" her country's destroyers. It meant something, in the thick of the early years when offenders were frequently beaten up on the spot, if they did not comply with the arm-stretching rule.

The professor in Munich who lost his chair and pension because he had steadfastly refused to bow to Hitler and his prophets is another I won't forget. He has been eking out an existence ever since, selling insurance, if and when he could. There was no social security, out of nazi coffers, for those who did not dance to Hitler's tunes.

Also, I must remember the newspaperman in Stuttgart who turned "black printer," doing secret night work in his home for the "underground" with a manual press. The Gestapo got him and he disappeared for a while. He wrote his mother from the concentration camp. Then he returned, released on condition of good behavior, the marks of fresh whippings on his back. But he went on printing until he was drafted into the army.

The world has almost forgotten heroes such as Carl von Ossietzki, the battling journalist, who suffered years of torture and a slow death in concentration camps. As a writer and magazine editor, he had opposed the nazis and never wavered. After he had been confined three years the Oslo Committee awarded him the Nobel Peace Prize — which caused Hitler to flare up in a frenzy of cold rage.

There was Wilhelm Sollmann, the distinguished social-democratic Reichstag deputy who went through a similar ordeal before he was able to escape to America. And Rudolph Hilferding, former minister of finance, who was never heard from again after the Vichy government had extradited him to the Gestapo just when he was about to sail from France, to a refuge overseas. There were hundreds and thousands of unknown, and yet unforgettable victims of nazi brutality who were caught in the mesh of arbitrary laws while acting as secret go-betweens for their comrades abroad, as tireless organizers of a counter-revolution against the brown-shirted oppressors.

After nine months of nazi rule the shadows of concentration camps stretched out all over Germany, unnoticeable to most people, and yet gruesomely omnipresent, a haunting menace constantly in everybody's mind.

A "People's Court" set up by Hitler himself became truly a chamber of horrors, handing out wholesale death sentences. Every vestige of resistance was suppressed without mercy. The regular courts could no longer afford legal guarantees to the citizenry. Defendants often found themselves acquitted, and yet taken into custody again by Gestapo agents who maintained that they were above every law. "Right is whatever is useful for Germany, wrong whatever harms Germany," said the nazi jurist Karl Frank, future governor of conquered Poland. Of course, in his and his associates' mind "Germany" was identical with the nazi regime. The German people had no voice.

However, the Gestapo did not find it so easy to stamp out all signs of incipient opposition. The "underground" forces were slowly becoming organized. You could be almost certain, when people walked around a block or two of city streets just to avoid saluting a swastika flag, that they "belonged." You could almost tell when you met men or women who had been held as hostages that they were potential supporters of the "workers in the dark." You could almost spot the many individuals in a crowd who ignored the never-ending nazi collections in public cafés, and who refused to wear the poppies and other emblems indicative of nazi sympathy.

You could almost tell, I said, but not really, for anyone holding his or her life dearly, or those who meant to keep their jobs, would not dare to disagree with Himmler's hench-men publicly. It was clear long before he declared war, that Hitler was on the war-path — on the war-path against the German people.* The home front for him was but a labora-tory, a testing ground to try out the methods of aggression and deceit which were to be applied to the rest of the world later on. The first battle-front of this war was set up inside Ger-many, between the "underground" and himself. The conquest of Germany became his pattern.

It remained to be seen whether the rest of the world would yield, whether the "appeasers" abroad could be depended upon to do as thorough a defeatist job as the Papens, Hugenbergs, Schachts, and Thyssens had done on their side of the fence.

---

* "The nazi dictatorship is waging war on its own people," said a *New York Times* editorial on June 8, 1942.

# Chapter 10

## THE ANTI-CHRIST

**M**Y LISTENING post in Basel was becoming more valuable all the time. Many of my sources of information in Germany had been tightly clamped down, but on Swiss soil, those who managed to slip across the border were less reluctant to open up and talk freely.

An English-speaking Swiss banker, a friend of mine, had this explanation to offer: "There is so much that's hair-raising in hitlerland that people must come to Switzerland to let their hair down!" he remarked facetiously.

He was referring particularly to Dr. Albert Hackelsberger, only Center party deputy still in the Reichstag, who happened to be chairman of the board of his firm and used his business as a convenient excuse to visit frequently on safe neutral ground.

I had originally met Hackelsberger in Basel. Subsequently, our ways crossed in Berlin as well as in Rome. For a while Hackelsberger was close to Bruening. Sometimes, when I was visiting the Doctor at his hospital hideout, Hackelsberger would happen to be around consulting with him about the next move in the Reichstag tangles.

Relations between the two men were not as harmonious as they might have been. Hackelsberger was a southern industrialist, a man of wealth, ambitious and fairly new in politics. His leanings were conservative, but he did not have the experience of a Bruening. Of the nazis he thought in terms of utter contempt.

"Riff-raff, that's all they are. Good-for-nothings. There's only one fellow you can live with; that's Goering. He'll swing a deal when the time is ripe."

That was Hackelsberger's favorite line of thought. Bruening

disagreed. He could not see any nazi "swinging a deal." To his mind none of them could be trusted. He had seen too much of the hitlerites to be under any illusions, but Hackelsberger was the only parliamentary contact man the Center party had left. Bruening now could only operate behind the scenes. So Hackelsberger came in handy as a go-between.

He arrived in Basel one morning, beaming.

"I'm on my way to Rome," he announced, while I was having breakfast with him at the popular station buffet. "I think we'll have the Concordat in the bag shortly."

"A Concordat?" I asked in surprise. "With the German bishops agreeing?"

"Oh, they'll come around — some of them have already. There is nothing to be gained by dilly-dallying."

It was true that the German clergy as well as the laity, among the Protestants no less than among the Catholics, had been divided and torn in their emotions, when Hitler came to power. On the one hand there was Alfred Rosenberg, the Russian-born former Moscow school teacher whose treatise on what he called *The Myth of the Twentieth Century* (to wit: the myth of racial rather than intellectual and spiritual trends determining the trend of history) had become the text-book of all the nazi pseudo-educators; and Julius Streicher, the neurotic Jew-baiter of Nuremberg whose lewd posters were displayed all over the country; and Baldur von Schirach (the son of an American mother), would-be bard of the nazi gospel; and Rudolf Hess, the future star escapist of the war who had even refused to let his son be baptized. On the other hand, however, on the Catholic side, there were men boosting Hitler, such as Abbot Alban Schachleiter (who is said to have recanted on his death-bed); and on the Protestant side, the former army chaplain Ludwig Mueller, who became the nazi "Reich Bishop" for an inglorious interval until he disappeared behind a merciful cloud of oblivion.

Responsible religious leaders, with hardly an exception, maintained a judicious reserve when Hitler made his solemn statement before the Reichstag, averring that he considered "both Christian churches as most important factors, and Christianity as the immovable foundation of the moral life of the people." Who, then, was right — the government, queer simpletons like Schachleiter and Mueller, or the Bishops who remained non-committal?

"It's going to work out all right," maintained Hackelsberger. "You've got to give us time."

"And how about the blood and soil theories?" I pressed him. "They can never be reconciled with Christian ideas, can they?"

Hackelsberger was impatient.

"My dear man," he interrupted. "You can't have your cake and eat it too. This is a revolution and we're dealing with a lot of crackpots. Do you want them to run wild, and do to the churches what the Bolshies have done in Russia?"

"Germany isn't Russia," I insisted. "All I know is that the nazis have been double-crossing everybody right and left, and they will continue to do so."

"That's why we've got to nail them down! Have them sign on the dotted line!"

And off he went, to Rome. To see this big, husky man, a picture of health and prosperity, confident of success and sure of himself, set out on a mission which involved delicate spiritual issues made me wonder. Like others, that were to follow in his path, he was not sufficiently aware of the demoniac forces in this world.

In Basel the German church struggle was being watched with a more than perfunctory interest. Dr. Karl Barth was a native son of the city, and he was now teaching at Bonn university. This eminent Swiss theologian, with heroic Pastor Martin Niemoeller, who was to become Hitler's very own prisoner, was leading the Protestant "confessional" groups in Germany. Just about that time they had issued an epochal declaration, refuting the nazi claim "that the state should and can become the single and total regulator of human life." There followed a wave of arrests of Protestant ministers who had refused to betray their faith. As usual, the police club, rather than the intellect, was the only nazi weapon.

A former Berlin radio official, now a refugee in Basel, because he had refused to desert his Jewish wife, happened to be close to the Barth group. He often asked me over to his house, when I was back from a trip to Germany, to inquire about the latest developments, and I was glad to pass on to him and his

friends the latest information I had been able to pick up.
Shortly after I had seen Hackelsberger, we talked over the
situation again.

"No compromise with the devil has ever worked," my ex-
colleague remarked, and there was a tone of deep conviction
in his voice for he was a sincere believer and had lost his job
through upholding his faith. "The nazis claim the totality of
the people's soul. They won't tolerate 'strange gods.'"

"Despite the 'positive Christianity' pledge in their platform!"
I added.

"Oh, that was just another ruse," he agreed. "Shallow
humanitarianism, that's all it amounted to, and not even a sincere one. Most people did not notice the reservation that religious creeds were to be granted freedom only 'in so far as they
are not a danger to the state and do not offend the moral
instincts of the German race!' There was the catch!"

"It looks as though religion is being cut off the German air
entirely," I observed, displaying the latest Berlin program
schedule. "One by one church programs are being discon-
tinued, and 'pagan' ceremonies are put in their place."

"That was to be expected," my friend nodded. "While I was
still handling some of those broadcasts I ran into trouble with
the new bosses. They did not want any church music. They
said it was too denominational, either Protestant or Catholic.
The 'German God' and 'Faith in the Fatherland' were to become the substitute!"

Naïve and trusting people like Hackelsberger would not see
all this. They allowed dust to be thrown into their eyes, or kept
at least one eye closed, refusing to look the facts squarely in
the face.

Pius XI was not of that category. He was a battling Pope, a
great fighter. He knew too much of the affairs of men to be
deceived by the suaveness of Baron von Papen who had come
to negotiate the Concordat. But in the end less farseeing ad-
visers prevailed. More bees, they thought, are caught with
honey than with vinegar! They should have realized that the
nazis did not go for honey either! If Hitler agreed to let Papen
negotiate a Concordat, that still did not make a sheep out of
the wolf, at best only a wolf in sheep's clothing.

"Didn't I tell you!" triumphed Hackelsberger when he returned. The Concordat had been signed and it meant a considerable gain in prestige for the nazi regime.

"What will Bruening say?" I asked.

Hackelsberger professed not to know, but I was satisfied that Bruening would not approve.

"He warned you to go slow on this, didn't he? But you and Papen went ahead just the same. Pray God, you'll never have cause to regret it."

The blind did not see. Returning from Rome, Papen, in a jubilant vein, addressed a radio audience, claiming that the world was "on the verge of a Christian revolution." With other befuddled Catholics he may really have believed that. A bitter shock was in store, for the ink had not dried on the signatures of the Concordat when Hitler's counterblows began to fall.

First came the law authorizing compulsory sterilization of "undesirables," meaning mentally deficient persons, epileptics, and even the deaf and the blind. The measure was a slap in the face of the church which is known to object strenuously to all artificial interference with the process of life.

Next came the decree paving the way for euthanasia, the killing of supposedly incurable patients. "The interests of true humanity," were given hypocritically as the motive. Everybody knew, of course, that the nazis were identifying such interests with their own, and were just providing an instrument to get rid of people they didn't want.

The capital blow followed when Hitler appointed Alfred Rosenberg "educator of the nation." The slanderer who had leveled every conceivable diatribe at Christianity, overseer for a government which had just entered into a solemn agreement with the Church of Rome! The demagogue who denounced the Christian churches as "Jewish tools" because of their "negative teachings" on charity, mercy, and universal brotherhood, in charge of national morale building!

The Vatican immediately put Rosenberg's book on the Index. A truly total war was on.

"What now?" I asked Hackelsberger the next time we met, in the fall of 1933. It happened to be in Rome, and one of the German Bishops was with him.

"Hold your horses, man!" he replied with some annoyance.

"Hold your horses! Rome wasn't built in a day, was it? We'll have to be patient."

Patient with whom? With Hitler, the aggressor? There were rumors in the Eternal City that Pius XI had almost reached the limit of his endurance. I had been given a hint that his Christmas address to the College of Cardinals was to be a flaming protest against the nazi breach of faith.

"Sit down with us," Hackelsberger invited me. "Let's have a bite of lunch."

We were in the Ristorante Umberto, frequented by Roman society. Hackelsberger had discovered that their food was of the best.

"You ought to try their *canelloni*," he suggested to the Bishop. "We'll have some of that Est-Est wine with it."

"Thank you," said the Bishop, a quiet, modest type of man. He was to go through untold suffering under the nazi persecution in later years. "I'll have just a small dish."

"What do you think, Bishop?" I asked him. "Will the Pope speak up?"

"The Holy Father knows best," he replied. "We must trust his guidance."

The *canelloni* had been served and proved to be delicious. Hackelsberger was helping himself and I didn't mind joining.

"This thing has happened in Italy before," he lectured me. "First it was the stage when fascists poured castor oil down the throats of their opponents, then the wild men quieted down and came to terms even with the Pope."

"You don't know your nazis," I objected. "They are wilder than the wildest fascists."

"And," added the Bishop, "in Germany the situation is quite different. Once before we had a *Kulturkampf*, which stirred up the people against the Church."

I did not remain in Rome for Christmas. We had scheduled a holiday broadcast from Beuron, the Benedictine monastery in the Danube valley, on the fir-covered slopes of the Swabian Alps, not far from the Swiss border. So I proceeded, leaving Hackelsberger to his troubles. He was not entirely unsuccessful. The Pope spoke out that year, but not until 1937 did the conflict come to a climax when Pius XI published his challenging encyclical on Germany which was followed up by his

allocution stating flatly that "seldom has there been a persecution (of the Church) so crushing, so terrifying, so grievous and
lamentable" as the one in nazi Germany.

The Beuron broadcast was an event. The Abbey church was
crowded with devout peasant folk of the region. The inspiring
chant of the monks at Midnight Mass blended with the pealing
of the bells that echoed deep into the silent valley.

Archabbot Raphael Walzer invited me to stay on. He felt
like talking to someone from abroad. This tall man of erect
posture looked like a Giotto painting in his flowing habit.

"It is not often these days," he remarked, "that we can relieve our minds."

Even this remote sanctuary had been invaded by the swastika. One or two of the villagers, the "black sheep," the Abbot
called them, had joined up with the nazis and were making
life miserable for the monastic community whenever they
could.

"They report our sermons to the Gestapo, at near-by Sigma-
ringen, and though we are confining ourselves strictly to religious activities, they find fault with everything — with our
financial affairs, with the way we run our farm, with the edit-
ing of our publications. All is done by subterfuge. The people
hardly notice it. They are not supposed to know, but in the
meantime these moles are attempting to undermine the very
structure of our lives. For themselves they claim freedom of
speech, freedom to vilify the Church, and we are left powerless to reply."

"I find some priests though," I said, "who seem to maintain at least a benevolent neutrality toward the nazis. Strangely,
Abbot Schachleiter isn't the only one." I was referring to the
prelate who had found Hitler's favor in the early days.

"The poor man has been a problem child in our order for
quite some time," replied the Abbot. "As for the others, remember what Bishop von Galen, of Muenster, has said: 'A
deception of hell is being perpetrated which may even mis-
lead the good.' Many trusting souls took Hitler at his word.
Now that the Concordat is just another 'scrap of paper,' with
every essential provision systematically riddled, they may begin
to see the light."

Archabbot Walzer was soon to become an exile. The Abbey

was eventually converted into a war hospital; many of the monks were drafted and died on the battlefields.

"We, too," a farmer's wife of the region told me after the outbreak of the war, "have our blacklists. We know everyone responsible for this misery. Oh, for the justice of God! When the day of vengeance comes, there won't be enough gallows in the land. . . ."

We, too, she said. These simple people were outraged at all the trickery and violence that had infiltrated their poor lives. They were hard working Swabian and Baden folks of a peaceful disposition, steeped in the mellow traditions of the land which they loved intensely. What Hitler has done to them they can't forget. They can't forget that church holidays were banned, sanctuaries profaned, ministers and priests dragged to jail, religious properties wantonly expropriated, and hospitals "nazified" with the appointment of "Brown Sisters" who frankly despised Christianity.

The next day I was in Munich to see Cardinal Faulhaber. To his people, who revered him, he was the symbol of all the best in their national life, a true leader deeply concerned with maintaining their Christian heritage, one who had never compromised with the betrayers of his country's highest ideals and who had never succumbed to their sophistry.

The great Prince of the Church stood erect in his study to greet me, an imposing figure with the red skull-cap on his gray hair. It was shortly after the first attempt on his life.

"There is the broken window," he explained quietly. "The stone missed its aim."

He would not discuss the matter further. Had he seen Hitler? Yes, but he had no comment. Would he broadcast? He shook his head.

"You don't think I'd be allowed to, do you?"

"Perhaps, Your Eminence, if we chose the right occasion. . . ."

He smiled, without replying.

"When you get back to America, ask our friends to pray for us. We will need their prayers — badly."

That was the only intimation he gave me of the deep worries on his mind. Reports kept reaching him from all over his diocese of nazi interference with the people's freedom of worship. Protests were of no avail. The appointed authorities did not dare to make a single move displeasing to the new rulers. If anyone spoke up it meant dismissal, and often worse than that.

During the struggle for the maintenance of Bavaria's parochial schools many a father and mother went to jail because of their convictions. Civil service officials forfeited their jobs on the same account. Bishops protested, and in the end an overwhelming majority voted against the nazi plan to abolish the schools. But ballots were tampered with and the results published were those the nazis had wanted. The people's will was completely ignored.

In other parts of Germany, it was the same story. In the rural districts of the State of Oldenburg, for instance, nazi fanatics removed the crucifixes from the schools, but enraged farmers restored them to their places. Afterwards the men marched to the provincial capital to stage a demonstration of protest on the market square. Every one of them was seized by the Gestapo and dragged into a concentration camp without trial.

"What could we have done?" asked one of the Protestant leaders in Stuttgart, the seat of the valiant Lutheran bishop, Theophilus Wurm. "Close the churches? That's just what the nazis would have liked to see us do. Undergo arrest? Many of us did. One by one our ministers were taken away, hundreds of them, always under a cloak of silence. With our press muzzled, we were helpless."

"Spiritually, however, you emerged unscathed from it all," I answered. "The recent manifesto signed by the three thousand clergymen was a fearless challenge to the tyrants."

"It was, but it never reached the people. In a sense it fell on dead soil although we did everything to have it circulated. The Gestapo simply confiscated and burned every copy they could lay their hands on. You know what happened, how they forced us to disband our youth organizations, how they 'purged' libraries of every Christian book and made that bitter foe of religion, Hanns Kerrl, of all people, a cabinet member in charge of church affairs!"

"It is serious," I granted. "But religion can't be defeated."

"It never will. Tell it wherever you can: the Christians of Germany have not capitulated!"

In Berlin, Pastor Niemoeller's church was crowded Sunday after Sunday, and so were many others. The issues were becoming more clearly defined, although the nazis made every effort to keep the people in the dark so they would not become aware of the fundamentals involved. The Goebbels-controlled press tried to make it appear as though it was all just politics, or as they termed it, "theological squabbles," and no matter what the pastors said, everybody had to keep his mouth shut and obey the "Fuehrer."

Many who had not shown any interest in religion for some time noticed that the church was fast becoming the only rampart to rally behind, and they returned to worship. A new zeal manifested itself among believers, and Protestants and Catholics formed closer ranks in the face of a common danger.

The pastor of a church in down-town Berlin had been bold enough one Sunday morning to denounce Gestapo snooping.

"The fellows in the back pews," he thundered, "who take notes and report on me to the police can save themselves the trouble. I'll be glad to hand them over a copy of my sermon after the service!"

He was questioned and given a warning. The next Sunday his church was filled to overflowing, and again he spoke out fearlessly.

"The police have questioned me," he announced to a breathless congregation. "They say I am playing politics in church. You know that is not so. I am preaching the Word of God, but there are people, too many people, who try to gag God's ministers. To them I say that God's Word cannot be silenced."

This time he was arrested. His assistant carried on for him, with equal courage. After a while, he, too, was taken into custody. Many similar incidents occurred, but not a word could be said about them in the press.

I came by St. Hedwig's Catholic Cathedral one evening, near Unter den Linden. No service was scheduled, but people were walking up the steps. I entered the church which is built in the shape of a rotunda reminding one of the Pantheon in Rome. Frederick of Prussia had wanted the cupola designed "like a reversed teacup." It was dark inside. Worshipers were kneeling in the pews. The only spot of faint light was the tiny flicker of the sanctuary lamp. Only one voice could be heard, a single voice of a priest imploring his God, like Job and Jeremiah — truly a *De Profundis.*

Once in a while he would pause and the people would respond.

"Lord, have mercy! Christ, hear us!"

Then he would be heard again with words that came out of the depth of his heart, beautifully spoken, moving, stirring.

There was no allusion to politics, to the affairs of the world, and yet every sentence had a meaning reflecting the troublesome times. It was like a protest of the crucified church against oppression, like the community of all the faithful crying out to God, in deepest distress.

The priest was Monsignor Lichtenberg. He was there every day at the same hour, and people came and prayed with him. Then, one evening, in 1940, he was missing. A brief anouncement in the press said he had been arrested, "because of subversive activities." His death was reported soon afterwards.

Out of the nazi night, voices such as Monsignor Lichtenberg's have pierced through to the whole world. Pastor Niemoeller's and Bishop Wurm's, Cardinal Faulhaber's and Bishop von Galen's and many others, triumphantly and gallantly upholding Christian principles in the face of a cruel and cunning persecution. The people knew what it meant when, in the midst of the war, Bishop von Galen denounced the Gestapo from his pulpit in Muenster publicly for "injustices that cry to heaven!"

Bishop von Galen was not arrested. Bishop Wurm and Cardinal Faulhaber who spoke out with equal force were not arrested. Not a single Bishop was arrested, with the exception of the Bishop of Meissen, Saxony, who was kept in custody a few hours only, without the public knowing it. The Gestapo feared the Bishops. Hitler knew that a powerful body of German opinion was behind them.

In spite of all oppression Christianity today is stronger in Germany than it ever was before. It is crippled, enchained, shackled, humiliated — but not downed. Christians were muzzled, ignored, ridiculed, harassed, but they did not give up. Hitler lost this battle long ago. His fury was the fury of a man who is aware of being beaten — beaten by something he does not recognize as a force at all: the force of the spirit.

Thousands of copies of the sermons and Pastorals of all these upright ministers of religion, of the Niemoellers, Galens, Groebers, Faulhabers, Bertrams, Sprolls, Bornewassers, Wurms, Kallers, and Preysings were circulated "underground." Millions of Christians in Germany never missed a divine service, and as everyone who has been there in war-time can confirm, the churches continued to be crowded. Nazis, real nazis did not go to church. But the people went, the masses of the people, the workers, the women, and young people, too. They were not nazis. They despised the nazis in their hearts. Some day the world will again hear from them, when they have reached the end of this swastika-strewn way of the Cross.*

---

* On August 28, 1944, the *New York Times* published a letter from an unnamed private in France who had witnessed twenty Catholic German soldiers bowing in prayer. "It made an impression on me," said the writer, "because it proved to me that not all nazis believe in Hitler as a god." The letter is significant because it shows how nazi propaganda has succeeded to an amazing degree in convincing the world that hitlerism is in complete control of the German people. Once the war is over, many Americans will be greatly surprised to hear of the struggle of the German churches in the midst of the nazi darkness. It is of vital importance that the story be told fully and become much more widely known than heretofore. — In this connection a Geneva report of the Religious News Service, published by the National Conference of Christians and Jews in New York, and quoting, under the date of September 19, 1944, the Swedish Protestant Minister Birger Forell who is serving with the War Prisoners Aid of the YMCA in Normandy, is of particular interest. It states that 90 per cent of German war prisoners attend religious services.

# Chapter 11

## THE GRUESOME HOAX

T HE trouble with you people, you look at us from the outside, rather than from inside," said Eugene Hadamovsky, the new radio boss in Berlin, while I tried to convince him that the broadcasts he wanted us to take were definitely not acceptable in America.

All dressed up in the nazi "elite guard" uniform, with high boots and numerous decorations, he sat behind his desk, in the office formerly occupied by Hans Bredow, the German radio pioneer who had done more to promote the new art in a month than the nazis ever accomplished in their whole tenure of office. Hada, as his staff called him, shortening his Polish name, was a subaltern type of a fellow. He tried constantly to "play big."

"If we were really allowed to look at you from inside, I think we could get some stunning broadcasts," I said, continuing the conversation.

"What do you mean?"

"Well, from a concentration camp, for instance."

Hada was boiling.

"What if I asked you for a broadcast from a prison camp in the States, interviewing a chain gang?"

It was easy to answer that.

"Don't you see the difference? On the one hand, a due process of law; on the other, the outright persecution of political opponents!"

There was no use arguing. The gap was too wide, but it was astounding to see how these newcomers were prepared to ignore it, if by so doing they could win a point.

Up to the outbreak of the war relations between NBC and the German radio remained virtually unchanged. We got the programs we wanted and were given all the help we needed in arranging them. At first I had felt like cutting loose entirely. What was the use of trying to work with people who were trampling down all freedom of expression? But soon I was to realize that the trampling was mainly domestic. In its relations abroad the German radio made every effort to appear civilized.

A man of unusual ability had been assigned to handle these relations. He was Kurt von Boeckmann, formerly program director of the Munich station. Though not a nazi, he had been drafted by the hitlerites who needed men of his caliber to make up for their own deficiencies. After his transfer to Berlin, of course, he had to accept party membership, but because of an accidental family contact with a Hitler bigwig, he remained singularly free in his movements. His pleasant manners, his knowledge of languages and his rare adaptability made him an ideal choice. It was nice to deal with him rather than with a man like Hada, or his understudies who were practically morons.

Boeckmann's was not an easy assignment. When he was sent to Amsterdam to attend a meeting of the International Broadcasting Union, shortly after Hitler's access to power, he was almost ostracized. Seats remained vacant on either side of him. No one wished to be so close to a nazi!

Boeckmann broke down the antagonism after a while, and it was a victory for him personally. Soon he was chosen as a vice-president of the Union. The nazis used him as a convenient "front," pulling strings behind his back.

The situation was awkward in every respect — like constant shadow-boxing. The nazis I came in touch with knew where I stood, as I never concealed my feelings. They did not seem to mind my frankness, and even got a kick out of arguing with someone who brought a whiff of fresh air into their narrow disciplined lives. These people needed us and we needed them, so touchy subjects usually were ignored. Broaching the concentration camp idea to Hada was an exception to the rule!

One of Hada's assistants liked to keep open house, to satisfy the ambitions of his wife as well as his own. As a man who had suddenly emerged from obscurity he enjoyed the amenities of social life immensely. There was not a diplomatic reception nor official dinner he did not attend when asked. Having the limelight thrown on himself, he soon became an accomplished

"climber." I was surprised to find that his own parents
thoroughly disagreed with their son.

"You know," said his mother, after dinner one evening, approaching me in the winter garden which she had invited me
to admire. "We are not all like that. You mustn't think we are
all nazis."

Perhaps her son had cautioned her that I was an "anti."

"Why," I muttered, "I hadn't thought so. . . ."

"I am glad," acknowledged the father, who had joined his
wife. "You see, our son was always somewhat eccentric. This
recent promotion must have gone to his head."

"And what's more," the mother added eagerly, "there isn't
one single nazi in our whole family. Only Ernst has joined up,
and we never knew it until recently. He kept it a secret. You
don't think it's right, do you?"

The good people didn't realize how revealing their apologies
were. It showed me again how the dividing line cut through
so many homes and communities, from the lower strata up to
the high and mighty, and how little we knew about it.

For practical purposes the division meant little because the
nazis were gaining control more firmly every day even though
they made use of the services of anyone willing to fall in line,
so as to bridge the gap between their own kind and a cold
world that had no smiles for them. They were satisfied, at
least in the beginning, to run the show and set the cast as long
as others could be found to act as protagonists.

During the early part of 1933, when Hitler was still feeling
his way, collaborationists abounded on both sides of the fence.
Those in the nazi camp were motivated by a desire to profit
by the advice of men of governmental experience who did not
bear the marks of too close an association with previous
regimes, and who could serve as stooges in dealing with other
countries. After some initial hesitation many an old-school
diplomat and government official gave up their reserve, too.

"Should we let these nitwits upset the whole applecart?"
was one man's excuse when I asked him how he could in conscience swear allegiance to Hitler.

One of Germany's ablest diplomats, Rudolf von Nadolny,
a man of real intellectual stature, and a deeply religious
Protestant, realized from the beginning that the nazi stream-

liner was war-bound, and that only "all-outers" would be able to stand the dizzy journey. He was unwilling to join his more fickle colleagues on the road to the holocaustal pyre, but he considered it his duty to go along as a brakeman for at least a stretch.

Nadolny was what may be called a "conservative liberal," then near sixty, of engaging manners and perfectly at ease in an atmosphere of culture and refinement. He was a gentleman of unimpeachable character, and an admirer of Anglo-Saxon political philosophies. When Hitler decided that the time was ripe to take the initiative in Geneva, Foreign Office "moderates" prevailed upon him to choose Nadolny as the German spokesman. After all, Bruening in the course of his negotiations with the British and the French, had secured the promise of an armament convention that would have meant real progress. The question was whether the offer still held good now that Germany was on the warpath again.

In Geneva Nadolny met with utter distrust. France and Britain would not think of talking further about disarmament as long as the nazi firebrands were shouting from every housetop that *Der Tag* was at hand. The best Nadolny could wrest from his opposite numbers was a commitment to maintain the *status quo* for a four-year period — a concession the Allies were to regret!

Trying to arrange a broadcast, I called on Nadolny at his hotel one evening. He had just spoken over long-distance with Baron von Neurath, Hitler's first minister of Foreign Affairs and another collaborationist who at heart despised the nazis and yet thought he could live with them.

"We could not expect," Nadolny told me, "to reach an agreement on Hitler's terms. I have tried to convince him that he cannot force the issue, that he might precipitate a major crisis. He refused to even listen to me. He thinks he can get anything he wants."

"Does that mean Europe is on the verge of another disaster?" I asked.

"Not yet," was all Nadolny was willing to say.

The next morning he was recalled. From Berlin came the announcement that Germany had decided to resign from the League of Nations and would no longer cooperate with the

disarmament conference. The day was October 14th, 1933.
The Reichstag was dissolved. New elections were to be held
November 12th, as a sort of plebiscite. In a manifesto Hitler
stated that the German people were "determined to accept
sufferings, persecution and oppression rather than to submit
further to a perpetuation of the conditions created by the Versailles Treaty."

Nadolny was a man of real courage. Upon his return to
Berlin he told Hitler that a policy of willful provocation was
bound to lead to war. He was not prepared to share the responsibility, and after a brief interval as ambassador to Moscow he resigned, and went to live on his farm. In July, 1944,
after the alleged plot to kill Hitler, he was caught
in the Gestapo "purge" — another martyr of the German
"underground."

Mussolini was dismayed by Hitler's sudden move. He had
banked on the Four-Power Pact which had been signed in
Rome on June 7th, binding Germany, Italy, Great Britain and
France to consult together and to cooperate for the purpose of
maintaining the peace. The pact stipulated explicitly that the
signatory powers had "no intention of departing" from the
League Covenant, and that boundary revisions were to be
discussed under Article 19 providing for the reconsideration
of such portions of the treaties of peace as might have become
inapplicable.

Hitler did not care. Commitments, treaties, promises to him
were just devices to be tossed aside when no longer needed.
He had now made up his mind to test his strength — and the
weakness of his opponents. Broadcasting to the world, he
insisted that Germany's withdrawal from the League had become unavoidable because of "the deliberate relegation of the
German people to a status of inferiority, the perpetuation of a
discrimination unbearable to them!"

Europe was now on the threshold of a new phase of history.
Germany had been a member of the League for only seven
years. The period of frail peace which had lasted since 1918
was coming to an end.

When the election campaign started, Germany was already
behind a figurative barbed wire fence which surrounded the
whole country tightly. Goebbels admitted that there were

twenty-two thousand political prisoners. In reality the figure was probably three or four times as high. There were over one hundred concentration camps, truly diabolical prisons where innocent people were treated like criminals by guards who ought to have been behind bars themselves. Under such circumstances the campaign was really a frightful joke. All the candidates were nazis, too, or at least nazi sympathizers.

Hitler's press agents did a perfect job. Over public address systems the radio kept going virtually day and night. From every lamppost and telegraph pole came, not sweet tunes of peace, but the shrill notes of martial music. Whenever Hitler spoke, all traffic had to stop, and no serving of patrons was permitted in restaurants. Whether they wanted to or not, the people had to listen. Hitler was electioneering all over the country, speeding across the land in his own tri-motored plane, or in a 200-horse power automobile.

It was not easy to understand why the nazis went to such extremes. They had the election in the bag anyway. No one dared to contradict them. Anyone venturing to disagree, and to disagree carelessly enough to be heard in public, was promptly locked up after summary court proceedings. The issue, as Hitler in effect defined it, was patriotism, and he himself wanted to be considered as the super-patriot, the only one who knew what was good for the country.

It was a "command" election, with no back-talk allowed, a vote as free as Hobson's choice, entirely managed by the unscrupulous nazi machine. Even inaction was dangerous. Shirkers were black-listed publicly. On election day numerous incidents occurred indicating the true state of affairs. In the state of Baden, for instance, various voters who refused to cast their ballots were taken into custody. In the village of Puppen, Ortelsburg, nine citizens guilty of the same "crime" were forced to parade down the main street carrying placards which said "I am a traitor to my country." In the village of Selow, Warthebruch, the practice was enlivened with a brass-band. There were many more instances of this kind.

Hitler's last speech, on the eve of the election was a masterpiece of showmanship. We relayed the broadcast from the dynamo room of the huge Siemens plant in Berlin. Factory whistles and buzzing machines provided the sound effects, and finally the "Fuehrer's" coarse voice came rolling over the air like an ominous growl reflecting all the vulgarity of the man, bent on arousing the evil spirits of a whole nation.

For a full hour, traffic, business, and the wheels of industry were made to stop throughout the whole country. No one was to have the opportunity of finding an excuse not to listen to the new prophet who stood in Caesar-like pose on a rostrum built over the hull of a huge engine, symbolizing the "workers regime" which the nazis claimed to have established.

One of the most interesting pastimes in those days was to watch the German public react to the nazi antics. There could be no question that Hitler as an orator knew how to "put it over." He was always blunt and outspoken, and this time his braggadocio was centered on a popular issue, the issue of "equality" for Germany. The nazi interpretation, of course, was equal rights to arm.

"It's going to be a cinch this time," remarked Werner Pratt at the Friday Circle. "Equality! What about starting at home? Let's have equal rights with the nazis!"

"Lots of people must have that same thought," agreed Otto Weltin. "Hitler's bombast just doesn't ring true."

"He's going to win just the same," I said.

"Of course," Weltin went on. "But watch the people on the sidewalks, listening to the broadcasts. Hasn't it struck you how they express anxiety and concern? There are no happy faces. Still, all these men and women take in Goebbels' diatribes. They must. Only the bravest dare disregard the dirty looks of nazi watch-dogs."

In the polling places, the next day, "Ja" buttons were handed out to those who had actually cast their ballots, making any objector who might have worn one feel like a liar. Even invalids and the deaf and dumb were carried to the polling places on stretchers and in official cars, under the threat of being branded as slackers, should they refuse to come along. What could be expected when rumors of secretly numbered ballot-papers were being spread, to intimidate potential opponents?

This joke went the rounds:

"Did you hear? This time its going to be 110 per cent for Adolf!"

And the figure was not far off. Almost 90 per cent of the

eligible voters went to the polls. Of these, the nazis announced, 93 per cent voted "yes" — forty million for, two million against withdrawing from the League. Regarding the nazi Reichstag slate, the dissenters were admitted to be more numerous, 3.3 million, to be exact.

The temerity of these three million was really astounding. "No" votes were even cast in concentration camps, where the unfortunate inmates had to hand in their ballots in open envelopes, under the very eyes of their guards. As it was, the three million probably represented only a fraction of the negative votes, not to mention millions of voters who were scared and perplexed, or had cast their ballots under pressure. It made no difference if they cast blank ballots for they, too, were simply counted as "yes" votes.

I went with some friends that Sunday to mingle for a while amongst a typical crowd, in a beer hall of western Berlin. Most of the patrons were more intent on food and drink than on the election results which came in a constant, triumphant stream, out of the public loudspeakers. It was as though the masses felt the impact of a gigantic steam roller, a sort of kismet beyond all human control.

"All these people may well have voted in the negative, just to protest," remarked one of my companions. "But to no avail. Goebbels orders 90 per cent yes-men and he gets 90. He orders 95 per cent and he gets 95. The next time he may make it 99.9! Who cares? We know we are *verraten und verkauft,* double-crossed, anyhow."

The process of totalitarian control was fast approaching overwhelming completion. It was almost a painless process. For the timid and the wavering, Goebbels provided circus after circus, a constant round of parades and mass entertainment. The martial spirit began to envelop the whole dazed nation like a huge, impenetrable cloud.

One of the few who saw the shadow of war behind the whole ghastly carnival was General Kurt von Hammerstein-Equord who resigned as chief of the German High Command shortly before the new year dawned upon a gasping and turbulent world. (He "died" mysteriously in the spring of 1943.) But in London, Lord Rothermere came out with a four-column editorial in his *Daily Mail* of January 14, 1934, asking for "the same directness of purpose and energy of method as Mussolini and Hitler have displayed." He insisted that Italy and Germany were "beyond all doubt the best governed nations in Europe!"

## Chapter 12

## DEFIANCE WINS

O N JUNE 30th, 1934, the grisly date, never to be forgotten by anyone close to the scene of the first major murder crime of the Hitler regime, I happened to be in Oberammergau. Anton Lang, the late "Christus" of the Passion Play, had asked me to meet him, to discuss the particulars of a broadcast. NBC had relayed parts of the play for the first time on May 13th, which happened to be Mother's Day, and that program had fittingly been introduced by a two-way conversation between Oberammergau and Washington, with Frau Lang, and various members of her family, speaking to her son, Dr. Anton Lang, Jr., a professor at Georgetown University. The broadcast was a unique experience. Youngsters with curly locks allowed to grow long for the performances stood curiously around the radio amplifier. It was the typical atmosphere of an unspoiled Bavarian village, surrounded by mountain scenery of ravishing beauty.

Arriving for a repeat broadcast, I had stopped at one of the village inns, carrying a portable radio with me. It was an RCA, and immediately attracted the attention of the villagers. A group gathered around me while I was waiting for dinner to be served on the garden terrace. To demonstrate the set, I tuned in on the nearest station. There was the martial music again.

"The usual *Krach!*" remarked one of the Oberammergauers dryly and all the others laughed. There seemed to be little appreciation of Herr Goebbels' propaganda efforts.

But then came a "special" announcement. The villagers listened in terror. The hotheads of the Storm Troop Command, who had never liked the alliance with the "money powers," were said to have attempted a "second revolution," decidedly more leftish than the fictitiously legal one which Hitler had

put across by his pact with Franz von Papen. Apparently the
"wild men" had sensed for some time that Hitler was going
to double-cross them. They knew him better than the appeasers at home and abroad! Now hundreds had been murdered
during the night. Stalwarts like Captain Ernst Roehm, Edmund
Heines, and Karl Ernst were represented as plotters against
Hitler. But others, too, like former Chancellor Kurt von
Schleicher and Catholic Action leader Heinrich Klausener,
were caught in the blood-bath. The "purge" was thorough
indeed. Only some weeks later on did the German people hear
through their rumor channels that the "Fuehrer" had thus
conveniently done away with some thousand potential rivals
and opponents.

We all stood there in Oberammergau, listening intently to
my portable as the horrid story was broadcast to the world.
The mayor of the village was with us. Not a word was uttered.
The men were pale and thunderstruck.

"My God! My God!," gasped an old farmer. "What will
happen next?"

He was obviously frightened, and some of the others tried
to hush him. There was no expression of approval. When the
announcer signed off, the men walked silently away.

The following morning the village church was crowded.
It was a reverent, devout congregation attending Mass. The
singing of the boys' choir was inspiring. That same afternoon
we broadcast the Passion Play.

The Passion Play after Hitler's "blood purge!" The contrast
was indeed symbolical. Here were two worlds in conflict. I
had spoken to Anton Lang the evening before. He was stirred
to his very soul by the dreadful news and yet was mastering
his emotion in the strength of his faith.

"They truly know not what they do," he said, his hands
folded.

Then he spoke of the impact of the nazi upheaval. In his
peaceful village there had been few nazis, very few. Mostly
those who had never made good, the trouble-makers, but also
a number of misled idealists who believed in Hitler and
thought he would "save" Germany. However, the large majority of the deeply religious villagers knew of the nazi hostility
to all religion.

Had not Cardinal Faulhaber, of Munich spoken of the enemies of Christ? The Oberammergauers understood what that meant. They had heard of the vile attempt on the Cardinal's life. No, these good people were not with Hitler, not then, and even less so later on when the nazi fury against the Christian churches was unleashed without restraint.

There had been apprehension lest the nazi bosses prohibit the Passion Play. Hurried assurances came from Berlin that there was no such intention. Tourist traffic was still being encouraged at that time. A "front" had to be maintained. The Concordat with the Holy See was barely a year old and had already been rifled. Nazi medicine was administered in small doses. One shot at a time, and then a period of rest to minimize the shock. The Passion Play fell into one of the "rest" periods. Hitler himself had planned to attend the opening performance, but the "blood purge" caused him to decide otherwise. He never came to Oberammergau.

"It is better so," said Anton Lang quietly.

The saintly man has now passed away.

\*    \*    \*

A few weeks after the "blood purge" Hackelsberger, my friend of the Center Party turned up in Basel again. He was not in a happy mood. Events were not moving in the direction he had anticipated. The nazi breach of faith with the Vatican hurt him deeply. Now the "blood purge" had completely upset his calculations.

"There is little left for me to do," he complained. "My position becomes untenable."

"Don't you think it will help to have the lines drawn clearly between decent people and — well, your government?"

"I guess so. Hitler's bed-fellows in the cabinet must feel ill at ease right now. So far they have forgiven him many faux-pas, hoping he would become civilized. They did not reckon with the real Hitler as he has now revealed himself. They thought he was their prisoner. In reality he has put invisible shackles on them."

"The 'purge' has made them visible enough, hasn't it?"

"I wonder."

Hackelsberger mused a while. We had just ordered two

*Café-Kirsch,* in our favorite corner at the station restaurant, and he was in no hurry.

Outside, on the square he had parked his car. It was only a short drive from his home across the German border, in the heart of the Black Forest. The fact that he was still a member of the Reichstag and could show his official pass, made these crossings simple, but Hackelsberger was foolhardy in making use of the opportunity. Often he would carry Swiss newspapers in his pocket, to take back to his family, although they were banned by Goebbels.

One day, after the war had broken out, and regulations were being enforced more strictly, he was caught for some minor infraction and taken to jail. Probably it was a pretext as the nazis had distrusted him for some time. Once in their clutches, he was lost. He died a prisoner.

That day, however, in the Basel Buffet, no somber thoughts were in his mind.

"You know," he picked up the thread again, "I don't believe we are on the right track. What do you know of the people? What do I know? What does anyone know? In America you've got public opinion surveys. Such a thing is inconceivable under Hitler."

"It'd certainly ruin the whole nazi show!" I admitted.

"Well, maybe. What you hear, and what I hear, comes from people who think more or less as we do, from people of a certain background and independence of mind, and especially from people with foreign contacts. They are not the ones who vote for Hitler. Of course not. What of those who did vote for him though? I mean the masses, the little men, workers, farmers, small employees — the 'unenlightened,' in other words. I wonder if they are not really with him."

"I am no Dr. Gallup," I replied, "but I believe I've got a pretty good slant. The people I talk to in Germany belong to all strata, and those who are outspoken, all tell me the same thing. As far as they are concerned, this whole nazi business is a big fraud."

"As far as I am concerned, too. You know that."

"Of course I do, and I think you are in no sense an exception."

"I wish you were right."

"Have you become a skeptic all of a sudden?"

Hackelsberger laughed.

He called the waitress. "Fraeulein! Another *Kirsch* for me!"

"Those Swiss cherry brandies certainly pep you up, don't they? Even a skeptic! But don't worry. I just want to get your reaction. You reporters hear the grass grow all right, but mostly you are out for dog-biting men and the like. After all, you are primarily concerned with the unusual, aren't you?"

"That's a compliment!" I acknowledged. "But the law of averages still applies. People can't be fooled all the time."

"Except fools!" chuckled Hackelsberger.

We got up.

"What do you hear from Bruening?" I inquired before saying good-bye.

"Don't you know? He is in England."

"What?"

"He made his escape just before the 'purge.'"

"Was he warned?"

"I believe so, but he did not want to leave. His friends had to use all their persuasive powers with him. Finally, during the Whitsunday holidays when there was considerable holiday travel around those parts, they whisked him across the Dutch border in a motor car."

"Thank God, he's safe."

"Yes, we must be grateful, but he'll be missed. I hope you can go and see him."

Bruening's escape certainly meant a big change. It indicated clearly that there was not a chance in a million to control the extremists. Within the short compass of a year and a half the nazi regime had fully consolidated itself. The German people had been completely disarmed, first psychologically and then juridically. The police, the courts, the state administrations, the political parties, the armed forces, the labor unions — they all were now either "co-ordinated," subjugated to the nazi will, or ruthlessly destroyed. The Gestapo's hold was now more firmly established than the OGPU's in Moscow, and the last vestige of independence, which the military thought they had preserved for themselves, disappeared when Hindenburg died on August 2, 1934. Immediately Hitler clamped down the lid. He was now absolute ruler, and by his own appointment supreme dictator of a still reeling German nation.

Officially it was announced that the Field Marshal had designated Hitler as his successor, but the text of his "political will" was never published in full. There was considerable room for doubt that Hitler had been mentioned in the original at all. Whispering informants all over Berlin intimated that shortly before his death the old man had expressed his serious concern over the ungodly trend of things under the nazis. However, there was no way of checking up, and as far as the citizenry was concerned all they could do was to take the government's word.

Quickly, Hitler bade the armed forces swear allegiance to him. The "unknown corporal of the last war" as the swaggering "Fuehrer" liked to call himself, taking the oath from the staid, gold-braided army and navy leaders! It was a show for the gods, as the German saying goes. From a mere glance at the official photographs one could tell that the generals and admirals must have felt uneasy, though they didn't budge. Trained proficiently in a rigid tradition, they were caught almost unawares. Most of them had never displayed much political imagination or independent judgment. Their hearts, with few exceptions* had at no time been with the democratic regime, and their ambitions were those of career men. As long as the nazis provided appropriations and the chauvinistic clatter to whip up the dormant enthusiasm of the masses for uniforms and parades, everything seemed all right to them.

Only a few of these men of high military rank knew what they had to expect of the new rulers. Most others, although aware of the nazi demagoguery, saw their own advantage in playing Hitler's game. They were the ones causing the most serious concern to Hitler's conservative partners. Who but the military could keep the "brown Bolsheviks" under control? How could they do the job, now that they had been tricked into an oath of allegiance to the very man who had invited most of the violence, now that they had agreed to wear the swastika on their uniforms in another attempt to compromise with the devil? What could they do now that the old imperial flag of black, white and red which they had hoped to see restored to its ancient glory was about to be substituted by a

---

* General Berthold von Deimling, an ardent champion of democracy, was one of them.

symbol of cruelty and hatred and prejudice and arrogant pride?

Old-line army men must have considered it the very apex
of humiliation when the vain, multi-be-medaled Goering celebrated his wedding in the spring of 1935, and five military
bands had to serenade the couple for hours. The wedding
present of the air force, Goering's very own baby, was a golden
sword studded with jewels, and Hermann's gift to his bride
a diadem of sapphires holding a diamond swastika. It was an
upstart affair in true nazi style. The four hundred guests at
the sumptuous Kaiserhof dinner had a good time just the
same.

His honeymoon was hardly over when Goering was brought
face to face again with the troublesome realities of life, for
new unrest had developed. The Jew-baiters were interfering
badly with business. The ordinary citizen could no longer
expect protection in the nazi-dominated courts. The brown-
shirted "liberators" were getting to be a serious nuisance everywhere. Even sincere patriots who had first hailed the "new
era" were now in a predicament. Corrupt reformers and all
sorts of rabble were now on top and running wild, with no
one in a position to check them. The deluded foes of democracy had scoffed at civil liberties and constitutional government. Now they learned what it meant to have conjured an
irrational mob.

Not long before Hindenburg's death, Colonel von Papen
had emerged once more as the spokesman of his set. At Mar-
burg University on June 17th, he had openly denounced the
radical trend and threatened to resign. Hindenburg had wired
Papen warm congratulations, but Goebbels had ordered the
press not to report Papen's speech and shortly afterwards had
warned all "grumblers" and critics. Less than a fortnight later
Papen himself was almost caught in the "purge." Two of his
own intimates fell as victims of nazi vengeance, and the
colonel had to appeal to his army friends to provide him
with a personal bodyguard. Now that the old Marshal had
passed away, even army powers were visibly curtailed.

Big business found itself no better off than the army. They
had backed Hitler as long as he was out to destroy labor
unions and to put the workers "in their places." They wanted
to be "bosses in their own plants," free to fix wages and work-

ing hours as they saw fit. All the democratic regime had done
to improve labor standards was to their utter distaste. But
now the nazi bosses went to what these industrialists and
bankers thought was an even greater extreme by making
Robert Ley's "Labor Front" and its omnipotent "trustees," the
arbiters of both workers and employers. That, Hitler's business
backers felt, was not part of the bargain. It was socialism all
over again, the very socialism they had hoped to eliminate by
helping an avowed "anti-marxian" regime into the government saddle, and even paying for the privilege.

The nazis must have been greatly amused, for their critics
had little with which to back up their criticism. There was
no Reichstag any longer to throw public invectives at opponents, and no free press and radio. There was only a nation
of willing, or unwilling, yes-men smarting under the whip
of swashbuckling bullies determined to give orders even to
the Thyssens and the Schachts.

On August 19, 1934, Hitler tolled the knell of German freedom. In another "plebiscite" election which was to validate
his regime after Hindenburg's death, he had himself confirmed by the nation as dictator for life. There were 4.2 million
negative votes out of a total of 43 million cast. It was little
short of incredible that the men at the controls should have
admitted that many, although, of course, the real total of
"No" ballots was never revealed. In any case, it did not matter
very much what size opposition vote Herr Goebbels conceded.

"The nazi machine is well enough geared," observed Karl
Nord at the Friday Circle, "to produce any kind of rabbit out
of any sort of a hat!"

"Elections!" scorned Werner Pratt. "Ballot parades, I'd call
them!"

"You wouldn't blame the people though, would you?" I
asked. "As long as the army and big business tolerate it all,
what can they do? There has not been a single peep out of
the ruling classes, in spite of the outrages of these past few
months. The individual is helpless. If he sticks his neck out,
all he'll get is a one-way ticket straight to the nearest concentration camp."

"Let's not forget," Karl Nord spoke up again, "that the
nazis are really doing things. When they took over we had

six million unemployed. They are now fast being put to work. Few questions are asked, and no gloves are used, but the job is being done. No wonder a wave of confidence begins to sweep the country in spite of the fact that throngs of people can't stand even the sight of Hitler."

Weltin still disagreed.

"Sounds good on paper," he growled, "but the nazi blue-print rests on flimsy pretenses, mainly self-advertising. Our national debt is skyrocketing. Once most of these public works are out of the way, bolstering armaments will be the only answer to the unemployment problem, and you don't think the world will cheer us on to that, do you? Not to mention that only by export trade can we obtain the necessary raw materials. I tell you, I smell trouble, plenty of it!"

Grumblers such as my Friday Circle friends were not too numerous. As long as people were kept busy, grumbling could be conveniently ignored. The nation as a whole was fast taking to the nazi-created habit of thinking as little as possible. Independent thinking meant trouble, and those indulging in the luxury found out soon enough that it only intensified their intellectual and emotional misery. There was no escape from the nazi net. So why flirt with death by black-listing one's self? Why not rather concentrate on the hope that eventually the whole nazi nightmare was going to collapse anyway?

Professor Kraus, for instance, had decided to fence himself in completely, to escape from the futility of it all.

"I now follow a moron's routine," he said, while we were taking a walk under the colored foliage of autumn woods around his home at Nikolassee. "I get up mornings, eat breakfast, go to work, keep busy all day, go back home, eat, sleep — and I never look at a newspaper, never listen to the radio."

"Why?" I asked in amazement. "How can you stand that? You have been intellectually active and public-spirited all your life!"

He replied in a tired voice:

"What's the use?"

Thousands of decent, intelligent, honest people in Germany were in a similar frame of mind. They were, as I said, disarmed physically, psychologically, and juridically. All thought of active opposition against the Gestapo had to be eliminated.

Men with families to support remembered what had happened to others who had been arrested and disappeared, or returned from fearsome, unknown destinations, emaciated, nervous wrecks, with beaten hang-dog countenances. Experiences of this kind could be had by the slightest provocation of the nazi overlords. The denunciation of a disgruntled neighbor, of a dismissed employee, of a jealous competitor was enough to destroy a man's livelihood. Perhaps the suspect had not stretched out his hand when "heiling" Hitler, or he had not given the prescribed salute when passing a swastika banner on the street, or he had told one of the many current jokes about the "top guys" without making certain there was no eavesdropper around.

Having become resigned to what appeared to be an overpowering destiny, the masses took to the whip-up showmanship of Goebbels gracefully enough. There was plenty of good-natured kidding about the "bosses" who were strutting about in gaudy uniforms, looking important and living at taxpayers' expense. But that was about all the articulate opposition there was. On the surface the country seemed to be on the upgrade. There was enough to eat for everybody, so why court trouble? It was more convenient to let things run their course.

To the visitor this remodeled German scene was bound to look impressive. The country was shipshape. Restaurants and theaters were crowded, and everyone seemed to be having a good time. The dirty linen, of course, was washed behind closed doors. Only the bright side of the picture was shown. Anyone bold enough to look behind the scene was "treated rough and told nothing."

The constant talk of a "new Germany" and her Hitler-made glories had an almost hypnotic effect on the crowds. Many a man would stop and wonder whether it was not all a make-believe world, but most people fell wearily for the Coué-type propaganda which was taking in the whole country.

On March 16, 1935 came another of Hitler's sudden strokes when he restored conscription. He killed two birds with one stone. On the one hand, a large number of jobless were absorbed. On the other, a fervor of restored national dignity was injected into a people who for seventeen years had felt downtrodden and second-rate, a people smarting under the stigma of restricted sovereignty and forced disarmament.

Now Hitler had flung a challenge at the whole world. It was just the right move to make military hearts beat faster, and to allay the soreness of the conservative groups who had felt neglected, and almost betrayed. Small wonder theirs was a mood of "forgive and forget." To them, Hitler now seemed to be back in the fold and on the right track again, instead of stepping on too many people's toes. Now, they thought, he concentrated on the only essential task: the restoration of the Reich's greater glories.

At Broadcasting House, Hada and the minor nazi "guns" were in their seventh heaven.

"Versailles is as dead as a door nail!" announced Hada.

I voiced a note of caution.

"Paris and London may be heard from, you know."

Hada roared.

"Aw, let them jump in the lake! The time is past when we have to ask for their good pleasure!"

The fact was that England, France and Italy protested on paper. That was all.

\*     \*     \*

Dr. Bruening had a close friend in Switzerland. On the way from London to Lugano he stopped over in Basel, while I was there. It was a pleasure to find him in good health, even though in exile.

"History repeats itself," he argued reflectively. "When Napoleon overran Europe, the powers made one concession to him after another. Though it failed before, appeasement will be tried again."

"So you think war will be avoided?" I asked.

The Doctor shook his head.

"War is now a certainty, the only question is how long can it be delayed."

"Do they realize it in England?"

"Some do, some don't. There is little real understanding of the German situation."

"Will they let Hitler do as he pleases?"

From behind his glasses democratic Germany's last Chancellor looked at me as though he hadn't heard what I had said.

"You know," he smiled, "one of Talleyrand's maxims was *Surtoût pas de zèle,* meaning: Let's not get excited! Governments frequently are motivated by a desire to leave things alone when they don't know what to do."

After the outbreak of the war Bruening came to Harvard to take the Littauer chair of government. He ate his heart out thinking of the tragedy that had overwhelmed his homeland. Gallantly, he had done his part to forestall it, but no one had offered him a hand. With all the others who had relied on negotiation and peaceful understanding he was now in the doghouse, by the connivance of those who ought to have been his best friends.

As Bruening had surmised when he spoke to me on Swiss soil, Hitler's announcement of the new conscription law which soon was followed by the restoration of a German general staff was not nearly so much of a shock to European chanceries as one might have expected. The editorial comment of the London *Times* following Hitler's speech on the subject seemed to indicate that the British were not really aware of what the move amounted to. "The speech turns out to be reasonable, straightforward and comprehensible," said the *Times.* "It is to be hoped that it will be taken everywhere as a sincere and well-considered utterance, meaning exactly what it says."

Shortly afterwards Sir John Simon, then the British Foreign Secretary, came to Berlin to sound out the new German rulers. Sir John tried to obtain a promise of an "Eastern Locarno," but Hitler flatly refused to guarantee the *status quo.* His basic argument was that Germany should be given a free hand in the East, and that she was to serve as "a bulwark against bolshevism."

The day the new German army marched into the Rhineland, in 1936, he repeated the same offer suggesting a twenty-five year non-aggression pact to France, Holland, Belgium, Austria, Czechoslovakia, and Lithuania, coupled with a formal engagement "to prevent attacks from the air," and to return to Geneva, provided the German colonies were given back. Lloyd George in commenting upon the move in a House of Commons speech said:

"I trust Hitler!"

Disagreeing with his erstwhile comrade in arms, Churchill

informed the House that Germany was building a hundred planes a month; and the French Secretary of War, General Louis Maurin added in a speech before parliament that almost the whole German industry was now producing for the army which would be 700,000 strong by the end of the year.

Soon it was Rudolf Hess's turn to proclaim "Guns for butter!" as the nazi battling slogan under the terms of an economic four-year plan of national self-sufficiency. German school hours were reduced to allow extensive pre-military training. A new armament race was about to be resumed at a feverish pace, but it was to Hitler's interest to mark time. The French were just as determined not to lose any! On May 2, 1935, they had entered into a mutual assistance pact with the Soviet government. Czechoslovakia, as France's ally, followed suit.

Hitler smelled encirclement. Was there danger ahead? He was a past-master at causing confusion among his foes. First he had tackled them one by one in the domestic field. "Keep your shirt on," Joseph Goebbels had scoffed. "We'll get you all in the end!" After the communists had been "taken care of," it was the turn of the mid-wing groups, and finally of the old-line nationalists. It was a hand-in-glove job. Now the same pattern was to be applied in the foreign field.

The Vatican had been the first victim in Hitler's pre-war diplomatic jockeying. Poland had been his next. Lured by the smooth talk of his emissaries, Marshal Pilsudski signed a ten-year nonaggression pact which was but another time-saving device to reassure a baffled nation left seriously in doubt on England's and France's determination really to back Warsaw to the hilt.

"Who would think of war with Poland!" Hitler said to G. Ward Price, of the London *Daily Mail*. In a speech he explained further that the Poles "cannot eliminate the Germans from Europe, and we would be showing little intelligence if we thought of eliminating them." Five years later came the attack on Poland.

By taking on his enemies one at a time, Hitler achieved his purpose. The pact with Poland gave him fair insurance against complete isolation in the East and left him free to put Austria and Czechoslovakia out of the way first. Yet the London

*Times* commented editorially, on January 26, 1934, that Hitler now had "shown he understands the difference between an agitator and a statesman!"

And in Washington, Congress adopted a neutrality law, giving the green light to all aggressors!

It took the Munich conference in 1938 and subsequent events in Czechoslovakia to open the eyes of an all too gullible world. But in the days of Hitler's first triumphs people were easily impressed when they heard him make statements such as: "I consider war in Europe madness"; "The colonial question can never justify a war"; "It is ridiculous to think that we are after Russian territory"; "We are not threatening France!" All were clever devices used by the "Fuehrer" to serve his main purpose of stalling for time.

He won the first big round when, suddenly breaking through the Franco-Soviet ring of steel, he suggested a naval treaty to England which the latter accepted.

It was truly a spectacular event. Great Britain tacitly agreeing to an open violation of the Versailles naval clauses and granting Germany 35 per cent of her own naval strength! Was she prompted by a desire to divert Hitler's attention to the East in accordance with his own wishes? Or was it just another move in the diplomatic game of chess, another device designed to gain time?

In any case, Hitler had now succeeded in restoring the coveted "equal rights" for Germany. It was only natural that the German people began to ask themselves whether defiance, rather than compliance was not really the better way. Now the nazis could assert triumphantly that they were right, and their predecessors wrong. The peace-lovers, the democrats, the true Christians in Germany had been checkmated.

German troops moved into the reconquered Rhineland amidst a frenzy of patriotic fervor. The military was overwhelmed by Hitler's success. Resistance or at least a firm stand on the part of France had been anticipated. Hitler had been warned that he was taking too big a chance. But he knew he could afford the risk. He knew that France was in the throes of a domestic crisis, that England and Italy happened to be at loggerheads over Abyssinia. His boldness was shrewdly calculated.

New converts were won for the swastika. Success was again succeeding, and few seemed to care that the public debt, still rapidly rising, was now near the fifty-five billion mark. Hitler's magic touch was supposed to cure all ills. Foreign boycotts directed against German goods, and the devaluation of the national currencies of France, Italy, Switzerland, and Czechoslovakia, which were causing a further contraction of Germany's foreign trade, were waived aside as paltry when compared to the "Fuehrer's" wizardry in organizing a strictly self-contained national economy along totalitarian lines. The *Voelkische Beobachter* had actually declared Hitler "infallible." So why worry? Having lost its moorings, half-blinded, half enslaved, a whole nation was merrily courting disaster.

*     *     *

As long as things went well, the enthusiasm engendered by Hitler's easy victories was contagious. Suggestions were reaching me from Berlin's radio headquarters in a fairly constant stream. The offers ranged from Hitler speeches to special pickups from the Rhineland, from interviews with nazi bigwigs anxious to tell America all about the wonderful things they thought they were doing, to feature broadcasts of every description meant to convince the world that under the sign of the swastika an age of everlasting bliss had arrived in the Third Reich.

The first chance I had to break away from the office in Basel, after the reoccupation of the Rhineland by German troops, I went to Berlin to confer with the radio people. It was an overnight ride in a comfortable sleeper, and the trip along the Black Forest ridges, through the fertile valleys of the Rhine up to Frankfort and beyond was always restful. The stream of German life was still flowing fairly normally under the boisterous nazi cloak.

I called at Berlin's Broadcasting House in the morning. Hadamovsky was out of town, speech-making. He had been superseded by a new general manager, Dr. Heinrich Glasmeier, a fat fellow, bald-headed, rotund, vivacious, and radiating confidence in himself. He had come from Cologne where he was manager of the local radio station for a while, after having been associated with a Westphalian genealogical society for many years. He represented the very type of middle-class burgher whom the nazis found the easiest bait, flag-waving, bragging, conceited. His simple-mindedness was pathetic.

"You must see for yourself," Glasmeier invited. "Go round and watch the people! We are entering a new era. The depression is over. Years of peace and prosperity are ahead of us. It ought to be reflected on the air. Why don't you take more of our programs?"

I muttered something about different tastes, and no time being available.

"But your people in New York must realize that this is the turn of a century. What is happening in Germany now transcends everything else in importance. Today, for instance, we are opening the radio exhibition. Have you been invited?"

No, I had not.

"Well, here is a card of admission. I hope you'll come. Dr. Goebbels will be there. Perhaps I could introduce you to him."

The radio exhibition was notable. The television demonstrations were amazing. They had small receiver models that were perfect wonders. Goebbels arrived at the appointed hour, surrounded by heel-clicking, uniformed bodyguards. Presently, Glasmeier was motioning to me, and I found myself exposed to the little man's penetrating gaze.

"You ought to come and see me," Goebbels urged. "We like to do everything we can to promote the radio program exchange with the United States."

We were taking quite a few programs from Berlin as it was, I explained.

"You could certainly take more," prodded Goebbels.

"It is somewhat difficult," I explained, "to produce the features we are really interested in."

"Why?"

"At the moment, everything in Germany seems to be politics, and we don't want so much of that."

"Politics is the apex of life!" exclaimed Goebbels excitedly. "How can you be a broadcaster and ignore politics?"

I tried to make myself plain, but I seemed to have hit a sensitive spot.

"This is a political era," Goebbels went on. "Everything else is secondary."

"That," I ventured to differ, "is perhaps a matter of opinion."

"Not with us, Sir," Goebbels rebuked me coldly. "When the time comes, people in America, too, will find that out."

I bowed sort of sidewise, and Goebbels stretched out his arm. It was my first and last personal encounter with him. I must say, he did look funny, all puffed up as he was, awkward in his movements and pompous in his manners.

The atmosphere in Berlin was unreal. Seas of flags everywhere. Parades of youngsters singing lustily. Had the people really out-lived their more normal past and accepted this nazi way of life as something that had come to stay?

"If you lived here," cautioned Karl Nord at the Friday Circle, "you'd understand that nazism is like a Roman bath. Once you are inside, there is one rubdown after another, and clouds of hot steam; there is no escape, until you're entirely exhausted and let them do to you what they please!"

"But don't these people realize that they have an antagonistic world all around them, that their so-called way of life is not wanted by the rest of humanity?"

"We who live here, most of us, I assure you, don't want it either, but it's here, a permanent circus! How could one stop it? I grant you, it's exasperating, but griping doesn't do you any good, so eventually you wind up by, well, just letting it happen!"

"Sounds like fatalism."

"Maybe. Do you know a way out of it?"

I didn't.

Neither did the rest of the world, at least at that time. As a matter of fact, the rest of the world was rather slow in making up its mind about the true significance of Hitler's moves. The ranks of the former Allies were split. England's naval pact with Hitler, and France's deal with the Soviet precluded a united front against a resurgent Germany. The question was whether she should be given a free hand in the East, or checked immediately by the application of force. There was no readiness to pursue either course, unflinchingly.

"You'll see," continued Karl Nord, "that all these diplomatic hustlers will swallow Hitler's medicine readily, though without gusto. The taste is bitter, but what should they do?"

"For once," I remonstrated, "you'll be greatly mistaken! The powers will stand for only so much of his game of bluff, and then there will be trouble."

The old Friday Circle was no longer what it had been all these years. Known nazis had been gaining admittance to the club, and attendance had been dwindling. The stalwarts of the good old days were now meeting in homes or offices where they could count on greater privacy.

"The next time you are in town," Nord suggested, "we'll have a *Bierabend* at my home. Just a few of us after dinner. We'll be able to talk more freely."

It was not until the following summer that I got around to calling on him. We met in what he called his "den" in the basement. The walls were panelled, with benches built in all around. Near the entrance stood an old-fashioned keg. On the sideboard, stacks of pretzels, slices of pumpernickel, and big hunks of cheese were neatly placed within everybody's reach.

We were six in all. Besides the host and myself, a Foreign Office official, a newspaper editor, a mining engineer and Otto Weltin soon gathered around the table.

"Help yourselves to smokes, gentlemen!" Nord opened the conversation. "And *prosit* to all of you! Who's going to be raked over the coals tonight?"

"May I recommend the foreign appeasers for a change?" Otto Weltin started in.

"Which ones?" I asked.

"Oh, all of them! All the dupes and sissies that are paving Hitler's roads."

"I think you are exaggerating," I said.

"Indeed he is not," Nord came to Weltin's aid. And all the others echoed:

"He certainly isn't!"

"You see, that's just the trouble," our diplomatic friend explained. "It isn't realized, as Weltin put it a moment ago, that unwittingly, all these people are paving Hitler's road to ever growing power, simply by being on speaking terms with him."

"Why, I ask you, do they have to come at all?" Weltin broke

in again. "Wasn't it enough of a lesson that Sir John Simon failed last year in his attempt to cajole Hitler? Yet, not much later Lord Londonderry accepted an invitation to one of Goering's hunting parties, and Lloyd George came to see Hitler and then wrote in the *News Chronicle* that Hitler is not planning any aggression at all and that war between Germany and Russia is impossible for the next ten years. Is he blind, or senile — or both?"

"And what about Lord Mount Temple who sponsors the Anglo-German, in this case Anglo-Nazi, Friendship League?" added the editor. "He throws dinners for Ribbentrop in London as though that were the most natural thing in the world."

"The list is almost endless," assented the diplomat. "There can no longer be any doubt that prominent men in various countries are in the mood to follow the example of so many of our own business leaders in making the best of the nazis. Sir Henry Deterding, the Anglo-Dutch oil magnate, gave us a gift of ten million guilders the other day. In Paris, Jacques Doriot wants to negotiate with Hitler. The Aga Khan extols his regime as a 'firm pillar of world peace.' George Lansbury, of the British Labor Party, publicly expresses the view that there is no danger of war, and to top it all, the British Ambassador, Sir Neville Henderson, tells us that nazism is being misunderstood, and that Hitler is doing a great job."

"I ask you," Weltin shouted at me as though I had been responsible for all these sad mistakes, "I ask you, what's the big idea of these men morally crushing the last remnants of our badly decimated democratic forces? All these visitors who appear to be so anxious to plead for fair weather with the nazis should never even have talked to them! They ought to have realized that they were being hoodwinked and bamboozled by unscrupulous politicians. They should have known that by remaining on speaking terms with these usurpers they were but contributing to the complete enslavement of the German people."

"Which," interrupted the diplomat, "is but an essential preliminary for the war of aggression Hitler is planning."*

---

* Richard Reid, editor of the New York *Catholic News,* in this paper's issue of September 30, 1944, made reference to those who hold peoples of enemy nations individually responsible for the crimes of their leaders, and then said: "The United

Far into the night we talked. The keg must have been nearly empty when we broke up, but no one was in a merry mood. In all our minds was the prospect of another cruel war. Inside Germany it was seen clearly, long before chagrin overtook the appeasers and they began to look back remorsefully on the days when they had let themselves be used as Hitler's tools.

Fortunately most of the men at the helm in London were wise to Hitler's game. They knew that he wanted a neutral Britain and an immobilized France that he might concentrate his entire strength against Moscow. They knew that he was prepared to pay almost any price to achieve this end. But it was also obvious that the British government could not have considered his deal. A successful campaign in the East would have provided Hitler with the weapons and resources he needed to set himself up as the arbiter of all Europe. As long as England was unwilling to grant him that privilege, all efforts at appeasement were eventually doomed to failure.

War was really the only alternative, as events have shown. Whether a "preventive" war after Hitler's march into the Rhineland could have changed the trend, as many observers at the time insisted it would, is a *post factum* question this writer does not dare answer. Even before Lord Halifax came as another British "explorer" to see him in Berlin, late in the fall of 1937, Hitler himself must have known that war was his only choice. He was not ready for it at that time, but ever since the Rome-Berlin "axis" *entente* was sealed on October 25, 1936 and supplemented a month later by the Anti-Comintern Pact with Japan, the die had been irrevocably cast.

States and Great Britain did business with Hitler for nearly a decade after he came into power. Had they realized Hitler's intentions, it is inconceivable that they would have negotiated with him as they did. Are our leaders, then, responsible for Hitler's crimes? And is it reasonable to expect the people of Germany to realize what Hitler was scheming when the world's most experienced diplomats did not know until it was too late?"

## Chapter 13

## A PEOPLE BLINDFOLDED

IN THE summer of 1936 the Olympic Games were held in Berlin. There had been opposition in a good many quarters against this world event being staged under nazi auspices. Opposition was particularly outspoken in the United States. But once more the "appeasers" won out.

Berlin gave a royal reception to the world, and everything was perfectly organized. Five hundred and eighty radio engineers were on duty. Thousands of miles of cable had been strung to link up with hundreds of microphones, to "feed" the sports page of the air in some thirty-five different countries, in twenty-five different languages.

The city was bedecked with flags. Every effort was made to avoid untoward incidents, even to the extent of preventing possible molestation of negro visitors. The latter measure proved particularly helpful when Jesse Owens won coveted prizes, to the discomfiture of the "Aryan" hosts.

Americans wearing their national emblem were received with real affection everywhere. Other nationals, too, felt strongly how much the average German welcomed the opportunity of establishing contacts with people from abroad, people who conveyed an atmosphere of freedom.

"It's hard to believe," said Bill Slater who had come as NBC's special commentator, "that this country is in the throes of a violent revolution. Why, if the people didn't speak German, and if there weren't all these swastikas around, you'd almost think you were back home."

His reaction was typical. Visitors from abroad easily gained the impression that the German people were the happiest in the world, perfectly satisfied with their government.

"I wish I could take you where the nazis certainly don't want you to go," I replied to Slater's remarks. "I wish I could have you meet Germans unafraid to talk to you."

"Why don't you?"

Like most other foreign observers, Slater was in no position to peek behind the scenes for himself. All he could see was the cheering crowds. Like other visitors, he was impressed by the "Potemkin villages," the massive buildings the new regime was putting up, the imposing motor-roads, the booming industries and gay resorts. He could not inspect the concentration camps. He could not be present at the secret trials of Gestapo tribunals. He could not even read the regimented nazi press which might have conveyed to him a faint notion of the immensity of the destruction wrought by Hitler upon the proud traditions of the nation of Bach and Goethe, of Kant and Diesel and Humboldt.

"Let's call on a friend of mine tonight," I suggested, and I made an appointment with Karl Nord who was always happy to see Americans, to revive happy memories of his own days in the States.

"If I could only go back!" he said after greeting Slater effusively. "You can't conceive of what it means to a man who has roamed all over the world to suddenly find himself blind-folded."

"But it can't be that bad," Bill wondered. "After all, you can attend to your business and move about freely, can't you?"

"I can. Yes, Sir, I can."

"Go ahead, Karl," I told him. "Don't be afraid. Bill won't report you!"

"Oh, I know that. Your introduction is his credential. But isn't it awful that I couldn't even talk to this friend of yours, if you had not brought him in? Would I hesitate in New York? Of course, not. Yet, here, we need introductions for safety's sake. Our whole lives are permeated with the insincerity about us. There is fear of being overheard on the telephone, of reading the wrong book, of calling on the wrong friend. There is always something to hide, something to conceal. I tell you, it's an inferno."

"The commotion I notice all over the place does not entirely lack spontaneity though," observed Bill.

"Not entirely. As a matter of fact, it's pathetic to see how the nazis go out of their way to make themselves liked. They have the power, but they are not popular, and they know it.

Otherwise they would dispense with terrorism, with mass arrests and regimentation."

"Haven't they made some progress in winning the people over?" asked Slater.

"Backward progress, yes! I wonder, if there were a free vote today, whether more than twenty-five of thirty per cent of the people would be for them. And this in spite of all the repressive measures, in spite of all the automatic 'must' saluting and the intellectual isolation from the outside world."

"The stranger certainly notices little of all this," Bill interrupted.

"That is exactly the issue," concurred Nord. "This discrepancy between the 'Third Reich' which on the surface appears buoyant and obstreperously successful, and the hidden Germany in chains, the Germany forced underground, has become the phenomenon so many of our friends from abroad fail to grasp. As a matter of fact, it is hard for us who have to live in this nightmare, to comprehend it."

"In other words," Bill concluded, "to get the facts, you've got to be a mind-reader around here!"

"A mind-reader of millions!" laughed Nord. "In America you can kick, you can complain, you can write letters to the editor. All of that is 'out' under a dictatorship. By the by, did you notice the stickers on our door?"

"I did," said Slater, "they're plastered all over!"

"And more of them are to come! Nazi pressure groups collect week by week, month by month, and 'stick' you. If you don't give, you get no sticker, and no sticker, of course, is a sign of lukewarmness toward the regime."

"And the one-dish days!" added Frau Nord, who had come into the room to offer us refreshments. "If we don't eat the meal Goebbels decrees, be it economical or not, and insist, say, on a plutocratic hamburger, we may have trouble! The cook could easily report us, if I should ever have to fire her."

"You really have to do a lot of mind-reading to find out all these things," Nord wound up. "People won't tell you, unless you know them intimately."

"Mind-reading," I elaborated, "is the very thing the nazis know how to forestall by scaring the life out of the people."

Bill said not a word as we walked down the street, on our way home. He was greatly upset by all he had heard.

"There must be people though who've lived here long enough to get at the bottom of this thing," he remarked while we had a nightcap at the hotel.

"Among the foreigners residing in Germany," I replied, "at least those concerned with political affairs, only a relatively small percentage are acquainted with the pre-Hitler state of affairs. Most of them arrived after Hitler came to power. They know only his world. They don't know what the country was like before."

"And the tourists, of course, can't find anything wrong; therefore many of them return home with glowing reports," Bill conceded.

"That's right. At the same time the whole of Germany is isolated. One after another of the doors leading into the outside are being closed. Every bit of information and opinion not bearing a nazi stamp is kept out of the press. That's the way Hitler has 'conquered' the German people. Since they refuse to love him, he subdues them, forces them into submission, killing all freedom and dignity of men. The country's real countenance remains sadly concealed from the world."

I would have liked to take Bill around to see other people so he could round out his picture, but there was no time. Besides, how many more "conducted tours" would have been in order for the thousands of foreign visitors who needed to be enlightened as to the true conditions! Even those trained in gathering information were running up against a stone wall when they tried to get the facts. Who but the most foolhardy of Germans would have dared to engage in conversations with unknown visitors from abroad? And after all, Berlin was only one city. As a rule foreigners did not go far beyond the capital. A few would go to Munich, perhaps to Cologne or Frankfort. They would see little, if anything, of the rest of the country. What could they learn of the people?

Crossing the border from France, or from Holland, or from Switzerland, they would ride on clean, well-serviced trains; they would stop at comfortable hotels and go to theatrical performances and music festivals of world renown. They would not be forced to salute in the Hitler style, and if because of their connections or their rank, they were the recipients of special attention, they would be given every privilege. Herr Goebbels and his attendants knew how to dispense this type of "sleeping powder propaganda" in sumptuous clubs amidst the glamor of extravagant dinner parties and impressive official receptions.

Of course, there was sufficient evidence to support nazi contentions. There were beneficiaries of the regime, misled, unthinking people, "collaborationists" and an incongruous mass of turncoats who could all be depended upon to "put up a front." Those coming from abroad would not often be able to establish contact with any other kind of people, and if they had such contacts, they had to be careful not to embarrass, or even endanger, friends of long standing. Only after pass-words were obtained, would doors open for those "in the know."

When Bill Slater left Berlin he had seen enough of the "hidden" Germany to discount all the nazi flag-waving and Hitler-cheering he had gone through at the Olympic Games. But there was one question he had on his mind that remained unanswered.

"Why don't they revolt?" he asked me time and again. "We wouldn't stand for all this browbeating and bullying in America. I know that. Why do they stand for it here?"

Then, on his last day, when Karl Nord and I saw him off at the station, it happened that three "Elite Guard" six-footers took over a table next to ours at the buffet. Cold-eyed and provocative, they paid no attention to anyone. It was as though a chill had come over those present.

"Look at them!" said Nord under his breath. "Our jailers! But they have guns! We have none."

In a nutshell, there was the answer to Bill's question. Himmler had the guns, and the torture chambers and concentration camps.*

\*          \*          \*

---

* "Obviously," says Father James M. Gillis, editor of the *Catholic World*, "there are people in Germany — I venture to think millions of them — who feel about Hitler as millions of Frenchmen feel about Laval. Americans, safe and sound here at home who ask 'Why don't they revolt?' can have not the slightest inkling of what revolt means under a totally tyrannical dictatorship. . . . When Germany

In Copenhagen, Dr. Herzberg had asked me to look after his aged mother whom he had been forced to leave behind in Frankfort. The old lady was ailing and would not have been able to withstand the rigors of exile.

As often as I could I interrupted my journeys back and forth from Switzerland, to call on her. She lived in a small apartment in the Sachsenhausen district of the Rhine metropolis. There she had been born and there she had remained all her life. "I can't get it into my head," said an old limerick, "that a man not in Frankfort is bred!" That was exactly how Frau Herzberg felt. She was a true daughter of her native town. She could not conceive of being happy anywhere else.

Frau Herzberg was a member of that Hebrew aristocracy which has contributed so much to the life of the German nation. She knew many of Frankfort's prominent Jewish families whose names are identified with its history. She knew the Mertons, for instance, whose memory I shall always treasure because of my own association with them in my college days, when the late Dr. Wilhelm Merton, Frankfort's great benefactor, had engaged me to do some work for him in the social welfare field. Frau Herzberg spoke of him when I first saw her, and of many other distinguished Jews who, like herself, had seen better days.

And she spoke of the three sons she had given to the fatherland, two of whom had lost their lives in the last war. Now none of that seemed to count. Now her proud and beautiful city, too, center of art and science, had become an object of racial persecution.

"They say I am no German," sobbed the poor old lady. "For centuries my people have had their homes in these parts — and they say I don't belong!"

I tried to comfort her. "Pay no attention to them."

"Oh, I wish they'd pay no attention to me, but look!"

And she showed me the latest "don't" circular from her Synagogue instructing the members on behalf of the nazi rulers that they should do no shopping except in the late afternoon hours, when everybody else had been taken care

---

is well rid of that fantastic madman, it will be well for us to remember those millions of Germans who wanted to revolt but couldn't, just as the French imprisoned in France were eager to break out but couldn't." (*Catholic News*, New York, December 5, 1942.)

of, that they should not attend theatrical performances, that they should sit only on park benches that were painted yellow and marked with the Star of David, that they should not use public telephones, that they should not leave their homes after dark.

"Pinpricks," said Frau Herzberg. "To make our lives miserable!"

"All this won't last. It's criminal stupidity," I encouraged her again.

"I know it won't last. But it will last long enough to destroy us all."

"Don't lose hope. The evildoers will eventually destroy themselves."

"That, too, I know. We all know it. But we will be the victims."

Not until the assassination of Ernst vom Rath, the German diplomat in Paris, on November 7, 1938, by a crazed young Jew did the antisemitic frenzy reach its climax. I happened to be in Berlin that day. Leaving my hotel near Fasanenstrasse I came by the synagogue which had been set on fire during the night. People stood around looking at the smouldering remains.

"Everybody move along! Don't stand around!" the nazi police warned them.

It was not advisable to look too carefully. Many a bystander had been arrested on the street because of careless remarks. The doorman of my hotel who knew who I was, stepped up to me and whispered.

"Walk around the next block! See for yourself!"

It was a fashionable street of the western district of the city. Every single show window had been smashed. Patrol wagons were parked in front of some of the stores which the day before had been the pride of their owners. Now they were heaps of rubbish. Jewish children sat on house steps with haunted, puzzled expressions.

One little girl was leading another by the hand. There was a horse-drawn milk wagon and the smaller child shied away from the horse who had stepped up on the sidewalk.

"Don't be scared, dear," said the older girl. "He doesn't know we are Jewish. . . ."

# A People Blindfolded 171

In Berlin alone some fifty thousand Jews were carried off to concentration camps that night. It was an organized pogrom, breaking loose at two a.m. sharp and led by carefully trained arson gangs.

"We'll have to pay for it some day," said my doorman after I got back to the hotel. "This is a terrible crime."

Most people reacted as he did. Not even at Broadcasting House where I dealt with avowed nazis did I notice much satisfaction with Herr Goebbels' assault upon a helpless minority.

"The Jews should have known better," was all Kurt Rathke, the program man, was willing to say. "They borrowed trouble, didn't they?"

Wherever people spoke freely they were incensed and out-raged, not over Jews, but over the nazis. "Aryans" I knew were doing all they could to help their Jewish friends, agree-ing to be their trustees, hiding their properties, helping them to escape. Few indeed were the fanatics who approved of the nazi brutalities, but the rank and file did not dare to inter-fere except surreptitiously, for open interference meant imme-diate arrest.

Then the exodus began. At the American Consulates throughout Germany long lines of applicants could be seen day after day, all Jews seeking visas to escape. Persons having American connections were eagerly sought after.

"You must help my nephew, Franz," Frau Herzberg im-plored me. "He is in hiding now; they have searched his apartment. Please help! He needs an affidavit of support. Will you please talk to your Consul!"

We managed to get Franz across the Swiss border, with an Albanian visa.

American officials did not know how to comply with the thousands of requests. American immigration quotas were limited, and not all applicants were eligible. Red-tape caused incredible delays although Consuls were doing their level best to meet the emergency.

Frau Kraus, the wife of the professor, who had relatives in Switzerland and had been visiting with them at least once a year, now was in a position to use these connections in the interest of her Jewish acquaintances. Gold watches, diamond rings and other valuables could easily be carried on one's person when crossing the border, and deposited abroad for the benefit of those who would soon leave the country and then pick up their properties on Swiss territory.

"I am inviting my Swiss friends, one by one, to come up here," Frau Kraus told me. "We now have a well organized traffic. The ladies arrive simply dressed, and with no jewelry and leave again wearing fur coats and diamond bracelets! It's a joy for us to help these unfortunate people."

In Frankfort, too, Frau Herzberg related incidents that were touching.

"It is a wonderful experience," she said, "to find so many kind hearts. The other day I tried to buy some fruit, but the man apologized: 'Sorry, Lady, you've got to come back at five,' and when I got home there was a basket of fruit at my door which some stranger had left for me."

Later on when rationing was enforced, the Jewish population was unable to have shoes soled, or to buy soap, or even to get thread to mend their clothes. Then indeed Frau Kraus' shuffle service became invaluable. I, along with other non-Jews, was enlisted as a helper, and it was a real thrill each time I managed to smuggle a few cakes of soap, or a few bars of chocolate, or some spools of thread across the Dutch, or Danish, or Swiss borders. I felt like Santa Claus the year around with bulging pockets, handing out the precious goods to those in need — and such need!

"The next time I want coffee, only coffee!" ordered Frau Kraus. "My wards haven't had any in months."

So I stuffed the linings of my bags with instant coffee and to get through I even bribed the customs men with some of it!

There was many a Frau Kraus; there were many men and women in all parts of Germany acting as good Samaritans, coming to the aid of the people with "wrong prayer-books," as the victims themselves put it so pathetically. The nation as a whole did not condone the execrable wrong a barbaric government was doing. Individually many tried to atone by just being humane.

As long as there were Jewish-owned stores, the nazis had to post guards at the doors, to prevent customers from gaining access, and Gestapo photographers were ordered to take pic-

tures for publication in the local press, of those who were
daring enough to brave the consequences, and to label them
"traitors of the race." Rarely was there a ready response of the
people to the vile propaganda the Jew-baiters were attempting
to put across.

"Yet," I warned Frau Kraus, "there are plenty of your
countrymen tolerating all this savagery, at least by their
cowardly silence."

"That's true," she admitted. "There's no excuse for those
who freely expose themselves to the nazi poison and shut their
eyes in the face of a criminal aberration. But don't you think
it is significant that the Himmler gang have to be their own
henchmen in the darkness of the night? They don't dare perpetrate all this terrible injustice in the light of the day! How
many people really know about it? The press tells them little,
and only those who have close Jewish friends find out the
facts."

"It's the same old method," the Professor agreed. "These
pogroms have to be engineered systematically by rabble-rous-
ing propaganda. They do not come about spontaneously. So
Goebbels mixes his own brew. Atrocity stories! Public scan-
dals! The slightest pretext is acceptable just to arouse the evil
passions of the mob; and still it does not work. This anti-
semitic hysteria is an artificial product. Less than one per cent
of the population responsible for all the ills of the world! The
people just don't believe that sort of thing. But what can they
do? What can anyone do? We've got as much of a chance to
do anything as a canary in its cage."

"The quitters and slackers in this struggle are in high
places!" Frau Kraus went on. "They are the ones that have
betrayed us. The Papens and the rest of them! They made a
pact with the devil and now the whole nation pays for it."

There were many upright men and women who refused to
swallow the quack medicines concocted by nazi brains. By
his own appointment and never charging a cent for his services, one member of the former Friday Circle, a courageous
lawyer by the name of Oskar Merkel acted as consultant to as
many Jewish people as wanted to use his services.

"Publicly," he told me, "There is absolutely nothing anyone
can do. This shameful thing can only be stemmed under cover,

and I consider it my duty to give as much of my time and
energy as I can to help these unfortunates, though when it
comes to an actual showdown, I can contribute but little."

What this man did, meant a great deal. His office was
crowded all day long and until late in the evening. Merkel
made out the required documents for his clients to leave the
country. He helped them with their visas, their money trans-
fers, their taxes. There were still loop-holes for those who
knew the intricate machinery of the wanton legislation the
nazis had set up; loopholes to save on the confiscatory levies
which were being imposed on every Jew; means to expedite
the annoying procedures devised by the police; devious ways
to escape the vexations of Gestapo snoopers who made it as
miserable for the poor people as they could.

Merkel carried on bravely for a while. Then one day he was
arrested. After being detained a few days, he was released.

"We can make it tough for you," the Gestapo men warned
him. "This is just a gentle hint!"

Nazi hints are broad enough. Merkel had to give up. Others
carried on. A lot could be done with bribes. Well-to-do Jews
could still be robbed. The poorer ones sometimes had such
treasures as stamps, or family silver, or antiques.

In the midst of the war a friend of Frau Herzberg's met me
one night in an alley, during the blackout, fearful of being
discovered, and handed me a valuable stamp collection.

"It's all I have left," the man explained trembling. "Do try
to take it with you! I want my daughter in America to have
it. It is my only possession!"

I tried. There was an attaché of a Balkan country who
"handled" assignments of this sort by using the diplomatic
pouch. His fee had to be paid out on neutral territory, in
Sweden, or Switzerland, and in this instance, he received it,
but the stamp collection never arrived.

The stamp collector had been a man of wealth, the owner
of a prosperous business.

"Now," he said, "I've lost everything. All day long my wife
and I sit in the one room they've left us—the rest of the
apartment was taken over by forced tenants. We hardly dare
go out, for fear of being exposed to humiliations. We wait until they come to get us, to be deported, to die. One of my

former employees comes once a week to keep me informed on my own business affairs which I am no longer allowed to look after. She has to come at night, at great risk to herself, and she always has a little gift for us. Some candy, or a cake of soap, or some fruit. Think of that! I was her boss! Now I am happy to take her alms. . . ."

Like the pogroms, the "mercy killings," too, were set in motion stealthily, under flimsy pretexts, and then carried out in the dark so the people would not know.

A physician I had met at a friend's home in Munich first told me about them. The story was hard to believe. How a bus with all the curtains drawn drove up to the door of an insane asylum one day, and the doctors and nurses were told that the inmates were to be "transferred."

"Orders from Munich!," the doctor said, was the only explanation. And transferred these unfortunates were — into eternity.

In the beginning, the instances were not numerous, but gradually they grew more frequent. I had all the facts, even to the names and addresses of individual patients given to me. Horrified relatives told the heartrending stories to one another.

How the nazis kept the information from the people was shown by the experience of two young women in a Rhenish city who related it to a friend of mine. While riding on a street-car one mentioned to the other the "mercy killing" of her aunt. When they alighted, they were followed by a man who soon identified himself as a Gestapo agent.

"I would not talk of such matters, if I were you," he warned them icily. "Might get you into trouble."

And with that he was gone.

People had to heed such warnings. They made every effort to keep away from all that was not strictly their business, and would not needlessly take chances. Fear is a mighty weapon. It does strange things to people. It can even put you to sleep.

In Berlin, Professor Sauerbruch, the great surgeon who had never been a partisan of the nazis, but because of his scientific reputation was practically beyond their reach, was deeply aroused when he heard of these murders of innocent people which the nazis were committing in the name of so-called racial purity. He had been apprised of all the details by Pastor von Bodelschwingh, the Protestant Minister and philanthropist, whose institutions for the feeble-minded in Bethel were models of Christian endeavor. After checking the facts carefully, Sauerbruch went to see Hitler personally.

"Coldly, he denied that anything of the kind was happening," one of Sauerbruch's close friends whom I knew, told me shortly afterwards, "although he himself had given the orders in writing!"

In this field, as in so many others, the German people were but Hitler's guinea pigs. The "mercy killings," the persecutions of minorities, the inhuman methods of the Gestapo to subdue dissenters — all was a mere rehearsal for the days when on a hugely enlarged scale, these same evils were to be inflicted upon conquered peoples. The history of the first six years of hitlerism follows the pattern that later on was applied by Himmler's legions in the war.

When the first hostages were executed in France, I remembered that in the earlier days prisoners in concentration camps had been held responsible for the behavior of their families still at liberty.

"For every storm trooper who falls a victim of these assassins I shall execute three communists," threatened Count Helldorf,* Berlin's nazi police commissioner on March 8, 1933 — and of course, everyone opposing the nazis was a "communist."

When Philipp Scheidemann, the Weimar Republic's first chancellor, was found to have escaped to Prague, his relatives were imprisoned in Germany and not released until he had publicly made "amends" for having told the truth.

Such were the measures which turned out to be but initial steps on a road finally leading to Lidice. In Germany itself there could be no Lidices. There the people had to endure gangster rule because it was clouded behind the constant beat of patriotic tom-toms. With Hitler in power, all Germany was

---

* Count Wolf Heinrich von Helldorf was one of the seven men sentenced to death by a nazi court on September 11, 1944, under the pretext that they were implicated in the attempt on Hitler's life of July 20, that year. How Helldorf could have joined forces with the opposition after having been one of Hitler's most active supporters and one of the worst Jew-baiters of the nazi party, is hard to explain. It may well be that he had become too strong a rival of Gestapo chief Heinrich Himmler and that a convenient excuse was sought to "purge" him. It appears most unlikely that the other alleged conspirators should have availed themselves of the services of so disreputable an individual as Helldorf.

a Lidice, morally and psychologically — and physically, too, in many individual instances — long before the brownshirted bandits were let loose behind the shield of conquering armies. The nation which treaded insecurely on a road taking it deep into a dark destiny had been "mercy-killed" symbolically, the moment the swastika had been raised as its emblem.

When we consider how it all came about, how by deceit and trickery, by brutal intimidation and complete psychological isolation the German people were lured into a state of sullen resignation to what seemed an inescapable fate, a fate countenanced by the ruling classes, and to quite some extent by the world at large, it is astounding that so many were able to hold out grimly in their nests of passive resistance against the overwhelming might of a party machine such as the world has never seen.

"Should not all this be evident enough to the mind of anyone not affected by prejudice?" Dr. Bruening asked me when next I saw him in his London apartment. He kept in touch with his British friends, trying to interpret the German situation for them in the proper light. Whitehall should have been pleased to have so competent an advisor close at hand.

"It is not easy to make them face the facts, and public opinion in England is divided, as it is everywhere," said Bruening. He had aged visibly since his escape from Berlin and was more deeply concerned than ever over the march of events.

"As one who can still move in and out of Germany," I remarked, "I am not surprised that the world is so slow to make up its mind about Hitler. You cannot conceive of the tremendous effect of Goebbels' propaganda even on foreign observers in Berlin who are resolutely anti-nazi. On some minds, it has a truly paralyzing effect."

"I know," Bruening agreed. "And it all rests on the false claim that the German people are united behind Hitler. Why then, one should logically ask, the controlled elections? the concentration camps? the regimented press? I understand that the membership of the nazi party, even at the time when latecomers were still admitted, never exceeded four million out of a population of 66 million!"

"That's the sort of thing," I said, "Goebbels refrains from mentioning on the air! The sound of frenzied mass meetings, the thunderous applause of his commandeered audiences — that's his favorite program material. Though only a few thousand may be shouting, the listeners are misled to believe that it's all Germany heiling Hitler!"

"And yet," continued Bruening, "it is simple enough to figure out how many individual Germans were caught in the Gestapo mesh. One has only to add up the totals from the nazi press! What incredible nonsense to term all Germans nazis when Himmler is locking up people by the thousands!"*

"You might as well say millions," I interrupted. "In concentration camps alone Himmler is now reported to be keeping two million political prisoners."

"It does not surprise me," nodded Bruening. "Of course, there is a limit to all despotism."

"What could the people do?" I asked.

"The people," he answered ruefully, "cannot do a thing. But Hitler can. He will go to war, as I told you before. It's his only way out. That's why he is making a chain-gang out of a whole nation."

Bruening was right.

There was but one way out for Hitler. He needed a war because he could never keep the peace. To keep it, he would

---

* Dr. Alfred Kantorowicz, a refugee German journalist and permanent secretary of the League of German Writers-in-Exile, reports in the New York magazine *Free World*, of February, 1943, that *during the first three years of Hitler's regime Gestapo-controlled courts sentenced 225,000 men and women to a total of 600,000 years in prison, for political offenses only!* These figures do not include concentration camp confinements. Anyone attempting to estimate the size of a potential German opposition will also have to take into account the families, relatives and friends of all these victims of the nazi tyranny. It adds up to a good many millions, particularly if one considers those who were astute enough not to let themselves be caught. — More recent figures were made available in an O.W.I. report from Washington dated August 8, 1944, which quoted the *Stockholm Tidningen* to the effect that *in the course of 1943 the Gestapo arrested no less than 250,000 Germans, 11,000 of them women*, throwing them into jails and concentration camps. — Louis Lochner, the former Associated Press chief in Berlin, correctly summed up the basic facts when he wrote: "There is a Germany submerged and inarticulate at present because every possibility of public utterance has been taken from it. It is a Germany which prays for deliverance from the nazi yoke as fervently as any member of the United Nations can pray for the end of Hitler's system. It is a Germany which still cherishes the normal, civilized ideals of equal and humane justice for all; of honesty and truthfulness in human relations; of sympathy for the oppressed, weak and infirm. It is a Germany which is ashamed and humiliated at the disgrace into which naziism has dragged the German name. When one considers how completely the instruments of power are in the hands of the nazi regime, one cannot but wonder that there is as much of 'another Germany.'" (*What About Germany?*, pp. 216–217, Dodd, Mead & Co., New York, 1943.)

have had to retrace his own steps, obliterate all he had done, throw open the jails, restore freedom to his victims, re-establish an incorruptible judiciary and — tell the truth! How could he thus commit political suicide, the would-be conqueror of the world and self-styled "liberator" of his people?

The alternative was a systematic preparation for war, for that war which the people certainly did not want, which he had to force upon them. For years he claimed peaceful intentions. At the same time he built the most powerful military machine Germany ever possessed, with the profiteers of big industry, in Germany and elsewhere, cashing in on the boom.* The people of all Europe were kept in the dark.

Every step the nazi regime had undertaken since 1933 was meant to be a preparation for the great revenge. The home front was to be made "secure," to avoid another collapse such as the one of 1918. Christian teachings of neighborly love, of forebearance and forgiveness did not fit into such a scheme of hate. No free speech could be allowed, no free press tolerated for it might have revealed too much. It might even have revealed the thorough disunity of the German people themselves. Regular court procedure, too, might have interfered with totalitarian principles of state idolatry. It had to be curbed for the sake of a more martial spirit. Summed up the whole nazi scheme was a super-colossal structure of purposeful immorality based on systematic distortion, on fists rather than consciences, on blood rather than the spirit — indeed an inferno within whose iron boundaries the average German felt stifled, manacled and unhappy, but completely helpless.

Satan is often a well-dressed man. Many a German liked his shining uniform without realizing that the devil's own

---

* "It was conservative Britain that aided the nazis to overcome some of these handicaps (in rearming), by extending credits for the purchase of such vital raw materials as nickel and copper, and by actually sharing in the erection of armament plants," says George N. Shuster in his book *Germany, A Short History* (co-authored by Arnold Bergstraesser, W. W. Norton & Co., New York, 1944, p. 207). Another pertinent comment was made more recently by Professor John Hanna, of the School of Law of Columbia University, when he wrote to the editor of the *New York Times,* on September 25, 1944: "Much nonsense about Germany's rearming after 1918 would be avoided if we recalled that Russia provided a training ground for German aviators while England and a good many other countries encouraged German rearmament as a protection against bolshevism. Disregarding Allied responsibility for creating the will in Germany to rearm and ignoring the sabotage of the League of Nations, any sort of Allied unity, even between England and France alone, could have stopped Hitler long before he became a menace."

symbol had been pinned on it. They were glad that they did
not have to walk the streets any longer, that they could work
in an atmosphere of renewed confidence. Many still thought
the "rough edges" of naziism would wear off, and they were
depending on the military to do the polishing job. There was
joy when storm troopers, too, had to report for army training
as privates, and stories were gleefully told of how the "brown"
fellows were given extra rough rides, just to make them realize
that they were not any better than others. Few were aware
of Hitler's persistence, of his fierce determination to throw
overboard every code, every moral commandment which
might block his road to a total war. The military themselves
were caught in the eddy, overwhelmed by the poisonous nazi
fumes, carried away by the evil forces with which they had
conspired.

In 1937 the number of those aware that Europe was drift-
ing toward another war was small. Like the diplomats and
the military and the politicians, most people thought the
world would somehow wriggle through the nazi emergency.
It was more comfortable to ignore unpleasant facts. Gaily,
Vienna was celebrating the 70th anniversary of the Blue
Danube waltz. London was aflutter with coronation, frolics,
and there were the Wimbledon tennis matches, and the Grand
National Steeplechase in Dublin. In Berlin the International
Chamber of Commerce was discussing world peace through
world trade, while the Soviet North Pole fliers were being
acclaimed in New York. Broadcast material proved ample,
and radio people were kept busy moving about the Continent
as though conditions were normal.

Then, in the spring of 1938, Hitler marched on Vienna.

# PART III

# THE HOLOCAUST

*"One can never corrupt the people, but one can often deceive them, and it is only then that the people seem to will the wrong."*

(*Rousseau, "Contrat Social," III*)

# Chapter 14

## THE SECOND VICTIM

SINCE Hitler had come to power, the less frequently I had to go to Berlin the better I felt, for it was no pleasure to associate with people of whose every thought I disapproved and whose political conduct I considered intrinsically evil. The old-timers in Germany who were my friends disappeared one after another, moving into the country, going into exile abroad, and often retiring completely from a world that to them was hostile and repulsive. More and more I tried to transact my business with the German Broadcasting Company by long distance telephone from Switzerland, where the air was fresh and clean.

To go to Vienna was another matter. There I felt so much at home that I often wondered if it was not an atavistic experience. My great-great-great-grandfather on my father's side had come from Steinach, a small Tyrolean village near the Brenner Pass, so I could really claim a sort of birthright among these people whom I liked for their carefree informality and natural charm. They always seemed to be perfectly at ease and on the best of terms with all the world, and I was on the best of terms with them instinctively, even to the extent of picking up their melodious dialect.

Austria had been left a torso by the treaty of St. Germain, a sorry remnant of the once prosperous Danubian federation. Deprived as she was of means of subsistence, and cut off from her natural markets by artificial tariff walls, she was lost amongst her bigger neighbors.

Yet, tourists were streaming across her borders from all over the world. Her mountains, her winter sports, the gaiety of her resorts, her inspiring music, the Salzburg festival, the Vienna opera were all so many attractions which at the same time provided tempting radio copy.

Erich von Kunsti, program manager of the Austrian Broadcasting Company, was my most frequent Vienna contact. A former captain of the defunct Austrian navy, he had been forced to take up a civilian occupation after the last war. He knew music, the drama, and good living. The first variety show ever produced on the air was his idea.

His choice of program offerings was astounding. Berlin was left far behind, and I did not hesitate doing all I could to promote the exchange which was to have a salutary effect upon the morale of the Austrian people, in bolstering their pride and self-reliance, while providing features for American audiences which could not be obtained anywhere else.

Kunsti had ideas and knew how to put Austria on the map. An interview with Franz Lehar. A program from the Vienna Central Cemetery in the shadow of the tombs of Beethoven and Schubert on All Souls' Day. A performance under Max Reinhardt. Mozart's and Schubert's own pianos. Johann Straus' violin. A merry sampling of Grinzing's vintage festival.

And, oh yes, that Christmas broadcast from Hallein, the sleepy little village near Salzburg, where "Silent Night, Holy Night" was born some hundred and twenty-five years ago. I will remember the scene forever. Roofs covered with deep white snow, and wreaths of smoke fluttering up from the chimneys toward the winter stars. If Santa Claus felt at home anywhere it was in Hallein on that Yule morning when the children sang Franz Gruber's immortal carol to the accompaniment of his well-preserved guitar for the benefit of American radio listeners.

But then came the days of internecine warfare, in February, 1934, when several hundred people were killed in Vienna and other parts of the country and workers' flats were shelled. Chancellor Engelbert Dollfuss, who had struggled valiantly to maintain his country's independence while rebuilding it on a solid foundation, termed this tragic blow to national unity "the most terrible time of his life."*

His was an almost superhuman task. Deserted by the western democracies, he had sought Mussolini's support, not knowing where else to turn, but whatever history's verdict will be, it is certain that he never meant to be a dictator, and looked

---

* Kurt Schuschnigg, *My Austria* (New York: Alfred Knopf, 1938), p. 222.

upon one-man government as an emergency measure to be
abandoned as soon as circumstances permitted. A great deal
of conviction was hidden behind his soft Austrian voice. Perhaps all this was not conveyed over the radio, but I still think
his broadcast, when he made an eloquent brief for a free
Austria, not long before his assassination, was as brave and
heartfelt an address as ever went on the air. Even in that
difficult time he kept his sense of humor. As he walked into
the studio, he noticed a sign intended for the employees:

POLITICAL CONVERSATIONS NOT PERMITTED
ON THESE PREMISES

"Well, gentlemen," he grinned, "I suppose this means I
can't say a thing!"

In those days a constant stream of vicious nazi propaganda was flowing into the country. Theodor Habicht, a
German heading Hitler's "Austrian Legion," had been given
the freedom of the Munich radio and kept pounding out
messages across the border to incite rebellion. Finally, on
July 25, 1934, a band of criminals led by Otto Planetta invaded the Chancery on Ballhausplatz. They forced their entry
into the building while the cabinet was in session. Planetta
pointed his gun at the little chancellor who faced him single-
handed. Although the bullet wounded him seriously, his life
could have been saved had the murderer allowed a physician
to be called immediately. Not even the victim's request for a
priest to administer the last rites and to comfort him in his
last hour was granted. So Engelbert Dollfuss bled to death
for his country.

"I wished only peace! God forgive them . . .," were his last
words.

After the Dollfuss murder, the nazi rulers silenced Habicht's
voice abruptly, and Colonel von Papen, appointed German
Minister to Vienna,  publicly feigned disdain of the crime,
at the same time disclaiming all German responsibility. He
must have had a hard time explaining why shortly after Dollfuss had passed away, Habicht and his aides were elected
members of the nazi Reichstag delegation.

I flew to Vienna for Dollfuss' funeral. The murdered statesman had become a national hero. At the southern border

Italian troops stood ready to intervene in case Hitler attempted to annex Austria by force. The atmosphere was tense. Facing a microphone in front of the City Hall, I described the cortege. When the bier reached St. Stephen's Cathedral, I continued from the nave.

The magnificent church, to me the most inspiring cathedral in the world, aside from Chartres', Cologne's, and Milan's, was packed with a reverent crowd. A flood of sunlight fell through the stained-glass windows upon the Gothic altars. The organ sounded the mournful notes of the funeral Mass, and a polyphonic choir sang the *Dies irae* while the celebrant prayed: "May light eternal shine upon him, O Lord." It was a solemn hour, the day of Austria's deepest grief.

After Dollfuss' death Kurt von Schuschnigg took over the reins, but the odds were against him from the start. In the summer of 1937 the Berlin government forced a "treaty of appeasement" upon him. All news unacceptable to the nazis was banned from the Austrian press. *Mein Kampf* was placed on public sale in Austria.

When I attempted to have an address of President Roosevelt relayed over the Austrian air, Kunsti was evasive.

"I'll have to check," he explained. "You know how careful we must be these days."

Then, after the broadcast was over, he arrived beaming at the Grand Hotel outdoor cafe. He sat down with a mysterious air, ordered his usual *Schwarzen,* a demitasse of black coffee, and lit his cigarette. Newsboys were shouting the headlines of afternoon papers, but although it was the biggest story of the day, there was no mention of Roosevelt's speech — the one in Chicago suggesting that aggressor nations be quarantined.

"I've got it for you," said Kunsti proudly, pulling a copy out of his pocket. "We had it recorded off the air."

"And you did not rebroadcast it?"

"Oh, we couldn't! Might get us into trouble with Berlin, you know."

It was not the only instance of this kind. Within Hitler's orbit the radio was kept simon-pure of any democratic thought, American or otherwise. The men in control were fearful that democracy might appeal to their listeners.

"If we were given support from you people, or from France

or England, it would be different," Kunsti elaborated. "But we are alone."

Yes, they were alone. In spite of Schuschnigg's brave stand the big powers did not rally behind the hard-pressed little country. Instead the London *Times* said editorially, on February 17, 1938, that it was not Britain's business to interfere with German expansion in those parts of the continent — a welcome cue for Hitler's provocative Reichstag speech three days later when he referred to Austria as a "German state." Schuschnigg's answer before his own parliament was straight from the shoulder.

"The limit of our concessions has been reached," he stated forcefully.

But his words were not backed by Paris, London, or Rome. Henri Flandin, exponent of high finance in the French parliament, even went so far as to warn his government that it was not its business to be "the policeman of all Europe."

Clearly, Hitler had nothing to fear. When he invited Schuschnigg to Berchtesgaden, it was the Austrian chancellor's doubtful privilege to be the first foreign statesman thus summoned "for consultation" to the nazi leader's mountain retreat. Hacha of Czechoslovakia, Beck of Poland, and many others had to follow in his path because the first caller was left in the lurch.

After his return, Schuschnigg was a nervous wreck. One of his friends who welcomed him back in Salzburg told me that he alighted from his train exhausted.

"It was terrible!" he said. "God help Europe!"

The tale Schuschnigg brought back from Hitler's Berghof was indeed alarming. How he was kept waiting two hours by the "Fuehrer" and then yelled at and lectured by him like a school boy, simply because he had dared to call on the Austrian people to preserve their freedom and independence. How Hitler roared: "No smoking in my presence!" and how he demanded peremptorily that Schuschnigg bow to his will by destroying the evidence of a nazi plot against Austria.

Schuschnigg returned to Vienna to tell parliament that he had turned down Hitler' request.

I vividly recall the tenseness in the hall when the chancellor arrived, greeted by thunderous applause. Outside, a crowd seldom before seen in such numbers had given Schuschnigg a rousing welcome, and when he left the building after his moving appeal to preserve Austria's freedom, thousands marched the city streets in a spontaneous demonstration, voicing their determination to fight for their country.

Dr. Seyss-Inquart, one of the quislings and future nazi boss of Holland, walked out of his stall with a sullen expression. He came by the press gallery where I had my seat — on his way to become a traitor.

In Austria, as in Germany, most people never had stomached hitlerism. But an aggressive minority, led by men such as Guido Schmidt and Seyss-Inquart, stole the march on the majority. Nazi bribes helped the subversive elements, and not unlike the German middle class, the Austrian burghers remained impervious to the experiences of their neighbors.

"Is it really as bad as all that?" Kunsti wondered when I was telling him of some of the things I had seen in Germany. "Many among us are impressed by Hitler's successes. Of course, they see only one side of the picture, but as long as we are facing such a bad plight in this country, it is hard to counteract nazi propaganda."

Oscar Czeija, the general manager of Austrian radio, was in a similar mood. Along with most of his compatriots he disliked the nazis intensely, but he was equally displeased with the status of his own country.

"We are like beggars," he said in his office one day, as I was trying to convince him that he should establish closer ties with America. "We beg in Paris. We beg in London. We beg in Washington. We cater to tourists. They have a good time among us, but when we come down to brass tacks, they kick us around and leave us in a hole."

The nazis knew how to exploit such resentment, and I decided to keep a watchful eye on Vienna.

On March 9, 1938, I was just winding up at the office in Basel, while listening to the news, when the Swiss announcer concluded with this item:

"Vienna — Chancellor Kurt von Schuschnigg has arrived in Innsbruck and will address a mass meeting there tonight."

I tuned in on Vienna. There was an opera on, so while

finishing my mail, I kept listening. Suddenly the music was interrupted by a "flash":

"Chancellor Schuschnigg's speech from Innsbruck will be broadcast at nine o'clock."

An hour later Schuschnigg's radio audience heard him rallying his people to freedom. With a voice full of emotion he told them that a poll of the nation was to be held the following Sunday.

"We want a free, independent and social-minded, a Christian and united Austria," Schuschnigg said. And clearly referring to Hitler, he continued: "Threats and pressure are not going to be tolerated. I demand from no one that he should put up with insolence!"

The crowd rose as one man and sang the Andreas Hofer song which tells of that great patriot bidding farewell to his beloved Tyrol before facing a Napoleonic firing squad. But Schuschnigg's defiance of Hitler turned out to be a boomerang. He had played his last card.

The morning after the broadcast I was on my way to Vienna. I had retired to my berth about the time the Arlberg express was half way between the ski resort of St. Anton and the Tyrolian capital. At midnight I was awakened by someone thrusting the door of my compartment wide open. Before I could ask any questions, a stranger's voice said, "Sorry!" The door closed and I was alone again.

I got up and looked around. We were in Innsbruck. Reassuringly, there were Austrian policemen on the platform. Were they really wearing swastika armbands or was I mistaken? The train stopped far behind schedule. It was all rather puzzling.

People walked up and down the corridor of the sleeper. They looked like detectives. Had Schuschnigg reached an agreement with the nazis? Had the nazis gained control of the country? The conductor did not seem to know. When we started moving again I decided to go back to bed. There was nothing I could do but wait until we had reached Vienna.

When I got up in the morning I began to rub my eyes. Was I seeing things? Nazi banners were flying on every housetop. Youngsters wearing swastika armbands were guarding depots and power plants. People on the streets were obliquely giving the nazi salute. Finally the conductor put in another appearance.

"Gentlemen," he said calmly, "the Schuschnigg government has resigned — the nazis are in control."

Hitler's ultimatum had done the trick. The "Fuehrer" was incensed by Schuschnigg's decision to let the people of Austria determine for themselves whether they wanted to be free men or slaves. He was afraid the Austrians would turn openly against him, that the plebiscite Schuschnigg had decided upon after his visit to Berchtesgaden would show the world that a David could still stand up against a Goliath. It might even have led to a revolt in Germany and to a declaration of war by the Western powers.

If only a peep had come out of the chanceries of Paris, London, or Rome! One single word to back up brave Schuschnigg! But he waited and pleaded in vain. To avoid bloodshed he finally stepped aside. Those were moving words in his last broadcast:

"I take leave of the Austrian people with a farewell from the depths of my heart. God protect Austria!"

During the night sixty thousand men of the German mechanized forces marched into Austrian territory. Some of them spoke freely after they had been quartered near the Vienna Ring.

"At the time we left Munich, there were demonstrations," said one of the older privates. "The women wanted to keep us at home. I heard shouts: 'Another war? We've had enough!' "

"As a whole everything went smoothly though, didn't it?" I asked.

"More so than we expected," the private replied. "When we got to Salzburg we were really uneasy. We thought the Austrians would fight, and I don't think we would have put up much of a resistance had they actually made a stand against us."

It was the same story as in the Rhineland. There the German troops had expected to meet with a French countermove when Hitler marched in. This time the German general staff had been even more doubtful that Hitler would succeed. They remembered how both France and Italy had committed themselves publicly to protect Austria's independence.

Hitler had sensed this reluctance in his own ranks. Shortly before the showdown with Schuschnigg he had dismissed General Werner von Fritzsch, the commander-in-chief who later on was to seek death in Poland. He also replaced the veteran von Neurath with the irresponsible upstart Joachim von Ribbentrop, as foreign minister. These were moves preliminary to the Vienna stroke. After it succeeded, the activists in the army backed the "Fuehrer" up fully. Had it failed, they might easily have got rid of him.

Had Schuschnigg but realized how shaky was the ground Hitler stood on, he would not have despaired of finding support outside nor would he have resigned under the nazi threat of invasion.

As it was, having refused to look after his personal safety, Schuschnigg became Hitler's prisoner. Now his pictures lay in shreds on many a Vienna sidewalk, trampled upon by the mob. All Austria was fired with excitement. Disorder spread, while the nazi columns swiftly gained the upper hand, routing their foes on the very streets of the capital. Schuschnigg's own guards fled to safety in civilian clothes. Antihitlerites hid in their homes. Foreign tourists rushed to the borders. At Graz, the Styrian capital, yelling crowds tore down the Dollfuss monument.

France started manning her borders, suspending all leaves for the forces guarding the Maginot line. Italy looked perplexed at the swastika flags adorning the Brenner Pass. In London a disillusioned Chamberlain cabinet delivered a platonic warning to Berlin and met to consider aid for Czechoslovakia. Hitler could now take time by the forelock.

Refusing to assume a risk where their own interests were not directly at stake, the big powers threw Austria to the wolves. They forgot that appetite comes with eating.

\*    \*    \*

Now that I had slipped into Vienna a few hours after Schuschnigg's resignation, all there seemed to be worth delivering was a *post-mortem*.

Hailing a taxi, I rushed to broadcasting headquarters in Johannesgasse. The military was all over the place.

Kunsti? Oh! He was under arrest! Yes, in his office upstairs, but he could not be seen.

Finally I flashed my American passport at the fellow who seemed to be top guy. Perhaps he was too tired after the all-night excitement bordering on civil war to argue with me any further. Or perhaps it was my smattering of the Viennese dialect that confused him. At any rate I forced my way through to the third floor and found Kunsti, with his usual *Schwarzen,* sitting seemingly unruffled behind his desk. He professed complete ignorance of what was going on.

"All I know," he said with some sarcasm, "is that I am locked up and I wish I could get out! Have you got a cigarette? I've only one left!"

Despite his predicament I had to laugh.

"Austria isn't lost," I said, "as long as there is such equanimity!"

But he put his finger on his lips, indicating that he was afraid I'd cause him trouble.

He'd had enough of it, as it was. All through the night he had been getting frantic telephone calls, virtually from all over the globe. The mild-mannered Viennese switchboard girls had put them all through to him as though it was business as usual. New York, London, Paris, everybody wanted to know what had happened and whether Vienna didn't care to tell the world. But Vienna was now under nazi rule, and nazi orders came from Berlin.

"You really mean to say I cannot broadcast at all?" I pressed poor Kunsti.

"Better ask the new bosses," he suggested. "It looks as though I am fired. Maybe Ehrenberg can help you. Why don't you ask him?"

Ehrenberg was his former assistant, now in charge of program operations as a nazi neophyte. I knew him slightly.

So I bade Kunsti good-bye.

"Don't forget the cigarettes!" he reminded me.

"What brand?"

"American, of course! Cheerio!"

I delivered the goods the same evening. By that time Kunsti was again a free man, as we shall presently see.

The Vienna coup was a perfect example of nazi strategy.

For months prior to the nazi invasion, the hitlerites had
planted "cells" among the police, the army, the press, and
naturally in broadcasting. When Hitler struck, everybody
knew where his or her place was going to be in the new setup. Kunsti's own secretary turned up as one of the "insiders."
In his case it proved to be an advantage; for all the employees
of his department, who now threw off their masks and emerged
with shining new nazi party buttons, liked him personally.
Reversing the totalitarian "principle of leadership," the employees intervened and finally obtained release for the boss. A
few days later he was even amongst the select few who were
not dropped from the payroll. He was only shorn of program
duties, and assigned to the accounting division instead.

"Maybe they want to see if I can put two and two together,"
he joked, "now that it's all over!"

Herr Ehrenberg was of service. He realized the importance
at that critical juncture of a report reaching the United States
directly. So he did not object to my broadcast, provided he
could see my text in advance. Fortunately, rules and regulations were then still being applied with a good deal of common sense, that same common sense George N. Shuster had
in mind when he once pointed out that the difference between German and French policemen is that the latter know
when not to enforce the rules! So by the time I succeeded in
calling New York to ask for a "period," I was all set to go
on the air with the first eye-witness account of Hitler's march
on Vienna, straight from the scene — and uncensored.

Things were quiet on the Austrian air during the first ten
minutes of my broadcast, when suddenly the engineer mo-
tioned me from his control booth.

At that hour nobody knew what fate was in store for
Austria. Was she to maintain a semblance of independence
under an Austro-nazi government, or was she to be annexed
outright by Germany? It was known that Hitler was on his
way to the Austrian border, but would he come to Vienna?

I had arranged for earphones to be connected with a studio
receiver. Now that the engineer had given me the cue, I put
them on. That very instant I heard the Austrian announcer
say excitedly:

"We have a special bulletin — Hitler has arrived in Linz — we take you now to Linz!"

I turned back to my microphone and passed the word on to New York.

Knowing Linz, the attractive capital of Upper Austria on the banks of the Danube, famous for its baroque buildings and fancy cake, I was able to insert an impromptu description of the scene, listening to the local broadcast all the while.

The noise of the crowd in Linz was now intense.

"He's coming! He's coming!" shouted the local announcer.

And out went my echo for American consumption:

"Hitler has just arrived on the city hall square, only a block distant from the Danube river."

The engineer in his control booth had been quick in making the most of a coincidence. Luckily he knew a little English and was able to understand what I was reporting to New York. Each time I waved at him through the soundproof studio window, he would throw the proper switches and link up with New York, so that listeners in America could be earwitnesses, from afar, to an historic event.

Presently I heard a voice and tried to identify it.

"Some local orator is now addressing the crowd of 300,000 people on the Linz City Hall Square," I said. "Let me find out who it is. . . . Oh, it's Hitler himself!"

And within a split second we turned over and broadcast the "Fuehrer's" three hundred word speech which sealed the fate of Austria by incorporating her into the Reich.

"We must prove to the world," the "local orator" asserted pugnaciously, "that any further attempt to part this united people will be of no avail."

The *Anschluss,* Austria's incorporation into "Greater Germany," was now an accomplished fact. Hitler's first public utterance on the soil of his native land had been the verdict of an Austrian who was no longer a penniless student in a decadent empire, but a dictator who had realized his boyhood dreams. Having first conquered Germany, he now had the second victim in his clutches.

That day and the next I witnessed the whipping up of mass frenzy on the very streets which had once seen the glittering displays of the Hapsburgs. I listened to Hitler's harangues from the balcony of the Imperial Hotel, amidst a sea of flags and serenades in his honor. I watched torchlight and military parades. I spoke to the man in the street, and went back on the air intermittently, in an attempt to cover every phase of the great story. It was a sensational drama filled with endless "Sieg Heils!" and the roar of airplanes over a city suddenly and strangely transfigured by stark discipline. Under the sound of marching patrols, the clatter of armored tanks, and machine-gun turrets rolling down the main avenues of her capital, Versailles-created Austria, temporarily faded from the map as an independent nation.

Four weeks after the nazi coup I went back to Vienna to report Hitler's "plebiscite." Swastika banners were now flying from every building. Austrian flags had disappeared. The easygoing Viennese were having a hard time getting accustomed to the nazi salute and the constant clicking of heels. Memories of a less martial past seemed alive in their hearts. But nothing could impede the mighty nazi steamroller. The German general staff was hard at work in the Bristol Hotel and the Gestapo had set up headquarters at the Metropole.

Some of my Viennese friends had disappeared. I heard of many being detained in concentration camps. Jails and military barracks were filled with political prisoners. The Jewish district looked as though it had just been through a locust plague. Windows were smashed, walls smeared, stores robbed wholesale. Under storm trooper supervision pitiful victims of nazi rowdyism could be seen kneeling on sidewalks, frantically trying to scratch off and rub out with knives and brushes the symbols of the Schuschnigg regime which his supporters had painted on almost every street corner. Onlookers turned away in disgust. The few who dared object to these scenes of indignity were arrested on the spot and forced to join in the "rubbing." Many Austrian nazis turned out to be more brutal than their masters.

Jewish people kept to their homes in fear, prepared to hear the door bells ring at any moment and to face "rubbing squads" of nazi hoodlums who would drag them into the streets. Others were so bewildered they could not bring themselves to seek refuge elsewhere. I found one of my Jewish friends peacefully tending the garden of his suburban home. Only my urgent pleading prompted him to proceed to Switzerland at once.

"Is it that serious?" he asked in complete surprise.

On the other hand, a writer of my acquaintance who had been militantly anti-nazi was miraculously "overlooked!"

While I was dining with Kunsti and his wife at the "Kerzenstuebl," a typical Viennese restaurant in the heart of town where true "Gemuetlichkeit" in the best tradition could be found even now, a man joined us who was a stranger to me.

"Oh, hello, Guido!" said Kunsti, and he introduced me.

It was Guido Schmidt, foreign secretary of Schuschnigg's last cabinet, star quisling and "collaborationist."

I could not restrain myself from asking him a blunt question.

"How is Schuschnigg, Doctor?"

He turned pale, and there was embarrassed silence at our table for a moment.

Then he said coldly:

"I have not seen him."

After exchanging a few pleasantries he found an excuse to say good-bye. Not much later he turned up in Berlin. He had received his thirty pieces of silver in the form of a fat job with Goering's mammoth industries.

Of course, the plebiscite was 99 per cent in Hitler's favor. One could not have expected anything else. I knew some of the people who voted "yes" in reply to the question, on the ballot, whether they approved of *Anschluss*. These voters did not approve. Still, they voted in the affirmative, dazed, confused, and misled as they were, along with thousands of others who were terrorized by the sudden impact of nazi fury.

"We'll remain Austrians just the same," observed my friend, the writer, when we met after the storm. "We'll outlive those Mexicans."

"Mexicans?"

"Sure. Don't you know? *Mag sie kaner!* Pronounce that with a Viennese accent! Sounds like Mexicans, doesn't it? and means: nobody likes them!"

Will the Austrian sense of humor survive the ordeal of these years? Now that the Moscow declaration has given new hope to these people who have suffered so much the world can look forward to a revival of Austria's distinctive traditions. For her errors she has atoned, and the world will remember its debt to Austrian genius as symbolized by Mozart, Haydn, Bruckner, and Johann Strauss. When brighter days return it should not be forgotten that Austria fell under Hitler's blows less because of her own faults than because of the blunders of those who could have saved her.

# Chapter 15

## A SHAKY AXIS

"DUCE, I will never forget this," Hitler wired his axis partner after the Austrian rape.

"Nor shall I!" the cynics suggested as the most appropriate reply. Instead, Mussolini wired back some meaningless generalities which hardly concealed his painful surprise.

One has to go back to their first meeting in Venice, in the summer of 1934, to understand why the personal relations of the two dictators had always been somewhat strained. Before becoming a "Fuehrer," Hitler had heaped boundless praise upon the man he considered his model. He adopted his salute (making it a bit more horizontal and stiffer!) — that very salute the slaves used in ancient Rome in making obeisance to their masters. He also took over the Duce's ideas of what a well-dressed party soldier should wear, only changing the shirts from black to brown, the color more adaptable to military uses. As for fascist philosophies, Adolf almost memorized every one of Benito's speeches he could lay his hands on and used them as a kind of master pattern during his early campaigns.

But when the two men got together for the first time, the master was little impressed with the pupil.

"A caricature of myself, Tyrolean style!" sneered Mussolini to one of his aides, who passed the remark on with relish.

No one was surprised by this reaction. Hitler looked unimpressive in his sloppy trenchcoat while facing a host all dressed up in fascist regalia. Even more important was the difference in the intellectual levels. While Hitler could not even write grammatically correct German and as a public speaker depended mainly on shrieks and shouts, the Duce was an accomplished newspaperman and a skillful orator who knew how to put the beauties of the Italian language to good, though demagogic, use.

When I first met him, on my newspaper mission to Italy back in 1919, in his shabby newspaper office in Milan, I could see that he was headed straight for the napoleonic complex, for in answering my questions he often referred to himself in the third person.

He was then editor of the *Popolo d'Italia* and was waging a violent campaign of vituperation against the constitutional government. His adherents were organizing for civil war, and there was considerable excitement because of the poet Gabriele d'Annunzio's comic opera expedition which was to wrench the Adriatic port of Fiume from the Yugoslavs.

"Mussolini says that the glory of the fatherland must be uppermost," declaimed the future ruler of the fascists, when I expressed my doubts that the venture was vital for Italy.

"How do you reconcile all this with international socialism which has been your tenet before the war?" I ventured to suggest.

I never received an answer to my question. To doubt Mussolini's infallibility was an unforgiveable offense. Good actor that he was, he got up and stretched out his arm.

"Mussolini says that Italy has been born anew in the great war!"

*La nostra guerra!* Our war! That was the theme that ran through all his writings. *La guerra italianissima!* The most Italian of wars! Like Hitler, the Duce had been through experiences at the front that changed his whole outlook on life and made a fanatical flagwaver, a jingo, out of the radical agitator and former socialist.

The Italian people did not fall for his antics. They thought he was picturesque and ever amusing, but a buffoon. The belief of admiring tourists notwithstanding, the rank and file of the Italians never became fascists. The typically Italian art of living could never be spoiled with imitated goosestepping and martial speeches.

"It's like this," explained my friend Armando Pettone, a well-to-do businessman of Milan who entertained nothing but scorn for the ruling regime. "You wear a badge and you stretch out your arm because that's the way you have to do business nowadays. But outside of that there is no such thing as fascism. Deep down there isn't."

"But," I objected. "It strikes me real enough in its applications."

"Applications to what? To corruption? To propaganda? To a highhanded conduct of foreign relations? All right. But not to the life of the people! They don't take it seriously. Very few of us do. Its alien to us. Italians are too realistic for all this ballyhoo."

Realistic was right. But Italians also like good showmanship and the Duce knew how to provide it, after the old Roman pattern of *panis et circenses,* meaning: plenty to eat and good entertainment, which applies no less in other parts of the world. Somehow both are prerequisites of peace and contentment, not to mention the more essential factor of stable government.

"This country must be run by people who know how to write headlines," Mussolini remarked the next time I saw him.

He was all dressed up that day. A broad-rimmed homburg, striped trousers, a carnation on his lapel, white spats, chamois gloves, and a big cane which he waved in the air furiously to emphasize his points. He was stodgy even then, with a fanatical gleam in his eyes, and liked to walk fast as though he was always busy whether he was or not.

"Headlines?" I queried. "That's not enough, is it? You've got to deliver, too."

"*Naturalmente.* Of course. And I tell you, I will! When I am the dictator of Italy, I will!"

He hailed a cab and rushed off for some meeting. It was shortly before the march on Rome.

The equipment of the newspaper office in Milan where he had written his fiery editorials was taken to the capital some years later to be shown in the exposition displaying the fascist "glories." The desk, the chair, the coal stove, the party banner, and the cuspidor. The headlines that were to revamp the globe were pasted all over the wall. Headlines they remained, to the day of the author's collapse.

It is true that Mussolini had been more practical in his approach to current problems than had any of the nazis. He had retained the monarchy, and was cautious in his dealings with the Church. Although expediency, and not conviction, was his motive, he knew his people well enough not to run counter to their instinctive sense of balance.

"Another *pagliaccio!* Another clown!" said the man of the street in Italy when he first caught a glimpse of the "Fuehrer."

In the beginning Mussolini felt the same way without any comparison to himself! But then came the murder of Dollfuss, and Germany's rearmament, and the reoccupation of the Rhineland, and finally the invasion of Austria. The *pagliaccio* was doing all sorts of crazy things.

When I saw Marconi one day at his office in the Academy of Sciences in Rome, to discuss some broadcast matters, not long before the crisis came to a head, he was emphatic in stressing Italy's desire to prevent another war.

"Mussolini is alarmed," the father of radio said. "We all are! Only a system of collective security can maintain peace, and we are farther removed from it than ever."

Was not fascism itself one of the causes of Europe's unrest? I asked.

"Fascism," replied Marconi, "is a consequence, not a cause. It is the consequence of the political and economic unbalance in Europe's setup. If we don't succeed in correcting it, by a common effort, it will eventually run wild, just as hitlerism has."

That was the moderate view, though it certainly was not shared by everybody. However, the Duce could not conceal his apprehension when he first became aware of nazi ultra-show-manship during his Berlin visit in the summer of 1937. Hitler was determined to impress his rival and displayed all his fireworks so Mussolini would no longer think he was dealing with a "Tyrolean," a poor second to him.

"We don't like all this showing off," an Italian close to the Duce who was my best source of information in Rome quite frankly told me when I asked for his impressions. "We can't keep up with it!"

But now the Duce needed Hitler. Germany had stood by Italy during the Ethiopian campaign when the Geneva League clamped down with half-hearted sanctions. Austria was the pay-off for Hitler, and the Duce had to pretend he was not looking.

At any rate, the Danubian as well as the African harvest was now in the dictatorial barns and mutual patting of backs was in order when Hitler finally arrived in Rome on May 3, 1938.

I had come, the day before, to "cover" this six-day visit of state. Radio reporters had assembled at the Italian broadcasting company's headquarters to receive their credentials. The Italians and the Germans were wearing special uniforms, similar to those of their respective parties.

I had not seen the men in this novel splendor before. More uniforms! I shook my head, without saying a word.

Raoul Chiodelli, the manager of Italian radio, must have noticed my astonishment.

"We've got one for you, too!" he kidded.

"Not me!" I shouted indignantly, eliciting a roar of laughter.

After the meeting Chiodelli buttonholed me in the lobby.

"You rebel!" he teased. "You know what we ought to do? Force you to wear a uniform! You need to be under control!"

"What do you mean?"

"I mean just that, after what happened in Ethiopia."

The reference was to an incident during the Abyssinian campaign.

We had obtained radio facilities from Addis Abbaba and real programming had started when Mary Moss Wellborn, then American representative with the Women's International League for Peace and Freedom in Geneva, now dean of women at Duke University, came into the picture.

Radio engineering had accomplished a real feat in getting a signal out of Ethiopia, triumphing over all odds. The glowing reports at the time of NBC men hacking their way through Abyssinian jungles were interesting to read, but in reality the job had been done the routine way, by long-distance management. The rigmarole of diplomatic conversations which preceded these exotic pickups was more involved than Livingstone's trails. Fred Bate, then head of NBC's London office, had pulled the wires at the Ethiopian Legation there, and I had done my part with the swarthy-faced delegates of the Negus in Geneva, but progress was slow.

I told Miss Wellborn of our problems in tropical Africa one evening while we were having an after-dinner walk along the shore of Lake Geneva — snow-capped Mont Blanc towering over the horizon.

"What about the empress?" asked Mary.

"What about her?"

"Well, why don't you get her?"

I wasn't used to just "getting an empress" and so far had only thought of the Negus, but Mary was for equal rights. If the emperor was to be given time on America's air, why not his imperial consort? Wiring Empress Menen on behalf of her organization, Mary clinched the deal the next morning.

"Am I good?" she 'phoned all excited. "Listen to this!"

And she read the wire: Her Majesty accepts!

It was Mary Moss Wellborn's scoop. And did we celebrate!

Thus the ice was broken by the intriguing voice of Empress Menen in Amharic. Haile Selassie was next to be booked on the transatlantic airlanes. But what about neutrality? The Italians were going to resent it if we gave time to one side only. So I invited Ciano, who was at the Erytrean front, to speak, providing a period for him right after his foe's.

When the Italian broadcasters found out what had happened, they were furious. They were not on speaking terms with Ethiopia except by means of bullets!

"The idea!" Chiodelli went on, now that he had the first chance to talk to me about the matter. "Do you realize that was an insult?"

"An insult? Why, we provided equal time, didn't we?"

"Equal all right. That's just the trouble. A member of the Italian cabinet treated on equal terms with the Negus! It's outrageous."

"Then perhaps I ought to be careful tonight," I mocked.

"How?"

"Well, in reporting your Hitler parade — on equal terms!"

Chiodelli had known me long enough to laugh that one off. I could not have risked such remarks in Berlin, but the Italians had a sense of humor.

"Watch your step, fellow," he said, bidding me good-bye unfascistically, without giving the salute. "See you after it's over — at the Umberto."

Hitler was welcomed in Rome perhaps with more splendor than even the Caesars had experienced. Remembering Hitler's displays in Berlin, the Duce evidently had resolved to outdo him.

The procession wound its way along festooned and troop-lined avenues from a new railway station especially inaugurated that day. The three-mile route had been gaily decorated. The glorious fountain on Piazza Esedra was never before so beautifully illuminated. The historic ruins were bathed in flood-lights, and from behind the huge arches of the massive Colosseum shone crimson flames, creating a magical effect against the background of the starlit Roman sky. In each of the archways, three stories high, stood a soldier with fixed bayonet wearing a shining steel helmet. All this for the man whom Mussolini in his heart despised and whom he was later to fear.

Along the whole route the onlookers were held back behind double lines of soldiers and police, one line facing the crowd, one the parade. When the car with King Victor Emmanuel and Hitler drove by, it was difficult to distinguish their features, so considerable was the distance maintained between the vehicle and the people.

I stood at a corner of Via Nazionale watching their reaction. The moderate applause was drowned in the noise of the motor-cycle escorts, and there was mild curiosity, but no enthusiasm. Perhaps the elaborate police precautions had dampened it. German emigres and other suspects were kept in custody until the guests from the North had safely departed. Dictators are never really at ease with the people even though they pretend to be their chosen leaders.

When Hitler and the king finally reached Quirinal Hill, the royal palace was ablaze with lighted electric candles. From the square one could distinguish the huge chandeliers reflecting their glow upon the great reception hall of state. Carabinieri in colorful uniforms and with drawn sabers were holding back a rather modest crowd of cheering, pushing Romans.

From the vantage point where the microphone had been installed for my running commentary I could see Michelangelo's imposing dome of St. Peter's. The Pope was not there. The week before Hitler's arrival, Pius XI, ahead of his usual schedule, had left for his summer residence of Castelgandolfo to avoid meeting the nazi dictator. He publicly expressed his regrets over the hoisting in the Eternal City of "the emblem of a cross which is not the Cross of Christ."

"Don't you think," I asked Chiodelli when I met him for dinner at the Umberto restaurant after the broadcast, "that this absence of the Pope is far more significant than the pageant at the Quirinal?"

It was a blunt question, and Italians don't like bluntness.

"If you were not like one of our own," said Chiodelli, "I would leave you right now, to eat your *antipasto* alone!"

"Of your own? You don't mean of your own, fascistically, do you?"

Chiodelli chuckled. He was an engineer who had fought in the last war against Germany and was limping from an injury in battle. His interests were mainly technical and his spare time was devoted to his family. Why he should ever have become a fascist I did not understand. Probably his patriotic sentiments had got the better of him and he was misguided into identifying them with those of the Mussolini regime when the latter set out to fight pretended bolshevism in Chiodelli's home town, Turin.

"That," Chiodelli went on, "is just the trouble. You insist on making a distinction between fascism and Italy. You ought to know better. You were born in this country and grew up as one of us."

"For that very reason I think I know what I'm talking about."

"I don't think you understand our position as Italians," insisted Chiodelli.

"Suppose you sum up what that position should be to your mind."

"Simple enough. We were 'gypped' of our victory in the last war. The Allies didn't keep their promises. An economic malaise ensued. We are overpopulated and poor and have no outlets. Should we pass around a hat like an organ-grinder instead of fighting for a place in the sun?"

"You think you will get the place in the sun by the Duce's calling everybody names and now particularly, by tying up with this maniac Hitler?"

Chiodelli looked around uneasily, but we were in a secluded corner of the restaurant and no one was paying attention to us.

"You don't think the Duce really wants to, do you?" he whispered.

"Perhaps not, but it doesn't matter whether he wants to or not. Facts alone count."

"Right, but it remains a fact, too, that fifty-one nations lined up against us in Geneva, and except for Japan and Brazil who are far away, Hitler was our only friend."

"Your only friend?" I interposed. "Should not that by itself indicate that you are in a bad way?"

Chiodelli did not reply. At heart he agreed with me. I could not expect him to admit it.

"Let me tell you about a scene in Geneva the other day," I said, changing the subject. "The Negus was there, and you should have seen the little black-bearded man standing in the council chamber of the League building where José Maria Sert has portrayed the liberation of the human race exhausted by war. 'Some day,' said Haile Selassie, 'the other nations, too, who are now condoning my country's destruction may be victims of aggression, some day they, too, may, like Ethiopia, have to climb the path to Calvary.'"

Chiodelli listened attentively. Then he got up and shook hands.

"I hope not," he said. "I hope not."

When he left me I had a feeling that he was sad and discouraged.

\*     \*     \*

Not long after Hitler's visit to Rome Pope Pius XI passed away. We had made arrangements to broadcast the funeral services as well as the election of the new Pontiff. It was the first time that radio had a share in the impressive function. Since Pius XI had been ill for some time, we had set up special wire-lines and planned appropriate programs for months. When the news of the Pope's death came from the Papal chambers, it was broadcast within a few minutes for NBC listeners in the United States.

The scene at St. Peter's was deeply moving. An almost endless silent procession of mourners passed by the chapel where the remains of the Pope lay in state, arrayed in the vestments of an Archbishop and with the mitre of gold filigree.

All through the right-wing colonnade of St. Peter's square, up the huge marble steps, and through the gigantic bronze doors the crowds kept moving, slowly, quietly, in perfect order, passing by the spot where, amidst lighted torches and between two rows of uniformed noble guards, rested the last remains of the beloved Pontiff. On both sides had gathered the prelates in their purple robes, and the Giulia Chapel choir chanted the Office for the dead.

The people of Italy showed unmistakably that their heart was with the Church, and that it remained uncorrupted by materialistic philosophies. A million visitors, at least, came during those three days, from every part of the country, young and old, members of every social strata. All were united in a last tribute of reverence and love for the man who was probably one of the greatest Popes the Church of Rome has ever had, the two hundred and sixty-first successor to St. Peter. His Pontificate had embraced one of the most trying periods in the history of the world.

Broadcasters will remember Pius XI as a sincere friend. Personally, he had supervised the installation of the Vatican radio station on a small elevation behind St. Peter's basilica, frequently consulting with Marconi himself about details of construction and operation. He was the first Pontiff to make use of the radio and throughout the world people knelt before loudspeakers to receive his blessing when his warm and strong voice first came across the ether, symbolizing the emergence of the Papacy from the retirement in the Vatican, which had lasted since 1870. The last broadcasts of Pius XI were impressive indeed. A feeble old man, shaken by disease and distressed by the plight of humanity, addressed words of peace and benediction to a world in pain. It is seldom that a moment of such sacred pathos descends upon the busy air, always so much like Martha, worried about many things.

In 1935, in the course of a private audience, John Royal of NBC and I were amazed to find the Pope so well versed in radio matters. We had been shown into his study, at the end of a long row of *anticamere* attended by ceremonious chamberlains, and found the head of the Church at his desk, going over some papers.

The Pope spoke Italian, quietly and earnestly. He looked fatherly in his white cassock, and made us feel perfectly at ease.

"I have just received a report," he said, "about the constant growth of broadcasting. It is a development of far-reaching importance and the Church must not lag behind in making the best use of it."

"May we," asked John Royal, "suggest to Your Holiness to elaborate on the practical application of this thought?"

"Indeed you may," replied the Pontiff smiling.

He picked up a volume from his desk which he seemed to keep in readiness for frequent reference. It was a collection of the odes of Alessandro Manzoni, the great romantic Italian poet.

"Now that the voice of man is multiplied an infinity of times through the instrumentality of wireless," he continued, "we must be aware of our responsibility. Those who make use of the new medium should use utmost discretion."

And then he quoted from Manzoni's "Ode to Carlo Imbonati":

"Never compromise with, or be a servant of evil men,
Never commit treason against the holy Truth."

Consistently the Vatican radio has observed this code through the critical years that followed. The inspiration it received from Pius XI has remained alive in this period of most severe stress. Bravely it upheld the truth against all inroads of deceit, "never compromising with evil men."

Three weeks after the funeral services for Pius XI, I was in Rome again for the Conclave. Not only spiritually but politically it far overshadowed the meeting of the two dictators. Here, indeed, was an occasion of world-wide significance. I saw the cardinals enter the Chapel of the Princes, twenty-seven of them from foreign countries, three from the United States, one each from Argentina and Brazil. The Cardinal Secretary of State, Eugenio Pacelli, was first. Since I had last seen him as a Nuncio, he had aged under the burdens of his office, though he carried himself erect. He proceeded to the Pauline Chapel and for a long time remained absorbed in prayer. It so happened that it was his sixty-third birthday. Soon the College was confined in the Sistine Chapel, behind sealed doors. Observers outside of the Vatican buildings were now watching the thin cast-iron pipe which projects beyond the roof of the chapel. According to a tradition dating back to the thirteenth century, straw is burned with the ballots. Whenever a vote is indecisive thick black smoke emerges from the pipe. But when a two-thirds majority of the cardinals agree on one candidate, only the ballots are burned, sending thin white smoke up in the sky.

In the corner room of a building on the very edge of St. Peter's Square I had a microphone installed, and right next to it, a telephone connected with New York. So listeners across the Atlantic were really given a front-window view of the grandiose scene when the election of Cardinal Pacelli was announced from the center balcony of St. Peter's.

*Habemus Papam!* The announcement by the cardinal giving out the news was relayed to the four corners of the earth, and the voices of three hundred thousand people gathered between the colonnades, on the square, and in the near-by streets responded, wildly acclaiming the new Pontiff.

"There are easily ten times as many here as turned out for Hitler!" remarked Philip Mackenzie, of the Baltimore *Sun,* who was sharing the assignment with me.

"Without regimentation and troop-lined parades," I agreed.

Pius XII now stretched out his hand to impart his first blessing to the Eternal City. In our running commentary, Mackenzie and I tried to reflect the spirit of that historic hour, but the cheers and the applause of the enthusiastic throng were more vivid than any description could be.

In conclusion, I held the microphone out of the window, catching the sound of the hundreds of bells that were ringing across the Seven Hills.

The "Pope of Peace" now wore the Fisherman's ring. Yet, the world was on the threshold of another war, a war that was to spell the doom of the dictators. But the Pope's reign would endure.

Mackenzie and I walked back to the city together. The Tiber reflected the golden rays of a Roman sunset. Newsboys were shouting the "extras." Precariously, the most skillful taxicab drivers of Europe were swerving around street corners. People were sipping vermouths in outdoor cafés before going home for dinner. Rome was profoundly peaceful.

"What would Mussolini have thought, had he been a witness to the scene on St. Peter's Square?" I pondered.

"Perhaps he would have remembered the late Pope's words about the swastika," said Mackenzie.

"Yes, he might have. What a contrast between the city of man and the city of God, right here in Rome!"

"Two worlds in conflict," remarked Mackenzie. "Side by side."

He knew what he was talking about. He had spent almost a lifetime in Italy and spoke Italian like a native. He was British, his wife American, and both loved the country like adopted children.

"I have been preaching all these years," he said, "but don't seem to get anywhere. The visitors from England, and from America, the butterfly tourists who learn all about Italy in a week, return home to sing the praises of fascism. They do not know what's going on behind the scenes, in the prison camps, the jails, horrid, dirty holes under brutal overseers, the penal colonies, where innocent victims of the tyrants have been languishing for years. But when they see a few hundred black-shirts shouting *'Viva il Duce!'* they go into raptures and think Musso is wonderful."

"Do you think the attitude of foreign countries had anything to do with stifling anti-fascist opposition right here?"

"It killed it! Just remember how Curzon helped the Duce out of the jam in Corfu! How Austen Chamberlain, shortly after the Matteotti murder, called on him in Rome, stiffening his back! How the same Chamberlain and others in high places extolled him as a great man! What chance did the opposition have with the outside world giving such 'build-ups' to their oppressors? Now that fascism bears its natural fruit all these appeasers begin to see the light. The swastika in Rome! It's the climax of aberration. The new Pope will have to carry a heavy burden."

At the hotel, Chechina, the maid, was sitting at the floor desk, knitting. She knew that I had been down to St. Peter's, for in the morning she had asked me for permission to come to our outpost to view the scene. Then she found she could not get away. Chechina had known me for years and she felt safe in talking freely to an *Americano*.

"Well," she greeted me expectantly. "How was it?"

I told her briefly of my impressions. When I mentioned the Pope's first blessing, she made the sign of the Cross.

"Now," she remarked devoutly, "we have a new Holy Father. Perhaps soon we will have peace."

"I don't know, Chechina," I replied. "Perhaps not for some time."

"*Forse che no.* Perhaps not. But the evil men won't last, Signore. God is not with them."

I noticed tears in Chechina's eyes and I had a feeling as though she were shedding them for all the good Italian people.

\* \* \*

As there was a visit to Mount Vesuvius on my schedule, I proceeded toward Naples in the morning. I had long had the ambition of broadcasting an eruption of the volcano, and the time seemed propitious.

When I drove up to the mid-way hotel, the old man in the mountain seemed as soundly asleep as Rip Van Winkle. Hardly a yawn was audible. The Italian engineers were wondering how the "crazy Americans" were going to make him growl.

Luckily, the volcano was active and in the midst of my commentary there was a tremendous roar. The crater was suddenly ablaze with crimson lava and one could well imagine how Pompeii and Herculanum had once been buried under its molten blanket. The mountain looked like a huge Christmas tree within the glow of its own fire.

One of our microphones was swallowed by the boiling elements pouring forth from the cone; and listeners in America heard the eruption more distinctly than most Neapolitans ever do. Who could know that American flying fortresses would soon eclipse the volcanic thunder in bombing raids more terrible and devastating than any paroxysm of Hephaestus!

In the course of my remarks on the air I introduced one of the guides, who happened to be New York born.

"You haven't lost your Manhattan slang," I complimented him after it was all over.

"Oh, I wouldn't!" he said proudly.

"Would you like to go back?" I asked.

The young man paused, and then he said: "I am homesick right now."

Like Chechina, he wanted none of fascism's blessings.

# Chapter 16

# THE FOLLY OF MUNICH

TO LOOK back on the successive stages of Hitler's aggressions leaves one gasping. "Some part of even the most impudent lie will remain and stick," he had said in his book. The trouble was that nobody thought he really meant it. "Germany neither intends nor wishes to interfere in the internal affairs of Austria, to annex Austria or to proclaim an *Anschluss*," he had asserted on May 21, 1935. After the *Anschluss*, he applied the same hypocritical deceit to Czechoslovakia. "We would not think of subjecting foreign peoples," he maintained on May 27, 1939, insisting that a border adjustment to "liberate" the three and one half million Germans in Sudetenland was all he wanted. Yet, the nazi agitation against the Prague government constantly grew more violent. Czechoslovakia was now the danger-spot of the continent.

In spite of his willingness to make generous concessions at Czech expense, Lord Runciman, sent especially to Prague by the British government to offer its good offices, finally had to admit failure. Prague was prepared to compromise and to satisfy Germany's legitimate aspirations, but there could be no doubt that Hitler had made up his mind to remap the whole of Central Europe, and the diplomats were not going to deter him from that goal. Was he going to use force to achieve it, or was there still a chance of peaceful settlement?

I went to Nuremberg, city of the "Meistersinger," to attend the 1938 "Nazi Olympics." Newsmen of all nationalities had made their headquarters in a popular hostelry, across the street from the main station. Nearly a million people had gathered for the congress. They had come in five hundred special trains and motor lorries from all parts of the country to attend Hitler's tenth national rally. There were parades

all day long and torchlight processions at night. Also brass-
bands and uniforms of all assortments. A mass meeting in the
Zeppelin stadium reached a climax when huge searchlights,
encircling the rigid nazi formations, reflected their candle-
power high up against the sky, creating the illusion of a
heavenly aura over the people's heads. It was Hitler's last
party convention before the war. There could be no doubt
about the meaning of the virulent speeches, nor the significance of the lavish military displays impressively staged for
foreign observers.

Hitler himself sounded the keynote in a broadcast when he
cautioned his listeners that Germany had "no more worries
about food, having stored away what is necessary to give full
security, so the idea of an economic blockade of Germany
can henceforth be buried." The echo came in the address by
Rudolf Hess, the "Fuehrer's" deputy, who proclaimed that
"whatever Hitler does is right, whatever he does is necessary,
whatever he does is successful, as manifestly he has the divine
blessing." And Hermann Goering led on with the same theme
in a violent speech when he spoke of Germany's alleged
invincibility and concluded with the phrase: "No one can
stop us!" On the closing day, Hitler flung the epithet of "liar"
at President Edvard Benes, of Czechoslovakia, and declared
it was "unbearable that the Germans in Sudentenland be
delivered to shameless ill treatment."

That was plain language. I walked back to the station.
There were no taxicabs or buses. A stream of exuberant
humanity was jamming the roads. While the cabinets were
deliberating in London and Paris, the fate of Czechoslovakia
seemed sealed — unless the Western Powers meant business
and declared war on Germany. No one thought they were
prepared for it.

The rapidity of events following the Nuremberg congress
was breath-taking. First, Chamberlain's visit to Hitler in his
mountain eyrie, to make a personal plea for peace. Then the
ill-fated meeting of the two men in Bad Godesberg on the
Rhine, followed by the spectacular Sports Palace gathering
in Berlin. And finally the great turning point at the Four
Power conference in Munich which resulted in nothing less
than the destruction of France's hegemony on the Continent.

England was then still in a mood of "appeasement." The British public was in favor of granting most of the German demands on Sudeten territory, but expected guarantees which Hitler was in no mood to give. Once more the eyes of the world were fixed on Downing Street. Many will recall Chamberlain's brief radio messages at that time, and how tired he sounded although he tried to convey confidence and hope for peace. For a few days the scales went up and down. Opinion in Czechoslovakia and throughout the world was hardening against further concessions to Hitler. In the Sudeten districts the tension grew to a point where ordinary police measures proved useless. A week after the Berchtesgaden meeting Chamberlain boarded a plane to Godesberg, to seek a solution of the tangle.

Preceding the British Prime Minister, I drove along the Rhine one sunny autumn morning, to investigate radio prospects. I found Fritz Dreese, owner of the leading hotel in Godesberg and, at that time, German national vice-president of the International Hotel Alliance, in the midst of hasty preparations for Hitler's arrival that afternoon.

Herr Dreese prided himself on a personal acquaintance of long standing with the "Fuehrer." After his release from prison in 1922 Hitler had found it difficult to obtain a refuge. In Godesberg where he had hoped to take a rest before resuming his political campaigning all the hotels, except Dreese's, refused him.

"The Fuehrer really likes it here," explained Herr Dreese throwing out his chest. "He is so appreciative of what I did for him. He is kindly, you know."

"Hmm."

"Everything he does is dictated by his love for the people."

"Except when he turns them over to the Gestapo," I interrupted.

"Oh, but those are only the criminals! The Gestapo protects us from the communists."

There was no use arguing.

About lunch time Hitler arrived and immediately retired to his quarters, which were now guarded by special storm troopers in heavy armor. Soon the hotel was crowded by nazi officials in jaunty uniforms.

"Where could we have our microphone?" I asked Herr Dreese.

"Right here," he said, "In the pantry!"

That was not a bad idea, for the pantry was just behind the main lobby and there was a glass oval in the door to peek through! Waiters were rushing in and out with pots of coffee and bottles of Rhine wine, but they didn't bother me. An open circuit to New York was all I needed.

Shortly before the arrival of the British delegation, Hitler showed up in the lobby, dressed in his brown coat and black trousers, hatless, and again with a single decoration on his breast, the Iron Cross. Paul Schmidt, a Foreign Office interpreter, was talking to him. Hitler stood in the middle of the room, his hands placed on his hips, a provocative expression on his face.

Various people came to meet him. He did not shake hands with anybody, just gave them his staccato salute and nonchalantly turned back to Schmidt. But then a lady appeared on the scene, who, I believe, was Frau Dreese. Hitler kissed her hand, smiling broadly. His moves were awkward, angular, unrefined, conceited.

After a while, Chamberlain and his party drove up to the hotel entrance, and everybody retired to the conference room.

Hours went by. A Rhine steamer was moored at the river pier, and presently Hitler went to inspect it. There was a recess in the meeting and it was rumored that the "Fuehrer" would invite his British guests for a trip down stream to show them the Lorelei rock. As the legend goes, Lorelei, the beautiful golden-haired maiden, threw herself into the Rhine in despair over a faithless lover, and became a siren whose voice lured fisherman to destruction. All this might have been inauspiciously significant to Mr. Chamberlain.

Eugen Hadamovsky had come from Berlin to supervise broadcasting. He was radiant in his uniformed glory, heavy boots, dagger, and sundry decorations.

"Not one word must go out of this building without my okay," he ordered.

"Now listen," I objected. "You can't censor the American air."

"I don't care where it goes, orders are orders."

Fortunately, there was not much to report, anyhow. It looked for a while as though the meeting would break down. Messengers were rushing back and forth between the British headquarters across the river and Hitler's hotel. The wires between London and Godesberg had been buzzing all day. Over the telephone I received radiograms from New York urging reports on the progress of the conference, but there was little to tell.

"The Fuehrer will handle this thing all right," Hadamovsky lectured us reporters. "Germany will come out with flying colors."

"It may mean war," I suggested.

"Oh, you mustn't even think of that word! No one wants war. The 'Fuehrer' stands for peace."

"On his own terms, I guess."

Hada turned his back on me.

"What you think makes no difference," he grumbled. "Wait and see."

I wondered what the British thought of the nazi world, of its affected dignity and boisterousness. Hada was a prototype of hitlerian arrogance and narrow-mindedness.

It was past midnight when Chamberlain returned to the Dreese Hotel to again call on Hitler. Germany's request that the whole of the Sudeten territory be turned over to her at once had been refused by the British. Further consultations in London were required.

In the morning Chamberlain flew back home. He looked worn and tired as he boarded his plane. The Prague government had just ordered general mobilization and the larger cities of Czechoslovakia were blacked out. At Godesberg I had seen interpreter Paul Schmidt carrying a map into one of the meetings. It was the map Hitler afterwards handed over to Chamberlain. The Sudeten areas, whose surrender Germany had demanded, were heavily shaded, leaving out a few "enclaves" whose fate was to be determined by subsequent plebiscites. Czechoslovakia rejected the terms. In an official Prague broadcast it was stated that France and Britain had passed the map on to the Czechoslovakian government without specific recommendations, thereby indicating, the speaker said, "that they themselves did not consider the new proposals a reasonable basis for securing an agreement."

The stalemate could not last long. The nazi press was raging. "Prague setting the world aflame," said one typical headline. Hitler was irritated by the delay. An "historic manifestation" was ordered to be held in Berlin's huge Sports Palace. "It will take in every city and hamlet in the Reich," the announcement said, "for all those owning receiving sets will be within reach. Those who do not have this convenience are instructed to foregather around public loudspeakers under the direction of local party leaders. No man, woman or child in the Reich must fail to be a listener or witness of this momentous proceeding."

The Sports Palace was filled by a frenzied crowd of fifteen thousand ardent nazis. The platform was jammed with government and party officials. Huge swastika banners were displayed all over the balconies, and there was an atmosphere of tense expectation. When Hitler arrived he was greeted by frantic applause.

Outside, on the streets of Berlin, convoys of troops, heavy guns, ambulances and army kitchens were rumbling to secret destinations. The people on the sidewalks were silent, watching with gloomy faces. Nobody said a word. There were no manifestations of joy. Was the world on the brink of war? Was mobilization at hand? Then Hitler spoke.

Perhaps there had never been as large a world-wide audience listening to a single speaker. A few days before, Mussolini had spoken from Triest: "In case of war Italy has chosen her side." And again from Udine: "Italy is ready to go to war." Litvinov was heard from Geneva. President Roosevelt addressed a dramatic midnight plea for peace to the nations of Europe. Now it was Hitler's turn.

Some readers may remember the broadcast. How the "Fuehrer" sailed full force into President Benes. How he thanked Chamberlain with veiled sarcasm "for all his trouble." How he mentioned having told the British Government "that there will be no further territorial problems for Germany," if only his demands on Sudetenland were satisfied. How he branded Czechoslovakia as having been "conceived as a lie and conducted as a swindle for twenty years." How he concluded by shouting that "the time has come to talk business."

I stood in front of a microphone, some twenty yards distant from the rostrum. My English summary was to follow the speech. I made notes, but could hardly turn my eyes away from the man who was challenging the whole civilized world. I had seen him in action before. Never had he sounded as violent and uncompromising as on that day. His words meant war. To my mind the only question was: When?

Something happened at that point which, I think, escaped the attention of many observers present.

After Hitler had spoken, Goebbels stood up to close the meeting in his capacity as Berlin's nazi district leader.

Goebbels pledged the German people's support to Hitler, without consulting them. And then he yelled:

"Never again will we witness our nation going down in defeat — as it did in 1918!"

That "never" was spoken with a penetrating emphasis and articulation. The moment it was uttered, Hitler jumped from his seat, lifted his right arm and with an expression which seemed to me one of extreme brutality, clenched his fist as though he was pressing a dagger against someone's back and screamed:

"Never!"

The commandeered audience applauded wildly. Then they poured out of the building, munching frankfurter rolls and lighting their smokes. Few seemed to realize the portent of the day.

By the time they had dispersed, the streets of Berlin were empty. The people as a whole remained sullen and apprehensive of the things to come.

That evening Chamberlain spoke in London. In contrast to Hitler's, his words were calm and controlled. He said he was "a man of peace to the depth of his soul," but he pledged Britain to fight any power seeking to dominate the world by force.

In Berlin, radio and press correspondents made plans to go to the front. From a window of the Adlon Hotel I looked out on Pariser Platz. Anti-aircraft guns had been moved onto house-tops. Field-equipped columns of artillery raced down Unter den Linden.

But, then, suddenly, came a temporary change of scene.

Chamberlain was addressing the House of Commons on the "present anxious and critical situation" when an invitation reached him from Hitler to attend a meeting in Munich. Mussolini and Premier Daladier were to be the other participants. An eleventh hour respite! President Roosevelt's intervention and Chamberlain's plea addressed to Mussolini had brought it about. Hitler postponed mobilization for twenty-four hours.

A fast plane took me to Munich just in time to be at the airport when Chamberlain arrived the following morning, September 29th.

Microphones were quickly set up, and soon the cheers of a crowd of Bavarians welcoming the British guests were broadcast across the Atlantic.

The main railway station was next on my schedule. Our microphones were in position, right in front of the special coach which had come up from Italy. When the German dictator alighted with his axis partner, they were greeted by a long line of officials. Schacht was conspicuous among them.

The Duce looked his best, all dressed up in fascist splendor. He always knew how to hold the center of the stage. But now he had to share it with someone else. As they walked out of the station, I wondered which of the two trouble-makers was the better swaggerer.

A year before I had come through Munich to view Hitler's exhibition of so-called "degenerate art." In a way, it was a repetition of the book-burning. Significantly enough, the "model show" set up by Hitler's amateur standards attracted only one third of the number of those looking over the "degenerates," the Gauguins and George Groszs and Picassos. Even in matters of art, the two thirds of the German people who had opposed Hitler ever since he had come to power had apparently not changed their minds.

The British and French delegates in Munich were not privileged to make such observations. They were not shown through the downtown section of the city where they could have seen the people walking around a whole square to avoid passing the nazi bronze memorial dedicated to Hitler's "martyrs." Everyone was supposed to salute it with outstretched arm, like the Gessler hat in Schiller's "William Tell," but few people did. These foreign visitors were given no opportunity to mingle with the people who could have told them, in hidden corners, how much they were averse to war and how little it mattered to them whether their country would gain or lose this or that strip of territory.

Diplomats often operate in a vacuum. In Munich it was evident that the governments were out of touch with the people. It seemed as though the fashionable hotel which served as the meeting ground of the kibitzers and as a trading post of news was the only ground the foreign delegates and newspapermen were anxious to explore. Nazi propagandists saw to it that curiosity was satisfied within those artificial fences.

A few blocks away was the "Brown House," inaccessible to outsiders. But there are no obstacles in this world which cannot be conquered, if conquered they must be. In the morning a group of American correspondents had managed to be shown about the building. We saw the huge lobby, the modernistic reception halls with symbolic wall paintings of German lore, the "Fuehrer's" study. Personally, I was more anxious to learn something about radio facilities. Inquiries produced valuable information.

There were cable lines connecting the "Brown House" directly with the Berlin radio station. There were microphones too, and amplifiers — everything we needed. But the equipment was reserved for German needs. Foreign reporters were supposed to go to the studio building, some twenty blocks away.

That evening I was having dinner at the "Vier Jahreszeiten" Hotel with Lord Derby who had come from London in a private capacity, and G. Ward Price, of the *Daily Mail,* when young Schmidt Hansen of the German radio, known to all of us as "Johnny," came by.

"The conference isn't over, is it?" I inquired.

"I don't know," he replied. "I am on my way over there now."

"Could I go with you?"

"Oh, they wouldn't let you pass."

"Suppose we tried?"

"Well," he laughed, "it won't be my fault if they throw you out!"

I was willing to take the chance.

When we reached the police cordon, near the Brown House, Johnny showed his credentials mumbling "Rundfunk." It was like a magic pass word taking care of both of us. We slipped by the main entrance of the building and arrived at the back door which allowed direct access to the radio room under the roof.

Once I was inside I had no trouble finding my way through the maze of corridors right into the main lobby. There, behind closed doors, the meeting of the Big Four was in progress.

It was a brilliant scene throughout the various reception rooms, although not a single woman was present. The male of the species was messing up the world all by himself! Showing off their uniforms, and displaying their glittering decorations, the nazi bigwigs paced the floor strutting like the peacocks in Munich's zoo.

Presently Heinrich Himmler, the Terrible, came parading my way. Was he going to seize me and fling me into one of his dungeons?

What a face that nazi superexecutioner carries around! And what an icy glare behind that pince-nez! I shuddered, but he paid no attention to anybody.

I went back to the radio room. Johnny was adamant.

"You've got to go back to the studio," he said. "This equipment is reserved for us."

But I was in no mood to give up. Pleading over the telephone with Johnny's superior in Berlin, I finally got permission to pass a message on to New York. Thereafter it was a battle of wits.

About one o'clock in the morning I noticed a group of Italian officers leaving the conference room. As they walked by I heard them drop a remark which seemed to indicate that the meeting was about to come to a close.

"*Andiamocene!*" said one of the men. "Let's pack our grips!"

That was my cue. I dashed upstairs and called New York once more.

"Stand by, NBC! Important announcement expected momentarily! Stand by!"

Back in the lobby, I could see that the meeting was actually nearing its end. I noticed Sir William Strang, of the British delegation, leaning against a railing of the big marble stair-

case. To him I was able to explain the importance of our securing the official English text of whatever communique was
going to be issued. He promised to do his best.

So upstairs once more! Another warning to New York.
And back to the lobby. But this time I seemed to be just
a couple of minutes late. The conference was over. And there
went the Duce! And there Daladier! Both on their way
downstairs.

Where were the British? I rushed through the lobby. That
very moment I could see Chamberlain leaving the building
with his group.

"Hey!" I shouted at the top of my voice. Forgetting all
diplomatic amenities I started racing toward them.

Sir William recognized me.

"Oh," he said. "That's right."

Turning to Sir Horace Wilson, Chamberlain's diplomatic
adviser, he whispered a word or two into his ear. Wilson
didn't hesitate. Under his arm he carried a batch of the official
communiques. He handed one over to me. I was the proud
possessor of the first copy of the official protocol which up to
that moment nobody except the participants in the meeting
had seen!

As though wearing seven-league boots, I dashed upstairs to
the microphone in no time, breathlessly asking for the air.

My German colleague was taken aback. He had not yet
received his text, so he doubted the authenticity of mine. It
all but ended in a fist fight! Fortunately we did not knock
over the microphone. Though somewhat peeved, the German
reporter finally withdrew his objections and five minutes
later the complete text of the Munich agreement was heard
by NBC listeners from coast to coast. We had scooped the
world! Lady Luck had been on our side.

\*     \*     \*

Before leaving for home the next morning, the delegates
should have canvassed the people of Munich. It might have
opened their eyes. Perhaps Daladier and Chamberlain noticed
at the airport that this time there were no cheering Bavarians.
The real feelings of the people were best expressed by one
of the more daring German newspapermen who had said
to me the night before:

"Isn't there anyone in the whole world to tell Hitler where to get off?"

Léon Blum, then the French Premier, expressed a view which was widespread after Munich when he said: "War has probably been averted, but I feel myself divided between cowardly relief and a sense of shame."

The Munich decision meant the ruin of Czechoslovakia, as Germany obtained the country's basic industrial resources and gained full control of its strategic frontier positions. Thomas Masaryk's republic lost almost five million inhabitants, one and a half million of them Czechs and Slovaks, and a billion dollars' worth of industrial raw materials, besides armaments and sizable reserves. Peace was temporarily saved by selling a small country down the river. Hitler's demands were met, and the world turned rather suddenly from gloom to relief.

In the House of Commons on October 5th, Winston Churchill spoke words that today sound truly prophetic: "The utmost the Prime Minister was able to secure has been that the German dictator, instead of snatching his victuals from the table, has been content to have them served to him course by course. The difference between the positions reached at Berchtesgaden, at Godesberg and at Munich can be very simply epitomized, to vary the metaphor: one pound was demanded at the pistol's point. When it was given, two pounds were demanded at the pistol's point. Finally the dictator consented to take one pound, seventeen shilling and sixpence, and the rest in promises of good will for the future! The idea that safety could be purchased by throwing a small state to the wolves is a fatal delusion."

But Chamberlain who had quoted Shakespeare's "Henry IV" — "Out of this nettle, danger, we plucked this flower, safety" — claimed to have achieved a "peace with honor" and insisted before Parliament that "the path that leads to peace is a long one and bristles with obstacles." The question of Czechoslovakia, he explained, was the latest and perhaps the most dangerous. "Now that we have got past it I feel that it may be possible to make further progress along the road to sanity." Yes, he said: sanity!

Major Attlee, leader of the opposition, had the proper reply: "Having decided to leave the League system to embark on a policy of alliances and power politics, Mr. Chamberlain has been the dupe of dictators. In the place of covenants and collective security we are left with two promises, one from Mussolini and one from Hitler."

I called on Professor Ketter before leaving Munich. He was a member of the faculty of Munich University, and another brave worker in the dark against hitlerism. That day, a local publisher happened to be visiting with him. Their conversation was interrupted when I entered the room.

"What were you talking about?" I asked.

"What would one talk about?" answered the professor — "The conference!"

"You don't seem to be happy over it."

"Happy?" the publisher scoffed. "Why, it's the worst letdown we've had in years! We are depressed beyond words."

"You ought to know," agreed the professor. "You were there, in the Brown House, weren't you? Tell us about it."

I did. And then I concluded:

"At least there will be peace for a while."

"Peace!" shouted the publisher. 'You don't mean it, do you? It's the green light for war!"

"A lady friend of mine," the professor took over again, "saw Hitler before he left town this morning. She had an introduction through the Gauleiter and was curious to see the great man. When she was allowed into his presence, she felt she had to say something because he barely shook her hands and just stared at her. 'Congratulations, *mein Fuehrer,*' she bowed. And he replied: 'On what?' The lady, not being the kind that's easily embarrassed explained that she felt he had saved the peace. Whereupon Hitler shouted: 'I don't want peace! I want war!' He said it, and walked out of the room. That's the kind of man that rules us. Let the world beware!"

"Have you heard of General Beck's resignation?" the publisher asked me.

I had not. General Ludwig Beck was known as one of Germany's best military minds. He was to lose his life in the "purge" of 1944.

"Well, Beck feels that Hitler is courting the most serious trouble. As a General Staff man, Beck was against the march on Vienna. Now he has warned Hitler that his moves on Czechoslovakia may mean war."

"What should the Czechs have done?" I asked.

"Fight, of course!"

"Could they?"

"Certainly. They are in splendid shape, militarily, but now England and France have stopped them. The big powers really don't seem to know what they are doing."

"They aren't prepared," I said.

"What do they have to be prepared for? Don't they know that all nazidom is built on sand? If someone will only call Hitler's bluff, it'll collapse."

"What's the use arguing now?" the professor broke in. "Certainly the friends of peace have missed a great chance. The democracies have lacked courage and resolution. They could have turned the tide. Instead, they have given in to the aggressor."

"And we Germans," concluded the publisher, "are completely delivered into his hands."

On my way to the station I passed by the Cathedral. It was nightfall, and there was a big throng in the square. Thousands of men, all bearing lighted candles and walking in silent procession. It was a mute demonstration of protest against the outrageous treatment of Cardinal Faulhaber by the nazi police. But Chamberlain and Daladier had left town. They were not witnesses of this remarkable scene. They had only seen the Brown House, and Hitler and Himmler and brownshirted guards. They had not seen the people.

## Chapter 17

## BLACK-OUT OF PEACE

TO RIBBENTROP, who was constantly pressing for action, both the Four Power protocol on the Sudetenland and the Anglo-German declaration of friendship which had been signed at Munich, were but means to gain time for further aggression. Barely six months after Munich, and just one year after he had marched on Vienna, Hitler marched on Prague. In true Blitzkrieg fashion he smashed dismembered Czechoslovakia and made her his "Protectorate." President Emil Hacha was summoned to Berlin. His last futile attempts at resistance were thwarted when Hitler threatened to bomb Prague to bits. That same night German motorized units moved swiftly across the border. The pledge of Munich was broken. The world woke up on the morning of March 15, 1939, to find the swastika banner flying over the venerable Hradshin Castle, once the palace of Bohemian Kings. Again taken by surprise, the Western Powers condoned the rape of Prague as they had condoned the rape of Vienna.

"We had expected it ever since Munich," said one of my friends at Radio Prague. "Our very allies have sold us out. Some day they will regret it."

The twenty years of the Czechoslovakian republic had been filled with achievement. The Czechs were patriotic to the core, at times ebulliently so, but who could blame them after the magnificent struggle for freedom they won under such true leaders as Masaryk and Benes? They had a right to be proud. Why should they be tossed out of the window, simply because it served the convenience of their partners?

"Do you remember how we mobilized during the Munich days?" my radio friend went on, reminiscing gloomily.

"I certainly do," I said. "I still see that taxi driver who took me to the station from the Alcron Hotel. 'We'll fight!' he vowed. 'We'll fight!'"

"Yes, we all were going to fight! We longed to fight. But they stopped us. Our friends stopped us. We had to take Hitler's blows lying down. . . ."

Now a nazi supervisor had taken over in the modern structure housing Prague's broadcasting studios. There many of our finest programs had originated: music by Dvorak and Smetana, descriptions of the famous Ghetto and Jewish cemetery, Moravian choirs — all voices of an exalted past and a noble present. Now the Gestapo ruled the land of the sokols, which might well have inflicted a Waterloo on the invaders.

Few people were aware of how completely Hitler had fooled the world. "We have assured all our neighbors of the integrity of their territory. That is no hollow phrase. The Sudetenland is our last territorial claim in Europe." Thus had he spoken on September 26, 1938. In the same speech he had said he was "convinced that the German agreement with Poland will bring about lasting peace." And in January, 1939, he had added that "the friendship between Germany and Poland was one of the reassuring factors in the political life of Europe."

For Poland, it was like a kiss of death, and for the German people it meant that with every move Hitler succeeded in "putting over," their fate under the nazi tyranny was sealed ever more irretrievably.

When I reached Berlin again on my way from Prague, I found Karl Nord of the Friday Circle in despair.

"After this," he said, "the people will swallow anything. It's a mass psychosis and it looks as though the Powers will continue to do all they can to promote it."

"You don't mean that in earnest, do you?" I objected.

"Of course, I do, and I don't have to prove it either. Vienna, Munich, Prague are proofs enough. And now comes Warsaw!"

"Don't take it for granted that the British will let him get away with everything!"

"I am taking anything for granted, after what's happened these past six years. It is as though the whole world was spreading out red carpets for the great 'Fuehrer.' We who are struggling just for air to breathe, have the props taken out from under our measly ramparts, and we are sinking, sinking, I tell you! Who cares?"

It was hard to provide answers for the men and women in Germany whose conscience had not been lulled to sleep. They despaired of ever again seeing the light of a day of liberty.

"Remember," said Nord, and I sensed almost a sob in his voice, "we too, we enslaved Germans, are let down, we, too, are thrown to the nazi wolves. What does the world care? It won't care until it has to face these monsters the way we face them right now."

Hitler's move on Prague had opened many eyes. Statesmen and diplomats who had stuck to ostrich tactics began to awaken to the imminent danger of war. The time was approaching when a stand would have to be taken. England was first in taking hers when she pledged full assistance to Poland on March 31st, 1939.

The wooing of the Russian bear was the next step. Both the nazis and the western powers courted him for his favors, but he was elusive. Hitler had openly proclaimed Danzig and the Polish "Corridor" as his next aims. He had forced Lithuania to surrender Memel, and scrapped the non-aggression pact with Poland along with the Anglo-German naval treaty and the Munich consultation agreement. "The German people are ready at any time!" he had bragged defiantly in a scathing speech at the launching of the 35,000 ton battleship "Admiral von Tirpitz." No one could doubt any longer that he was out for big booty.

The Moscow government was not ready to take chances. Stalin was playing for time, and Hitler willingly surrendered to his claim on the Baltic states which the British and the French had not been prepared to grant. The two dictators buried the hatchet temporarily when they signed their non-aggression pact on August 21, nailing Poland to the cross for the fourth time in her history.

By air, it was just a hop from Berlin to Warsaw, so I decided to check up with my contacts there. Polish broadcasting was ambitious. Their links with the Poles in America were close, and through their good offices we had secured many a rare program feature. International Chopin concerts, Eva Brandowska-Turska, the great singer, popular music enlivened by the Cracow trumpeter, and one of the most bizarre of broadcasts, the election of a gypsy "king."

But now I had to give thought to matters of graver consequence.

Life in the Polish capital was normal. Only few people realized that a crisis was impending. Festive summer crowds strolled by Chopin's monument in the Lazienki Park. The meals at the Europejski Hotel were still among the very best in the world, and Hungarian Tokay wine, served as the specialty in a local inn, stood out as one of the rare treats in the east of Europe — which meant a great deal when we remember that the Poles are among the most hospitable people on earth. The most hospitable and I must add, among the most deeply religious.

Anyone who has ever seen the Polish people at prayer will treasure the memory with a sense of reverence and admiration. A broadcast arranged from Czestochova, the famous pilgrimage shrine which, to so many Polish immigrants in the United States, is the symbol of their home land's greatness, had offered me the opportunity to grasp some of the meaning of that innate religious fervor of their nation. It is a fervor touching in its simplicity and at the same time truly inspiring because of its sincerity and depth. The haunting chant of the pilgrims in Czestochova which followed the sound of silver fanfares signalling the lifting of the curtains before the sacred likeness of the "Black Madonna" was as sad and strange and moving as is the history of Poland.

The shrine is part of a monastery built on a hill. A long street lined with drab little shops selling all kinds of devotional articles, souvenirs and refreshments leads up to it. Peasant women trudge past with wicker baskets fastened to their shoulders. I was told that in those baskets they carried the festive costumes donned only when, after hours of walking from some distant rural village, they had actually reached the church. It is a scene never to be forgotten when this colorfully garbed crowd, many of them stretched out on the chapel floor, join in singing the rosary — yes, singing it, as a slow, imploring litany.

Like the Czechs before the nazi invasion, the Poles, too,

were confident. In their case, there had been no "Munich," no sellout. They were not alone, but their friends were far away.

"We are not afraid," said Edmund Rudnicki, the radio producer who had spent several years of his life in the United States and loved to tell of his experiences.

"Are you aware that Hitler's armies are ready for action?" I asked.

"So are ours."

"But his are stronger."

"Ours are on home soil."

"See what happened in Austria, in Czechoslovakia."

"It won't happen here. We won't capitulate, even though we may have to fight to the last man."

It was the spirit of Poland, indomitable, heroic.

My next stop was Danzig, still a "Free City," as artificially and untenably set up at Versailles. Clearly, the Poles were on the defensive. The nazis of Danzig were shouting and parading and while people were enjoying glorious summer days at the Zoppot beaches, thick clouds were gathering fast on the political horizon.

To get a complete picture, I went to see Dr. Karl Burckhardt, a prominent Swiss jurist and then the League of Nations' High Commissioner in the "Free City." He had just returned from a visit to Berchtesgaden.

"How was it?" I inquired.

"Well," replied Burkhardt, "it was an unusual experience."

"You are putting it mildly, aren't you?"

He laughed.

"Probably so, but I mean it. It was certainly unusual for Hitler to listen to me."

"He really did?"

"He did. I had gone to see him because I felt it was my duty to impress him personally with the tremendous responsibilities involved in this Danzig situation. I explained it to him fully and frankly, pointing out the determination of the Poles to fight."

"And what was his answer?"

"He didn't answer for quite a while, just stared at me and listened. When I had finished he got up, walked across the room to one of the bay windows which afford a stupendous view of the Bavarian mountain scenery and stood there for quite a while, looking into the landscape, silently. I wondered what I should do. Then I pleaded:

" 'Your Excellency (the only way I could address him as a foreigner whom he was receiving on official business), won't you say a word to save the peace of Europe?'

"At that, suddenly, he turned around, his face livid, grabbed the heavy window drapery with both hands and tore it to the floor with a violent gesture, shouting: 'No!' Whereupon he turned his back on me and walked out of the room."

"So there is no hope for peace?"

Burkhardt did not answer my question. He probably felt his story had answered it.

The next morning came the news that the nazi majority in the City Council had proclaimed Danzig independent. The local nazi boss was appointed head of the "Free City" by the insurgents. It was a challenge flung at Poland, premeditated and carefully timed.

Armies all over the continent started to mobilize. Hitler called off his annual Nuremberg circus which this year had been announced as a "peace convention" — presumably to camouflage the preparations for war.

But in Paris, Marcel Déat, future Vichyite, even then was playing into Hitler's hands, "Why die for Danzig?" he asked in his *Oeuvre*. Five years later he was reported to have been killed at the Polish front. Unwilling to die for Danzig when it might have meant stopping Hitler from the outset, he met his just deserts as nazi cannon fodder.

\* \* \*

All through the years since he had fled to hospitable Holland, and almost to the day of his passing, a bronze bust of William II, last of German Emperors, was kept in a niche of the pompous Adlon hotel lobby in Berlin. Spiked helmet, up-turned mustache, martial look, and other appurtenances of imperial glory were displayed on this anachronistic relic which somehow had survived two revolutions and the vicissitudes of the era between two wars.

No one paid much attention to His Majesty's bust, for the corner was dark, and the hotel guests were more intent on imbibing tea and cocktails and on the gossip of the day. The bar was just around the corner, a meeting-place of the capital's eavesdroppers. On September 1st, 1939, it was packed and it was hard to get service. Too many people were crowding into the small room for comfort.

Excited voices were engaged in analyzing a bulletin just received over the ticker at the porter's desk:

"Hitler annexes Danzig! Warsaw bombed!"

"Let's go!" said Otto Weltin whom I had met for lunch. As we walked across the lobby someone hailed him.

"Oh, there is Countess Erdner!" he acknowledged. "You've met her, haven't you?"

I had not.

"Well, she is one of the best informed socialites in town, the daughter of former Ambassador X., and now married to a scion of the West."

At the Countess' table there were three men. Weltin introduced me to her and she in turn presented me to her husband, to an official of the Foreign Office, and to another civilian whose name sounded like "Von Werner." It did not take long before we were all engaged in a lively conversation.

"What do you think this means?" the Countess asked Otto Weltin.

"The bombing?"

"Yes."

Weltin was non-committal.

"In the bar," I remarked, "the newspapermen seem to have no doubt but that it means war."

We all sat silent.

Then the mysterious Herr von Werner spoke up.

"Not only does it mean war. It is war. It's the beginning of World War II."

The Countess was almost beside herself.

"Oh, if the British would only come tonight and destroy this whole city! Smash everything and us, too! What would it matter, if only these mad dogs could be stopped!"

"They can't be stopped," Werner went on. "Not now anyway. They have planned it well."

On the way out I asked Weltin:

"Who is this fellow Werner?"

"An army officer."

"Then he ought to know what he is talking about."

"Particularly since he is with the General Staff."

"Really?"

"Keep it under your hat. I'll have you meet him some other time, alone."

I had a broadcasting date and said good-bye.

Unter den Linden was quiet, normally busy. Back in 1914, the declaration of war had been received with enthusiasm. There were patriotic street demonstrations. The crowds sang the national anthem over and over again. Flags were on display everywhere.

No such symptoms could be discovered this time. There was gloom in the air, and the faces of the people were serious. There was no singing, no flag-waving. True, the country was still on the verge of war. It had not been formally declared, despite Hitler's aggression in Poland. Most people were inclined to think that he might again get away with it.

The optimists had some facts to point out. The mass meeting of 150,000 nazis which was to be addressed by Hitler, on the battle-field of Tannenberg in East Prussia where Hindenburg had won his most spectacular victory against Russia in the last war, had been called off. Goebbels cancelled his broadcast. Behind the scenes diplomats were working frantically, hoping to achieve a compromise. Hitler conferred with the ambassadors of the big powers. Sir Neville Henderson had flown to London, and Mussolini was known to be bending his efforts on stalling the German war machine at the last hour. In London, however, children were being evacuated. In a broadcast from Waterloo station they were heard singing the Lambeth Walk.

Diplomatic cars were parked all day and late into the night of September 2nd at the Foreign Office in the Wilhelmstrasse. High-ranking military could be seen rushing in and out of conferences. A diplomat who was "on the inside" came down the steps of the press department.

"Yes," he said to a small group of us, off the record, "there is still hope, but it's as when a mouse nears a trap — the only hope is that the trap won't work!"

Sand bags were being piled up around public monuments.

Works of art were about to be removed from museums. People began to think of evacuation. Emergency food rations were being checked, air-raid wardens mobilized. The railways announced war-time schedules. American tourists scurried for border stations and airports.

Then Hitler spoke, addressing his yes-men in the Reichstag. It was another gasconade, a speech full of threats and bullying, bombastic and contradictory. And the scene was pathetic, almost unreal in its stiff and staged solemnity. "From now on bomb will be met by bomb!" yelled the "Fuehrer." "I have put on my old soldier's coat and will not take it off until we achieve victory!"

While driving to Broadcasting House I tried to concentrate. What could I report? What would I be allowed to say? Hard and fast censorship rules were now striking at the very roots of radio. How tempting it would have been to arrange for random pick-ups and street interviews! Some people might have spoken their mind. They might have told how they really felt, how they loathed the very thought of another war. That is, the plain people, not the ones in gaudy uniforms and heavy boots who claimed to represent the people — without giving the people the slightest chance to vent their feelings!

By the time I reached the studio I knew what I was going to say. The five hundred words required for the early morning spot in New York were soon typed out. Formerly I would have stepped up to the microphone without further ado. Now there was a censor.

"Let's see," grumbled the little man whom Goebbels had appointed to check American copy. "What've you got?"

He was a former instructor of a college in the Middle West, had lived several years in the States and considered himself an expert on things American.

He started reading:

"American commentators," I proposed to say, "are handicapped just now. There are limitations imposed by the present situation, and more discretion must be used than ever before. All I am saying, therefore, implies a certain reserve."

The censor looked at me.

"What do you mean by this?"

"Exactly what it says."

"Limitations, discretion, reserve . . . I don't get it."

And out went the whole paragraph. Clearly he did not like my warning to the listeners that under the circumstances they should not expect straightforward reporting. Came the next paragraph:

"Hitler today spoke to the Reichstag almost exactly in the same vein as the Kaiser did to that body twenty-five years ago. . . . Without a declaration of war, war is actually on between Poland and Germany. . . ."

The censor was furious.

"I won't stand for this," he fumed, and his blue pencil crossed out one sentence after another. Out went the reference to the Kaiser, out the statement about the undeclared war. It was useless even to attempt a report.

That same afternoon I went to complain to Karl Boehmer, head of the nazi foreign press section.

"This sort of thing," I insisted, "makes it impossible to do a decent job."

Boehmer was Goebbels' appointee, a former newspaperman who had travelled in the United States and Mexico, a friend of good living, of wine, women, and song, but not the worst of the nazis by any means. Proudly he was wearing a second lieutenant's uniform.

He had a copy of my script on his desk.

"Listen," he remarked coldly, "you didn't really expect we'd let you get away with all this, did you?"

"Why not?"

"Comparing Hitler to the Kaiser, to a Kaiser who suffered defeat?"

"That's an honest opinion."

"I don't care how honest it is. You can't say it. This time it isn't a Kaiser! This time we won't crack!"

Boehmer landed in jail at a later stage of the war because he had "spilled the beans" of Hitler's forthcoming attack on Russia, after just one drink too many. Eventually he was allowed to pay with his life at the Eastern front for having spoken out of turn.

Insecurely, I kept going for a few more days. Then I gave up and suggested to the boss in New York that we stop all broadcasting from Berlin. Unfortunately, it was found impossible to reach an agreement with everybody concerned, and radio reporters had to make the best of distasteful conditions, resorting to "baby talk," and depending on the ability of the audience to "listen between the lines." We should have quit after the first failures for in the end we were all losers.

And here we had dreamed of radio doing a bang-up job when Mars ran amuck! A job on battlefields with portable transmitters, on men-of-war describing engagements at sea, on bomber planes equipped with our own microphones! Our fancy came to naught in the blackout of truth.

\* \* \*

"You'll see," Hans Nord, who fondly remembered his days in America, had warned me the day of the first Warsaw bombing. "It'll be like a prairie fire with a high wind blowing."

So it was. The desperate attempts to localize the conflict came too late. On September 3rd at 11:15 o'clock London time, in the midst of a long American Labor Day week-end, Neville Chamberlain went on the air. In a measured and solemn voice which hardly concealed his deep emotion, he announced that "this country is at war with Germany — it is the evil things we shall be fighting against — brute force, broken promises, bad faith — but I am certain that right shall prevail."

And from Salt Lake City Senator Key Pittman spoke words which ought not to be forgotten: "Possibly Hitler will destroy the Polish nation, but he will never win. He has proved the instability of dictatorship. He is unworthy of the German people."

Now war had again come to Europe, and the Polish campaign was but the gruesome prelude to the great conflict. Hitler had wanted this war. He had long planned for it. Ribbentrop who had assured him that England would not fight, who had predicted that the "Polish incident" would be a matter of days, like the occupation of Austria and Czechoslovakia, wanted it.

Who else wanted it? The army? Some of the leaders, undoubtedly. Not all. The steel barons? Some of them, yes, but not many. The people at large most certainly did not want it. Many individual Germans were again caught by surprise, as in 1914, befuddled and confused by nazi propaganda, but even among the rabid nazis, most had thought that the "Fuehrer's" lucky star could continue to carry him through his adventures, without shooting.

In cafés everywhere the newspapers were being devoured avidly. People were stunned. One could sense the anxiety in their minds. What would the British do? and the French? All borders were manned. The first death notices came in from the Polish front. I received one directly, from Irma, my school-teacher friend. Her younger brother was one of the early casualties. I wrote to convey my sympathy. Then she came to see me, in tears.

"I never would have thought this could happen," she cried. "Never!"

"In what state of mind was your brother when he left you?"

"Oh, he was so confident! Full of enthusiasm. He believed this to be a just war. Danzig is a German city, and the Poles had ill-treated our people in the border districts. You know that."

The poor thing had to justify her own misery.

"Irma," I tried to calm her. "This is only the beginning. Is a border issue really worth it? You mustn't believe all the papers tell you."

Irma did not understand. There were many like her, over-whelmed by the suddenness of it all. Many more, however, could see through the maze of propaganda. Public reaction to the war news was not at all what Goebbels wanted it to be. The Danzig issue had always been popular and the Poles were generally blamed for most of the troubles at the Eastern border, ever since the last war. But die for Danzig? Die for the "Corridor"?

"No," admitted Irma, "It isn't worth our blood. There must be another way to adjust these claims."

There might well have been another way. Now, of course, it was too late to think of it. Now things had gotten completely out of hand. The diplomats were packing up, leaving the job to the generals.

In less than three weeks the German juggernaut of a million men conquered Pilsudski's Poland. Half a million poorly equipped Poles suffered a smashing defeat at the hands of an enemy who was their superior in numbers as well as in arms. The "suicide garrison" of the Westerplatte near Danzig held out six days under constant shell-fire, but while that small group of heroic fighters made a stand, the main body of the Polish army was in retreat before the huge, mechanized force of the Germans which sped on relentlessly. Soon Germany's eastern borders of 1914 had been restored. Silesia's coal fields and industries were again in German hands. Then Warsaw was shelled and encircled. The ordeal was over.

Our radio friends in the beleaguered city held out bravely in the midst of the worst gun-fire. Every broadcast specially arranged for American listeners seemed an imposition on those people who were fighting for their lives. And yet, they did not turn down a single request until their station's voice had been silenced. When Soviet troops crossed the Polish border in the East, on September 16, the battle had become hopeless. Then only did radio Warsaw start dismantling equipment to prevent its falling into enemy hands, and most of the staff moved on to Wilno.

Edmund Rudnicki, the producer was left behind. He refused to leave when all the others left. I hate to think what may have happened to him. Always I shall remember his smiling face and how he used to tell the stories he had picked up in America, good-naturedly and with real human understanding. He was as kindly a soul as I have ever met, and as brave.

After Hitler had staged his victory parade in battered Warsaw he saw the foreign correspondents.

"I only wish," he said, "certain statesmen who want to turn the whole of Europe into such shambles as these were aware of the real meaning of war!"

Whereupon he flew back to headquarters.

The next day came his offer to stop hostilities on the western front, in a speech broadcast from the Reichstag. Both London and Paris said "no" emphatically. The first peace offensive had failed.

A few weeks later I saw Poland's grand old man, Ignace Jan Paderewski in Geneva. Previously I had had the unforgettable experience of arranging his broadcast to America from Lausanne. When I had asked him what his wishes were with regard to the studio setup, he reflected for a moment and then replied:

"Just so long as I can remain by myself, all alone, it'll be all right."

He finished smoking his cigarette before walking up to the grand piano. When the engineer gave him the cue and the circuits were opened for the direct shortwave transmission to the NBC in New York, his venerable face was aglow with light as though he had been inspired for the performance. His eyes were closed when he touched the keys, and then the notes his master hands evoked from the cords of the instrument carried Chopin's score across the Atlantic, a majestic outpouring, as it were, of Poland's soul, of all its sorrow, grief, and beauty.

Now he had come to attend the last session of the League of Nations, the last one for the duration of this war. Finland's complaint had just led to Russia being deprived of her membership. Paderewski sat in the diplomatic gallery of the council chamber listening attentively while the vote was taken. He had no word of comment on the decision, but kindly smiles for the many well wishers who gathered around him. Then he took the train to Paris.

When he passed away in New York, these were his last words:

"Poland shall live again. . . ."

*　　*　　*

# Chapter 18

## THERE WERE TWO FRONTS

THE morning Warsaw fell I mentioned the news to the elevator man in my Berlin hotel.

"Oh, really?" he said gingerly, "Then there'll be peace soon, maybe."

The sentiment of the people could not have been expressed more exactly. Now that Poland was crushed, they hoped for an early end of the war. There was no hatred of England, none of France. As in the case of the anti-semitic campaigns, the war spirit had to be whipped up, and Goebbels found it a hard job. The victories in Poland left the people cold and unresponsive, and the news that was now trickling across the eastern border made them shudder. Even nazi fellow travelers began to wonder whether they had bet on the wrong horse, when they heard of Himmler's "elite" battalions swarming through the conquered lands on the heels of the regular troops, arresting, torturing and executing civilians, wholesale. Martial law was covering up the most heinous of crimes against a beaten, helpless foe.

Otto Weltin had relatives in Poland who were Polish nationals.

"The other day," he told me, "a German railway man came to see us to bring greetings from our cousins in Poznan. So far they have not been bothered, but the man was terribly upset. He said what the Gestapo was doing to innocent Polish people was outrageous. If he could help it, he never wanted to go back."

There were others receiving reports of this sort, reports of mass executions, of brutal persecution of Polish Jews, of wanton discriminations against the conquered people. It echoed experiences of the early Hitler days when Himmler set out

240

gagging, shackling and ill-treating his German victims, but now all this happened on a huge scale in another land.

Irma, too, had heard of it when a young officer who had served under her brother came to see her in Berlin to bring news of the last hours of the deceased.

"It sounds horrible," she reported to me. "And I believe it because this lieutenant is sincere. How is it possible? Our army leaders can't approve of it. The Fuehrer would certainly stop it, if he knew."

Of course, I disagreed, but I wondered if she meant what she said.

"Goodness, you don't think he'd approve of such brutalities, do you?" Irma went on.

I did not tell Irma the story I had heard from another army officer just back from Poland. It told of a German major and a Himmler guard who had been court-martialled and sentenced to face a firing squad because of the cold-blooded murder of three Polish women. On appeal Hitler had not only personally squashed the sentence but even promoted the men.

Those who knew the truth were horror-struck and indignant.

"I wish I could talk to that fellow Werner," I said to Weltin. "What do you suppose a man of his caliber thinks of it all?"

"We're having another get-together in Karl Nord's 'cave,'" answered Weltin, "and Werner is coming, too. Next Monday, at nine. I'll pick you up and we'll talk about it there."

Now I knew something of Werner's background. He was a veteran of the last war, and had earned many promotions. His sympathies had been with the democratic regime all along, but he had kept his contacts with the officer class.

Nord was as jovial as ever. His "cave" had been converted into an air-raid shelter. The keg was still there, and there were pretzels and smokes, all that could be had without ration coupons. Of our old gang only Werner Pratt, the stage-manager, had come.

"They'd indict Schiller for high treason if he lived today!" he remarked bitterly.

After Werner had arrived it did not take long before we were in the midst of a heated argument. "I heard a report of hostage executions again today," said Weltin, "and it came from an eye-witness. The details I have not the heart to repeat. Why does the army let that sort of thing go on?"

Werner was puffing at his pipe. We all looked at him. Weltin's question was uppermost in the minds of all of us.

"The worst of it is," he replied after a while, "that you get only part of the story. I see official reports every day that are simply revolting."

"And no one does anything about it?" I asked.

Werner was pale. He was struggling with a deep emotion. Then he said, almost under his breath:

"We were caught in a trap. The Gestapo is above the law."

There was another moment of silence. Then Weltin spoke again:

"Gestapo! Is that an excuse? Gestapo above the courts! Gestapo above the army! Gestapo *ueber alles!* You can't tell me that your powerful, well organized and highly trained Reichswehr has to stand for this outrageous situation, against its will!"

"It isn't as simple as that," Werner came back. "First of all, we are at war. We may deplore it, we may blame it on the nazis, but it's a state of war we are now confronted with. Secondly, things get out of hand. The hoodlums are too numerous."

"You mean to say," I objected, "that the army does not dare make an issue of it with Hitler? Is that what you are driving at?"

"It's putting it somewhat bluntly . . ." hesitated Werner.

"But it's the truth, the sad truth," Weltin agreed. "It's the same at home. These Himmler guards have become an actual nightmare to all of us. They are the brutes we've loosed on those poor Poles!"

"Do you realize," continued Werner, "that this is really Hitler's private army, his Praetorian Guard kept in readiness for the Third Reich's doomsday? There are hundreds of thousands of them. They spread all over Austria, Czechoslovakia, and now Poland. They are the 'Fuehrer's' fairhaired boys and he has them all equipped with modern weapons. Many of our military leaders are as much shocked by what is going on as you people are. Others are just callous, indifferent, and selfish.

Others hope that by winning victories they can secure such influence for themselves that eventually they will have the power to tell Himmler where to get off."

Everybody jeered at this point.

"It may well be the other way around!" observed Karl Nord. "Some day Himmler may be the one to tell the army which way the wind blows!"

"Let's look at the facts," I insisted. "This campaign in Poland was not a Himmler affair, was it? The army organized it and put it across. They were the ones dropping death on Warsaw."

Werner interrupted me.

"The bombings, you must remember, are Goering's business. He is the Luftwaffe boss, and his men are trained according to the ruthless nazi code."

"The infantry and all the other troops weren't missionaries though, were they?" observed Weltin. "And they are doing the job, obeying every order, good or bad."

"In the long run," added Karl Nord, "the men are bound to be taken in by the warrior atmosphere. They will lose their fears, their hesitations, even their humanity. Himmler will gain the upper hand completely, and the longer this war lasts the more securely will he take hold. God help us all, if it lasts too long! The nazis are beasts and they are determined to make beasts of everybody else."

"Unless," said Werner, "Hitler is stopped!"

"Who will stop him? Who can?" Weltin asked eagerly.

"It can't last," sighed Frau Nord.

"When it is darkest," concluded Werner Pratt, "you see the stars best. We must not give up hope."

I walked over to the subway station with him. The streets were blacked out. The skies were overcast.

"No stars tonight," I observed.

"No, but they are there," replied Pratt, "beyond the clouds, and we'll see them again. Some day!"

\* \* \*

Few people realized, as Werner Pratt had that night, that the war wasn't over, that the surrender of Poland was not the end of it. The first winter of war was approaching, a long, dreary German winter, but the western fronts were quiet.

There were peace rumors afloat almost constantly. They were wishful, for the people had enough of the war, more than enough. Austria, Bohemia, Danzig — these were issues the people understood emotionally. "Greater Germany!" "The reunion of all Germans!" were convenient slogans. It was another matter when it came to France and England. There were no German brethren to be liberated there. The Polish war had certainly not been popular. The war in the West was far less so.

Herr von Werner had dropped a hint at Karl Nord's house that only now were the Allies getting ready for war in earnest. The people as a whole began to sense it when naval engagements became more frequent. The blockade was effective. Merchantmen were sunk by the hundreds. Neutrals began to suffer heavily. Again it was a question of the freedom of the seas, and American shipping was heavily involved.

I had had some fairly quiet weeks at my desk in Switzerland when late in the fall of 1939 a radiogram from New York put me on a "hot trail" again.

"City of Flint in Russian waters. Wish you check."

That was not much of a clue. Newspaper reports had first referred to the daring American freighter when a German cruiser captured her in Polar waters on October 21, as a supposed contraband carrier. With a German prize crew aboard, and the nazi flag at her stern, she was commandeered to Kola Bay on the Arctic. There had been no dependable news of the ship since. Following the New York lead, I decided to fly to Moscow, with a faint hope of locating the boat at Murmansk.

It was not my first visit to the Soviet capital and I remembered that it had always been difficult to establish contacts with the Russian authorities. Kipling's words on the East and the West remain true, "and never the twain shall meet." Even in this modern world when the physical approach between nations is so much easier than ever before, man remains a stranger to man.

One of my first attempts to open an avenue of understanding between America and Russia had been the broadcast arranged on the day the Soviet government was formally recognized by the United States, November 16, 1933. Maxim Litvinov, then Soviet Commissar of Foreign Affairs, had come to

Washington to complete negotiations with President Roosevelt, and I happened to be in New York.

"Get that Russian!" ordered the program director at NBC, as though it was a routine proposition.

I had met Litvinov on previous occasions, at diplomatic conferences, and I knew his secretary, Constantine Oumansky, now the Soviet Ambassador to Mexico. Litvinov was a man amenable to suggestions, an interesting conversationalist, and appreciative of the good things in life. In Washington he could sometimes be seen in a pensive mood walking along the paths of a public park, holding a cane in hands crossed behind his back.

Oumansky was more of a realist, a practical man without illusions who never liked to cross bridges before getting to them. When I talked to him about a broadcast he thought it was fantastic. It was like talking about a trip to Mars, wasn't it? Finally, to make it tempting, I suggested a two-way conversation between Moscow and Washington.

"Suppose it could be done," said Oumansky. "To whom would Litvinov talk?"

"Why, Kalinin, perhaps, or Stalin, or Voroshilov," I suggested.

"Is that all you want?" scoffed Oumansky. "Don't you know that not one of them speaks English?"

"They don't?"

"No, Sir."

We paused for a moment. It looked like a stalemate.

"Really, not one of them?" I questioned once more.

Oumansky became reflective.

"Let's see. Of course, there is his wife, but . . ."

"His wife? Great! Just what we want. But will she accept?"

She did, and her husband was plainly enthusiastic.

Litvinov was in conference with President Roosevelt at the White House when he was called to the telephone. The call was from his secretary.

"We've got Moscow, clear as a bell," Oumansky informed the Commissar.

Litvinov rushed to the studio. "Give my regards to Madam Litvinov!" the President had told him, and the simple phrase inaugurated wireless communication between Russia and the

United States. Then there was talk about the weather, about their state of health, and about Junior Litvinov just home from school. The girls in NBC were astonished that a Russian should talk with his wife "just like any other husband!"

This memorable broadcast turned out to be the first and last one ever carried from the Soviet capital to the outside world, uncensored. To us it had been a "special event," a new experiment in communications, a thrilling adventure into unknown spaces, and we had hoped it would open at least one of the many gates hiding Russia from the world.

"There is the language barrier," said the program manager in New York, "and there is politics, but there is also great music, and there are lots of things we want to know about the Bolshies, how they live, what they think. See what you can do."

The gentleman had no idea how hard the sledding was in Moscow for anyone accustomed to American methods. I sat through endless conferences, and argued with officials who no doubt were quite amused by my zeal, but did not show it. I waited and waited for decisions that never came, although I had explained at length how we conceived of program exchanges, and how anxious we were to present radio versions of Russian life to American audiences. Most of my efforts came to naught or brought only meager results.

"Moscow," I reported to New York, "is the hardest nut to crack."

"Crack it!" the program manager flashed back unimpressed.

On my arrival in Moscow this time, I was again confronted with the usual stone wall of official aloofness. The Congress of the Supreme Soviet was in session. Worker and farmer delegates from all over the Soviet Union had assembled behind the crenellated walls of the Kremlin, in the historic hall of St. Andrew where once Czarist society used to gather for sumptuous festivals. Ruby soviet stars shone from the slender spires of the Kremlin towers, and at regular intervals "Great Ivan," the carillon, rang out the International. Neon lights around the Red Square reflected the profile of Stalin.

Moscow street scenes to me had always been fascinating. As a rule they were drab to the Western eye. There were no fashionable districts. Show window displays were almost unknown and anyway, there was little to buy. The people were dressed simply. "Looks" counted for little. Most of the passers-by seemed busy. They walked along paying little attention to one another. They gave the impression of being careful not to meddle with one another's business. It's enough, these men and women seemed to think, to worry about one's own affairs.

At the Metropole Hotel, Natalia, who served as my interpreter during my first visit to Moscow in 1932, was still on duty. Each time I came to Russia I found her in a different job. This time she was handling accounts for the official tourist agency; but tourists are scarce in times of war.

"Not much doing, is there?" I asked.

She smiled.

"Oh, there is always work."

Russians are not used to extreme statements. It can never be hopelessly bad for it has been worse; and it can always get better, can it not? I found this philosophy widespread. Those few who came in touch with foreigners were following a strict line of conduct, refraining from what could be construed as loose talk.

"What is there new I haven't seen?" I inquired of Natalia. She was a woman of about thirty, slender, petite, with expressive dark eyes and a winning smile.

"Oh, the subway!"

"That's right. I didn't have a chance to see it the last time I was here."

"You mustn't miss it," Natalia said proudly. "It is magnificent. There is nothing like it in the world!"

"How do you know?"

"I know."

That last sentence was spoken condescendingly as though I just did not appreciate the finer values. Natalia had never been abroad. She knew little beyond what she had got out of her doctrinaire school books. Yet, she had a sincere pride in what her people were doing, a perfectly natural pride, though it was indiscriminate.

"I also want to have another look at the godless museum," I remarked.

Natalia became formal.

"I'll get you a ticket, if you wish."

"Thank you. I have a friend who will take me tomorrow."

These anti-religious mockeries which formerly had been part and parcel of ordinary guided tours are now relegated into the background, but they will be remembered as exhibits of incredible ingenuity. I had often watched the people going by the graphs and posters and technical displays meant to prove the "foolishness" of all religion. Some inspiring ikons were hung on the walls in between, and when the guards were not around, one could see peasant folk making the sign of the Cross in front of them and saying a furtive prayer.

"The soul of Russia is still *soborny,* that is all-embracing in a spiritual sense," said Father Leopold Braun when I saw him that night. This lone American priest of Moscow had been through the whole phase of the slow, but steady reawakening of the religious spirit of the masses.

"No people can truly live, if it is confined to the superficial realms of politics and economics, and this applies to Russians even more than to other peoples," he added. "But the pendulum is now swinging back from its extreme position. There will be a renaissance."

The heroic missionary knew more of the people of Russia than many a diplomat. They came from afar to meet him, mostly at night, to have their babies baptized secretly, to seek his counsel and material help.

No one who has seen these Russian people, at work or at play, can help loving them. To me they seemed so helpless, so careworn in their constant struggle for the bare necessities of life, and yet so unspoiled in their ways. There was a shy, even dejected look in many faces, and again an expression of childlike wonderment in others. Of course, Russia is more a part of the East than of the West. The masses are fatalistic. They have never known the better life, the true freedom of a living democracy. They are grateful for the modest gains they have achieved at so heavy a price.

And they are heroically patient. Patient when they have to ride in street cars that are constantly taxed beyond capacity; patient when they have to live in over-crowded apartments; patient when they stand in long queues day after day, waiting just to buy the afternoon paper, or a head of cabbage, waiting at government offices to get passes, as indispensable as the daily bread, for travel, for hospitalization, for practically every move they make. There is no grumbling. They just wait, the old and the young, the women and the men. There are no high and low. They are all low. And they know that for most of them it will always be so as it has always been. The nostalgic sadness of the Volga boatman song is all over Russia. The tragic note of Dostoevsky, the tormenting quest of Solov-yev, the suffering of mankind as expressed in Tolstoi is all over Russia.

There was a practice blackout the day I arrived. The pact with Hitler was still in force. To most Russians, as to the rest of the world, it had come as a surprise. It was hard for them to make out the motives behind it.

"All the people want," said one of my American friends who had lived in Moscow as a language teacher for some time, "is to stay out of the war, but they fear the nazis."

"In spite of Stalin's pact with Hitler?"

"That pact was born of the desire to remain neutral, and not to be drawn in."

"The sudden about-face must have been a shock to many, though."

"It was. Almost overnight text-books in the schools were revised. The tenor of radio broadcasts changed. But you will notice, the swastika has not invaded Moscow. It is to be found nowhere, except on nazi embassy flags!"

"Strictly a marriage of convenience, isn't it?" I concluded. "They are the ones that break up easily!"

For the present, of course, playing with Hitler served a purpose, and I was not surprised to find no mention at all of the "City of Flint" in the Moscow papers. It was an embarrassing incident which might have caused trouble with both America and Germany, so every effort was made to dispose of it quietly.

Over American Ambassador Lawrence A. Steinhardt's protest, the merchantman had been released and she had slipped out again, with the German crew still in command, to parts unknown. The Soviet authorities, not wishing to be involved with any of the belligerents, let her go.

As the ship had left Russian waters there was little for me to do but to pursue her elsewhere. I decided to take the next

plane to Stockholm. On previous occasions I had travelled by
train to Leningrad and then over the border to Finland. It
was always a unique experience to cross that frontier line into
the western world. The contrast was even more marked if one
covered the distance between Moscow and the Swedish capital
by air, some fifteen hundred miles in little over five hours.

It was pitch-dark when I got up, and bitter cold. I drove to
the Moscow air-port through flurries of snow. Early risers all
huddled up in woolen scarfs, were hurrying to work. Many
were already standing in line at the stores, to buy food. On the
runway the plane of the Finnish delegation which was nego-
tiating with Molotov, stood poised for another take-off. A German plane was parked nearby.

It was a dismal day, but the Soviet pilot who was wearing
the decoration of the Red Order of Lenin on his lapel steered
clear up to the five thousand foot level, beyond the heavy ceil-
ing of wintry clouds. The trip was really but a hop across the
Baltic Sea. I was happy when I reached teeming Stockholm,
queen city of the North, bathed in the twilight of a wintry
sun.

Swedish radio friends welcomed me with the information
that the "City of Flint" had been reported from the North
Cape, where we had originated a weird broadcast not long
before, and that now she was headed south, sailing along the
Norwegian coast in an attempt to elude the British blockade.
There was no time to lose. I rushed on by train as fast as I
could and arrived in Norway's capital just as the phantom
ship pulled in where she was not expected at all, at Haugesund.
The day after, she reached Bergen, proudly flying the Stars
and Stripes. Her epic voyage had come to an end when the
Norwegian government decided to release the ship to her
American master, interning the nazi crew.

It was a lucky break, for now I could establish contact with
Captain Joseph A. Gainard. Within a few hours after his arrival at Bergen I had him broadcast his experiences to the
folks back home.

In concise seaman-like fashion the plucky skipper told what
had happened to his ship while she was chasing about between ports. He himself had foiled the nazi plan to turn her
over to a German prize court, by maneuvering across the three-

mile limit and then staging a single-handed surprise attack on his captors, knocking them out of control.

"Some of those fellows," he added with a twinkle, "seemed pleased to find a neutral haven!"

Two months later the "City of Flint" was on her way home again. In Washington, Captain Gainard was awarded the Navy Cross for distinguished service and the Congressional Medal. In 1943 his ship was torpedoed and sunk by the Germans in the Atlantic. Soon after that the Captain, who had retired some time before, passed on to his eternal rest.

\* \* \*

I should have liked to linger on in Oslo, but it was time to get back to the office. Crossing Germany on the way to Switzerland, I stopped over in Berlin, to check up on things.

"Well, well," Hada greeted me at Broadcasting House, "how's the Moskovite?"

The undertone in his voice was sarcastic, but formerly it would have been belligerent. How quickly the picture had changed! Since August 21, hammer and sickle had been admitted to the social register of the hooked cross, and the *Mein Kampf* version of the rulers of Russia was tacitly shelved.

I could not argue this out with so stubborn and dogmatic an opponent as Hada. Like all the hitlerites, he was swayed by prejudices and pet peeves. In the case of Russia, too, they were liable to vary with the weather.

I changed the topic. "Anyway, you people seem to be just as pleased as the Russians that the 'City of Flint' episode is out of the way."

"Sure, one headache less!" laughed Hada.

He did not want to concede that Berlin had no desire to jeopardize American neutrality, if it could possibly be helped; 1917 was still too fresh in everybody's memory.

"Don't you think," I asked, "that this is a good time for you people to make a statement of policy? The Norwegians saved you quite a bit of trouble when they released the 'City of Flint,' but your navy is sinking neutral ships right and left."

"Not our fault, is it?" objected Hada who had been rather cocky ever since the Polish war. "They are warned to stay out of the war zone."

"Are you going to have another Lusitania case?" I persisted.

"We don't care," Hada brushed me off. "We've got to keep the sealanes open at any cost."

"Even at the cost of ultimate defeat?"

"You are crazy! We know we will win this war. Look at the western front! It's a *Sitzkrieg,* a sit-down war, with no one fighting. The French and the British as well, know that we can hold out as long as we like."

"Not everybody feels that way," I challenged him.

Hada looked at me.

"All right. You want to go and see for yourself?"

"Certainly, if you'll let me go."

There was an angle of prestige in Hada's suggestion. He liked to show his influence in putting things across, so he got busy. Early in December I received word that permission had been granted for a broadcast from the Siegfried Line. New York decided to take it on Christmas Eve, tying in with a similar pickup from the Maginot Line.

When I arrived in the combat zone, south of Karlsruhe, the *Sitzkrieg* atmosphere was evident enough. There were tank-traps, gun towers and barbed wire fences, but though it was an active battle-front, there was no action.

"All we see down here is minor skirmishes," explained the captain who had been assigned as my guide.

I had visualized this front expedition in a more martial light, but the Karlsruhe sector was really quiet, and there were no secrets to discover. I was not restricted in any way and was allowed to climb over cat-walks and ditches as much as I pleased. No one even mentioned blind-folding. When we finally reached the banks of the Rhine, it was thrilling to stand on slopes affording a clear view of the other side of the river.

"Watch out!" warned the captain. "They might shoot!"

But only the sound of French rifle practice could be heard in the distance. Had it not been for that far-off rumble, I might have had the illusion of watching some peace-time maneuvers.

That very afternoon German soldiers were practicing Christmas carols on their accordions. On the other side of the river French soldiers joined in lustily, shouting "Merry Christmas!" across the water. Christmas trees which were clearly visible to the Germans, had been set up on their pill-boxes. There was no problem of language. The French troops in those parts were mostly Alsatians familiar with the tongue of their opponents.

Dinner was served in "Bunkershausen," a fancy name given to a military reservation centering around a main line of fortifications. *Bunker* was the name for a new type of iron-reinforced, concrete pill-box, thousands of which formed the Siegfried Line. The commander lived in a block-house hidden away amidst fir tree woods, and there he welcomed our radio group for a homey Christmas party. Goose was served with the season's trimmings, and a local wine made everybody feel warm and chummy.

By nightfall I was anxious to get going. Everything was set for the broadcast. I checked with the engineers. They had strung telephone wires from Karlsruhe to "Bunkershausen," so we were connected directly with Berlin, and thence with New York.

At the given hour the cue came through as planned. NBC was ready. A portable microphone had been set up right in front of the pill-box we had selected as our emergency studio. I took over. Now I could see the engineer's flash-light giving me the "go-ahead" from the amplifier car near-by.

"Hello, America!" I opened my commentary. "The Siegfried Line is calling!" Crawling on the ground, I slowly entered the pill-box through a small passageway, so small in fact that I had to bend very low, not to knock my head against the iron bars. Presently *O Sanctissima* was heard. Twelve soldiers had gathered around a table in the center chamber. There were gas-masks and steel helmets on the shelves. Cots were strung along three sides. In the corner stood a gaily decorated Christmas tree.

To describe such a scene, straight from a European battle-zone to far-away America, and on Christmas Eve at that, was more than an ordinary experience. But even more revealing was the contact with these soldiers and officers. They liked the idea of the broadcast to the United States. Some had relatives there and wanted to be remembered to them.

As for their enemy — somehow he didn't seem real.

"We get along swell with the *poilus*," said one of the German boys. And when they sang their songs there was no war-like spirit in them, just a longing for home and for the girls they'd left behind.

Indeed, this was a *Sitzkrieg*. War on this front had not yet started in earnest.

In talking to the higher officers I was struck by their reticence about politics.

"We are soldiers," explained my guide, the Captain. "Our business is the war."

Beyond that there seemed to be little for these men to think about. Their minds were attuned to a traditional patriotism which could be applied to any ruler, to the Kaiser, to a democratic president, or even to Hitler. In that very obtuseness lay the danger of their becoming willing instruments of a political power operating like an infernal machine. Hitler needed such instruments. If they were not available, he would create them. He was determined to fashion the armed forces of the nation after the model of his storm troopers: men submitting mechanically and blindly to discipline, with regimented minds and souls, and trained to obey without hesitation, for good and for evil.

In the car, driving back to Karlsruhe after the broadcast, the Captain sat silent beside me. The countryside was at peace. Christmas trees could be seen behind the windows of almost every farmhouse. In the villages people were on their way to Midnight Mass.

"I'll be late trimming our tree at home," said the Captain after a while.

"Where is your home," I asked.

"Frankfort."

"That isn't so far."

"Oh, no. I am fortunate having holiday leave anyway. Think of the others!"

"I know."

"Away from home — thousands! Fathers, husbands, sons. Who knows how many of them will be alive next Christmas?"

"And remember the others, too, the French, and the British, and the Poles . . ." I said calmly, but with an intent.

The Captain did not reply at once.

"You are right," he said after some thought. "The others, too. All of us. Christmas! Peace on earth and good will to men! And what do we make of it! Why does it have to be this way?"

"Why does it?"

"Oh, who knows! We are caught in the stream and we can't escape. We'd rather tend our gardens and live in peace. Did you hear those boys in the dugout singing melancholy songs of the fireside, of love and romance. At dawn they will be on patrol again, with rifles and hand-grenades. And it's the same with the French. It makes me miserable when I think of it."

"Perhaps that is the answer. People are not thinking . . ."

"I don't know. Even if you think, what good does it do? You cannot change the course of events by just thinking about them. As I said, we are all caught, and there is no escape."

"Not now," I observed. "But there could have been."

The Captain looked me straight in the face.

"You think so?"

I just nodded, and he remained silent.

At the hotel he bade me good-night.

"You are right. There could have been an escape. Now many of us see it."

I shook his hand.

"I am glad you see it, Captain."

But he immediately stood at attention rigidly, saluting.

"We are soldiers. We must do our duty."

Then he drove on to Frankfort, to join his family, for his last Christmas. He fell in Belgium.

# Chapter 19

## THE NORWAY COUP

DESPITE Hada's boast, the state of lethargy and inaction at the western front did not help the nazi regime. Hitler had to "deliver," if he wanted to maintain his prestige with the masses. He needed constant motion. Sitting behind pill-boxes was not heroic enough to divert the people's attention from their plight at home. Clearly, they were despondent over the war. The first few enemy air-raids had been irritating. The black-outs were getting on everybody's nerves. The ruling clique was being more openly criticized within the narrow precincts of many four walls.

Peace rumors were again afloat. Was the nazi war machine going to bog down in a stalemate? Was there a chance of a popular uprising against Hitler now that he seemed stumped?

"With millions of men in uniform," said former Chancellor Wirth whom I went to see once in a while in Lucerne, "the nation is well under control. Soldiers don't revolt unless their armies are beaten."

"Inaction means frustration though," I observed. "Don't you think this is the time when the opposition might get organized?"

"A British industrialist was here to see me a few days ago, with the same question," replied Wirth. "He is not the only one 'feeling out' the belligerents. There are go-betweens all over the place."

"How serious are these efforts?"

"It is hard to tell. Of course, everybody is in agreement on two points: that we should get rid of the nazis, and stop the war before it engulfs the whole globe. Unfortunately, I cannot see a tangible prospect of translating the desire into action, as yet."

"So the war must go on?"

"I am afraid so."

And the war did go on. Its next phase involved Finland, the land of a thousand lakes. When Red Army troops crossed the Karelian border on November 30, 1939, while Soviet bombers flew over snow-covered Helsinki, the "white city of the North," I remembered my last visit there. Riding over the border bridge on the way from Leningrad, underneath a red banner stretching across the tracks, I had arrived at the spic-and-span Finnish frontier station. Neat waitresses were serving fresh strawberries and cream to the passengers. It was like going across a barrier that stood between the East and the West. Here was a progressive land, contented and peace-loving, forging an enlightened destiny of its own, one that gave a promise. Caught between two military rivals, both striving for supremacy in the Baltic, it became a pawn of power politics.

The white-hooded battling Finns who were facing their gigantic foe alone could draw only meager comfort from the speeches made on their behalf in London and Washington. On skis and armored sleds, amidst blinding snowstorms, they fought fierce battles all along their eastern border. After losing fifteen thousand men, they had to give up. Stalin got the strategic bases he had been after.

Molotov had given "security" as the impelling reason for the break with Finland. Everybody knew that the four million Finns were no menace for the Russian colossus of 180 millions; but behind Finland stood Germany. Stalin's pact with Hitler had been born of fear. Now it was bearing fruit. To gain time for their Eastern thrust, the nazis had agreed to the sell-out at the expense of Finland and the Baltic states. Temporarily at least, the Soviet quest of security was met by Hitler's connivance. After a brave fight the land of Sibelius and Mannerheim saw its flags go down to half-mast, on March 13, 1940.

There had been some real war reporting from the Finnish front. On New Year's Eve gun fire was relayed over transatlantic radio channels from an NBC microphone placed in the very trenches which saw hand-to-hand fighting, and reports were broadcast directly from the Rovaniemi sector, high up north. Our radio friends in Helsinki held out heroically under constant air bombardments.

When I phoned Dr. Heikenheimo, the Helsinki program

manager, from Switzerland one night, he interrupted me in a routine way:

"Can you hear the sirens?" he asked.

Distinctly, the wailing sound came over the telephone line.

"It's our sixth raid," explained Heikenheimo quietly.

"Don't you go to the shelter?"

"Oh, it's all right. I can wait. When do you want your next program?"

He reminded me of Rudnicki in Warsaw. Many true heroes in radioland remain unsung. Along with their comrades of the press, they have stood the test.

I had a strange feeling after the Finnish war. Things were ominously quiet.

"Hitler is brooding," remarked Hackelsberger, who was in Basel on one of his periodical visits.

"What's your guess?" I asked.

"Yours is as good as mine, but you should really go up and find out for yourself."

And, after a moment's pause, he added:

"Have you ever met Goerdeler?"

Yes, I had, and I was not surprised to hear that Hackelsberger knew him too, for he was close to most of the prominent business leaders in Germany.

In a sense, Dr. Carl Friedrich Goerdeler was a mystery man. His friends rarely used his real name when talking of him. To most of them he was just "Mr. X." for Goerdeler was recognized in opposition quarters as the potential leader of a movement to overthrow the Hitler regime. It was vital that he be guarded against needless risks.

There were various groups operating under cover, but none was as influential as Goerdeler's. His was a spontaneous movement of German patriots resolved to get rid of the nazi shackles. It was made up of people from all camps, conservatives and socialists, politicians and educators, military and civilians, Protestants and Catholics. All these men and women were fervently pursuing but one aim: to free Germany of the tyrant!

"Mr. X." had rallied them systematically, one by one, ever since he had first clashed with the brown-shirted oppressors in 1936. That was in the sixth year of his term as Lord Mayor of

the city of Leipzig, the center of the famous fairs and home of
the Reich Supreme Court. A year before, when he was on
leave as Federal Price Administrator, he had already reached a
dead end in his dealings with the nazi bosses. His efforts to
make ordinary decency prevail in governmental affairs had led
to constant friction. It was evident that the new rulers had
been out to "get him" ever since. Now they insisted that the
Mendelssohn monument in front of the great concert hall be
destroyed. Mendelssohn was not "aryan!" Carl Goerdeler maintained that that did not matter, and that if they touched the
monument, he would resign. During the night the monument
was removed, and in the morning Carl Goerdeler did resign.
His protest was public, emphatic, fearless.

Soon his counsel was sought by leading industrialists.
Robert Bosch, of Stuttgart, the man who had refused to shake
hands with the "Fuehrer" when he was first invited to meet
him, made Carl Goerdeler one of his executives. From that
time on "Mr. X." travelled the length and the breadth of the
country, looking, like Diogenes, for real men.

He had long foreseen the war and predicted Germany's
defeat as inevitable. To forestall a catastrophe, he spared no
effort warning the appeasers at home and abroad, the blind
who could not see, the selfish who thought they could compromise with evil, the ignorant who were befuddled by
Goebbels' propaganda. And many listened to him.

Abroad many knew of "Mr. X." In London and Paris, in
Brussels and Stockholm, in New York and Washington he
had kept in touch with leaders of government, business, labor,
and education. He visited America in 1938. The Gestapo was
constantly on his trail. They did not trust him. His pretended
business interests seemed to be just a camouflage for suspicious
contacts. So nazi agents shadowed him wherever he went.
But he had good friends in the German army who provided
him with alibis and undercover protection. A very special
Guardian Angel must have been watching over him, too.

By the time Hitler struck against Austria, Carl Goerdeler's
name had become a household word in the chanceries of many
capitals during off-the-record conversations. Among the government leaders who had met "Mr. X." personally were the
King of Belgium, Premier Daladier of France, Secretary of

State Cordell Hull, Foreign Secretary Anthony Eden. All were impressed by his personality.

He was then a man in his mid-fifties, distinguished in appearance, energetic in manner, utterly free of self-consciousness because he was sincere, honest, straightforward. He was a Christian, a Lutheran of high ethical convictions, tolerant of other faiths, a moderate conservative who loved his country deeply, but to whom the moral law and considerations of right and justice meant more than the flag-waving pseudo-patriotism of so many of his own social class.

I had been introduced to "Mr. X." by Otto Weltin who knew him well through his home firm, the Robert Bosch Company, and it meant a great deal to me to establish this contact. I knew others in the opposition camp, but access to the legitimate "underground" was hard to gain. Only those with friends of long standing among them could hope to be taken into the confidence of these brave workers in the dark.

They had started their resistance movement at the very beginning of the Hitler regime, and its motivation was as intense as that of any of the resistance movements organized later on throughout the countries Hitler invaded. Carl Goerdeler had been in the forefront from the beginning. The ramifications of his group were widespread and even penetrated the army general staff, the intelligence services and the dreaded Gestapo. He knew prominent people in every walk of life and in all parts of the country, and they trusted him implicitly. He could meet them on equal footing. It was not long before he had become the focal point of all those willing to do their part when the time would come to throw off the nazi yoke.

Naturally, the organization was loose. There were no meetings. Names were never mentioned over the telephone. But there was a common goal, a strategy to which all the participants subscribed.

"He is the keyman in the picture," Otto Weltin had explained to me after describing Goerdeler enthusiastically. "I'll arrange for you to meet him."

A week later I was on my way to an appointed place in the very heart of Germany. I got off the train at a way-side station and went straight to a telephone booth. Weltin had given me a number which had been easy to memorize, and I had to use an assumed name.

Goerdeler's wife answered the telephone; and she called her husband. He said he was expecting me, and told me to wait at the station — that he'd be right over.

Presently he arrived in a buggy and we rode through the sleepy village, up a road along hilly orchards, to a farm house hidden behind two huge oak trees. Frau Goerdeler, a dainty woman of refined manners, was there to welcome us.

After dinner we retired to the library. There were family portraits on the walls, a whole gallery of them.

He was a country squire, a tall, hardy type, of healthy complexion, and engaging in his demeanor. I was struck by the expression of his clear blue eyes, those of a straight shooter and a gentleman.

In conversation Goerdeler showed a logical mind. He had been a lawyer before entering public life, so he knew how to parry questions. It was a pleasure to hear him talk. His sentences were concise, clearly thought out, full of a sincere conviction.

"Tell me about America!" he said.

He knew many prominent people in Washington personally. His perspective was world-wide, that of a man who had travelled far.

"When this nazi calamity came about," he explained, "I went to Paris and London, to Brussels and other capitals. I know some of the top officials and I warned them, but they did not seem to appreciate my intentions. So much of what I had to tell sounded incredible to outsiders. The Hitler nightmare has to be lived through to be understood."

"But you had facts to tell them, didn't you? Couldn't you get them across?"

"Only to some extent. They knew me long enough to take my word for what I was saying, but they just did not grasp the full significance of events in Germany. Perhaps they felt my thinking was wishful though sincere when I referred to the potentials of anti-nazi sentiment. Perhaps they thought I was gullible when I told them of the many Germans who were as unhappy about the nazi mess as they were. Since I mentioned specific possibilities of breaking through that great wall of propaganda, they may even have felt that I was being used as an instrument to disseminate confusing information about the true state of affairs in the Reich!"

"In the early days, of course, it was all terribly puzzling," I threw in.

"Quite," agreed Goerdeler. "But it was exasperating to me to find outside observers judging Germany with a nazi perspective as it were. Because Goebbels said that all Germans stood behind Hitler, world opinion appeared to be satisfied that he was telling the truth."

A maid entered the room at this point, to serve coffee. After she had left us alone again, Goerdeler went on.

"You see," he said, "to us who have to live in this nauseating atmosphere of lies and distortions it appears incredible that the average person abroad should conceive of us all as being infected by the Hitler poison. Don't they know that we in Germany are ordinary human beings, too? Can they really believe that we are so different from the rest of the world? That there is a streak of nazism in every one of us?"

"Only the misinformed would maintain such a view," I interrupted.

"I hope you are right," he replied. "Still, I did not find many people abroad who understood that we Germans were the first people conquered by Hitler,* and I mean conquered! overwhelmed! shackled! By election frauds, the Reichstag fire, terrorism, and devilish propaganda! We were the first, right here, to suffer from the brown plague while the civilized world looked on almost impassively, and even dealt with the nazi gangsters as equals. Bearing that in mind you will agree that you have to be a German to really hate the nazis."

"I believe you will find many people abroad granting you that Hitler never had a majority behind him," I said. "However, the fact remains that the nation as a whole was swept almost completely by this evil tide, so that now the gangsters really have full control."

"That," agreed Goerdeler, "I admit without hesitation, and I

---

* Anne O'Hare McCormick, about a year and a half later, used a similar expression when she wrote: "Germany was the first country defeated and occupied by Hitler" (*New York Times*, November 27, 1941).

cannot find a single word to excuse the cowardice of so many
Germans who should have known better, who should have
shown what Bismarck called civic courage. Yet, the fact remains, as Vernon Bartlett, the distinguished British journalist
has pointed out, that no nation can be normal that has gone
through so much.\* The war, the defeat, the revolution, the
monetary inflation, the disappointment of those who worked
sincerely for democracy and found no support abroad, the
reparation tangle, mass unemployment. Why, it was really
just too much!"

"Still it does not justify nazi brutalities, racial persecution
and policies of aggression, does it?" I asked.

"By no means," replied Goerdeler. "Do not think for a
moment that I am attempting to excuse things that are intrinsically evil. I have stood up publicly, as you know, to
protest against the indignities of this regime. But I wish those
who point the finger at us now were willing to see present-
day events in the light of history. It has all happened before."

"Certainly not on such a scale."

"Probably not, but this is the mechanical age. There was no
radio at the time of the Sicilian Vespers, otherwise the horrors
might have spread far and wide even then. The Roman
Spartacists had no motor cars, or else they might have won!
Basically, all the terror phases of history are the same. Whether
it's the Jacquerie, or the French Commune or the Indian massacre in the Americas, we must realize that cruelty is a major
element in human nature. In civilized society, man's animal
instinct is subdued, but it's still there. It will spring up and gain
the better of us time and again, if the social and economic balance is upset."†

"I can see your point," I conceded. "But isn't the argument
somewhat specious? Other countries, too, have had their unemployment cycles, their defeats in war. Yet none of them

\* The statement was made by Mr. Bartlett on p. 39 of his *Intermission in Europe*
(New York: Oxford University Press, 1938) — a book which should be considered
essential reading for all those concerned with European problems. Take sentences
such as this: "The history of the treatment of the vanquished powers since the
Armistice is so packed with blunders that one hardly likes to write about it." Or
this: "People still do not realize the extent to which the growth of National
Socialism in Germany has been in direct ratio to the number of empty bellies."
When he contributed his relevant article for the *New York Times Magazine* of
July 23, 1944, Mr. Bartlett must have forgotten what he wrote six years before.
† Cf. Appendix II.

has produced as horrible a monster as Hitler! As you know many feel that this is not an isolated instance, that Hitler is but another expression of the *furor teutonicus*, of prussianism, which time and again has disturbed the peace of the world."

Goerdeler paused for quite a while. He got hold of a pipe, taking his time to light it.

"It is difficult to enter into such arguments," he finally admitted. "Let me just try to point out some of the essential facts that people are inclined to forget. Hitler a German product? Why, he was born in Austria, and some say, partly of Czech stock. Take his cronies. Hess born in Egypt; Darré in Argentina; Rosenberg in Russia; Goering and Himmler are Bavarians; Goebbels is a Rhinelander. Yet, all this hodgepodge is being charged against so-called prussianism! Well, I for one am a Prussian, but I object to being thrown in with that gang!"*

I pursued my argument: "As a rule when this subject comes up, it is traditional Prussian militarism that people think of, the sum total of the philosophies embodied in such men as Colonel Nicolai and General Bernhardi who stand out as preachers of aggression."

"I know. And I can well see how the argument comes in handy to simplify the issue. But don't you think it all depends on the emphasis? Take Russia. Is Dostojevski, Bakunin, or Ivan the Terrible representative of that country? In France, is Robespierre and Danton, Joan of Arc?"

"I should think that all of these, and many others reflect the image of each and every country."

"Of course. Posing such questions suffices to show that in all things human there are not only either-or situations. It is a risky thing trying to define a national character, and we easily succumb to generalizations when we attempt it. Too many of us are inclined to spotlight only the worst in other nations, to use only black paint when brighter colors can be had."

"Unfortunately, Hitler has done his very best to confirm the view of all those to whom the Germans are but Huns and barbarians."

"That I grant you, but when we think soberly we should insist on proper distinctions. As for the Huns, it may be well

* Cf. Appendix III.

to remember that from the fourth century on Germanic tribes were alone in opposing them. And those who like to quote the Nibelungen Song to prove the alleged barbaric strain in the German race should not forget that Krimhild's vengeance occurs at Attila's court in Hungary! Other peoples, too, have their cruel sagas. Take the great epics of Norway. Berserk is a Norse, you know!"

I laughed. "Wait till Hitler finds that out!"

"Oh, he'd build him a monument!"

Goerdeler was now pacing the floor of the large room, walking up and down past his library shelves.

"Look at these books!" he said. "Humboldt, Master Eckart, Leibnitz, Goethe, Kant! Isn't that the true Germany? Yes, I know, there is Treitschke, too, and Nietzsche. Does it not prove that there are two souls in all nations, just as in most individuals? Jekyll and Hyde are multi-national! There are those depicting the *deutsche Michel,* the German 'Mike' as a good-natured, somewhat clumsy simpleton, as a homebody wearing a nightcap, while others conceive of him as wearing the spiked helmet abed!"

"What you are driving at," I tried to sum up, "is that no group of people, and certainly no nation, should be judged wholesale."

"Exactly. When I hear all this silly talk of a German master race which the nazi theorists are spreading I always remember Goethe's *Weltbuergertum* and how strongly his thinking has influenced German literature. Take Schlegel and Wieland, or the tremendous interest we Germans have always shown in the literary and artistic achievements of other nations, indicating our strong desire to assimilate rather than scorn foreign thought."

"Of course, you cannot ignore the pan-German maniacs. The trouble is that they probably made more noise than the sensible people!"

"Crackpots! They talk of *Herrenvolk.* The 'Herren,' the overlords, are there all right, the party bosses pushing everybody around. The 'Volk,' the people, certainly want none of them and their nonsense. World domination? Let nazi scribes rave of it! The German people, I assure you, would be happy, if they could be just free citizens in their own country. They don't want to be hyper-Germans of the nazi brand at all, but just plain people leading ordinary lives."*

That very moment the telephone rang. Goerdeler went to the next room to answer it. He was back after a few minutes.

"They want me in Berlin on Wednesday," he said. "You are to be there too, aren't you?"

"Yes," I replied, "I will be there the day after tomorrow."

"That would be just right. Let me suggest that we meet Thursday morning. I will be at the Eden. Now it's about time for your train anyway, so let us continue next week, if you like."

There was a directness about the man that impressed me deeply. I felt that this was the most important contact I had made in a long time. My own "underground" began to expand!

Again we drove through the hills in Goerdeler's buggy. He held the reins like a man firm in his purpose and unperturbed.

After this first meeting I saw Goerdeler frequently. We had agreed on various cover names which could be used conveniently in different circumstances. Both he and I had to be careful to keep Himmler's men off our trail!

One evening, having just arrived from Holland at my regular Berlin hotel, I found a message which was easy to decode. Goerdeler expected me at his office, in a western suburb of the city. He did not know I was expected that day, but had taken a chance, leaving word for me to call if I was in town.

It was during the first winter of war. The blackout made it

---

* The *Herrenvolk* notion of the nazis and their pan-German precursors was never taken seriously by the majority of the people, and the whole super-race theory was always considered the product of insane brains, by educated Germans. Even in the midst of the present war it was vigorously repudiated by German Bishops, and in the last war its adepts were an insignificant minority although, like cranks and fanatics everywhere, they succeeded in creating constant commotion. The hitlerites, who like to quote Nietzsche as their authority for the theories of racial superiority, ought to be reminded of the pungent passage from *Thus Spake Zarathustra* (part 3, chap. 56,12) which says, "O my brethren, a new nobility is needed which shall be the adversary of all mob and tyrant rule and which shall inscribe again the word 'noble' on new tables!" — Master race concepts are, of course, not confined to Germany by any means. Those who think so might well heed the remark made by Archbishop Robert E. Lucey, of San Antonio, Texas, in the course of a sermon, on March 18, 1943, when he said that "even today many of our citizens cling to the empty myth of the master race. They feel that the man whose skin is brown or black is somehow inferior and must be held in subjection. As though Almighty God were concerned with pigmentation!"

easy to move about unobserved. When I reached the appointed place only a doorman waited.

"The Doctor is upstairs," he said. "Working late again!"

Goerdeler was alone. He was always cordial, pleasantly informal and immediately made a caller feel at home.

"What did you hear in Holland?" he asked.

"Not much," I replied, "except that there is much anxiety."

"Over what?"

"Over Hitler's double talk!"

"I see."

Goerdeler remained silent for a while.

"What is your guess?" I asked.

"It depends on who will take the initiative."

I wondered what he meant by that.

"It has been Hitler's initiative so far, hasn't it?" I remarked.

"That's right," replied Goerdeler. "But what are the Allies waiting for? Hitler isn't going to hibernate forever!"

Goerdeler, normally optimistic by temperament, a man of action who did not believe in sitting back and just letting things happen, was visibly depressed that night.

Finally I asked:

"What could the Allies do?"

Goerdeler got up. Always, when in a tense mood, he used to walk up and down the room, his hands in his coat pockets, erect, but with his head bent slightly as though making a special effort to concentrate.

"You are right," he said. "I suppose I should answer specifically. What could they do? Well, my friends abroad have posed the same question when we made our plans earlier this winter. There never was any disagreement as to the goal. Hitler is Germany's evil spirit. It is imperative that he be removed. But I am not in favor of aping his methods! If he were killed, he would only become a martyr. So that is not the way we must tackle our problem."

"But is there a way so long as he holds all the power?"

"Yes!" replied Goerdeler with that specific emphasis which often made his speech distinctive. "Yes indeed, there is! But we need the army! If we can win over some of the commanding generals, if they will only see what my friends and I see so clearly, that Hitler is Germany's ruin, then they will act. And they are the only ones who can."

"Act? What do you mean by that?"

"It means a coup d'état!"

Goerdeler said it coldly and he was perfectly composed while he said it. Yet, what tremendous import there was in his words! Could it be that he was expressing more than a mere hope?

But then he spoke at length and told me how far the plans of his group had progressed. A trap was to be laid for Himmler. Once the Gestapo chief was behind lock and key, Hitler was to be unseated and put behind bars, too. Everything depended on the cooperation of the army which was to divert a troop movement from east to west. Thus a state of siege was to be clamped down on Berlin while the nazi bigwigs would be completely shorn of their power.

Wouldn't they put up a fight?

Of course, they would. But the people then would be able to rise! If only the army was behind the move! Everything would hinge on that.

And what were the prospects?

"We needed assurances from the Allies as to what support we could expect from them," said Goerdeler.

"You actually approached them?"

"We did. One of my friends is just back from Stockholm."

"And what is the word?"

"Utterly negative! They seem to think it's our funeral! And they don't trust us."

I was fortunate to see Goerdeler that night, just when he felt the need of talking to someone, to a confidant who would appreciate his state of mind. He was plainly upset, but by no means despairing. After lighting his cigar again, he said:

"You can't blame me, can you, if I feel that a great deal depends on who will take the initiative?"

"Certainly not," I answered. "But don't you think that the Allies have a right to expect the first move from your side? You cannot blame them either, in view of all that has happened, if they are reluctant to trust mere words! If some of the army leaders see eye to eye with you, and if they are aware of the tremendous risk implied in their support of the nazi regime, they ought to act on their own, without waiting for assurances and promises from abroad."

"That is true," Goerdeler granted. "But can't you see that the generals, too, are human? To them, it's a gamble either way! With or against Hitler! He has friends among them who will stick by him no matter what happens. Others, the older ones particularly, are hesitant, and they are the ones I am counting on, but they are the ones who need the hypodermic!"

"Then," I concluded, "I am afraid we've again reached a deadlock."

"I am afraid you're right."

Goerdeler did not give up. All through that first winter of war he continued his efforts "underground." The civilians in his camp knew exactly what they wanted. Some of the military did too. General Hammerstein, for instance, and General Beck. Both are now dead, so their names can be mentioned. But there were others, right at the top of the High Command whom Goerdeler knew well and who consulted with him.

Most of these men were uneasy. They were distrustful of whatever bore the mark of the swastika. To them, the victory over Poland meant nothing. They knew that the war had not even started, and they remembered the last war. How could the nation be drawn back from the precipice?

While Hitler was brooding over new conquests the patriots did not give up hope, and their underground network rapidly expanded. They needed help, hypodermics as Goerdeler had put it, and more than anything else, moral support from abroad.

But little of it was forthcoming. Hitler had destroyed all faith in Germany. In the six years of his abhorrent rule he had done a thorough job. On the face of the evidence the world had decided that the Germans were a bad lot, the whole kit and boodle. Few were in a mood to make exceptions. Goerdeler's task was like Sisyphus'.

\* \* \*

When Hackelsberger suggested that I look up Goerdeler again, several weeks had passed since I had last seen him.

"It's just a hunch," Hackelsberger had said, "but I wouldn't be surprised if you found Mr. X. in Berlin right now."

Hunches are important, I thought! So, the next day I was on my way north.

When I arrived at the Anhalter station I checked my bags and went straight to a public telephone booth in one of the near-by cafés. I called the Eden hotel in the fashionable western district where Goerdeler always used to stop. No, said the room clerk, the Doctor was not in town, but he was expected the next day.

The next day was April 4, 1940. When I met Goerdeler he was visibly nervous.

"Let's go across the street to the Zoo Park," he remarked casually.

We dropped our conversation until we had reached the miniature bridge which stretched over the Swan Lake. There we could not possibly be overheard.

"What happened?" I asked.

"They are striking tonight," was Goerdeler's blunt reply.

"Who? Where?"

"German troops are being embarked in Stettin and other ports. They will start out immediately for Norway!"

This was four days before the invasion. The import of the news did not immediately dawn on me. I stood there stunned.

Goerdeler looked at me.

"Don't you understand?"

"Why," I said, "yes, of course. But how will they do it? How can they do it?"

"There isn't anything else I can tell you just now," replied Goerdeler. "Suppose you drop in again this afternoon. Then I'll have the whole story."

When I came back he had it. And what a story! A hit-and-run double-barreled bombshell! Denmark to be invaded. Norway to be occupied. Goerdeler had obviously tapped a general-staff source.

But why was he telling me? I knew I could trust him fully. Still, I felt hesitant. My primary interest was to get the news and to put it on the air. But this news? I could not think of writing it down. There was bound to be trouble for anyone tampering with military secrets even though as a reporter.

"What are the chances of this move?" I asked Goerdeler, who had again taken me to the Zoo Park and was now standing near the main gate, looking out on the busy street, absorbed in his thoughts.

He turned to me again.

"Hitler is putting this over against the advice of his top military advisors," he said. "They think it's foolhardy. Admiral Raeder has threatened to resign."

"What do you think?"

"I think the move will succeed, unless . . ."

"Unless what?"

It seemed as though Goerdeler was in a daze, still under the impact of what he had been told.

"You see," he went on, "these transports will move up through Danish waters tomorrow. Once they leave the Kattegatt they will be exposed to enemy attack."

"That might mean a battle."

"Naturally, perhaps a decisive one, if . . ."

Again he hesitated.

"You mean," I tried to complete his sentence, "if the British are prepared for it?"

This time Goerdeler did not answer.

"I hope you'll excuse me," he said finally. "I think I'd better go and see my friends at once."

"Should I drop in later again?"

"Perhaps you'd better not. There is nothing we can do now. We will have to see what comes of this."

We shook hands. This was a crucial hour for Goerdeler. I understood his anxiety.

"Good-bye," I said. "I will get in touch with you."

On the way back to my hotel I tried to make up my mind. The information I had received was dynamite. I had to consult with someone, but did not feel like remaining in the country much longer. Where could I go? Whom could I talk to? Was Denmark going to be the pivotal point of the war in a day or two? Then the best thing would be for me to go there at once.

I called the airport. There was a seat available on the early morning plane to Copenhagen. I booked it.

It was Friday evening when I arrived in the Danish capital —three days before the invasion. Everything was quiet. No one seemed to have an inkling of the impending threat. I remembered an amusing incident of the year before. Denmark reputedly boasts the largest number of storks in the world, and since these birds play so important a part in our lives, I had made plans to broadcast a "message" from clattering mandibles. I had visions of picturesque nests on dozens of chimneys, but for some reason or other the storks refused to put in an appearance. The broadcast had been set for. Mother's Day — but what a "flop" it was! Now the time of frivolities was gone, but I still could not quite fathom the thought that I had arrived on Danish soil to report a war.

In the morning I had a talk with one of my friends at the American Legation. The United States, it must be remembered, was then still a neutral, and I realized that I as an American citizen, had to exercise the utmost caution in planning my moves. At the same time, of course, it was my duty to make proper use of important information in my possession.

After consulting with my Legation friend at length I decided to pass a warning on to my office in New York, hoping that the date line of the radiogram would be a broad enough hint.

"Stand by," I wired them, "am trailing big story."

While awaiting further developments I reserved transmission lines to Geneva, just in case I needed them for a broadcast. Also, I secured the various visas to proceed to Norway, or back to Germany on a moment's notice, and tentatively booked accommodations on trains and planes in various directions.

Monday morning there were extra editions of the Copenhagen newspapers. The British had mined the Skagerrak during the night! Did they know what was up? After all, the German men-of-war steaming through the narrows couldn't have remained unnoticed, and it was hard to conceal major German embarkation moves from enemy agents.

Perhaps, too, these agents had noticed, during the month of March, the mountaineer troops concentrated in the Berlin area, most of them Austrians openly wearing the Edelweiss emblem. Obviously these troops could not have any duties to perform where there was nothing but plains and sand dunes and water. British intelligence might well have drawn its conclusions from that and it would not have been surprising, if the British mining operation had been decided upon as the counter-move, in an attempt to block Hitler.

The suspense was tantalizing, but later in the morning, a news flash came over the teletype of the radio station, in the old building next to the opera. I had dropped in, coming over from my hotel across the street, when Harald Rud, the press contact man, was hurrying upstairs.

"Come along!" he yelled. "They've just called me to the news room."

There stood three men around the ticker reading the bulletin.

"Not for publication," it said. "Nazi transport planes sighted off the coast. German naval units approaching from Kattegat. British cruisers standing by behind mine barriers."

The story was about to break. Would the Danes clamp down a censorship, too? It was risky to wire New York again. All avenues of communication seemed barred. Here I was with one of the biggest "scoops" in months and unable to deliver the goods!

There was no time to lose. I realized now that I had to wait for an official announcement. Berlin was most likely going to be the place where it would come out first, so I rushed back to the airport. Three hours later I was in a studio again, on "Adolf Hitler Platz."

I went on the air that same night, tight-rope walking! The censors acted innocent, or perhaps they had not received their instructions as yet. They allowed me to say that "an expansion of the war on all the fronts was now in the offing." It was only six hours later when the break finally came.

At five o'clock in the morning, on April 9, the moment nazi troops crossed Denmark's southern border, and while others were being landed on Norwegian soil at the rate of 8000 men per hour, Goebbels' aides phoned the foreign correspondents in Berlin, summoning them out of bed for an immediate press conference. Every bit of Goerdeler's report turned out to be correct.

The poise of the Danish people was amazing. The German landing force in Copenhagen had only been a thousand men. They were steered through the harbor mine fields by an unsuspecting Danish pilot.

"Of course, we are tourist-minded!" said a witty Dane when he heard it.

Professor Niels Bohr, the Nobel Prize Winner, carried on

undisturbed in his Institute for Research in Physics. He had once helped me arrange a broadcast from the laboratory where he was engaged in experiments with atom-splitting. Had he but split one at the right moment, the explosion might have destroyed the invader! Instead, the professor eventually became a refugee in Britain.

For almost a century the people of Denmark had not had a war. They had counted on their avowed neutrality. A year before, their government had signed a pact with Germany which stated that the two countries would "under no circumstances resort to war or any other form of violence against each other." Now the partner was within their gates.

Bravely, the Copenhagen radio carried on in the midst of the sudden crisis. The last words heard were about the nazi bombers flying over the city. At Tivoli, Copenhagen's amusement center, the bright lights were dimmed. Along with black-outs came butter rations in this land of milk and honey. And the storks? None of them were around. It was too early in the year, but perhaps they had a hunch that the nazis were coming!

Norway, too, was taken entirely by surprise. Had the people offered resistance, Oslo undoubtedly would have suffered the fate which later befell Rotterdam. Kurt Braeuer, German Minister to Norway, had invited Norwegian and other diplomats to his legation the evening before to show them a motion picture of the bombing of Warsaw — a plain forewarning in an atmosphere of respectability, between cocktails and demitasses!

A few hours later, in the light of a new spring moon, Oslo was bombed. Only military objectives outside the city, and the harbor defenses were hit, but the roads leading out of the capital were crowded with evacuees. The people who had remained in town watched the nazi troops march down the main avenue, past the same broadcasting house where only a few weeks before I had arranged a trans-atlantic broadcast with Sonja Henie in an atmosphere of perfect normality. Now, after 126 years of peace, Norway, too, was suddenly swept by war.

"All German ships in the Skagerrak and Kattegat will be sunk," said Winston Churchill in a broadcast from London.

But naval warfare was now raging along the whole extent of the Eastern shores of the North Sea and in many of the fjords. The French and the British were facing the tremendous task of invading the mainland from the sea. Narvik was hidden behind a blinding snowstorm. For several days there were claims and counter-claims until it became clear that the nazi air force was supreme. Soon they had conquered the strategic points which could be used as submarine bases and airfields — within three hundred miles of Scapa Flow. On June 10, King Haakon capitulated and became an exile in England.

Major Vidkun Quisling still stands in the public mind as the main factor causing Norway's defeat. To him and to his followers are attributed all the sabotage and "fifth-column" work which seemed a prerequisite of Hitler's success. However, fake orders sent by radio, probably from German cruisers, to the Norwegian military commanders were at least equally effective in creating the confusion at Oslo which ended in disaster. When the spurious character of these orders began to be suspected, it was too late to thwart them.

The "Trojan horses" had played their part in the drama, but they were by no means the only, and not even the main explanation of how fifteen hundred nazis took possession of a city with a population of a quarter million. Only a superior air power could have broken the strangle-hold of the invaders. But the British were unprepared, and Hitler must have known it. When he overruled his generals, he broke the spell again. Many among them had hoped, like my friend Goerdeler, that this daring venture would break his neck. But he won.

# Chapter 20

## AVALANCHE IN THE WEST

AFTER the Norwegian invasion there could be no question that now it was the Netherlands' turn. Diplomatic quarters in Berlin were buzzing and bets were no longer made as to where, but when Hitler would strike next.

Many remembered his sneering remark in a Reichstag speech not long before the war: "The assertion that Germany will soon attack North or South America, Australia, China, or even the Netherlands is on the same plane as the statement that we intend to follow it up with an immediate occupation of the moon!"

"Or even the Netherlands . . ." The reference now began to take on dire significance. It was time to watch the Low Countries. I flew from Berlin straight to Amsterdam.

For weeks the Dutch army had been engaged in constant maneuvers. In the southwestern part of Holland the dykes were mined so the land could be flooded instantly in case of an enemy invasion.

"Do you object to a broadcast from that district?" I asked Colonel Versluys in the war department at The Hague.

"Not in the least," he replied. "We want the whole world to know that we are prepared and that we will fight to defend our neutrality."

To think that a few months before we had "covered" Crown Princess Juliana's wedding to a German prince! The famous Dutch synagogue choir had been heard by NBC listeners coming from Amsterdam, and girl workers in a diamond factory on the banks of the Achtergracht, against the background of the hum and whistle of their motors cutting and polishing the precious stones, had sent radio greetings to the June brides in America.

Our friends at Hilversum had been among the most progressive broadcasters of Europe, setting the pace in the radio art with the finest of studio equipment and the best of radio engineering.

To me, the Hollanders were symbolic of economic and political security, a great colonial power entrenched on a solid foundation, morally no less than temperamentally. Only the refugees that had crossed the borders from Germany were worried and uneasy and found it hard to understand why their hosts were not panicky. Of course, the Dutch were taking their precautions. Queen Wilhelmina had consulted with King Leopold of Belgium. A joint defense of the two countries was being envisaged. Studiously, Holland avoided all but legitimate contacts with the belligerents, depending on her neutrality.

Churchill had warned the neutrals. "Each one hopes that if he feeds the crocodile enough, the crocodile will eat him last," he had said. But in the case of Holland it wasn't that. No attempt was made to appease the potential aggressor.

"As far as is humanly possible," remarked Prime Minister Dirk Jan de Geer in a speech, "we rely on ourselves."

For the first time in almost a century of Dutch history, Queen Wilhelmina signed a decree extending the state of siege through the whole country. On May 6, all army leaves were canceled, and telephone service to foreign countries was stopped "as a matter of precaution." In Washington, Dutch Ambassador Dr. Alexander Loudon was made paymaster for his government, just in case . . .

"If Hitler succeeds," Goerdeler had told me before the Norway coup, "things will run their course, and none of us will be able to do anything to stop the mad whirl."

Hackelsberger, whom I met when I got back to Switzerland, had seen him at his country home the day after the British had given up at Narvik.

"Now Hitler can do anything with the military," he had remarked. "He has taken a chance and won. Now he can gloat and march on. Before he is through marching, Europe will be a shambles."

On May 9, Mussolini's "Cavour," a precocious attempt of his earlier years at dramatic writing, was presented in a gala performance at the Berlin State Theater. Goering was conspicuous in his uniformed splendor. The camouflage worked. At three o'clock the next morning German troops crossed the Netherland border. The Dutch opened their dykes, flooding large sections of the country. Anti-aircraft batteries bagged six nazi planes. But the Amsterdam airport was bombed. "New and large formations of planes are arriving from Germany," said the speaker of radio Hilversum, while Hitler's parachutists were landing at Leiden, at The Hague, at Eindhoven, at Rotterdam. Brussels was raided from the air.

It was almost all over when Ribbentrop sent for the Berlin foreign press in the early morning of May 10. He announced to a horrified world that Germany had issued orders "to safeguard the neutrality of Holland and Belgium with all the military means of the Reich," for, Herr Goebbels explained, they had "plotted" with France and Britain against Germany. Little Luxembourg, too, was to be "protected."

In London, Chamberlain resigned. Churchill took over. British troops landed at Dutch ports. French contingents crossed the Belgian border. Hitler, in an order to his army, declared that "the fate of the German nation for the next thousand years is now at stake." Then he left for the front, and the super-blitzkrieg was on.

Under the command of General Henri Winkelman a half million Dutch put up an heroic resistance along the Yssel and Maas rivers. But soon the German high command announced that Maastrich and Malmedy had been taken, that The Hague was in German hands, and that all resistance was being crushed. Savage fighting was in progress over a two hundred mile front. A ten-minute bombardment left the center of thriving Rotterdam in ruins. Thirty thousand innocent and helpless civilians were killed in this treacherous assault which had been planned to destroy, block by block, one of the trade centers of peaceful Holland.

In Amsterdam, Margaret Rupli stood by for NBC while air-raid sirens were wailing, and enemy bombers were flying over the city.

Over the shortwave circuit connecting with New York she asked:

"What do you want to know?"

"Everything! Just tell us what you see!" replied the program director.

That moment the hisses and screech of falling bombs were heard.

"I've got to run!" said Miss Rupli.

"Oh, don't leave! Let's hear the bombs!" was the program man's reply.

He had some nerve, speaking from the safety of a New York studio!

Miss Rupli probably didn't even hear him for she had scurried for shelter.

The invasion was a thorough job, and even to the point of radio coverage, prearranged in every detail. Mobile vans followed in the wake of the German invaders. They carried complete record libraries of over one thousand Dutch folk songs, sufficient to build programs for at least a fortnight. Announcers and commentators on the Dutch stations were immediately pressed into service, while armed nazi guards watched them at the microphones.

"You don't sound cheerful enough," was the complaint of one of these supervisors imported straight from Berlin. The poor Dutchmen tried hard, but to be cheerful when you go on the air at the point of a gun was asking too much. Soon cheerfulness was provided in "canned," recorded versions, straight from the Reich, and the Dutch announcers had to look for other jobs.

The strength of the invaders was overwhelming. After six days the brave little country was completely overrun. Having suffered the loss of one fourth of its men, the intrepid army surrendered. Queen Wilhelmina, Crown Princess Juliana, Prince Consort Bernhard, and their two daughters became refugees in London.

Hitler's armies marched on. Soon Antwerp, Brussels, Malines, Louvain, and Namur had fallen.

"Conquer or die!" said General Maurice Gamelin in an order of the day.

French and Belgian refugees jammed the roads, terrified by nazi dive bombers. Thousands of roaring tanks were engaged in a death struggle. Total war was over the fields of Flanders and the Champagne. Gamelin resigned, and 73-year-old General Maxime Weygand took over, while British and French forces were in retreat, and half a million of their men in danger of being caught in a trap.

Eleven days after this lightning war in the West had got under way with a fury unequaled in history, Premier Paul Reynaud of France admitted "disaster" in a speech to the French Senate. He promised punishment to those responsible for "unbelievable faults." Fifteen French generals were relieved of their commands in the midst of the battle.

But it was too late. The swastika was flying on the Channel coast near Calais. In an Empire Day broadcast from Buckingham Palace, King George VI called on the British people: "The decisive struggle is now upon us — it is the issue of life or death for all of us." Boulogne fell. Dover was within reach of German long-range guns.

Then, after Belgium's surrender, came Dunkerque. Most of the British expeditionary forces withdrew from the Continent on listing destroyers and barges, through curtains of continuous, pitiless enemy fire from the air. The retreat was a success. It saved a half a million men from annihilation. But the German push toward Paris was now practically unchecked. Everywhere the French lines were crumbling. Fear paralyzed the Army of the Republic. On June 3, less than a month after the offensive had opened, Paris was bombed for an hour. Some twelve hundred people were killed. One of the bombs narrowly missed American Ambassador William C. Bullitt, who was lunching at the Air Ministry.

"God must be with me," he told the President afterwards in a transatlantic telephone report.

The new "Weygand Line" was pierced. "Inasmuch as the enemy still spurns peace," said a broadcast from Berlin, "the fight will be carried on to its total destruction." The German radio could barely keep track of the news bulletins pouring in from the front in a steady flow.

"Bombs fell like rain," said one of the nazi war correspondents.

People started evacuating Paris in a panic. Anti-aircraft guns sounded all over the city. Barricades were put up in the streets. The Paris radio announced that smoke from incendiary bombs was so thick that it completely enveloped the Place de la Concorde. The city was now half empty and totally blacked out at night. The government had left for Tours, while every hour the German iron ring closed more tightly around the capital. Nazi troops crossed the Marne River. Refugees by the thousands were plodding south in a confused and hopeless stream. It was all over. Hitler had conquered his ninth capital since coming to power.

On June 14 Ambassador Bullitt phoned from Paris to his colleague, Mr. Anthony J. Drexel Biddle, United States ambassador to the Polish government in exile, then at Tours. It was 7 p.m. Paris time, and Mr. Bullitt said that the German army was now "inside the gates of Paris, but the city is quiet." Mr. Biddle passed the message on to Washington.

Retreating further before the nazi avalanche, the French government moved its seat to Bordeaux, and resigned shortly thereafter — just five weeks after the invasion of Holland. Marshal Pétain took over. The "grand old man of France," the victor of Verdun who had coined the famous phrase "They shall not pass!" went on the air to tell his countrymen — on the 125th anniversary of the Battle of Waterloo — that he had sued for an armistice. "I have given myself to France," he said, "to better her situation in this grave hour. . . . It is with a heavy heart that I say we must cease to fight."

The armistice was signed on June 22. Three days later, at 12:35 a.m., came the order to cease firing. French flags were at half mast, and Hitler decreed a ten-day holiday in the Reich to celebrate "the most glorious victory of all time."

# Chapter 21

## THE INSIDE ANGLE

I WAS not present in Compiègne when the armistice was signed. Shortly before the event, while my colleagues were carrying on, I had rushed to New York to consult with NBC regarding the future coverage of the war.

People in America were stunned. The holocaust had been too sudden. France's collapse and the deadly peril England was now facing seemed almost unreal in the far-off perspective. As President Roosevelt had put it, on the very day of the invasion of Holland, Americans "thought that a distance of several thousand miles from a war-torn Europe to a peaceful America, that that distance itself gave us some form of mystic immunity."

I was talking to an influential United States senator in Washington the day after Dunkerque, trying to impress upon him the extreme seriousness of the emergency. He was reluctant even to listen to me.

"A world is falling apart, Senator," I said.

"Not our world," he replied distractedly.

"It is one world today, Senator," I insisted, "and oceans are no longer barriers. This is America's crucial hour."

"Unless we are attacked, we should keep out of this mess," he dismissed my pleading. "The war is not of our making."

I was again reminded of Churchill's crocodile story. Now the Europeans had learned their lesson and were wondering whether Uncle Sam would benefit from it. William Allen White's Committee to Defend America by Aiding the Allies was hard at work to put the lesson across. "Stop Hitler now!" was its slogan. But there were too many deaf ears, too many cold hearts.

A high Washington official was well acquainted with Goerdeler, whom he had met on various occasions before the war. I told him of the German opposition to Hitler, and how Goerdeler and his friends were pinning their last hopes on American intervention.

"The nazis are aware," I said, "that the United States can tip the scale, but they are confident we won't come in. They think they will win the war before we are ready."

"I know," answered the official, "but public opinion in this country is not concerned with the war as a pressing issue. People are loath to face the facts. They were disillusioned in the last war and are distrustful of propaganda."

"And Hitler counts on that," I agreed. "He thinks this country is divided and soft. If we could only strengthen the decent elements in Germany by giving them moral support!"

My friend shook his head.

"The time isn't ripe."

Disheartening as it was, it was a correct appraisal of the situation. The American people were not really concerned about the war. They felt safe and protected, and distrusted even legitimate reports from the other side.

"I barely look at the headlines," remarked Jim, the Wilmington garage man, while he was fixing my tire. "Too much propaganda, I tell you."

"It's not propaganda that the nazis are on their way to Paris, is it?"

"Well, I suppose not, but it's not our business. We've got enough trouble at home."

It was the people's voice, one that echoed far and wide. American complacency was the same as it had been in Berlin before the nazi darkness enveloped the hapless land, or in Vienna before Hitler marched in. The "crocodile" took on its victims one by one. Destroying it would have been simpler had they but stuck together before it had grown all of its ugly teeth.

"You don't know," I said to Jim, "what we'd be up against if England does not hold firm."

"Aw, I wonder."

He didn't care, and like so many others was passing the buck. There was a baseball game on that afternoon. That was all Jim and his kind were interested in — until Pearl Harbor. Then, at last, the American people began to realize that both the Atlantic and the Pacific ocean would be dominated by enemy powers, if Germany conquered Britain, and Japan overwhelmed China. Now they could see that this was really our war, and that we could not stay out.

I "clippered" back to Europe after a month's absence, just in time to join a group of correspondents who had been invited by the Berlin Foreign Office to visit "conquered Paris."

My earlier requests to be allowed to inspect nazi-occupied areas had been turned down. Independent observers were not wanted where there was much to conceal. One of the radio bigwigs in Berlin gave me the reason.

"Too many snoopers around," he said.

I had not been keen to attend the ceremonies in the Forest of Compiègne when a prostrate France had to sign on the dotted line. Dictated terms are never respected. France would be better off today, had she been more generous at Versailles, had Clemenceau not inflicted the first humiliation upon Germany on that same spot twenty-two years before, the humiliation which Hitler was now paying back in more than full measure. The lesson of history was lost on the "Fuehrer." Compiègne became just another milestone on the road to revenge. Now that the blunder had been committed, I wondered how the French people were taking it.

I had been in Paris just a few weeks before Hitler struck in the West, in the winter of 1940. Then the city was the least "blacked out" of all the belligerent capitals. Restrictions were unnoticeable. French food was as tasty as ever. Few people seemed to think of impending dangers. To most, victory was a foregone conclusion; just a matter of time, a fruit of the blockade. All France had to do, these deluded dreamers said, was to sit tight behind the Maginot Line. Soon enough hitlerism was going to collapse anyway.

Under the surface of French public life unrest and discord had long been smoldering. Politicians played their irresponsible game in defiance of national unity. Ever since 1934 things in France had been going from bad to worse. It was as though the country's decline had started with Hitler's rise to power. In February the government had intervened to suppress street demonstrations. A tumult ensued in which shots were fired and heads broken.

NBC happened to be short a man at the time, and I was asked to hurry to Paris as a pinch hitter. Edgar Mowrer, then of the Chicago *Daily News*, was willing to help and together we set forth in his car, one of the few still functioning in the huge city. The streets were crowded with an angry mob. To avoid flying stones, and perhaps bullets, we stuck pretty close to the floor of the car while our heads bobbed up and down at the windows like marionettes in a Punch and Judy show.

The circumstances were such that friends in America assumed we had been through all kinds of peril and even fighting on street barricades. One writer spun a nice yarn about one of my eyes having been closed by a stone that came crashing through the car window. Just why the stone should have given me only a "shiner" I don't quite know. The fact of the matter is, nothing happened to spoil my looks!

Edgar and I saw a good deal on that exciting ride, and we were able to give American listeners "an earful." It was a report from the scene, more colorful perhaps than any written account of that day, in a broadcast delivered by candlelight. Electricity had been shut off, and Paris Americans were sitting around at the Ritz in the glow of what served their ancestors in times before kerosene and Mr. Edison.

Those Paris riots were symptoms of more serious trouble to come. After war had broken out, observers on the spot had good reason to distrust the seeming confidence of the French leaders. They knew that French army equipment was inferior and outdated; that there were only some five hundred up-to-date war planes as against Hitler's five thousand; that only one million of the six million mobilized French soldiers was stationed on the northeastern border, with the rest in garrisons at home and overseas; and that the military leaders, torn by petty rivalries, were lost in a fatal atmosphere of *laissez-faire*. These observers also knew that the Lavals and Doriots, the Déats and de Monzies, the Quislings of a later day, were boring from within. They knew that the Maginot Line was no defense against domestic enemies, on the right and on the left. But warnings went unheeded.

Now, just a few months later, I was back in a Paris that had fallen under the conqueror's heel. I returned to a world capital which suddenly and at least nominally had ceased to exist as such. To anyone who had known the city in normal times, in times of beauty and glory, it could but appear unreal. The very waters of the River Seine seemed to flow by Notre Dame Cathedral at a slower pace. Had I half closed my eyes, divorced myself of all that happened in a single month, physically the city would have appeared as majestic as ever. But blinking away an aura of fantasy I had to face the reality. This was definitely not the Paris I, or millions before me, had ever known.

Germans were all over the place, military in armored cars, sentries clicking their heels and giving the nazi salute. The smartness of the Champs Elysée and downtown sections of Paris had disappeared. Paris had become almost a provincial town, without tourists, a city of Parisians, strange to say — that is, if you excluded the conquerors who were having a fling at window shopping and buying perfumes and silks with their "credit marks," the worthless currency created for the use of the German army in occupied territories.

In the air raids, Paris had virtually been spared, but in some of the near-by towns we drove through all was ruin and destruction, the mute misery of war. We saw miles of wheat and barley that was not harvested, and everywhere untilled fields. The farmers had fled, or were prisoners, or had drenched the soil with their blood, leaving widows and orphans behind.

Think of being a prisoner in your own country! It was a sad sight to watch Frenchmen being marched to this or that task, groups of fifty or a hundred, led by one or two heavily armed Germans.

On Sunday I strolled along the avenues in a charmingly bourgeois world. Gone were the "upper classes," the famous writers and artists. The simple people, the workers and the middle class, the *midinettes* and the small shopkeepers, who are so sober and so right in their living, now dominated the scene. What did they know of the crookedness of their politicians?

As I drove out to Chartres, I found a stream of motor-cars, most of them decrepit, and an assortment of trucks and wagons loaded with bewildered people and their household goods. The stories these refugees told were heartrending: of a panic-stricken stampede to escape the bombings.

I was particularly anxious to ascertain the condition of Chartres Cathedral. The famous stained-glass windows had been stored away at the outbreak of the war. They were now replaced by plain glass which allowed daylight to flood the huge nave with an unfamiliar brightness, but the sculptures, the carvings, the spires remained intact. The heart of France was still breathing.

Some day, I said to myself, I was going to be back, in happier days of peace when I could again dig into libraries and archives, searching for my lost French ancestors! In previous years I had discovered some of their traces. If only the war did not wipe out indispensable records, I would yet succeed in completing my family tree!

From Paris we proceeded straight north, by Compiègne, and through the battle zones around St. Quentin and Maubeuge into Belgium, often amidst the shattered ruins of villages and towns which had been through the same ghastly experiences of shelling and street fighting so many times in their history, and twice in this present generation. Evacuees were returning home from the South, to start all over again, having barely saved their lives, and perhaps a few of their belongings.

When we arrived in Brussels I had to think of Cardinal Van Roey who later on was to brave the invaders. "Mercier only barked, Van Roey bites!" the Belgians chuckled in their days of oppression.

The city was teeming with humanity. What was in the minds of all these German soldiers who were strolling around in the business districts? Their behavior was good. Taking snapshots of the city's monuments was a favorite pastime, and shopping, of course. So many of the good things in life which were hard to get, or rationed in Germany, could still be bought in Belgium and France without any restrictions. Candy, silk stockings, leather goods, soaps, perfumes, coffee, tea. All these were welcome presents indeed for wives, mothers, and sweethearts back home. But there was no stampede. Despite the language handicap, the boys managed their purchasing urbanely, and they seemed in good spirits.

I approached some of them at random.

"On furlough?" I asked one of a Bavarian group.

"*Jawohl,*" he grinned.

"Having a good time?"

"Sure."

"Where are you going from here?"

"Don't know."

"Home, perhaps?"

"Oh, I wish we were!"

One of his comrades broke in:

"I'd rather be home today than tomorrow."

"But look at all the food you're getting here!"

"Home is still home," the third in the group averred nostalgically.

In a small restaurant I sat with some marines around a brass rail, husky fellows talking freely. They seemed to be having an argument.

"I bet you we'll be home by Christmas!"

"Wish you were right."

"Don't you see how we are cleaning up all over the place? Another couple of months and England will sue for peace."

"I wonder . . ."

"You do? Why, there can't be any question!"

"Now listen, think what you like, but I tell you this is going to be a long war. We are just starting."

The other men nodded. The optimist ordered another round of beers.

"How anyone can be such a killjoy, I don't understand," he said glibly. "After all our victories . . ."

"Victories all right," another fellow remarked, puffing at his pipe, "but what do we get out of them?"

"Oh, you're a fool! There'll be peace this year, and after we've won, there'll be plenty for all of us."

"Plenty more trouble, I guess," said the smoker.

At that point two M. P.'s could be seen emerging from behind the door. My marines quickly changed the subject to the merits of sundry brandies they had tasted in France.

It was the same story everywhere. The war had gone well so far. Casualties were few. The loot was ample. And yet, there was no exuberance of feeling among the German troops. The average soldier and officer seemed pleased, and even surprised, that there had been no setbacks, but their behavior was one of restraint, sometimes almost apologetic.

All these, of course, were observations preceding the Gestapo stage which was to follow the military invasion. As a rule, foreign reporters had little to do with Himmler's toughs, but after this trip, rather unwittingly, I had a taste of their methods.

I had just returned to Berlin from Paris, and drove up to Broadcasting House. There was a regular period to be filled on the air, and I was late. Dashing past the reception desk, I was stopped by a "Black Guard" on duty.

"*Halt!*"

"What's the matter?" I said.

"Where's your pass?"

I had forgotten the pass. Ordinarily, the guards knew all of the radiomen, and there was no need for passes. This seemed to be a new man on duty.

"Never mind," I shouted, "I've got to make a broadcast."

"Over my dead body!" — and he pulled his gun.

"Are you crazy, man?" I yelled, and beat a retreat.

Fortunately, at that very moment one of the military censors came downstairs. He identified me, and I went on the air just twenty seconds late.

Guards with loaded guns were not only at radio head-quarters but all over Hitler's Germany — in uniform and steel helmets as well as in mufti. There could be no better explanation for the reticence of the rank and file of the Germans to vent their feelings. But Berliners have always been plain-spoken, and somehow they became more daring and articulate during the campaign in France.

Although Germany was winning spectacular victories, the people did not seem to care. When Paris fell, on a week-end eve, bathers were crowding the beaches near Berlin, basking in the sunshine. Newsboys were rushing around to sell their "extras," but few people were willing to relinquish a nickel.

"Paris? Fine. Then the war may be over soon."

"Has the armistice been signed?"

These were typical remarks. Later on they became stereotyped, always with a growing emphasis on early peace. Those who picture a German nation wildly enthusiastic over Hitler's conquests, and willing to go to the hilt in overrunning all Europe, must have read *Mein Kampf* from cover to cover,

but not the mind of Hitler's people. That mind was plainly
revealed the day of the "Fuehrer's" triumphant return from
Paris.

Expecting Berliners to turn out en masse, and stage a rousing
welcome for the new Caesar, I had gone to Anhalt station to
witness the scene. But I found no gay, milling crowds. It happened to be a Saturday afternoon, another glorious summer
day, and most of the people, instead of jamming the avenues
through which the home-coming conqueror was expected to
pass, were jamming suburban trains to reach beaches and resorts. Those left behind were nazi storm troopers, commandeered workers delegations, "Hitler Youth" boys and girls
"on duty," and an assortment of police. They were the ones
lining the sidewalks, waving miniature swastika flags and
shouting their "heils" to the point of hoarseness. All the while,
the plain Berliners were enjoying week-end sports, or hiking
and picnicking in the woods.

"You missed a grand show today," I said to one of my
German friends in the evening.

"So what?" was all he had to offer in the way of a comment.
He happened to be a foreign service officer of the Hitler
government.

"Let them have their fun," he added dryly.

"Them . . ." Yes, that was typical too, that so many Germans
were getting used to speaking of their government in terms of
"they." If "they" were waging war, it was "their" business.
Too bad the people could not do much about it. It was none
of their concern anyway. "They," the nazis, had started it all.
It was "their" responsibility, and the people did not consider
themselves "their" partners. In spite of all of Goebbels' shouting, the German nation was less united than ever. United in
silence perhaps, under Gestapo threats.

* * *

Barely a week before the collapse of France, "the hand that
held the dagger stuck it into the back of its neighbor," to
use President Roosevelt's words. Mussolini, afraid of coming
too late to share the spoils, had declared war on Britain and
France at the last moment. It did not seem to make sense.
As a nonbelligerent, Italy had enjoyed a unique standing. Her
technical neutrality had helped her reap sizable profits from

continued international trade and shipping. Hitler himself had been aware all along that a fighting Italy would become a liability. His general staff had warned him of the inadequacy of the Duce's war machine which could only be kept in gear by German supplies of coal, iron, and other vital materials.

A few days before the Duce flung his trumped-up challenge against the democracies, I had spoken to an Italian friend who had good connections in fascist quarters. Let's call him Vittorio.

"It's going to be next Monday," he said mysteriously.

"What?"

"Well, you'll see."

My informant happened to be in Berlin on a visit. His people had just completed arrangements with the nazi government whereby they were to strike whether Hitler liked it or not. The tip-off could not be disregarded. So I rushed to Rome.

The scene in Italy's capital could well be compared to the one in Berlin. The people indifferent, inert, confused, had their minds made up for them by a small but noisy minority. War was forced upon them. They did not want it. They were afraid of it. Most British were popular in Italy, much more so than the Germans. As I have said before, Hitler at first was considered a joke by the man on the street. Now that he had shown his might, he was feared. German penetration was feared. Businessmen saw the tourist trade ruined. As Churchill put it, correctly and effectively, in his radio message to the Italian nation on December 23, 1940: "It is all because of one man, one man who, against the Crown and royal family of Italy, against the Pope and all the authority of the Vatican and of the Roman Catholic Church, against the wishes of the Italian people who had no lust for this war . . . resolved to plunge Italy into the whirlpool."

And all this, in spite of Hitler's assurances to the Duce, at their last meeting on the Brenner Pass just before the outbreak of the war, that Italy was not expected to join in military activities until after the "World's Fair" in Rome which was planned for 1943.

"By temperament the Italian people are anything but belligerent," I tried to say in a Rome broadcast. "They have a sense of proper balance, and if their reaction to this war is neither false enthusiasm nor serious concern, it is mainly due to their instinctive sense of proportion."

"Well, well," smiled the censor when he looked at my copy. "You think you are smart, don't you?"

"Apparently you don't think I am," I retorted.

"Why, certainly, Mister! But I can't let that pass."

"Then I'd better do it more smartly, eh?"

He laughed.

"I see we understand one another, but this won't do."

"Hmm. So you don't like my paying a compliment to the Italian people?"

"Not if you make it a compliment of insinuations!"

"Suppose I say flatly, the Italian people don't have their heart in this war."

"*Bene!* Precisely. Now you give me your official interpretation of that cryptogram! Sorry, but there is really too much being said between the lines. Why don't you state in so many plain words that the Italian people take this war seriously?"

This I was unable to do, so the blue pencil ruined my broadcast.

Italy was at war with France for a fortnight only. The Duce did not get much glory out of his gesture, but he insisted that after Hitler had enjoyed his triumph in Compiègne, the French armistice commission come to Rome to make a bow. Then, at last, was the order of *cessez-feu* relayed to the battlefields.

The bugle which Corporal Sellier had sounded on November 11, 1918, is being preserved at the Hotel des Invalides in Paris. On Armistice Day in 1935, NBC secured permission to have it taken out of its glass case, to be played in a broadcast across the Atlantic. Now the cease-fire order came by German trumpet calls, preceded by the somber rolling of drums. Hostilities had ended between France and the two axis powers. But Corporal Sellier's bugle is still there. It will be used again.

\*  \*  \*

During this visit in Rome, following Italy's entry into the war, a bugle call of a special brand was sounded for me, personally. Vittorio, who had given me so timely a warning in Berlin of his country's forthcoming plunge, was now back home and asked me to come to see him.

"You'd better leave," said my friend after he had made certain that the doors of his study were shut tightly.

As a rule, we met in his office, but this time he had suggested that I call at his apartment. He was a man of about forty, the prototype of a Roman, with gracious manners, eloquent in his speech, and gifted with that innate dignity reflected in so many Italians of all social strata, the culture of centuries behind them. Through his marriage to a Roman lady no less attractive than himself he had cemented his contacts with the powers that be and often had "inside slants" that proved invaluable. I had every reason, then, to mark his words but I was anxious for an explanation.

"Why should I leave?" I asked.

I was frankly puzzled. My conscience was clear. What in the world could have happened? Of course, anyone traveling about in war zones is bound to become the victim of distrust and gossip. Few escape it, but it is always difficult to trace the cause of the trouble.

"I saw a Berlin report about you," said Vittorio. And he told me that I was under suspicion by the nazis and that my movements were being watched!

I could not help laughing.

"My goodness, don't you understand what that means?" he exclaimed. "If I were you, I'd beat it straight back to America!"

"Well," I replied, "maybe I will. But I think I'll go to Germany first."

Vittorio shrugged his shoulders.

I thanked him — and took the next plane to Berlin, prepared to tackle the Gremlins.

After an exciting trip from Venice, straight across the snow-capped Alps at an elevation of fifteen thousand feet, we had a perfect landing in Munich, and the reception there, to put it mildly, was thorough. I missed the connecting plane to Berlin because the border police insisted on stripping me to the skin. Of course, the results were negative.

It really mattered little what Himmler's sleuths thought of me. I was going about the legitimate business of a radio reporter. "Contacts" were essential to my trade. Information I could obtain from confidential sources was a prerequisite of my job. Had our broadcasts merely consisted of what propaganda bureaus of the belligerents were handing out, they would have been meager enough. Besides, we were interested in hearing the grass grow. There were "undergrounds" in many places. One or the other group might some day emerge on top. To have been in touch with it might have meant "scoops" by the dozens.

On the other hand, I had to admit that the ordinary border police could not very well see eye to eye with me. My passport, issued in Washington, was suspiciously voluminous, all cluttered up with visas and stamps. To unfold its many pages and find the proper entry was somewhat exasperating to the immigration boys. Toward the end of 1940 formalities at European frontier stations had become overintricate anyway.

Gestapo masterminds, too, however, are just human. I noticed a slip-up on their part many times. After all, how can any secret police track down each and every one they consider suspicious, particularly those who know their way about and who may at times succeed in beating even a Heinrich Himmler at his own game?

Outside of the border incident, nothing happened to me on this trip. Apparently I was only being observed, but after Vittorio's warning I watched my step more carefully than ever. To look up Goerdeler, even under black-out protection, now seemed foolhardy. He and I could have been caught "in the act of conspiracy."

Strangely enough, air raids were a help to the "underground." Shortly before the fall of Paris, in 1940, Berlin had been bombed for the first time, as a retaliation for the June 4 nazi raid on London which marked the opening of the Battle of Britain. Berliners were taken entirely by surprise. Had not Hermann Goering promised that no enemy planes would ever reach German territory? These raids indicated clearly enough that he had been very much mistaken, and also that the war was by no means over. Opposition elements made good use of such arguments. Karl Nord was actually jubilant the morning after the second raid.

"I wish the British came every day!" he whispered to me.

"You really do?"

"Why, that's the only way to teach these usurpers a lesson!

I cheered the British last night when they were flying over my roof!"

"Suppose you'd been hit by one of their 'eggs'?"

He laughed off my query.

"Germany is ruined, anyway, as long as these bandits remain at the helm."

There were many who felt exactly like Nord. I went through air raids in various German cities during 1940 and 1941. Always the people crowded in the shelters seemed depressed, but not angry. They would play cards, smoke, engage in whispered conversations, but never did I overhear anyone cursing the enemy.

"You should listen to the women," said a woman employee of Broadcasting House in Berlin when a sudden alarm kept us at the studio late one night.

"All my friends agree that we've got it coming to us, and that we'll get plenty more, she explained.

Gestapo agents were on duty in every air-raid shelter, so no one dared speak freely in the presence of strangers. But there could be no mistake as to how the people really felt. The "underground" was making headway constantly, thanks to the RAF.

# Chapter 22

## NONE COULD ESCAPE

ON JULY 19, 1940, Hitler delivered his "final warning" to England in his Kroll Opera speech, following the British attack on the French fleet at Oran, Algeria. Once more, Hitler said, he was appealing "to reason and common sense in Great Britain and elsewhere." But neither London nor Washington was impressed. Along the white cliffs of their seacoasts the British took up the nazi challenge. Churchill had given the lead when he spoke after the fall of France: "Let us, therefore, brace ourselves to our duty and so bear ourselves that, if the British Commonwealth and Empire last a thousand years, men will say: this was their finest hour!"

In August nazi air poundings of London reached their initial climax. It was truly a strategy of terror, but despite all-day bombings the British people remained stubborn and unresponsive to Hitler's bluff of invasion threats. The RAF returned blow for blow, blasting nazi bases, plants, and communication centers, scoring hits on docks and factories, in constant, relentless attacks.

When Hitler had begun to realize that the war was not going to be over soon, he ordered huge air-raid shelters built in many of the larger cities. No mention of this was made in any newspaper, but the man on the street was aware of Hitler's plan to attack Russia long before it materialized. It was impossible to conceal the gigantic construction work going on in the capital city of East Prussia. In spite of Goebbels' censorship, almost the whole country knew about the Koenigsberg shelters from the first spade work in the fall of 1940. Moscow could hardly turn a deaf ear to these reports. Perhaps they prompted Molotov's visit to Berlin in November, the day the RAF chose to drop explosively effusive greetings around the very square where the hotel of the Russian guests was located.

None of the shelters were really safe. In a western Berlin district a warden ordered me off the street one night. I took to a doorway, but almost the same instant I heard a terrific detonation in the adjacent block. A five-hundred-pound bomb had hit a shelter. The death toll was twenty-seven. Only two people in that building had not gone downstairs. They were found safe and unharmed in their apartment. Certainly air-raid time was not exactly the best time to walk your dog, for anti-aircraft shells often caused more damage than enemy bombs.

The first summer of aerial warfare, some fifteen hundred Luftwaffe planes dropped almost five million pounds of bombs over London alone, but the threatened invasion of the British Isles never came off. To stir up the populace the nazi radio had played the poet Hermann Loehn's song of the last war for weeks.

> "Give me your hand, your dear white hand,
> Farewell, my sweetest love.
> Farewell, my sweet, farewell.
> Farewell, for we sail, farewell, for we sail,
> For we sail against England."

But the German people were not impressed. They were war-weary and had no desire at all to sail against England. For the present, all they could notice of Hitler's proposed channel drive were ack-ack guns and sirens, none of them pleasant to hear. The nazi bosses were talking constantly of reprisals, but reprisals were only causing more reprisals, and there seemed to be no end to it.

When finally Hitler decided he had to deliver something since he could not deliver the trip to England, and the rabbit from Ribbentrop's hat turned out to be a ten-year political, economic, and military alliance with Italy and Japan, many Germans wondered whether peace was ever again to be the blessing of their days.

It was at that stage that President Roosevelt spoke at Dayton, Ohio, on Columbus Day. "No combination of dictator countries," the President said, "of Europe or Asia, will stop the help we are giving to almost the last free people fighting to hold them at bay." That was America's reply to the Axis.

It was like an echo of Churchill's broadcast after the fall of France: "We shall defend our Island until the curse of Hitler is lifted from the brows of men." No totalitarian triangle could change that determination, and as if to put a joint seal on it, the United States presented England with fifty destroyers. In London the people sang:

> "There'll always be an England,
> And England shall be free . . ."

Goerdeler had suddenly turned up in Switzerland. We had not met for months. He had a lot of news this time. I told him why I had avoided calling on him inside Germany.

"I knew," he said.

"What?"

"That you were being watched. I wanted to warn you, but I had no means of getting in touch with you, and this is my first chance to meet you on neutral ground."

"Can you tell me anything I may not know?" I asked.

"Oh, plenty!" he laughed. "You were caught in a solid trap."

"Trap?"

"Certainly. Don't you remember the man who came to see you in Basel claiming he was a refugee and a victim of the Gestapo?"

"I do."

"Well, he was a stool pigeon. He gained your confidence and . . ."

"But, he didn't," I objected.

"Just the same, he was your house guest and must have got enough information to pass on to the Gestapo. I have seen the report."

I remembered the case distinctly. The person in question had come to see me, armed with an introduction from a man whose integrity I had no reason to doubt. I had done all I could for the visitor, who was in distress, or at least said he was. He had impressed me favorably, but I did not acquaint him with anything of a confidential nature.

"That's all right," Goerdeler interrupted, "but he reported you, arousing suspicion. Then after the Gestapo had gone through the many official and semiofficial files they confiscated in Paris, it seems that your name came up again."

It is astounding how careless some people were at this critical juncture. Many a German opposition worker was caught because their friends in France and elsewhere left documents and letters behind which should never have been kept on file in the first place, and certainly should have been destroyed before they fled from the invaders.

Goerdeler seemed to know quite a bit about all this.

"You left carbons of reports you had sent friends in America with someone in Paris for safekeeping, didn't you?"

"Why, yes . . ."

"Well, those papers were found by the Gestapo. Tying them in with your 'refugee' guest's report, they could make out enough of a case to justify your being black-listed."

"But why then did they let me go in and out of Germany after they had obtained what they thought was evidence against me?"

"Because there was not enough of it to justify an uproar. Even now you may be able to move about Germany freely — until they decide to clamp down on you."

The papers in Paris were lost. They were carbons of my reports on the religious persecution under the nazis which I had sent from time to time to the Catholic press in America, through the *NCWC News Service* in Washington. Stopping in Paris, during my last trip to New York, I had left this material with a friend who wished to go over it. I meant to pick it up again later on; but when the nazis entered the city, my papers were left behind, without proper safeguards. Now they were interesting reading matter for the Himmler boys.

Under these circumstances, the opportunity of talking to Goerdeler in Switzerland was a great help. Our meeting, of course, was camouflaged. The house of a Swiss friend in a lonely countryside was the appointed place. I could drive there at night. There were many convenient side roads to confuse possible pursuers, and no onlookers for miles around.

But how did Goerdeler manage to leave Germany at all? He dropped a few hints on that score, but these were sufficient to indicate his connection with an opposition group within the general staff itself. Whenever they wanted him to scout around, they could give him an intelligence assignment which was none of the Gestapo's business.

It was a risky game. Some of these men were carrying water on both shoulders and trying to "insure" themselves in two directions. Others were sincerely disgusted with Hitlerism, but groping in the dark, looking for straws to grasp, and lacking courage.

"My friends are fighting with their backs against the wall," said Goerdeler. "They know Germany cannot win this war. They know Hitler is planning to attack Russia. Their protests fall on deaf ears. All they seem to be able to do is to hold on to their jobs, to prevent the worst — the worst being that the nazi desperados gain full control of our armed forces."

"What could the Allies do to help you people?" I asked.

"Hardly anything just now," Goerdeler replied. "They missed a chance before the invasion of Norway. As I told you at that time, a coup d'état was within the realm of possibility, but England and France failed to size up the situation properly. Now we have to deal with a victorious Hitler. No active opposition can be organized with men in uniform subject to the starkest discipline."

"But," I objected, "all these men are fighting, aren't they? There have been no mutinies in the armed forces. How do you explain that?"

"Have you ever seen soldiers rebelling as long as they are not beaten in the field? Of course, they fight. What else can they do? If they don't, there is the 'jug' and the firing squad, and, of course, the Gestapo, to look after the families of recalcitrants back home."

"But what will happen if Russia is attacked?"

"Nothing. Our men in the ranks are good soldiers, too good to think of anything but obeying orders, that is, unless they suffer a serious reverse."

"You don't see such a prospect, do you?"

"Not for quite a while yet, but ultimately, yes."

"When?"

Goerdeler shrugged his shoulders.

"Everything now depends on America. If she enters the war against us, it will be the beginning of the end for Hitler. And our general staff knows it, too."

"But knowing that, why don't they act before it is too late?"

Goerdeler smiled wryly.

"Haven't you read of the promotions? Brauchitsch, Rund-stedt, Leeb, Bock, List, Reichenau, Milch, Keitel, Kluge, Witzleben, Sperle, Kesselring — twelve field marshals! That did the trick! Hitler knows how to play the fiddle of military vanities. And then, remember, so many of these generals are just technicians, rather narrow in their outlook, brought up in rigid traditions, political ignoramuses, you might say, who have no conception of the world at large."

"But, my goodness, they can't all be imbeciles! At least they ought to realize that Hitler is courting disaster for the country, and they ought to react to his criminal madness as patriotic Germans."

"They ought to, yes. But they are caught in the maddening whirl of this war. The glamor of the quick victories Hitler has won blinds them almost completely."

"And the people?"

"Remember how isolated they are. Nazi propaganda has been pumped into them for seven long years, day in and day out. In their eyes events seem to justify Hitler. If one country after another collapses before his might, what hope can they have of resisting him successfully at home?"

It was a dismal picture my friend was drawing. What could anyone do? Was the only answer fighting till all Europe was bled white?

"No," said Goerdeler, "but we who are carrying on this struggle inside Germany need support, moral support, particu-larly from America. It is our only hope. Speeches are not enough. The United States government ought to sever diplo-matic relations with Germany at once. Such a move at this stage of the war would have a tremendous psychological effect. It would hearten the conquered peoples and give new hope to the German opposition."

I was unable to offer Goerdeler much encouragement. Things were moving slowly in the United States. Even the Axis pact with Japan had failed to impress the isolationists.

"Just the same," said Goerdeler, "we won't give up. I may not see you again for it is not safe for either of us to meet in Germany, and who knows whether I can ever return to Switzerland. They almost caught me the last time, you know."

The story will be told some day. It is a story of bravery and daring that reveals how true German patriots never lost courage in the blackest night of hitlerism. They fought an almost hopeless battle against heavy odds, alone, with no help from outside. Workers and businessmen, churchmen and scholars, teachers and artists, military and civilians, women as well as men — all united by the common ideal of freedom, and hoping, praying, to overthrow the tyrants who had robbed their nation of its dignity and honor.

\* \* \*

Hitler could not stop his war. He had to continue. The evil flood he had unleashed was dragging him on in spite of himself. Another winter of suffering seemed unavoidable. Hitler had visited with Marshal Pétain and had met General Franco, hoping to convince both that the time had come to hold a "European Congress" in Berlin under nazi auspices. The two men gave him the cold shoulder.

Then, because the Duce had felt the urge of rehabilitating himself in the eyes of a disdainful world, Italy suddenly invaded Greece, without Berlin's permission. The opportunity appeared favorable, and no one seemed to be looking. The Duce thought he might as well grab some land while the grabbing was good. But soon enough his *Alpini,* who had crossed the Albanian mountains, were caught in Balkan snow and ice. General Mud helped the brave Greek defenders on the plains. It had been a badly prepared hit-and-miss campaign. Marshal Badoglio resigned in protest. Italian reverses in Egypt soon made matters even worse. The fascist "Empire" in Africa was about to collapse.

Mussolini was really in a bad way all around, but Hitler left him dangling. He probably thought it would teach his partner a lesson, and it did. Italy had now lost her freedom entirely. The abortive campaign in Greece proved to the whole world what few had been willing to believe the day the "Axis pact of steel" was forged. "Italy — betrayed," as the great Arturo Toscanini expressed it in changing the text of Verdi's Hymn of Freedom.

Betrayed. . . . Could this not also be said of Germany? If the German people were heart and soul behind the wily "Fuehrer," why was oppression continued now that the people had won Hitler's victories under his banner? Why were concentration camps still crowded? Why did popular enthusiasm have to be whipped up artificially time and again?*

On November 8, Hitler spoke once more. It was the anniversary of the 1939 Munich beer hall bombing. But this time the fireworks came from on high, with the RAF spoiling the celebration. Hitler had just finished his usual ranting when the missiles, meant as a special salute for him, dropped from the wintry sky. "I am the hardest man the German people have had for many decades and possibly for centuries," Hitler boasted. Strange language coming from a leader supposedly beloved by his people, and not too reassuring on the eve of the second winter of war!

Dense fogs were setting in over the Channel. All hope of downing England that year was lost. In Washington, Congress was asked to appropriate funds for the biggest defense force the United States had ever had in peacetime.

Shortly after Christmas, I decided to look around in Berlin once more. The holidays had been dreary, but in spite of Alfred Rosenberg's and Joe Goebbels' war on religion, the churches were more crowded than ever before. Pagan winter solstice celebrations had been decreed for the Hitler Youth and the storm troopers, but somehow they fell flat. After all, the

---

* Any calm observer will agree with the editorial writer of the *New York Times,* who said on July 13, 1942, that "no referendum was taken at any time to establish whether the majority of the German people actually wanted war, . . . whether the German people wanted Warsaw or Rotterdam or Belgrade destroyed, or innocent hostages shot by wholesale, or whole villages put to the sword. An unintimidated vote would at the very least have shown large minorities against those actions, possibly majorities. Just as Austrians, Czechs, Poles, Hollanders, Belgians, Frenchmen and men of other nations have been forced to collaborate with Hitler to save themselves from starvation, the concentration camp or the firing squad, so Germans have been forced into line in the same way."

In this same connection a report by Thomas Kernan, who was interned as one of a group of American diplomatic hostages in Baden Baden, Germany, from January, 1943, to March, 1944, is illuminating indeed. "Do not the German Catholics," says Mr. Kernan, "share in the guilt of the German people for the atrocities in occupied countries, for the death chambers for German Jews, and death ditches of the Polish patriots? This question is not difficult to answer. The German Catholics, and for that matter the common German people, share no guilt for the German atrocities, for the simple reason that they have never heard of them. No one within Germany has the slightest idea of the atrocities that are reported daily in the American press. . . . They (the German people) believe, because they have been told so, that there are great concentrations of Jews in the Gouvernement General (Poland), where Jews are being settled on the land and set up as artisans. . . . The average German is blissfully ignorant, and he would be genuinely shocked to hear of the frightful conditions under which this settlement has been made." (*The Sign,* National Catholic magazine, Union City, N. J., May, 1944.) Cf. Thomas Kernan's book, *Now With the Morning Star* (New York: Scribners, 1944).

Christmas tree had its origin in Germany. So had Kriss Kringle and Santa Claus. Deeply Christian traditions such as these cannot be torn from a people's heart by wanton edict.

On my way north I stopped over in Karlsruhe, but the room clerk of the hotel called me early in the morning to say that the police had taken my passport along, and I was to call for it at headquarters. Why? He politely professed complete ignorance.

At headquarters things were rather pleasant, sort of southern style.

"May I have my passport?"

"Your nationality?"

"American."

"Don't you know you are not supposed to stop over in the war zone?"

"But I have the right kind of visa."

"No, you have not. You are supposed to travel straight to your destination, without stopovers."

The good man was mistaken. Visas for foreign correspondents were issued by the Berlin Foreign Office, upon approval of the Propaganda Ministry. Once a correspondent was formally accredited, he was given exit and re-entry visas as though he had been a resident of Germany — a convenient procedure for those of us who were engaged in frequent travel. These special visas did not prescribe specific travel routes. The bearer could leave Germany and re-enter the country by whatever border he liked, and he was not bound to carry a "route order" such as was given travelers coming into Germany from abroad.

After this explanation, the Karlsruhe inspector let me off with a reprimand.

"Don't do it again," he warned me. "In spite of what you say, you are not supposed to stop over in war zones without a special permit."

I caught my train rather relieved. Obviously my name was not on a general blacklist — as yet! But one could never tell. In Berlin I told Hada what had happened to me.

"Serves you right," he remarked in a grouchy mood. "They should have kept you behind bars. All you fellows are doing is spying around. . . ."

The altercation that followed was not pleasant. I sensed a growing antagonism to all Americans. The time had passed when, in order to gain our good will, we were granted privileges of all sorts.

For a good while I had given up broadcasting from Berlin, as well as from Rome. Instead I would gather information in the two capitals and then return to Switzerland, where freedom of speech was unimpaired, within the reasonable bounds imposed by the country's neutrality, and broadcasts to America presented no problem. The United States, too, was technically still a neutral. But President Roosevelt had said publicly he could not "ask that every American remain neutral in thought," which made me feel justified in saying things over the Geneva transmitter which no censor would have passed in the lands of deadly totalitarian silence.

A case in point was Pierre Laval's arrest in Vichy. The sudden change of scene in the temporary French capital did not immediately become known to the outside world. Telephone communications had been cut, and only vague rumors had trickled across the border. I was just about to go on the air from Basel, to deliver one of my weekly reviews, when Paul Archinard, NBC's correspondent in Vichy, finally got through on the telephone and confirmed the reverse in Laval's fortunes, giving me all the incidental details which he had secured as an eyewitness in the Park Hotel.

It was a honey of a broadcast! Being on neutral soil, I could freely discuss the implications of the event with all the incidental drama at a time when other news sources had dried up.

When I think back, I believe that Laval broadcast was the last honest-to-goodness report I was able to deliver from Europe. They did not like it in Berlin. They had disliked some of my previous ones, too. Soon a formal protest was lodged with NBC by the German Embassy in Washington. If I carried on, said the nazi spokesman to John Royal, vice-president in charge of NBC's international relations, the German government would have to consider me *persona non grata,* and I would be denied access to German territory.

No wonder, then, that Hada had been in so offensive a mood. I found out before long that Goebbels himself had put

NBC on his black-list, which meant no trips to the fronts, no interviews with governmental and military leaders, no consideration for special features.

"Does this mean we are in the doghouse?" I asked Dr. Harold Diettrich, now the operations chief of the foreign division of German broadcasting.

His answer was straight from the shoulder.

"I'm afraid so."

The doorman of my Berlin hotel who had known me for years was surprised when I handed him an oversized tip.

"I may not see you for some time," I said casually.

He stared at me.

"You are not leaving for good, are you?"

"Well, for good as far as the Third Reich is concerned."

"So you are really going back to America?"

"Yes, I am going back. I long to go back. There'll be work to do. When Hitler is gone, perhaps, we'll meet again."

There were tears in the old man's eyes.

"You are leaving us, all of you, one after another," he said, grasping my hand, "and we are left behind amidst ruins. . . ."

No, it was not a happy Germany that I bade good-bye, not an exuberant, confident Germany, by any means. Rather a Germany which seemed to be wearing an ill-fitting uniform. On the streets, in the department stores, in the theaters, the atmosphere was sullen. People were morose, excitable, jittery. But most indicative of their mental state, they were inarticulate.

One could travel on streetcars or subways in any big city and find them crowded with silent people. During these war years I covered considerable distances by train, from one end of the country to the other. Passengers would sit in their compartments for hours and not say a word. Groups of people traveling together would whisper, or if they did engage in conversations that could be overheard, they would deal with such innocuous topics as Aunt Bessie's birthday party, or how Sonnie could trade in his roller skates for a pair of skis.

What a ghastly farce it all was! What a perversion of the inner life of the people! What a distortion of all the concepts of civilized government! But now every hope was gone for finding a way out of the mess. Stupidly, blindly, too many of the Germans had fallen into the nazi trap, dragging the whole world along with them — into disaster.

When the German conductor left our train at the Swiss border, it seemed as though he was merging into a no-man's land of darkness and fear. He and the brakeman, the engineers and the dining-car personnel were glumly going back to the calamity of the swastika.

* * *

The events of the spring and summer of 1941 were but the prelude of that huge anticlimax of the battle of Russia which marked the beginning of Hitler's reverses. England had withstood his assault. She had ignored his threats. Hitler could only hope to hold his conquests for a while by making a fortress of the whole continent. In the Fall he had taken over Rumania. Early in March the nazi vise closed on Bulgaria. Both these moves as well as the blitz into Yugoslavia, the thrust on Greece, and the battle of Crete, were but preliminaries to that end. Of course, Hitler had to give another reason. In his order of April 6, the day he struck against Yugoslavia, he proclaimed that his aim was to "defeat the legions of plutocracy and to fight until the last Englishman is driven from the soil of Europe."

In twelve days Yugoslavia was conquered. Radio and press correspondents had no chance to do a legitimate reporting job, for a blackout of news set in the moment Hitler's panzer divisions started rolling across the border. Joseph Goebbels' shortwave services were telling the world that Belgrade was "a sea of flames" as a consequence of pitiless aerial bombardments. The Balkan powder-keg was blasting once more, but at the same time Europe's last independent granary was being burned to the ground.

In Budapest, Hungarian Premier Count Paul Teleki committed suicide. He chose death rather than being ordered to fight side by side with the German army against the Yugoslavs. Soon the swastika banner was foisted on Mount Olympus, and nazi troops marched into Athens. A fortnight later Rudolph Hess flew to Scotland in a last attempt to enlist British help for the assault on Russia.

"If the Reich gives a guarantee, that means that it also abides by it," Hitler had the effrontery to state on June 22nd, 1941, the day his armies were smashing across the Soviet borders. Yet, on September 1, 1939, after having negotiated a nonaggression pact with Stalin, meant to protect the "Fuehrer's" rear, he had "seen no reason that we ever again will take a stand against one another." Molotov who had signed the agreement with Berlin twenty-two months before had proclaimed publicly that it was "putting an end to the enmity between Germany and the USSR." Now he found himself appealing to the world against the "clique of blood-thirsty fascist rulers of Germany."

The cataracts of total war had engulfed the whole continent. No longer could there be any thought of trading radio programs across the Atlantic. Soon, too, the few remaining neutral outlets would not longer be available to us. Until the nazi nightmare was over we could not expect to resume a free broadcasting exchange with any of the countries within Hitler's orbit.

I decided to return home and closed the office in Basel. A ten year assignment had come to an end. The parting from the gallant friends in Switzerland was sad indeed. They felt as though they were being left behind, one American after another abandoning them. But we knew we would be back, the day Europe had won its freedom again, the day when the oldest democracy in the world whose flag bears the emblem of the Cross, may become the pattern for a new Europe.

Coming through Madrid, I found beggars crowding about the cafés on the stately Prado Boulevard. Few of the ruins of the civil war had been rebuilt. Beautiful Spain was still sadly bleeding from many wounds, and the acrimonies of the past were bitterly alive.

Then came Lisbon, the maritime queen of the West and air terminal of the great clipper ships. What a wonderful host Portugal has been to the world all these years, when there was no other gateway, freely accessible from and to the Continent!

On the boat, homeward bound on my twenty-fourth crossing of the Atlantic, the Stars and Stripes were rippling in the breeze. Europe was behind us. Darkness and ruins were behind us. But ahead of us was America and freedom and light and hope.

# PART IV

# TWILIGHT OF THE GODS

*"I should be false to the very foundations
of my religious and political convictions, if I
should ever relinquish the hope — or even the
faith — that in all peoples, without exception,
there live some instinct for truth, some attrac-
tion toward justice, some passion for peace —
buried as it may be in the German case under
a brutal regime.*

*"We bring no charge against the German
race, as such, for we cannot believe that God
has eternally condemned any race or humanity.
We know in our own land, in the United
States of America, how many good men and
women of German ancestry have proved loyal,
freedom loving, and peace loving citizens.*

*"But there is going to be a stern punish-
ment for all those in Germany directly responsible for this agony of mankind.*

*"The German people are not going to be
enslaved. Why? Because the United Nations
do not traffic in human slavery."*

— *Franklin Delano Roosevelt, in an address
before the Foreign Policy Association,
New York, October 21, 1944.*

# Chapter 23

## WHY SO HELPLESS?

FOR a while after my return from Europe it seemed as though all my ties with the folks left behind were to be cut entirely. I could not write them for America was now at war. The die was cast at Pearl Harbor. Germany and Italy had become enemy territories. Only through Switzerland, Sweden or Portugal could news filter across the borders. I was wondering whether I should attempt getting in touch with my friends through the Red Cross when a letter arrived from Sweden, post-marked Gothenburg. It was from Irma, and written early in 1942.

Shortly after I had last seen her she had become a nurse's aid with a field ambulance. She had been sent to France at first, and then to Poland, but now she was assigned to Norway, and while one of her hospital transports was passing through Swedish territory she had managed to post this letter.

"You may never get this," she wrote, "but I am trying just the same. You have no idea what it means to me to just think of you as a friend far away, in a free land where there is hope and light. We have lost all hope, and lost all light.

"This winter is horrible. Our losses in Russia are staggering. Almost every family at home has had its share. Everybody thinks this war will be long, and victory is not in sight.

"Often I think of you. Now I understand much of what you told me. Then I would not believe it. I just did not know. Now I have seen for myself, and I shudder when I think of all the evil that is being done by my own people.

"I had thought we were fighting for freedom and now I see that we are stealing the liberty of others. Many see it as I do. I was home on leave last month and I found no smiling faces anywhere. People don't trust the government. Too many promises were made and not kept. Many eyes have been opened.

"The troops are brave, but they lack incentive. The men have become cynical. War makes man brutal, inhuman, and the longer it lasts, the more readily the restraints of civilization are dropped. I have seen so many men die, and in their last hours they often reveal themselves. They reveal their despair, their despondency.

"Why does all this have to be? Why are we so helpless in all this misery? Is there no light to shine through the darkness?

"And when will I see you again? When? . . ."

# Chapter 24

## THE LIGHTS ARE OUT

IF IRMA who had been among the blind, the confused, now, under the impact of adverse experiences was beginning to see the light, in what mood would my more discerning friends be? Goerdeler, for instance, who had foreseen the setback in Russia, and Otto Weltin and Professor Kraus and all those who were kindred in spirit?

At long last, in the summer of 1942, just before nazi troops took over the whole of France, another letter came. It had been mailed in Fribourg, Switzerland, but there was no indication of who had sent it. The signature it bore was scribbled illegibly. Nevertheless the source was unmistakable for the writer was sending greetings from "Karl," and the contents left no doubt in my mind that it was Karl Nord. I remembered that he had spoken to me of relatives in Fribourg, so it may well have been that they had visited him, or he with them. Amazingly, the various censors let the missive slip by for it bore no marks of having been opened or checked until it had reached American soil.

Here is the full text.

"Dear Friend:

"When we last met I thought Europe had almost emptied the bitter cup of its miseries. Not that I expected an early end of the war, but I must admit I did not anticipate that we would face disasters of such magnitude as are now in prospect.

"There can be no question that Hitler's attack on Russia was the turning point. The declaration of war by the United States all but sealed his fate, and the air-raids on Cologne, Bremen and other cities brought home to the wildest of the nazis that they were meeting with the determined resistance of the democracies on all fronts.

"To my mind, and to the mind of many of my friends, the

only question now is how soon we'll experience the final crash. We all know that Germany's defeat is inescapable, but what chaos and anarchy will envelop this bleeding, hapless continent once the nazis collapse?

"The German people know all this. They probably know it better than anyone else for they have been in the darkness of hitlerism longer than anyone else. They know that a fearful vendetta is in the offing. They have their black lists ready in every town and village. The thousands of Gestapo overseers in our factories, the nazi block wardens and all their sycophants are marked men.

"We who are confined in this huge concentration camp, behind the figurative barbed wire fences the Gestapo has woven about the German borders, often feel as though we were muzzled and gagged, locked up in a dark room. We wonder what the world outside thinks of us. It is hard for us on the inside to read our own domestic barometer. How much more puzzled must you people be who are far away! You hear Hitler's voice, Goebbels' voice, but not the voice of Germany. For she is wrapped in a deadly, dreadful silence behind the double and triple concrete dam, ramparts of brutal repression, her masters have built around her. The real image of the German nation can no longer be seen. It is concealed under bristling armor and blaring propaganda. The lights of truth are out.

"I know you would want me to give you some news. Some real news such as seeps through from the lands Hitler has enslaved. News of the 'underground,' of passive resistance, of sabotage. But alas! there is little I can tell you. We learn hardly anything about conditions in our own country, for we are isolated one from another, in constant fear of our lives. And it is not the enemy across the borders that really scares us. It is the enemy at home.

"For almost a decade now we are in slavery in our own land. It is true, as you know, that many were not aware of it in the beginning. There had to be a war to wake them up, to make them conscious of their shackles. Quite a few are still taken in by the distortions and misrepresentations that are flung about them day in and day out, but facts begin to speak for themselves.

"What will come of all this? As a German I am under no illusion. I have no apologies to offer. I only hope that the rest of the world will not be swayed by prejudices as violent as those that have brought about this unspeakable tragedy. I hope it won't brand us all as brutes and misfits. I hope it will believe that a feeling of national disgrace has gripped our souls. Cancer has taken root in our body politic. If only the patient is not identified with the ailment in the minds of those who have to suffer from it!

"Do you remember the days when you used to visit with us? The good talks we had in my 'cave?' Then there were still people like yourself who could move about to unearth the facts. Hitler had besmirched the German image, and the ordinary avenues of intercourse with our friends abroad were blocked, so it was difficult for them to obtain a true picture of the country. Necessarily, theirs was a half picture, a twisted one, awkwardly focussed on the swastika which was never the true symbol of our nation, but rather a disfigurement of its best traditions. The Germany that remained accessible was nazified. The other Germany was hidden and almost beyond reach.

"Now, that we are completely cut off from the civilized world, we live in so dismaying a vacuum that I am at a loss for words to adequately describe it. Now it is truly a hateful Germany because it is only Hitler's, Goering's, Himmler's and Goebbels' Germany. The atmosphere of this nazi world within whose prison walls we are confined is stifling and depressing, unfit to breathe!

"You have known Germany in normal times, you would hardly recognize her now. You know that hitlerism was always but an artificial veneer, a violent pretense put over with gigantic trickery. You have seen how Hitler conquered and subdued us while our neighbors looked on unmoved as though it was none of their business. You would not throw out the baby with the bathwater and conclude that all Teutons are just God-forsaken Huns.

"However, were you to come back now, you'd be horrified, even as we who have to carry on under this nightmare of violence and bluff and colossal deceit. But in the midst of all the destruction we have not lost our souls.

"Now that Hitler's bombs are coming home to roost the people are taking their sufferings stoically. I have heard no expressions of hate for the enemy even during the worst air-raids. And the churches are filled, despite the anti-religious campaign of the maniacs on top. Concert halls are jammed by crowds listening to serious music such as Bach and Handel, which helps them to bear the ignominy of these days.

"Sometimes I wish I were among Hitler's victims in Poland, or Norway, or Czechoslovakia. Somehow I would feel happier, in spite of all the tortures the invader inflicts on these people. Here at home I am subjected to similar indignities in the name of patriotism, and I find my own government, though it is one of depraved mountebanks, responsible for them. My own government, my own country involved in such unspeakable wrong!

"My family send you their best. So does the whole Friday Circle — what's left of it at any rate.

"Do pray for us all! For unless these days are shortened, no living creature may be saved (Math. 24, 22)."

# Chapter 25

## LET'S NOT APE THEM!

A FEW weeks later the air mail brought a letter from Cuba. Dr. Herzberg, my Jewish friend who had managed to escape from Germany in the early days of the nazi terror, and whom I had last seen in Denmark, had finally made his way over and he gave me the odyssey of his flight across France and Africa.

"You cannot conceive what I went through," he wrote.

"I got away from Denmark shortly before the nazis moved in. France seemed safer! You know what happened. How so many of us were almost caught in Paris and trekked along with the retreating French. In the Pyrenees I found a temporary refuge. Like others I had thought of myself as being in the Allied camp. I thought to be among friends. But how were we treated! Interned, harassed, deported, jailed!

"I finally eluded the Gestapo by the skin of my teeth and flew the coop — to Africa! I was spared the experience of Himmler's concentration camps, but people who have been in them, tell me that they are almost summer resorts compared to the hell-holes of the African desert where some of us were kept and treated like chain-gangs before we were rescued.

"You remember our friend David Nathan, no doubt. I saw him in Tarbes, near the Spanish border, with his wife and three children, after his escape first from Berlin, then from Paris. The French ought to have appreciated how much he had done for them, how he had been in the very forefront of the anti-nazi underground, as brave as any of the workers in the dark!

"He made frantic efforts to come to America. Friends in New York had braved interminable formalities on his behalf. They failed. Now it's too late. The Gestapo is all over France. Himmler's men picked up the Jews and other refugees alike. We will never hear from Nathan again.

"I had always thought that there was an instinctive solidarity among men of good will everywhere, like a great family stretching across the globe. Of course, you have to have credentials — the ones supplied by your record! If you were a fighter for democracy in your homeland, your spiritual blood-brothers elsewhere ought to have stood beside you, to help you, to open the way for you.

"Instead, we have witnessed shameful failures on the part of governments and organizations who should have considered it their bounden duty to reach out welcoming hands to the persecuted and the oppressed. Nathan was one of thousands who could have been rescued by concerted international action, but he was left in the lurch and abandoned to Hitler's henchmen because some bureaucrat thought he had to play safe, because visas were refused, or delayed, because men and women of proved sympathy for the cause of the Allies, people who had risked their lives in fighting Hitler and Mussolini, people whose names were known as champions of democracy, found themselves discriminated against, without even a hearing.

"I know you personally can do nothing about all this, and I beg your pardon for unloading my grievances on you, but this is my first opportunity for expressing them freely. I think some day a black record will reveal incredible failures in this tragic scramble when thousands of human lives were at stake, and so many hearts were cold, and so many minds as prejudiced as those of the worst nazis.

"Indeed, despite radio and aviation, the world has gained little in mutual understanding. We still know miserably little about one another, and we are only too ready to pass quick judgment upon our fellowmen. No matter how much superficial progress humanity achieves, most people remain homebodies who like their precious selves and their own peculiar ways better than anything else. 'Furinners,' it seems to me, continue to be the most unpopular and most misunderstood people on earth, no matter where they are!

"I clipped a sentence out of a New York newspaper the other day. It said that the theory of the iniquity of an entire race is a nazi theory, and that we should not ape it. That sums up pretty well what I have in mind. Will this war help us all to get the idea of tolerance into our heads, or are we just fighting intolerance with intolerance?"

# Chapter 26

## "NOW I HAVE SEEN . . ."

IN THE fall came the American and British landings in Africa. Marshal Rommel was on the run. And then, in Casablanca, Roosevelt and Churchill proclaimed the terms for the axis: unconditional surrender. Since the fall of France the scene had completely changed. Now again, there was a letter from Irma, post-marked Malmoe, Sweden. She was desperately unhappy.

"I am on my way home on furlough," she wrote, "and I will try not to return. Never had I believed it possible that my own countrymen could be guilty of such crimes. I am writing you again because I constantly remember our talks at the time the war broke out. Now, with my own eyes, I have seen some of the things you mentioned. Now I know that there are wicked men in all camps.

"I cannot tell you how many deserters we have. I have seen them escape almost on every transport I was on. Whenever we come near Swedish territory there is shooting. Gestapo guards after our men! But many get away. If they are caught, they are treated worse than beasts.

"The men are tired of the war. They want to go home. They feel instinctively that we can't win. There are some here who have been through the hell of the Russian front. As a people we are being bled white. I think I can do my part much better at home than in a foreign land where we have no business anyway. They tell us we are protecting Norway from the British. I wonder!

"I admire the Norwegians. If we were in their place, we, too, would fight for our freedom.

"I recalled the other day what Hitler said in *Mein Kampf*: 'If people but fight for freedom, weapons will grow in their hands.' Eventually, he may find he was right — when the weapons grow against him! But just now I see no hope.

"For the present the Gestapo remains supreme, at home as well as in the occupied territories. If the people we have subjected cannot revolt, much less chance have we! How can we revolt against armored tanks and bomber planes!

"But the day will come! That day when we will do precisely what Hitler has said in *Mein Kampf*. The passage is almost forgotten and the author never expected to see it applied to himself! It says that 'whenever a nation is led to disaster by the government, revolt by every member of that government (and he should have added: of the people!) is not a privilege but a duty.'

"A Swedish nurse is helping to smuggle out this note to you. I hope it reaches you safely. I may never be able to write you again. Good-bye! Don't forget me. . . ."

# Chapter 27

## SATAN'S PASSPORT

MONTHS went by, and I had no further word from any of the friends over there. The nazi ring of steel seemed to hem in the continent more and more tightly all the time. But then came the landing in Sicily, the first crack in Hitler's fortress. Not long after, a letter from Lisbon arrived.

It was Goerdeler's first message to me in three years.

One of his friends had succeeded in slipping out of Germany for a brief visit to Portugal. He signed with the pseudonym Goerdeler had used most frequently in his dealings with me. There could be no mistake about the authenticity of the document. Its most significant passages can be quoted:

"Our defeat at Stalingrad was the turning point in the last phase of the war. Hitler cannot concede defeat. He and his henchmen will attempt to fight 'to the last German.'

"You have no idea of the hatred surging through Germany. Not hatred of the enemy, but hatred of Hitler. Never in our history was any man hated so much. In the early days of the nazi calamity, clever propaganda had made him appear as the unselfish leader who, motivated by love of the fatherland, certainly would not approve of the evil things the underlings were doing in his name.

"All such illusions are now exploded. Those of us who had given warning all along now find ourselves justified, but it is a grim satisfaction. Complete disaster is impending, but Himmler's bullies keep us all in submission.

"Were you to visit us now, you would find a Germany bleeding from a million wounds. Between us and France, or Poland, or Greece there is really no difference. We are all 'occupied.'

"There is darkness all about us — not only on the streets. The people are breaking under the endless suffering which is

even more intense morally than physically. We know it won't
end when the war is over.

"What hope is there left? None, I think, for our generation.
I know too well how much guilt we have to expiate as a nation. I know that the innocent must suffer with the guilty.
But I wish I could at least have some hope for the future. My
two sons were killed in Africa, and my only daughter has
lost her husband in the battle of France. My wife and I are
old, much older than our years.

"You will remember our talks, back in '41. Things run their
course as I had anticipated; as a matter of fact, they move
faster. What the nazi bullies and the military clique inflicted
upon helpless cities in Holland and Poland and Yugoslavia we
now experience ourselves, and rightly so. Ruins, ruins, everywhere! Force always begets force, and violence begets violence.

"We hear little of what is going on outside of our borders.
We are too tired, too despondent to make an effort to obtain
information as we might, if we dared to play with death by
listening to foreign radio stations. After sitting up in bomb-
shelters all night one is too exhausted. And we are fearful,
cold, and bitter.

"The Gestapo shoots sight unseen. Grumblers are executed
on the spot. In the midst of air-raids, I have seen people ma-
chine-gunned within the debris of their own homes, when in
frantic rage they speak out against the man whom they now
blame for it all.

"I don't get around much these days. There are too many
wrecks, and travel permits are hard to get. But I pick up reports here and there. The story of the Catholic students in
Munich who were court-martialed as 'traitors' is making the
rounds of the whole nation. It happened last winter when the
Gauleiter cynically insisted that girl students had the 'patriotic duty' to bear children out of wedlock. Two former
Stalingrad fighters and the sister of one of them who stood
up to protest were summarily guillotined. Remember their
names: Scholl! Hans and Maria Scholl! And Adrian Probst!

"A similar incident occurred at the University of Greifswald,
while in Stuttgart a woman was thrown into jail because she
had sent flowers to a Canadian prisoner of war. In Koenigsberg
five women were sentenced to (I don't remember how many)

years in prison because they had given shelter to Jewish children whose parents had been deported.* In Essen an eighteen-year-old girl was given thirteen years because she had helped Polish prisoners of war to escape. A workman in the Ruhr district suffered a similar punishment because after an Allied air-raid he had suggested not vengeance, mind you, against the Americans and the British, but a monument to Hermann Goering, who had promised no enemy plane would ever fly over Germany!

"With that sort of thing going on, you may ask about our morale. Slaves have no morale.

"How I wish I could have a talk with you! I can scarcely visualize normal living conditions anymore. There is no one who would not want to escape from all this misery, but we are utterly helpless. Our youth dies on the battle-fields, and those who do live through the holocaust will not be the same. War unleashes the animal instincts of humanity on a gigantic scale. Millions become beasts when their only business is to kill, and everybody must look after himself in this death-struggle of a world gone mad.

"I wonder what people in America think about it all. Of course, I know they cannot be of one mind, just as we are not of one mind. There are hate-mongers in all nations. If only the hate-mongers would fight their own wars amongst themselves and leave the people alone who prefer peace and quiet living! We should have learned by now that Satan can travel on any passport. The main question is, will we visé it! In other words, will we allow conditions to arise, or to prevail, which make it possible for the devil to secure the right of way, driving the moral forces into retreat?

---

* The *American Hebrew* carried a report on May 28, 1943, stating that nazi anti-semitic propaganda "with all its madness and fierceness produces no effect in Germany," and that "the German people have become so used to and disgusted with the nazi anti-Jewish campaigns that they no longer pay the slightest attention to them." The *Religious News Service*, published by the National Conference of Christians and Jews in New York, said on July 27, 1944, that one of the main achievements of the Christian churches in Germany "has been not only to create a 'secret public opinion' against nazi anti-semitic measures, but to organize various activities on behalf of persecuted Jews, and . . . to facilitate the escape of the Jews to other countries, or to provide refuge and shelter in Christian communities." The report adds: "In various parts of Germany, thousands of Christians signed pledges not to recognize the so-called Aryan clause in their churches. That this was done in clear defiance of the Gestapo was an implied proof of the growing strength of the Church."

"Have you heard that we have special concentration camps for deserters? First Himmler had them for the Jews, and the dissenters among non-Jews. Now he keeps them for deserters as well. No one knows how many there are, but the fact that they exist is indicative enough of the true state of affairs in our huge prison camp which is all Germany.* The world probably knows little of it, even less than we know. There are plenty of firing squads to dispose of mutinies.

"This time, when it is all over, we Germans who are left will have only one chance — to throw ourselves on the mercy of the victors. Amid a heap of ruins we will be fighting wholesale starvation and probably epidemics. The flower of our manhood will be gone. Women and children, too, victims by the thousands of the mass bombings of our cities.

"I know that retribution cannot be avoided. I know that even with Hitler and the warlords out of the way, and his companions in crime dangling from every lamp-post, those who have suffered so unspeakably at the hands of the invaders will still harbor vengeance in their hearts.

"Can we hope that statesmen will rise above the hatreds engendered by years of battle, that they will think of future generations and sow the seeds of peace and good will, rather than the dragon teeth of new wars. Theirs may well be a righteous wrath, but also a convenient self-righteousness. May they be granted the light to see that any attempt to eliminate the devil with Beelzebub, Hitler by a hitlerism in reverse, is bound to fail in the end! For as we sow, so shall we reap."

---

* Anne O'Hare McCormick once summed up the situation convincingly when she wrote: "No one who knows Germany can doubt that there is another Germany, feeling itself as much occupied as France, and hating the horrors the nazis perpetrate as a policy . . . Wherever the nazis go they bring concentration camps — and the biggest, oldest, and most crowded of these are in Germany itself." (*New York Times,* December 30, 1942). A report by James Cassidy, NBC correspondent, from the First Army front (October 26, 1944) states: "The latest story, quite authentic, concerns the new way the Germans are posting guards. In one platoon twelve guards are put on duty each night, each connected by a wire tied to his left wrist. From this wire, another leads to a German sergeant [Gestapo commissar?] in a dugout. The wire is given a pull when the sentries change, informing the sergeant that all is well; but the main purpose of the wire is to keep the sentries from deserting. Needless to say, however, a lot of Germans are going over the hill in spite of this novel, tied-on-a-leash method of trying to halt them."

# Chapter 28

## POOR PEOPLE . . .

THE Duce had fallen, ignominiously rescued by his nazi partners. Allied troops stood on Italian soil. The axis had cracked. I wondered about my Italian friends. How would they survive the ordeal? A letter from a war-prisoners' camp in Montana brought the first news. It was from an officer captured at Salerno, a friend of Vittorio who had asked him to convey greetings to me, "should you be captured."

"I have just arrived in the United States," he wrote in Italian. "It's three months since I last saw Vittorio in Rome. I presume he is still there, probably in hiding for he was one of Grandi's men, as you know. Maybe he has escaped into allied territory. Now our country is truly an inferno. Our former Allies have become our enemies.

"As a prisoner of war I am safe in this country, but what will I have to go back to?

"Such strange questions we are asked in this camp: Do we still believe in the Duce? Do we want the Allies to win? Are we glad that Hitler is being thrown out of Italy?

"What can a prisoner say? What would American prisoners of war have to say in similar circumstances? Every man loves his homeland and he is reluctant to express his innermost opinion to a stranger.

"No doubt German prisoners react as we do. We who have fought with them know that. Most of them are the same kind of human beings made miserable by this war. There are fanatics among them, just as there are among us.

"You must have heard of Badoglio's statement after our collapse. How the Germans in Rome celebrated when the false rumor was spread that Hitler, too, had been thrown out!

"We are all our mothers' sons, aren't we? The Americans

and the British and the Russians and the Germans as well as we Italians. We all had to fight because we were told to. Most of us did not know what it was all about. Our soldiers had to swallow the propaganda fed them. They knew nothing else.

"Now most of us are awake. Over there we were told New York was in ruins, bombed by the mighty nazi air force. I wonder what the nazi prisoners have to say who were brought over to this country. They were so gullible. Few of them thought for themselves. Few of our men do. It's the way people are. Poor people.

"Vittorio asked me to greet you. He hopes to see you again. The collapse of fascism has not taken him by surprise. He had foreseen it from the day we entered this terrible war. Why did we enter it? Mussolini wanted it. The people of Italy never did. You know that, for you were with us often in happier days.

"Send me some newspapers in Italian, please, and books, if you can. Anything that's not fascist! We are starving for reading matter that is unpolluted. We haven't had much of it all these years when the sacred traditions of Italy were perverted by grandiloquent upstarts.

"It is quite an experience to attend divine services in this camp. So many were surprised to find Chaplains on duty. They had been told America was a land without religion, materialistic. It is a revelation to them.

"Please remember me in your prayers, and also Vittorio and his family, and our tormented Italy!"

# Chapter 29

## THE WAY IS CHARITY

THEN came the bombings, the big bombings. On Genoa, on Turin, on Vienna, on Munich, on Frankfort, on Berlin. The march of death was being stepped up.

And another letter came, from another prisoners' camp, down in Kentucky. It read as follows:
"Dear Sir:

"My aunt, Frau Goerdeler, whom I saw while home on leave shortly before my batallion became engaged in the Tunisian fighting, has asked me to give you her regards.

"She wants you to know that her husband disappeared on a business trip shortly before reaching the Swiss border. We don't know where he is, but have every reason to believe the worst.

"The most dreadful terror has engulfed my country. I have been through some of the bombings. The people are in a daze. The Gestapo is machine-gunning anyone who dares to complain. The executioner's axe never rests.

"Since I have arrived in this country as a prisoner of war I have had an opportunity to do a lot of thinking. We are allowed newspapers in this camp and I can assure you there is much shaking of heads among us when we come across reports on Germany.

"Strangely enough, it seems that writers with German names, or of German background and origin, or people who have never been to Germany, are the most biased. Their quick-on-the-trigger judgment makes me wonder whether they can appreciate what we have been through.

"In our camp, the other day, a vote was taken to determine who was nazi and who anti-nazi. Well, you know how Goebbels' propaganda has indoctrinated the people so that they identify hitlerism and patriotism. As long as we are prisoners of war, many of us feel that it is treason to take a stand against Hitler, even though we may be utterly out of sympathy with him. I know it is all wrong, but our critics should appreciate our dilemma.

"I have been here only a short time, but I read all I can lay my hands on. I am amazed to find that so little is known of the situation inside Germany. You have known my uncle and some of his friends. I don't have to tell you how they stood up against the nazi tyranny from the early days. You can well imagine how they must feel thrown in now with the very people whom they have so consistently opposed.

"I read statements in some of the papers here expressing doubts that Germans as a whole have any moral sense whatever. How about the appeasers in various countries who gambled on Hitler? How about the millions of Germans who have paid with their lives and their freedom for their democratic convictions? And the Christians of Germany who have taken a stand against the despots with unflinching courage?

"And what about the people who sing paeans of hate in America? The same sort of indiscriminate, violent hate which they condemn in hitlerism?

"We Germans have seen where mass prejudice can lead. Now we are paying for it as a nation. Utter disaster is the result.

"I hope to return home when the war is over and I hope that my uncle and men like him will be at hand to guide the work of reconstruction. We must try to help our neighbors who have suffered so much anguish at the hands of our militarists.

"We have everything we need in this camp. The treatment is excellent. But it is sad to be a prisoner, and most of us are terribly homesick. We think of our loved ones and their sufferings. Will we ever see them again?

"It would make me happy, if you would write me.

Yours sincerely,

Peter Ringer."

*    *    *

# Chapter 30

# WHICH WAR NEXT?

PETER RINGER'S letter arrived shortly after New Year's, 1944. Presently came the Allied landing at Nettuno, and a little later the Fifth Army marched through the gates of Rome, pushing on toward Florence and Milan. General Eisenhower had assumed the invasion command in the West, and in one of the greatest and most successful military operations of history our troops landed on French soil, firmly entrenching themselves on the Normandy beach-head. The thrust to Paris was on.

Now Hitler and all the denizens of nazi darkness were facing their doom. Light began to pierce the suffocating blackout of all Europe. The *Goetterdaemmerung*, the twilight of the "gods" and of their idols was fast approaching.

For quite a while I had been completely out of touch with the other side. No mail was coming through any longer, and only privileged neutral travelers with diplomatic passports could afford to cross nazi borders.

My friend Basil Lipps, a Swiss businessman with important interests in the United States was in that rare category. A governmental mission brought him to New York just about D-day. Naturally I was delighted when one bright summer morning his cheery voice came over the telephone, greeting me as though we had last met only yesterday.

Basil had traveled by rail through southern Germany, via Paris to Spain and Portugal, and then by air across the Atlantic. To think that here was a man who had just emerged from behind the nazi fortress and could talk freely! I looked him over as if he were a rare animal when we got together at his hotel on Park Avenue. He had not changed since the days when we used to see a good deal of each other in Geneva. Short, stocky, and affable in his manners, he still wore his immaculate dark coat with striped trousers, thoroughly "continental" in his appearance.

"It's more than three years since I last talked to you," he remarked, "but it seems so much longer, doesn't it?"

"Indeed it does," I replied. "Like ages gone by! I cannot visualize present-day Europe at all. How much it must have changed!"

"Well, we've managed to keep alive — so far anyway!"

"Sounds as though you were not too sanguine about future prospects," I said.

Basil twiddled his thumbs, pondering. As a Swiss he was not prone to mince words, but I could sense disillusionment in his whole attitude.

"You wouldn't blame us, would you?" he said after a moment of silence.

"But isn't the end in sight? Certainly, the worst of this war seems over," I insisted.

"I wonder. It all depends on whether the end will really end all this misery. People in America take too much for granted, I'm afraid, when they look at Europe. As one of our papers said the other day, the Old World cannot be measured by its surface alone. Its depth is more important."

I concurred. "I know what you mean. There are problems which transcend the economic and political spheres. Traditions, modes of thinking, cultural values which defy simple formulas."

"Exactly. But over here, who stops to think about that?"

"Perhaps because we get to know so little of what goes on below the surface, so little of what you call the depth of Europe."

"That I grant you, but let me be specific. On my way through France, just a few days ago, I met a Polish underground worker who had escaped from a nazi labor camp with the help of German soldiers. He told me of many others who have had similar 'breaks.' Poles, Frenchmen, prisoners of war of every nationality who succeed in escaping because German soldiers, farmers and others civilians make it possible for them! Even some Allied airmen parachuting over Germany manage to return to their home bases with the aid of this German underground which looks upon them as friends rather than as foes and which cooperates systematically with the foreign 'slave' workers inside German territory."

"But aren't these exceptions to the rule?"

"Less so than you would think. There is an instinctive solidarity of the 'underground,' a European common front of decent people which cuts across all border lines in spite of the Gestapo brutes. That's something I find people in America unable to grasp. They haven't lived under a dictatorship. They cannot conceive of its meaning — which is that it rules *against* the will of the people!"*

"Yet, what you say indicates that if there is only a will to resist, resistance can assert itself. Why, then, do not these 'decent' elements act and throw off the yoke?"

"It's too soon. They aren't organized sufficiently as yet. There were some recent instances of Germans helping Jews to escape into Switzerland. They had to pay for it with long terms of penal servitude. What can unarmed people do against the two hundred thousand men of Himmler's SS?"

"That may apply to civilians. But what about the armed forces? They appear to fight for Hitler with as much fanaticism as ever."

"True. You must not forget, of course, that the younger men are imbued with nazi propaganda. Their minds are warped. All they know is what Hitler tells them, and that's a meager and 'screwy' enough diet, as you know. As for the older men, you must have read of Hitler's win-or-die orders at the Anzio beach-head, of the machine-gunners in the rear of the German advance columns near Nettuno, of wounded Germans shot by their own officers at the Russian front when they tried to surrender, of the executions of German officers in those same parts because they had suffered reverses, and of mutinies quelled by Himmler's firing squads, of the captured German soldiers who had been told that the Allies were torturing and killing their prisoners. . . ."

"What were your observations on your way through Germany?"

"There isn't much to observe. Apathy is widespread. Hardly

---

* Cf. Chapter 17 of Louis Lochner's book, *What About Germany?* (New York: Dodd, Mead & Co., 1942), where the author discusses the anti-nazi "front of decent people" at length.

anyone gives the nazi salute. The people are listless, sullen and resigned. Many are in blank despair. Only a few men are left. Women do the men's jobs. Now even station masters are women. Everywhere in towns such as Stuttgart, Pforzheim, Karlsruhe, huge signs are displayed on the ruins caused by Allied air raids. They read defiantly: 'Let them come!' But the current saying among the German people is: If only they do come! — meaning, of course, the Allies. All the German people really want, is peace although few dare say it aloud."

"And yet," I asked, "life goes on amidst the ruins?"

"After a fashion," replied Basil Lipps. "What sort of life is it when even the teen-aged and the crippled and the blind are drafted for forced labor in underground ammunition factories and on the bastions of front-line fortifications; when those left behind in the battered cities have to put up with homes deprived of heat, running water, gas and electric current; when ration coupons are no longer honored, and there are no means of transportation except, perhaps, bicycles; when ministers of religion are not even permitted any longer to visit prison inmates, and to hold services in larger churches because the Gestapo fears all assemblies of the people?"

"Dr. Charles Merriam, of the University of Chicago," I interrupted, "came out with a statement the other day that the greatest potential fifth column in the world is within the German borders. Would you agree with that?"

"Unreservedly. But at the present time it is a fifth column immobilized by fear. It is nonsense to say that the German people are silent in the face of the crimes committed by their rulers, that they support them willingly although they might stop them. Those who heap all the blame on the German people forget that they themselves are victims of the most brutal tyranny of modern times."

"The nations who were overrun by Hitler's armies won't make such distinctions, I am afraid. They will judge by what they had to go through at the hands of brutal conquerors."

"Undoubtedly, they will, but again, we profit little by generalizing. I noticed in Paris, for instance, how even the French were dealing differently with nazi 'elite' guards than with the rank and file German soldiers. After all, the French have their own quislings, men obsequious to Hitler and not a few of them, so they are not inclined to subscribe indiscriminately to the black and white theory. The scoundrels, fools and knaves are not in one camp only, and mass frenzies and phobias can be traced in the history of many a nation."

"So there is hope?"

"Well, it will depend entirely on the leadership. People everywhere can be led and misled. The question now is will we make a fresh start, based on the enlightened self-interest of us all. If not, sooner or later, there will be only one question: which war next?"

Basil Lipps would not be drawn out any further. As a neutral he was apt to be cautious and as a businessman he preferred to keep out of politics.

"You see, I have to go back," he explained.

"And remember," he said in conclusion, "that Hitler is one of the shell-shocked of the last war. There were many like him. Look at the result in lunacy! We will have to watch our step, if we are not to see a repetition of the horrors on an even greater scale. There will be shell-shocked aplenty after this war, too. . . ."

The next morning came the first report of Hitler's robot bombs. Basil's words rang in my ear: Which war next? Victory and peace are now in sight. But will they lead to the dawn of a new and better day? Will the twilight of the nazi idols teach a lesson? Or will it all have been in vain?

# Chapter 31

## BEYOND ALL FRONTS

THE events of July 20, 1944, had suddenly thrown a bright light on conditions inside the Reich. With defeats inflicted upon Hitler's armies on every front, a scapegoat had to be found. After the pattern of June 30, 1933, a new "Reichstag fire" was engineered by Himmler's men. Now it was the "reactionary clique of aristocratic generals" which was supposed to have thrown a bomb into the very headquarters of the "Fuehrer" — a convenient pretext, to do away with the remnants of domestic opposition.

When the news of the alleged plot came blaring over nazi shortwave transmitters I immediately thought of Goerdeler and his friends. If he was still alive, would he not be in immediate danger? I took it from his last letter that he had maintained his "underground" contacts with dissenters in the German army. They could provide him with a certain amount of protection. But now, the army itself was caught in a trap.

By the middle of August a message came through from Turkey, dated Istanbul, and again bearing as the sender's name the pseudonym Goerdeler had often used in his dealings with me.

The letter was brief and without signature. It was clear from the context that Goerdeler had not posted it himself. Someone was writing on his behalf, explaining in a roundabout way that Goerdeler had been in hiding for some time.

"We are safe for the moment," said the writer, speaking for my friend. "My wife is with me. The Gestapo has been searching our home, but they found no clue as to our whereabouts. With this new 'purge' in full swing, it would mean certain death if we were discovered.

"This, of course, is the end — the end of Hitler. It won't

be long now. No matter what they do, the nazis face complete defeat. But their gang will never acknowledge it. They will crash in a fearsome holocaust and will try to drag down into their pit all that there is left of civilization on this hapless continent. Even after their destruction, some of their cohorts who may go 'underground' will remain a constant potential threat to society.

"When the nightmare is over there will be nothing but ruins about us, moral and spiritual ruins even more than physical ruins, and the German people will weep as the sons and daughters of Israel wept at the sight of destroyed Jerusalem. I for one know that they will disown the evil deeds of their rulers once they emerge from their coma.

"Many will not realize it until the crash that the nazis have broken every rule of the game and thrown all morality and legality overboard. The awakening will be terrible, but at least there will still be the foundations of the past, which even the usurpers could not demolish completely, to build upon anew. Then German thoroughness and discipline which overdone, are a curse, may again be a blessing!

Beyond all the fronts, and in the midst of the havoc, I believe a solidarity of decent people was maintained in the spirit. Let us hope that it will stand the test when it comes to wiping out the black record, and to restoring lawful government. We who went through this long night know well that we must pay the penalty for what the evil men have done to all the world, and to ourselves. Let us remember though that the task ahead is a common responsibility.

"This generation has been through two terrible wars. They have cost humanity some eighty or ninety million in casualties, not to speak of the material ravages. The graves of the legions who lost their lives because of this collective madness are a mene-tekel of fearful portent.

"To my mind there can be only one conclusion: that our best efforts ought to be concentrated on preventing the recurrence of these horrible catastrophes.

"Two wars in one generation should teach the lesson — beyond all fronts!"

\*     \*     \*

Beyond all fronts. . . . These were the last words Carl
Goerdeler sent me. They were written a few days before he
lost his battle with the nazi beast. Now allied forces were closing in on the Siegfried Line. As Germany's military machine
crumbled, no one in her army could afford undercover protection any longer. Facing Himmler's men alone, Goerdeler
had only a small chance to escape, for over the years they
had accumulated a sizable file on him. They needed no further
evidence when they finally tracked him down.

After the alleged attempt at Hitler's life Goebbels announced
over the air that Goerdeler was a fugitive. Perhaps we will
never learn what happened during this last tragic phase when
a colossal manhunt was staged against all German patriots
and prices were put on their heads as though they had been
the worst of criminals. Nazi reports claim that Goerdeler
was arrested at an airport and that a woman air warden col-
lected the reward. Were his friends about to provide him
with a plane to escape to Sweden? Was he trying to find a way
of crossing the border into safety?

Roundabout information indicated that he was hurriedly
leaving German territory when he remembered that papers in-
criminating some of his friends had been left behind, and
that he returned to his home town Schneidemuehl to destroy
them. Others insisted that the Gestapo, by holding some of his
relatives and friends as hostages, forced the exile's return. But
all this may well be just hearsay.

Then, on September 11, came the official report over the
Berlin radio that Goerdeler and six other men had been
sentenced to death. Those who paid the supreme penalty with
him were Ulrich von Hassell, a retired ambassador known for
his personal integrity and exemplary moral character; Adam
von Trott zu Solz, a young diplomatic official who once had
served in New York; Dr. Paul Lejeune-Jung, a former Catholic Reichstag deputy and industralist of Cologne; Wilhelm
Leuschner, ex-Secretary of the Interior of the State of Hesse,
a socialist and trade-union leader who had languished in many
a concentration camp because of his loyalty to democratic
ideals; and Josef Wirmer, a Berlin corporation lawyer.*

Of course, the list was incomplete. This time, too, many were

---

* Cf. footnote on p. 176 regarding the seventh name on Goebbels' list.

delivered to the hangman's noose whose names Himmler did not even bother to reveal. Rudolf Nadolny, for instance, the former ambassador to Moscow, as straight a man as the Lord makes them.† Hundreds, thousands of others, anyone not known to be died-in-the-wool nazi, were proscribed and executed without due process of law.

The attempt on Hitler's life provided the pretext to do away with every conceivable opponent to, and possible substitute for the nazi rulers. Goerdeler, undoubtedly, could never have been a part of any terrorist scheme. He had expressed himself consistently against murderous nazi methods. He knew that two wrongs do not make a right, and he did not think killing Hitler would help the situation, because obviously it would only have made a martyr and hero of him in the eyes of the gullible masses, and might have provided the excuse for another stab-in-the-back legend to explain away the defeat. All along Goerdeler had felt that the German people had to empty the bitter cup of hitlerism to the last drop, that they had to go all the way in their misery if there was to be any hope of regeneration.

Most certainly, Goerdeler was not in the same category as the men who discovered Hitler's wickedness only after his armies were beaten! Goerdeler and his friends were rebels not only when Germany was suffering defeats. They had been rebels, too, while she was winning victories, and even before the war started. As a matter of fact, they had seen the light much earlier than so many of the appeasers abroad. What they had wanted was not just "a Badoglio," in the eleventh hour, but a hard and fast alliance of all the forces of justice in the world, including the front of decent people in Germany. They had laid the groundwork for such cooperation under the most adverse circumstances, under the permanent threat of bloody reprisals. To the very last they had hoped that those of one mind with them in other lands would come to their aid before it was too late to prevent a universal conflagration of unheard-of magnitude.

The Schachts, the Neuraths, the Papens, the Keitels and their ilk got their just deserts when at last they tried to throw

† Cf. pp. 137–139.

the gears in reverse and to get rid of the men whom they themselves, in their folly, had raised to power. Carl Goerdeler was not of their lot. Hassell, Leuschner, Nadolny and all the others were not. They, rather, were the ones who fought the good battle with clean hands from the first day. They were the Maquis leaders of Germany, and there is only this difference that their enemy was not an alien overlord, that it was an inner foe entrenched in the very citadel of their homeland's fortress.

Beyond all fronts, indeed, these brave men were our allies. They were the vanguard of a better Germany, the fifth column of democracy in Hitler's depraved domain.

Now Carl Goerdeler and many of his friends are dead.* In the eyes of the world, they have failed. Hitler, for the time being, has won the race which will end in the most terrible disaster of German history. When the German people emerge from the ruins, they will bless and revere the memory of the heroes of their "underground."†

---

* As this book went to press, unconfirmed reports received by radio intelligence from abroad indicate a possibility that Carl Goerdeler may still be alive and safe, and that the Berlin announcement of his execution is a falsehood. This would be wonderful news and would of course in no sense necessitate conclusions different from those reached in this chapter.

† The *New York Staatszeitung* of October 22 and 29 and November 5, 1944, carried the full original German text of a "political will" Dr. Goerdeler had left behind with an American friend in the course of his visit to this country in 1938. This is a remarkable document which no historian of World War II can afford to ignore.

# PART V

# PRIMER OF PEACE

*"The anger of man worketh not the justice of God."*

(*St. James the Apostle*)

*"I bear him no hate. Hate is no consolation beyond the grave. I bear his people no hate. For no people is to be held to account for what the wicked do. I affirm before God that no race has been created without beauty and without ugliness."*

(*"The Last Inca," radio drama of Morton Wishengrad*, "Lands of the Free" *series of NBC's University of the Air, July 11, 1943.*)

# Chapter 32

## THE GREAT CHALLENGE

THE issue is the peace, and whether this time we shall win or lose it. I submit that we can only hope to win it by sincere reconciliation, and by magnanimity in the Christian spirit.

But is not the risk of postwar "appeasement" far too big? Could not the beaten foe prepare for another war under the cloak of a restored democracy? Should the aggressor remain unpunished despite all the wrong he has done?

Let us get this straight.

Unavoidably, there will be retribution. But will it be vindictive, or corrective? Will it be punishment for punishment's sake, after the nazi pattern, or punishment for the purpose of bettering the culprit and re-integrating him in society? In other words: what motives will determine the peace? Will they be narrow-minded, or far-seeing? Pagan or Christian?

Eric A. Johnston, president of the United States Chamber of Commerce made a strong point in his commencement address at the University of Virginia, on June 14th, 1943, when he warned of the danger that the enemies' moral corruption may touch our blood stream. "Even where we are forced to use their methods," he said, "we must not allow their attitudes to pollute our philosophy of life. Victory will avail us nothing if in the process of attaining it we lose our perspective and permit the contagion of totalitarian amoralism to infect our own hearts and minds."

What else can this mean but that there must be a change of heart, a *metanoeite* in its deep Pauline meaning, before we can hope for a better world? Europe today is afflicted with what might be called "brutalitarian cancer." An operation is imperative, if the infection is to be checked. But should we kill the patient in order to perform it? Should we burn the

barn to kill the rats? It certainly is not the whole body that
is sick, and there is good reason to hope for recovery once the
evil growth has been eliminated. To defeat the evil forces in
the enemy camp is not enough, and to destroy the nazis is not
enough. We must try to get at the root of the evil which
caused this war. This evil merely found its expression in para-
noiac and destructive forces which could have been held in
check, had not conditions arisen where the floodgates broke
down, and humanity, on a rudderless ship, was swept down-
stream, straight into the whirlpool.

An understanding of this interplay of forces will help
materially in preventing the recurrence of conditions which
always and almost inevitably must lead to revolutionary outbreaks and military aggression. We cannot expect to bring
about fundamental changes in human nature, for it is a known
quantity in its negative as well as in its positive aspects. But
we can attempt to change conditions which have a bearing
on the manifestations of human nature. It is not likely that the
world as it is constituted will ever be entirely safe and secure.
We have reason to hope, however, that it can at least become
safer and more secure than it is now. For the best is the enemy
of the better.

To bring such improvement about we must try to gain an
insight into the symptoms of this crisis.

The present world struggle is predominantly ideological
in character. Often the fronts seem confused and overlapping,
but across all boundaries and around the whole globe we can
trace the basic issues at stake, which far outrank strictly
political or economic considerations of governments. The
battle is between pride and charity, between a universal acceptance of the brotherhood and dignity of man, and a frankly
proclaimed selfishness of individuals and groups who profess
an historical or biological materialism aiming at the very
destruction of the rights of the human person, and at the
uncompromising denial of the equality of all the children
of God.

It is not merely a struggle of our day, of this age and
generation; for our age is but a mirror of the past. The present
crisis of civilization is by no means accidental. If we think of
Francis Bacon, John Stuart Mill, and Auguste Comte, of their

empiricism and utilitarianism, of Kant's moral rationalism, of
Herbert Spencer's hedonistic relativism, and of Nietzsche's
"will to power, above good and evil," we can see that there
is an almost straight line linking together all the modern
naturalistic and pragmatistic philosophies which have weakened man's metaphysical outlook on life. We must not forget
that Machiavelli and George Sorel and Joseph Gobineau were
the teachers of Lenin as well as of Mussolini, that Hume and
Hobbes and Fichte inspired Houston Stewart Chamberlain,
the Germanized Briton who in turn became the spiritual
father of hitlerism.

Thus the "age of reason" has led to chaos. The schools of
thought which made all values relative, or strictly secular and
profane, developed of necessity an anarchical individualism.
The nihilistic philosophers were the torch-bearers of a modern
paganism which found expression in the totalitarian political
systems of our day. All the Western nations have had part in
that process. Their leaders of thought did not realize that
philosophies have a habit of percolating down to the lower
strata of society. Madmen like Hitler know how to carry them
to absurd extremes, for their own selfish ends.

Long before it was being uprooted socially, economically,
and politically, the modern world had apostatized morally and
intellectually. Because it had become spiritually hollow and
indifferent, brutal fanatics, irresponsible demagogues, and
naïve reformers easily found the mental vacuum thus created,
ideally receptive. Out of their despondency and their despair,
the masses were finally lured into accepting stones for bread.
In their helplessness they sought salvation in what has aptly
been termed the escape from freedom.*

Similar views were recently voiced by so eminent a Christian statesman as the Earl of Halifax, who said that "no
Christian can contemplate the present disorders of the world
without feeling how largely they are the outcome of the
continuous erosion to which the Christian traditions of society
have been subjected." It is, to quote the Ambassador further,
"the cumulative effect of this mass movement of thought
away from old anchorages" that has led to "the nazi phi-

---

* Erich Fromm, *Escape From Freedom* (New York: Farrar & Rinehart, 1941).

losophy, the culmination of this destructive process."* If this is true, and no student of history will deny it, a broad perspective in contemplating the causes and consequences of this, as well as the last war, would seem in order.†

Now comes the time once more when we can retrace our steps, when we can plan anew for a better world. After the schemes of chaos and despair have failed we need a convincing alternative, a real hope for the future. Reverting to the past and its errors is not the answer. The task resolves itself in an examination of conscience, for the lesson of this war is an object lesson, and there has probably never been as cruel, as grim a lesson in all history.

Europe, and large parts of Asia, are in ruins. These ruins are physical only in part. Mostly they are moral and spiritual. They are also social and economic. The European continent will emerge from this war an almost total wreck. In facing this disaster, is there anyone not moved to pity? Who would think first of retribution, rather than of healing the wounds, and of repairing the immense damage?‡

Charity ought to be our prime motive in approaching the issues of the peace. Ours will be a victory over evil, therefore

---

* Address at Laval University, Quebec, Canada, May 29, 1943.

† In calling for "a spiritual crusade" and for "a wide sweep of deep religious feeling" which, he says, "would enormously augment the possibility of gaining sound foundations for international peace," Dr. James Rowland Angell, President Emeritus of Yale University and NBC Public Service Counselor, has emphasized that "we have allowed our control over the physical world in which we live wholly to outstrip our control over the motives, the ideals, the beliefs by which men guide their lives" ("Education in a World at War," Penrose Lecture, April 24, 1942, reprinted in the *Proceedings of the American Philosophical Society,* July, 1942).

‡ In a letter to the editor of the *New York Times,* dated September 25, 1944, Professor John Hanna, of Columbia University, has pointed out that "at the end of this war Germany will have suffered more comprehensive devastation than any country in Europe. Her industries will be destroyed. Most of her cities are already in ruins. Her proportionate loss of man power will almost certainly be greater than that of any of her enemies. With the extirpation of nazi leadership, the demolition of German fortifications and the destruction of German armaments, Germany would be completely helpless for at least a generation, even if the Allied armies should immediately abandon the Germans to their own devices within their 1919 boundaries. When one considers that at the very least Germany will be entirely occupied by Allied armies, with a gradual rebuilding of German local government from which nazis are eliminated, any threat from German militarism becomes a chimera."

Professor Hanna's statement is corroborated by a recent O.W.I. report quoting *Die Nation,* of Zurich, Switzerland. This paper estimates that so far Germany has had 8½ million war dead, 63 million disabled, and 13 million homes destroyed. Twenty-one million Germans are seriously ill from undernourishment, and as a consequence of air raids, 18 million are homeless. Only two of the larger German cities (Breslau and Dresden) have escaped major damage in the bombings so far.

it must be a victory for good, a constructive rather than a destructive victory. A fresh start is needed, one contingent on mending the ways of the past. No nation can consider itself exempt from this task. Gangsterism does not come to the top in a community, if the citizens maintain an orderly government. Will the victors see to it that "it won't happen again" by establishing a true new order, a moral order which will be a bulwark against international bandits running amuck?

Not all those who concern themselves with the problems of the postwar world seem to be prepared for such an examination of conscience. Altogether too many are unwilling to mend their own ways while they are enthusiastically prepared to make others mend theirs. There are those who insist that the fresh start ought to consist in tearing to pieces the meager stability that will be left after these years of horror. Their schemes, if carried out, would amount to a change of political regime, but hardly to a change in method. It would substitute one name for another, but would in effect be just another escape from freedom.

We have seen in these past years how humanity was left stranded because it has relied upon itself entirely. Mussolini was not the only one insisting that a nation, and man, can *far da sé!* With many, a shallow materialism had replaced conceptions of a higher destiny of mankind. All the while the soul was left empty, the heart cold. Man cannot live by bread alone, not by the mere satisfaction of his material appetites. If he attempts to organize a society which is a mere end in itself, conceived as a man-made panacea, the result will be a sense of frustration, time and again. For there is no stability in things human. Man is no assurance to himself. Sooner or later everyone is bound to find this out. Then we lose our bearings, and grope in the darkness and feel lost, if we are without an "anchor" as the Earl of Halifax called it, a faith transcending ourselves.

The masses in postwar Germany were largely in this frame of mind until, after years of confusion and agony a leader emerged who claimed he could fulfill their longings. By regimenting them, he thought he would quench their thirst for stability. By telling them what to think, he hoped to relieve them of their sense of insecurity. But all of this was just

*Ersatz,* all a miserable substitute for a real faith of the spirit, a faith in a destiny beyond mere human destinies. This, the people soon found out, and because the new leader feared to be deserted by them once they were disillusioned, he put them in shackles. He shackled their bodies, but did not succeed in shackling, entirely, their minds and souls.

The oppressed people of Europe, once they are liberated, will not want to try new shackles, no matter how attractively forged. They have all gone through experiences which have made them realize that class distinctions and caste privileges mean little, if man is deprived of his innate dignity. So it is that in Germany today, it is not labor alone that fights the heroic underground battle against hitlerism. All strata of the population share in it, with the Christian churches in the very forefront where the fundamental issues of freedom, justice and liberty of conscience are at stake, and with members of the professions and a large sector of the educated middle-class forming the vanguard of revolt against the tyrants.*

---

* Dorothy Thompson has correctly pointed out in her book, *Listen, Hans* (Boston: Houghton-Mifflin Co., 1942), p. 75, that "not only the democratic and socialistic political parties and their materialistic ideologies, have most stubbornly resisted the totality of hitlerism, but the Christian Churches and the Christian ethos." This is fully confirmed by a report of the *Religious News Service,* published by the National Conference of Christians and Jews in New York which was received from reliable Scandinavian sources on June 11, 1943, disproving that the Christian churches in Germany had followed a policy of resignation and inactivity in the face of the nazi tyranny. An impressive array of facts was adduced to show the widespread cooperation of all Christians in Germany in opposing the nazi regime. The same agency reported on July 27, 1944, that "German churchmen played an active and vital role in preparing the ground for the final overthrow of Hitler." Previously, at the Princeton International Roundtable of Christian leaders, Dr. J. B. Condliffe, of the University of California, paid tribute, on July 9, 1943, to the Catholic and Protestant churches in Germany for their "valiant opposition" which Stewart W. Herman, Jr., a Lutheran Minister, had termed "one of the most amazing records of spiritual resistance in the face of political pressure that the history of Christianity has to offer." — *It's Your Souls We Want* (New York: Harper & Bros., 1943). — On May 22, 1943, the *New York Times* carried a dispatch from Berne, Switzerland, which said that in the Spring of that year there were estimated to be 3000 Catholic German priests interned and illtreated in the notorious Dachau concentration camp alone — Cfr. *The Persecution of the Catholic Church in the Third Reich* (New York: Longmans, Green & Co., 1940), an essential source containing documentary material smuggled out of Germany. — Strangely enough, James P. Warburg, former deputy director of the O.W.I., in his otherwise excellent article on "Can the Germans cure themselves?" in the *New York Times Magazine* of August 20, 1944, appears to subscribe to the theory that only "a few" among the German clergy can be counted as "true anti-nazis." In view of the evidence available from both Protestant and Catholic sources, indicating the tremendous opposition Hitler has had to meet from the churches, it is

Once it is all over, the people of Europe will want to work out their destiny in their own way. They have suffered too much to be desirous of new upheavals. They long for peace, peace, peace. They will be suspicious of Trojan horses, no matter of what color, and of all fifth columns, irrespective of their allegiance. They have had enough of the theorists and fanatics, and above all, they will want none of the philosophies of abject materialism which leave the human soul orphaned. They have endured so much inhumanity that they will seek one blessing only: to be human again. They long for a truly fresh start for *they* have learned the lesson amidst a carnival of blood and tears.

It is safe to predict that the exhausted masses everywhere will be more amenable to constructive, practical thinking than most outsiders expect. There are indications, for instance, of teamwork between the "underground" movements in France and Germany giving hope for an eventual reconciliation between the two countries. Also a growing solidarity among true believers of all religious denominations who see the necessity of a united front, irrespective of national and class boundaries, promises much for the future.

Once the barbed-wire fences artificially set up by secret police tyrants are torn down under the impact of the United Nations offensive, the world will hearken to new voices which cannot now penetrate the clatter of arms and the clamorous bawling of vicious propaganda. It will hear the voices of men and women who have borne a cross together and have suffered a passion that has shaken them in their innermost beings. These men and women were cleansed in the fire of expiatory sacrifice. They are now spiritually aware that the enemy is within, everywhere and that there are allies in all camps for the cause of true civilization. Only if they should again be disappointed, would there be a danger of their relapsing into that state of despondency and desperation which would breed a new disaster.

---

surprising that no greater credit is given them by observers such as Mr. Warburg who certainly must have access to authentic and comprehensive material. When the day of liberation comes for Germany, genuine anti-nazis, men and women who never have compromised with the forces of evil, will be found in larger number than any of us who had to watch most of the struggle from the outside could possibly anticipate. And the clergy, all true Christians, will be in their very forefront.

There is a realism which takes into account the positive as well as the negative elements of human nature, one that is not full of skepticism and distrust, but leaves room for a confidence that the evil forces can be checked and the good forces promoted. Woodrow Wilson's faith in humanity was not based on unpractical idealism. His hopes might well have been fulfilled, had the League of Nations only been given a real chance to live. Nationalistic selfishness, the blindness of statesmen, the lack of courage of parliaments, the lethargy of their constituencies caused its failure, but as a method of peace enforcement by peaceful means it was never earnestly tried. Not a single member was prepared to sacrifice even an iota of its presumed sovereign privileges and prerogatives, for the common good. By stubbornly protecting their ill-conceived self-interests and refusing the least compromise, all nations lost in the end.*

Are we to go back to where we started, and fail again? Should all hope be abandoned of achieving a just and durable peace by practical means? Should we admit defeat and revert to schemes of power-politics which, as history shows conclusively, are never stable and bound to breed new wars? Human society was "bitten" by war not only once, but hundreds of times and should be "shy," not twice as the saying goes, but forever of outworn and fallacious methods of peace enforcement. In the case of Europe, we cannot go back to 1939, or to 1914. The *status quo* is not acceptable to anybody, but neither is the *status quo ante*. There must be a new plan of international solidarity, to overcome anarchy and to slowly integrate the divergent tendencies of the continent in a higher organic unit: the United States of Europe. The Holy Roman Empire had originally been conceived as a united Christian Europe. The great ideal was perverted later on into one of world domination, but the tradition is still alive. Unity may yet come to pass, for now it is the only way.

The peace-makers might as well not think of peace at all, if they are unwilling to keep in mind the fluctuations of human destiny. Balance of power is a most insecure foundation of peace, and no settlements are tenable which are im-

---

* Cf. Appendix I.

posed by force alone. Hitler has supplied ample proof of that. He was doomed from the outset because the peoples he meant to subdue would throw off his yoke at the first opportunity. It will be the same story, if Hitler's methods are applied to a defeated Germany. And as for alliances that could keep her in check forever, was there any in all history that was not corroded by recurrent rivalries?*

Wilson was right. Clemenceau, the "Tiger," who wanted a ruthless peace was wrong. Once more the issue is whether the victors want an armistice as the substitute for a real peace. It is the concern of generations to come. It is the great challenge for us all.

---

* William Hard, one of America's most experienced journalists, whose authority in the field of international relations is unquestioned, in a masterful article entitled "Are We On the Wrong Road Toward Peace?" in the *Reader's Digest* of September, 1944, tells the story of how power politics has always failed. And here is his conclusion: "The whole history of the world for the last 130 years teaches us that, when the power of the great powers is made the primary thing and when it is exalted into being the one central pillar of peace, it crashes in blood."

# Chapter 33

# THE ONLY ANSWER

WHAT sort of peace?
For those who have experienced the ravages of war, for those who have suffered its immeasurable grief it will indeed be hard to think in terms of peace at all. They are the ones who will be moved by a wrath arising from righteous indignation over the diabolical evil wrought by the aggressors. With British Foreign Secretary Anthony Eden they will insist that "Hitler is not an accident, but a symptom." With him they will demand that "in kind and generous moments after the war," we never relax in our determination to "see the problem of Germany through until a complete solution is reached."*

But is there such a solution, and how could it be "complete"? It would only be that, if it meant the prevention of another war. The question is whether another war can be prevented by adopting nazi ideologies, by exalting a peace of the strong, a "peace of the conqueror," to use a typical Himmler phrase, "the peace which holds the beaten adversary under its heel?"†

It has been said that the great lesson of history is that men do not profit by its lessons.‡ Fortunately, there are exceptions to this rule. We know of at least one instance in modern history where statesmen were guided by the lesson of the past. The situation with which they were confronted was described by a contemporary in these terms:

"We have seen a great high-spirited nation rise in its might and burst the bands of its government. . . . We have seen it in the uproar of anarchy and atheism. . . . While thus weltering in its own blood and seemingly in its last agonies, we have seen it spring forward in the

---

* Speech at Glasgow, October 30, 1942.
† *Schwarzes Korps*, January 1, 1943.
‡ Rev. Jos. F. Stedman, *My Sunday Missal* (Brooklyn, N. Y., 1941), p. 245.

paroxysm of rage — bearing all before it with irresistible might, binding the surrounding nations in fetters, and spreading havoc and ruin far and wide. We have seen a young man of no name or family, an adventurer, a foreigner, who had fed upon the bread of public charity. We have seen him step forward, put his bit in the mouth of this furious nation, scourge it with his whip and goad it with his spurs. . . . We have seen them, all as one man, become the tools of his ambition, a mighty engine in his hands that has been wielded hither and thither at his pleasure. . . . We have seen this modern Alexander moving in his career of victory with astonishing rapidity, shaking the pillars of every government within his reach . . . and still adding nation after nation to the train of his conquests. . . . All this we have seen, already, and what will be the next act of the drama or what its catastrophe, Omniscience alone can foretell."

It sounds like a newspaper editorial of our day, does it not? And yet, it was written over a hundred years ago for the *Connecticut Courant* of October 25, 1809* The adventurer of whom it speaks is Napoleon who then was disturbing the peace of the whole world. His was the same vain-glory, the same conceit which once more in our age, as so many times before in human history, attempts to postulate the might of man.

Frederic von Gentz, an Austrian publicist of Napoleon's time tells us that the French Emperor was moved "by revolutionary immorality, by revolutionary propaganda and by a new system of revolutionary strategy raised to such superior force and supremacy that the rights of states and individuals, neutrality, alliances, treaties, justice, gratitude, humanity — everything was swept away."† The result was the situation which Talleyrand describes as follows in his "Memoires":

"France was invaded from all sides at once . . . by numerous armies, composed on the whole not of mercenaries, but of entire people animated by the spirit of hatred and vengeance. For twenty years they had seen their own territories occupied and ravaged by French armies; they had been forced to pay all sorts of levies; their governments had been insulted and treated with utter scorn; there was no outrage for which they might not have sought vengeance, and if they were resolved to satisfy their hateful passions, what means did France have to resist them?"

In spite of all the evil that France perpetrated under Napoleon's rule, Austria, Prussia, Britain and Russia, at the

* Quoted by Dr. Max Fischer, in *The Commonweal,* August 2, 1940.
† Ibid.

Vienna Congress of 1814, granted her an honorable peace with justice. It was a peace that lasted more than forty years.* Europe was indebted to the Duke of Wellington for this farseeing and generous settlement. At a stage of the Congress when punitive territorial demands were made of France by Prince Metternich of Austria and Prince Hardenberg of Prussia, the Duke wrote Lord Castlereagh, then Britain's Foreign Minister and later its Premier:

"If we ask France to make the great cession (of territories), we must consider the operations of war as deferred till France shall find a suitable opportunity of endeavoring to regain what she has lost; and after having wasted our resources in the maintenance of overgrown military establishments in time of peace, we shall find how little useful the cessions we have acquired will be against a national effort to regain them. We ought to continue to keep our great object, the genuine peace and tranquillity of the world, in our view, and shape our arrangements so as to provide for it."

As in the days of the Vienna Congress, there are again skeptical people today who feel that no risks must be taken. Filled with distrust of the enemy they propose a "strong" peace and want to see stern measures applied so as to check all potential aggressors, now and in the future. However, if I am not mistaken, an even larger number of people see eye to eye with the Duke of Wellington. To them, the peace to come, and the tremendous challenge which it entails for the victors, will be the great test of statesmanship. As at the time of the Vienna Congress, "the peace and tranquility of the world" must be the goal. To achieve it after the most cruel and devastating war in history, the leaders of all nations will be taxed almost beyond human endurance. Their wisdom and farsightedness will be put to a test. To use a phrase of Dean Inge, they must beware so that Philip Sober will not again be ashamed of Philip Drunk.

President Roosevelt sounded a key-note when he said in his Lincoln Day address of 1943, that "unless the peace that follows (the war) recognizes that the whole world is one neighborhood, and does justice to the whole human race, the germs of another world war will remain as a constant

---

* Cf. Guglielmo Ferrero, *The Reconstruction of Europe* (New York: G. P. Putnam's Sons, 1941).

threat to mankind." Former President Hoover stressed the same point in a recent article when he pointed out that "we cannot have both revenge and peace, but we must make such a settlement as will give the decent elements in the axis peoples a chance to lead their countries onto the paths of peace."*

Stewart W. Herman, Jr., former Pastor of the American Church in Berlin, and a member of the American Embassy staff in the German capital, since 1939, has stated bluntly that "there are only two ways to forestall an eventual revival of hitlerism in Germany: first, by annihilating the entire nation, or, secondly, by applying a truly Christian policy of forgiveness."† Such forgiveness (which Mr. Herman advocates) rests on the premise that the "good" Germans can be trusted to restore their country to the status of a worthy member of a world society.‡

There can be no argument with those denying these premises and insisting that Germans as a nation, or any other people as a nation, are innately evil beyond redemption. To these protagonists of nationalistic prejudices and the holier-than-thou attitude in international relations Dorothy Thompson has given a cogent reply:

"There are no 'good' and 'bad' nations. In all nations there are good people and bad people, good people who seek power and Satanic people who seek power. . . . The only thing that will make the Germans 'good' is their integration into a new 'good' European society. If they are dismembered, de-industrialized, subjected to foreign rule and foreign 'education,' they will not become better, they will become worse. If, on the other hand, our occupying forces assure order; if their factories are kept going; if their children are fed; if every democratic and orderly tendency is encouraged; if such a program offers them, as a State and as individuals, the

---

* *Colliers*, June 19, 1943. — See also Appendix IV.

† Stewart W. Herman, Jr., *It's Your Souls We Want* (New York: Harper and Brothers, 1943), p. 281.

‡ From England, the voice of Harold Laski has been heard stressing the same point: "Ever since Mussolini and Hitler began to plan the conquest of the world for the principle of 'counter-revolution,' the one rock upon which the prospect of a decent future of mankind could be set was the insistence that distinction could be drawn between those who were their avowed and eager disciples and those who were compelled in less or greater degree, to the acceptance of their tyranny." — (*The New Statesman and Nation*, London, February 21, 1942.)

greatest opportunities for happiness and security, they will go with us in that direction."*

If we assure order, if their factories are kept going, if their children are fed! Yes, and this applies to all our present enemies, then "they will go with us." Then we need no guarantees of good behavior, enforced by bayonets, no probation periods and no guardianships. If the victors encourage the peaceful and democratic, the "decent" people in the countries that will surrender, then the "other" Germany, the "other" Italy, the "other" Japan, which are strongly alive behind the façades of tyranny, though temporarily silenced by inhuman, despotic ruling cliques, will find it possible to come to the fore. Then these "better" Germans, and Italians, and Japanese will not be weak and impotent at all, but they will grow in strength like flowers grow on this good earth, in freedom and in the light of the sun.†

In the case of Germany (which is at the core of the present world crisis and may well become the core of peace) the forces which were alive in the days of the Weimar republic,

---

* *American Mercury*, June, 1943.

† A remarkable statement, corroborating this view, has come from no less an authority than former U. S. Ambassador to Japan, Joseph C. Grew, who said in a broadcast on August 28, 1943, under the auspices of the *N.B.C. University of the Air*:

"It is my belief that when Japan's war with the United Nations is over, even in their defeat, the great majority of the Japanese people will give a sigh of profound relief and will welcome a new orientation and outlook so long as they are not deprived of the hope of better things to come. Just as we must not deny to ourselves hope of better things to come, so we must not deny them or anyone else, that hope. I have no sympathy whatever with those who hold, as some people hold, that before we can find permanent peace in the Orient, the Japanese common people will have to be decimated. Man for man, the Japanese people at home in their own land are not inherently the wolves in human form which some of our own people who do not know them believe. Once caught in the military machine they are taught brutality, cruelty, trickery and ruthlessness as a matter of high strategy — in the mistaken belief of their leaders that these things will break the morale of their enemies and lead to victory. Little do those Japanese leaders seem to realize that such methods of warfare have an effect precisely the reverse of that intended. The Japanese people are going to learn to their sorrow that crime and brutality do not pay, and once they have learned that lesson, the finer qualities which I know that many of them possess will have the opportunity to come to the fore. The Japanese in their own Japan are naturally a thrifty, hardworking, progressive people with great recuperative powers. Throughout their history they have become inured to and have surmounted great disaster — disaster wreaked by fire and flood, by earthquake and typhoon. Given the opportunity, they will likewise overcome the ravages of war, even with their substance spent and their cities destroyed. Those recuperative powers must be wisely directed into the healthy channels of peaceful economic and cultural pursuits and away, forever, from military enterprise."

but were weakened and rendered impotent because of the blindness of the victors and the obtuseness of communistic as well as jingoistic elements at home — these forces can be counted upon again when the day comes, provided they are given effective support in their swaddling period, and not pushed around and discredited in the eyes of their own people.

There is, as Prince Hubertus zu Loewenstein, himself a leader of German democracy put it, "only one way of dealing with the German problem — to give German democracy a chance to develop."* If Germany's democratic and peace-minded elements are given a real chance this time, they will make popular government as workable as it can be in any other part of the world. Then the jingoes and sabre-rattlers who hate peace constitutionally will have no chance to emerge, but truly democratic forces will gain ground and take root. As in the case of the Vienna peace of 1815, a beaten foe who is not penalized and humiliated will ultimately be redeemed as a friend. Once more we will have an opportunity to show whether, in the words of Horace Walpole, we "know at once how to conquer and to pardon."†

---

* Letter to the editor of the *New York Times,* dated May 24, 1943.

† Quoted by George N. Shuster in his address on "The World After," to the Association of the Junior Leagues of America, New York, May 7, 1943 — an address, incidentally, which deserves to be read and re-read.

## Chapter 34

## THE CROSSROADS — THIS TIME

BY AND large we are all aware of what seems a desirable goal for the postwar world. Who would not be lured by the mirage of permanent peace? But when it comes to defining the method whereby it may be secured, opinions differ as widely as tastes in food. It is granted at any rate that at the end of this war a state of peace cannot immediately follow the cessation of hostilities. There will have to be an intermittent period devoted to the most urgent tasks of reconstruction and rehabilitation. How long such a period should last will depend in the main upon the state of affairs after the collapse of hitlerism, and on the extent of cooperation the liberated peoples will lend to the allied authorities.

The magnitude of the Allies' task is evident. There are some twenty different nations, some forty different races and some fifty different languages and dialects in Europe proper (excluding Russia), and its population totals 350 million. To restore the order of such a continent after this devasting war is an objective of overwhelming proportions. What with group vengeance, mass recrimination, border claims, demands for property adjustments, and destitution on a scale such as the world has never seen, it will be immensely difficult to avoid anarchy. In the former enemy territories, the occupying armies will be the only stabilizing influence. On their conduct and policies will depend how soon a relative normality can be restored.

The Balkan story of the Lord and the farmer could now be applied to all Europe. The farmer, it seems, was asked by the Lord one day to indicate the thing he most desired, and it would be granted, but with this one condition — that his neighbor was to receive twice as much as he. The farmer pondered for a while and finally said:

"O Lord, please remove *one* of my eyes!"

It is a prewar story, but ten times more apt now! It intimates how Europe is steeped in an agony of hate, jealousy, bitter rivalries and almost irreconcilable ambitions. Wishing one's neighbor evil instead of good has become so habitual over the centuries that it almost looks as though there were no cure for it. At the end of this war antagonisms will flare up again, and the wisest of leaders would not know how to please everybody. To create a federation out of those conglomerated hates will at first appear beyond the range of mere human capacity.

The immediate objective will have to be palliative. The patient will require infinite care, and the physicians, both those of the body and those of the soul, rather than being taskmasters and overseers will have to be angels of mercy, albeit with firmness of purpose and a clear determination to restore order. If they tackle the job in such a spirit, the cure may take hold sooner than can now be anticipated. In Germany and Italy, and the other axis satellite countries, it will be essential that the full and voluntary cooperation of the people be enlisted. The authorities of occupation can only be helpers, advisors and mediators. The Germans and Italians and Hungarians, and all the others, will have to work out their own salvation, and it will be a slow, tedious and painful process.

Punitive and discriminatory methods applied against the rank and file of the vanquished people will defeat the main purpose of ultimate pacification. Now the large majority of the German and Italian people blame Hitler and Mussolini for their misfortune. There let the blame rest! Nothing ought to be done which might appear as a belated vindication of the evil works of the dictators.

On the other hand the punishment of those guilty of brutalities and atrocities — nazi and fascist party members in responsible positions, quislings and government and military officials against whom evidence can be produced to justify their being put on trial — will provide an opportunity to remove the last remnant of doubt in the mind of the people with regard to the criminal guilt of their former rulers. If they could be tried in their own courts by their own countrymen, the moral and psychological effect would be excellent. Property restitution, too, would best be carried out by regular court procedure

under Allied supervision, and the full spotlight of publicity
should be thrown on all these measures in order that the
vanquished people can satisfy themselves with regard to all
the facts involved.

Beyond this, it would not seem wise to "rub in" the defeat.
After all, horse thieves are not mainly hung for stealing horses,
but that horses may no longer be stolen!*

*"We shall win this war and in the victory, we shall seek
not vengeance, but the re-establishment of an international
order in which the spirit of Christ shall rule in the hearts of
men of all nations,"* said President Roosevelt in a letter addressed to the Catholic Hierarchy of the United States at
Christmas 1941. The spirit of Christ! Do not these words
sum up all that can be said about the peace we are hoping
for? If it is truly a peace in the spirit of Christ, it will leave
nothing to be desired. Then President Roosevelt's promise
addressed to Pope Pius XII on July 10, 1943, the day of our
invasion of Sicily, will be fulfilled: "In common with all other
nations and forces imbued with the spirit of good will toward
men and with the help of Almighty God, we will turn our
hearts and our minds to the exacting task of building a just
and enduring peace on earth."

Once all axis territory is occupied, the peoples will be found
without leaders. Numerous would-be leaders will arise, representing as many factions as there are lobbyists in Washington,
and they will cater to the authorities of occupation. The
upsurge of the oppressed will be tremendous, and the world
will have its eyes opened when the full, appalling truth is
revealed of what has been going on inside the various axis
borders.

To feed the starving, to rehabilitate the refugees, to care
for the sick, to reorganize transportation and production —
these must come first. But then, a little later, our armies of
occupation will find that there are still many able people
around, going strong despite the privations of all these years;
men and women who did not betray their ideals of democracy
and Christian fellowship. Some may have been confined in
concentration camps or prison islands, others may just have
been in hiding, quietly biding their time and awaiting their

* Cf. Appendix IV.

opportunity when the madness of war had subsided. They will come forward with deep lines in their faces, carved by unspeakable sorrow, matured in battle, spiritually exalted through experiences that we who were not there cannot fathom. Perhaps some of them will ask us what we have done to forestall the tragedy which was theirs as much as ours. Have we helped to shorten or alleviate it — by wisdom in our political conduct? by an unselfish concern for our neighbor's welfare? by being his keeper when he was persecuted and maligned? by taking a stand against despotism and aggression even when it did not affect us, and we were far away, safe?

When the oppressors are gone, when the fiends are put out of the way, the nightmare will be over. Then punishment will have been meted out to those who were guilty of horrible crimes against all humanity, against Jews and Poles and Frenchmen, against Greeks and Norwegians and all the others, but also against millions of German and Italian men and women and children of whom so many will not survive the ordeal. Those left behind everywhere will need our charity and our help.

America gave it the last time. America will give it again. This time, even more than the last, when we did not see the job through, the obligation to win the peace will be incumbent on us all. If the immense suffering humanity now experiences is not to be in vain, we must learn the lesson of these thirty years and wipe the slate clean after this war. We must learn again that human hearts speak the same language everywhere, under the blue skies of Tuscany and on the banks of the Rhine no less than on the mountain ridges of Norway or Greece, and in the valleys of Tennessee.

Soon the awful, depressing black-outs will be of the past and the lights will be on again — after some two thousand nights of pitch-darkness! When the day of liberation will be at hand, and when the Yanks see the misery all about them, the pale and worn-out women, the undernourished children, the shambles in the bombed areas, no, then they will not think of punishment and brow-beating, but they will remember that the whole human race is one. Our men will be human. They will find that now is the time of compassion, now the turn of this generation to prove its worth.

# EPILOGUE

TO CONCLUDE and by way of summing up the arguments which have run through this book, directly and inferentially, I should like to relate just one more radio experience that stands out in my mind as symbolically significant.

All these years I have been intrigued by the use of broadcasting in the field of religion. The "pulpit of the air" is truly world-wide, but the surface has barely been scratched in making it an effective instrument of religious inspiration.

With this in mind, not long before the outbreak of this dreadful war, NBC undertook a broadcast from the Roman Catacombs.

There had been a good deal of headshaking when the plan was first suggested, just as on previous occasions when precedents were to be established. To make the bells of Bethlehem ring around the globe; to let the ceremonial silver trumpets of King Tutankhamen echo from the burial chamber of an Egyptian pyramid; to broadcast from the very Shepherds' Field where the glad tiding of good will to all men first went forth into a darkened world; to describe the French gypsies' pilgrimage to the crypt of Saintes Maries de la Mer — all these had been ventures into new realms of the radio art.

Many doubted the wisdom of placing a microphone in an ancient subterranean cemetery, and even questioned its propriety. But Dom Michael Ducey, of the Benedictine community in Washington who was then studying in Rome, and had originally conceived of the idea, allayed all misgivings. He, who is now the *spiritus rector* of the Liturgical Conference in Chicago, guided us wisely in bringing to life again one of the most dramatic phases of early Christianity.

It is known that the Catacombs were not only Christian burial places, but also great Roman cemeteries where rested the bones of many who had once acclaimed Caesar and Augustus.

The earthly remains of Christian martyrs were laid above the dust of those who may once have been the pupils of Cicero, the wives of consuls, and veterans of the Punic Wars.

I trust that at least some of that sense of historical continuity which the Catacombs impress upon every visitor was conveyed in our broadcast to the American fireside. This continuity we stressed by inviting as a participant in the program Bishop Joseph F. Busch, of Minnesota, a prelate who on the one hand hailed from a country of which ancient Rome had not so much as heard, and yet who may claim that his office came down through an endless chain of consecrating hands from the days when Tertullian was preaching fortitude to the Christian victims in the Colosseum.

We stood there, fifty feet beneath the soil of Rome, in the city of the dead, and the liturgical chant of the Benedictine monks reverberated through the labyrinth of tombs. America heard music familiar to the early Christians long before the days of Pope Gregory the Great, and perhaps the same words and the same melodies had been used by bands of harassed disciples who worshipped in the days of Diocletian and Marcus Aurelius.

In the soft glow of flickering candles the Bishop described the scene. The austere Roman pillars supporting the vaulted roof, the ancient inscriptions in Latin and Greek carved on the walls and floor, the religious emblems traced upon the marble slabs of the altar and on the primitive oil-lamps, the stone coffins richly adorned with sculptured biblical figures — indeed it was an impressive setting for a broadcast, carrying the listeners back to an age which, like our own, had its freedom of worship challenged by brutal tyrants. As Bishop Busch expressed it, "Bethlehem's cave and these crude Christian caverns seem alike in the message they bring and in the fidelities they inspire: both Christ and His first followers were unwelcome and unwanted in a pagan world."

While I stood listening, I reflected how out of the sacred darkness of the Catacombs shone the light of salvation. The martyrs won the good battle. By bearing the Cross, the Christian underground of old gained the Resurrection. Because so many lights pierced the darkness, the darkness did not prevail.

Once more today hate is triumphant, and the children of light have taken refuge again in catacombs that of necessity are deeper and vaster than even those of ancient Rome. Once more the oppressed and the persecuted keep the flame alive, the flame of the faith in an eternal destiny of man. It is a destiny not of this world, not of earthly victories, not of conquests in terms of armed might and political power. It is a destiny beyond mere human scope.

Would that we understood this symbolism so full of consolation! Once the light of peace shines forth, once Nemesis has overcome the evildoers, the legions who have suffered valiantly throughout these years of darkness will rise from the catacombs of our days. They will be witnesses to the darkness they found everywhere, but also to the light that was always in their very midst.

When victory is won, the struggle will go on. We must pray that strength be given to the champions of light who time and again, throughout all ages, and beyond all fronts, are called upon to be torch-bearers for renewing the earth, that peace may abide in the hearts of men.

# Appendix I

# LESSONS OF THE PAST

TO AVOID the mistakes of the past, we must first try to understand them thoroughly. In 1919 when the destinies of Europe could have been wisely shaped, the warning voices were not popular. Had they been heeded, World War II might well have been averted. Men like Herbert Hoover had anticipated the inevitable result of an irrational policy of retribution. He predicted, as was revealed many years later, that taking more than the surplus of Germany's economy, as the Versailles treaty-makers set out to do, would "plunge Europe into economic chaos."* He knew that with regard to the German people two courses were open — "either to hold continued repression or to nurture democracy and a new outlook to them."†

Neither course was chosen. Mr. Hoover foresaw the consequences. Writing in 1934 and describing the grievous mistakes of Versailles, he said:

"The reparations and controls stifled German recovery, and ultimately her collapse dragged the world into economic depression. . . . More important, the subsequent conduct of the dominant Powers contributed greatly to destroying the growth of democracy in the old enemy areas. The words of many British and French statesmen could be cited to show that this is understatement. There are a hundred incidents to prove it. For instance, in the Spring of 1932 I received appeals from the democratic leaders of Germany to aid them in securing a modification of certain parts of the Treaty of Versailles which were endangering the survival of the republic. At that time they were being pressed by the communists on one side and the nazis on the other. The dangers were real and great. The changes they desired in no way endangered any other nation. But the response of the French Prime Minister (Laval) to my urging through Mr. Hugh Gibson, who was acting as our Ambassador 'at large,' was: 'I will not consent to changing one atom of the Treaty of Versailles.' Six months later, Hitler overthrew the weakened democratic government."‡

All this happened as Mr. Hoover points out in another paragraph of

---

* *Saturday Evening Post*, November 8, 1941.
† *Ibid.*, November 15, 1941.
‡ *Loc. cit.*

this same article,* "although the acceptance of democracy was genuine with the men who had led the revolutions in those countries. . . . The hope of the world rested upon sustaining their strength."

Indeed, Vice-President Henry A. Wallace was right when he summed up the whole problem of the causes of this war with the words that "the seeds of the present world upheaval were sown in the faulty economic decisions that followed the war of a generation ago, . . . by the unwise management of the peace."† Mr. Wallace added the thought in his commencement address at Connecticut College on June 6, 1943, that after the last war "the Allied Powers had no interest in the glorious hopes among the German university youth of that day. They provided no incentive for education in democratic traditions and so the German youth fell into the hands of retired army generals, monarchist professors, and politicians."

To quote a voice from another camp, Senator Burton K. Wheeler, of Montana, shares Mr. Wallace's view with regard to the factors which brought about this war. "It is not enough," he said in a recent article "to annihilate Hitler. We must eliminate the factors which gave rise to Hitler. I myself am in no doubt that the social and political convulsions which shook so many countries, especially on the continent of Europe, during the pre-war years are primarily due to the economic distress of those countries, that is, to the debasement of their standards of living. . . . It is equally evident that the disastrous economic war which began almost immediately after the Armistice in 1918 and continued with slight intermissions for two decades lies at the base of the present conflict."‡

Those who were in the midst of the turmoil at the time agree fully with these conclusions. Let us listen to just one of the observers on the spot, Sir Andrew McFadyean, who was Secretary General of the Reparations Commission and of the Dawes Commission in Berlin during a five year period after the war. He can hardly be accused of bias.

"The statesmen of Great Britain and France," says Sir Andrew, "showed no realization of the callow nature of the republic or the difficulties under which successive German Chancellors labored. They did nothing by well-timed concessions to strengthen the parliamentary regime. Appeasement which became a word of ill-omen when it necessarily appeared indistinguishable from the product of fear, a movement of retreat, and a composition with blackmail and felony, was never wholeheartedly tried with republican Germany.

"Some major concessions there were, but not of a character or so timed as to compensate for past mistakes. Concessions in the reparation question, for instance, were little more than an acceptance of the inevitable when irretrievable mischief had already been done. Concessions

* "The First American Crusade," by Herbert Hoover, *Saturday Evening Post,* November 1, 1941.
† "Foundatons of the Peace," by Henry A. Wallace, *Atlantic Monthly,* January, 1942.
‡ *New York Times Magazine,* June 6, 1943.

in the occupation question were linked up with and dependent upon a fictitious final settlement of reparations and not granted on their own merits. It is at least possible that a gift to Bruening of a fraction of what Hitler was afterwards allowed to take without more let or hindrance than was contained in a diplomatic note of protest might have maintained him in power and secured the continued existence of the tottering republic."*

Those who believe that Hitler was the only cause of this war ought to remember that there are always causes behind causes. The law of causality applies to politics and economics as well as to physics! In this sense hitlerism was a result, not a cause. It was the consequence of piled up errors and mistakes, almost incredible in their magnitude. Herbert Hoover and Hugh Gibson have reached the same verdict in the light of their experiences over two decades.

"Hitler," they say, "was a product, not a cause. . . . We must constantly realize that the causes of modern wars arise only secondarily from wicked dictators or perverse peoples. They arise primarily from deep-seated and destructive dynamic forces. . . . The causes of this war, and of war in general, have been obscured by a tendency to oversimplification. . . . Wars result from no simple causes, but are the result of the interplay of long-antecedent dynamic forces."†

And so indeed they are. Stringfellow Barr states it correctly: "Rather than face anarchy, men will always accept tyranny."‡ Out of the post-Versailles anarchy arose the nazi tyranny. It arose amid a state of dissolution in society. All Hitler had to do was to center his attacks on its weak spots. It had been disintegrating long before he appeared on the scene — disintegrating from an economic bad conscience, from a chronic corruption of international morality and from the intellectual and spiritual sterility of those who should have been leaders.§

---

* Sir Andrew McFadyean, "Don't Do It Again!" *Atlantic Monthly* (Nov., 1941).
† *Colliers,* June 5, 1943.
‡ *Tomorrow,* October, 1942.
§ Cf. Thomas A. Baily, *Woodrow Wilson and the Lost Peace* (Macmillan, 1944); also Harry R. Rudin, *Armistice 1918* (Yale University Press, 1944).

# Appendix II

# THE PART FOR THE WHOLE

IN SPITE of Edmund Burke's warning that we should not "draw up an indictment against an whole people" and Dumas the Younger's insistence that "all generalizations are dangerous, even this one," there are a good many observers of the contemporary scene who find it difficult to make a distinction between the rank and file of the German people and their nazi oppressors.

President Conant, of Harvard, termed it "evident" in his Baccalaureate Sermon on June 7, 1942 "that man's nature is such that all men at some time, and some men at all times will feel and behave not as though they were true Christians but as though they were devils incarnate." Yet, so many of us are quick to condemn nations wholesale, heedless of historical precedents.

"Once upon a time," said John Chamberlain in a recent book review,* "the French were the scourge of Europe. Once upon a time Napoleon was the Antichrist. Going back beyond the early nineteenth century, who was it that murdered the French Huguenots? It wasn't the Germans. Who condemned men to death for disobeying the injunctions of mercantilist manufacturing? It wasn't the Gestapo. Even Sweden, gentle land of the Middle Way, once terrorized Europe. And when the Elizabethian sea rovers hi-jacked the galleons of old Spain they weren't exactly obeying international law."

The list could easily be expanded. Aristotle, twenty-three centuries ago, said that "Greeks owe no more duties to the barbarians than to the wild beasts," and we don't seem to have learned much since ancient Greek times! Recall the horrors of the Sicilian Vespers, in 1282, of the Jacquerie in 1358, or the murders of Henry III and Henry IV! Consider the era of Marius and Sulla in ancient Rome, or the Spartacist revolt and its suppression! Did not the French Commune, a century and a half ago, initiate a reign of terror under Mirabeau and Danton? What of the Belgian misrule in the African Congo, or the massacres of millions of Indians in this hemisphere, both North and South, by British, French, and Spanish colonists?

To speak of the present, could any one justify the unspeakable cruelties committed and countenanced by French authorities in the hell-hole prison colonies of Guiana, and more recently in their concentration

---

* *New York Times*, March 14, 1944.

camps for German refugees?† And can we entirely gloss over the conditions in Soviet Russia described by Ambassador Joseph E. Davies in his *Mission to Moscow** as "tyranny over life and liberty," as "the horrors of the 'terror' "?

And our own country? We certainly would not countenance a wholesale condemnation of the American people because we have had carpetbaggers and Kukluxers in our midst, or because some Americans kept slaves for more than two centuries, and others cheated and murdered Indians, because some indulge in bitter race prejudice and brutal treatment of minorities to this day.

Westbrook Pegler can suitably be quoted in this connection, without subscribing to all he says. In his column on June 29, 1943, he admitted bluntly that "racial and religious prejudice are common and characteristic" among Americans. "We are not a harmonious or homogeneous people, and we have a long record of sporadic blood-shed and burning in fights between groups who found themselves set apart by differences of race or religion or national origin in Europe. We have had the Ku Klux Klan twice, anti-Catholic and anti-Irish riots and church burnings, union terrors of more recent date equal in ferocity to any other outbreaks in our history and, with diminishing frequency and fury, conflicts between white and Negro Americans. Gentile persecuted Mormon and the Mormon in his turn got hunk with the Gentile. . . . We deceive ourselves, if we believe that bigotry and intolerance are un-American. Prejudice flows in the blood of humankind and we have never been free of it nor ever will be."

The late Gustavus Meyers' "History of Bigotry in the United States" (Random House, 1943) provides ample material proof for Mr. Pegler's assertions. In reviewing this book for the *New York Times,* Orville Prescott wrote on June 25, 1943: "In every nation the forces of barbarism and evil are always present. . . . When restraint slackens, men turn upon each other with infamous vituperation, persecution, torture and massacre."

On the other hand as Maurice Hindus has pointed out, one cannot see the French Revolution solely or chiefly in terms of the guillotine, the Cromwellian revolution solely or chiefly in terms of the massacres in Ireland and the American Civil War solely or chiefly in terms of the depredations of the Northern forces.† One might add that present day Russia, too, must be understood against the background of the past. But should not the same be said of Germany? Are not the Germans part Franks and part Slavs? Are not the British partly of Saxon descent? Are not the Czechs a mingling of Teuton and Slav? Is not the whole of Europe, for that matter, as Nietzsche said, a "race hodge-podge"?

---

* (New York: Simon and Schuster, 1941), pp. 400, 406.

† *New York Times Book Review,* October 26, 1941. Those in the holier-than-thou mood should read Arthur Koestler's *Scum of the Earth* (New York: Macmillan, 1941), to appreciate that nazi Germany is not the only country in the world where inhuman treatment was meted out to political prisoners.

It is in the light of such considerations that we are prompted to caution those who are all too willing to identify Hitler with Germany, and to make him the very symbol of that country. Yes, he is nazi Germany, the one possessed by an evil frenzy. Once the true Germany shakes off the hysteria, the neurosis, and awakens from the hazy and false romanticism which has led her on the road to crime, she will be herself again. The superficial critics who apply ready-made formulas to a complicated problem by asserting that the "good" Germans constitute an impotent minority, or those who admit with Herbert Hoover that the German majority is "no more militaristic than any other," but see them "constantly overridden by their warrior group"* might well be reminded of the remarkable editorial of the *New York Times* occasioned by Otto D. Tolischus' impressive account of how Japan was driven into war with the United States. It deserves extensive quotation.

"It is a tale" says the *Times,* referring to Japan's preparation for war, "of the terrorizing of a government by a band of military fanatics and ultra-nationalists, one group maddened by the lust of conquest, the other hynotized by the ruthless success of the nazis. . . . In normal times and circumstances, such a disclosure of the seizure of power by a gang of reckless men, bent on using a whole people to achieve their own violent ends, would seem too fantastic to be true. But the same thing has happened in Germany and Italy. We know that great nations can be taken over by gangsters in the most stupendous racket the world has ever seen. Modern techniques, the mass production of machinery of war, have made it easier to seize control of key industries and rule by force and terror. Savages armed with bombers and machine guns cannot only carry war into peaceful countries; they can bludgeon their own people more effectively than they could in the days when buccaneers had to depend on simpler weapons.

"What we are learning from this terrible reversion to barbarism is that there can be no order in the world while peoples can be shocked and surprised by the actions of rulers over whom they have no control. We see that some form of popular government in every country is the first prerequisite for the peace of all countries. This is not to say that democracy is the guarantee of law and security; but the example of Japan, plunged into a career of plunder and destruction by the will of a group of wild militarists, is another proof that no one can live in a world in which the will of such desperados can prevail over the reason and interests of nations. The earth is a shambles because men and war parties are acting as if they were nations, and the first of war aims and peace aims is to get rid of despotisms forever."†

Despotism! Indeed, that is a better word to describe what happened than "Prussianism" or "Fascism." The basic concept is the same, but the meaning ought to be made clear, now that the whole world has once more experienced it in all its horror. It is a meaning which holds

---

* *The Problems of Lasting Peace* (New York: Doubleday, Doran & Co., 1942), p. 17.

† *New York Times,* July 30, 1942.

true in all countries. If there is one obvious lesson of this war, it is that dictators and tyrants are bred by revolutionary conditions. Were it not for these conditions, there would be no tyrants, and given identical conditions, even under different material circumstances, tyrants are liable to come out on top in any land, at any time.

James P. Warburg, formerly deputy director of the O.W.I., has ably expressed this same view in an article for the *New York Times Magazine* of August 20, 1944. "Recently," says Mr. Warburg, "there has been a spate of books and articles written to prove that the Germans are paranoid, or bloodthirsty, or militaristic, or aggressive, and that they must, therefore, be rendered forever harmless by drastic means. These books have been written about 'the Germans' in exactly the same way as Hitler and his followers have written about 'the Jews.' They have been written as if all Germans were alike — or even the majority of Germans. They maintain that all, or nearly all, Germans have certain precise racial or national characteristics.

"It must be recognized that this is sheer nonsense. The Germans are a people composed of both 'good' and 'bad' individuals, just like any other people. The individual German is made up of 'good' and 'bad' components just like any other individual. He has the same instinctual drives, the same sort of conflicts between what he is and what he thinks he ought to be, as we have ourselves.

"It is undeniably true that in the eighty years since Bismarck's first war of aggression Germany as a nation has behaved with increasing lawlessness and brutality, and that under National Socialism she has sunk to a point of bestiality and criminal brutishness unique in modern history. During this period the 'bad' in German society has dominated the 'good' — increasingly so in recent years. But this is a matter of behavior and not of inherent racial or national characteristics, and other nations, too, have gone through decades of 'bad' behavior. The evil which has made Germany what it is today is inherent in all human beings of every race and every nation; in Germany it has become dominant, partly owing to the vicious circle created by the German people themselves and partly owing to the behavior of all Western society after World War I.

"To think intelligently and usefully about 'what to do with Germany' now, it is well to remember the mistakes made by the victorious Allies immediately after the conclusion of World War I: how the Army of Occupation and Allied Military Government operated in Germany immediately after the armistice; how, under the armistice terms, the local Governments established by the democratic revolution were everywhere turned out and the functionaries of the Kaiser's regime reinstated; how Germany was partly disarmed, but by no means demilitarized; and how the German armies on the eastern front were left in being, in order to aid the Allies in their attempt to overthrow the new bolshevist Government of Russia.

"It is well to remember how fear of the bolshevist revolution, and of its possible spread into Europe, dominated Allied thinking at the time and overflowed into a fear of any revolutionary movement; how, as a result, the Weimar Republic established the forms of constitutional democratic government, but remained a hollow shell; and how, in their anxiety to 'preserve law and order,' and in their fear of 'chaos,' the Allies played into the hands of the same reactionary clique which had led Germany into World War I and which was later to deliver the German people into the hands of Hitler.

"It is essential to recall that the most important mistakes made by the Allies after World War I were made long before the much-blamed Treaty of Versailles was written. And that the mistakes of Versailles, particularly the reparations blunder and the failure to revise the treaty, provided excuses for the subsequent behavior of German leadership, but did not create that leadership, since it was the old reactionary leadership already firmly reestablished in the social and economic structure of the German nation."

So much for Mr. Warburg's arguments, which we can adopt with only minor reservations.

There are those who persist in wholesale nationalistic prejudices, those who are unable to make distinctions, those who generalize wildly without the slightest consideration of historical facts. But there are others who are not swayed by emotion and approach the issues of this war and of the peace to come in a spirit of true charity. They are the ones who search their own consciences and think constructively of a better world along the lines of an encouraging pronouncement of our own government recently released in Washington.

"Our enemy," says this official statement, "is the German-nazi, the Italian-fascist, the Japanese militarist. At the same time our enemy is not necessarily the German, the Italian, or Japanese people. They have been misled by despotic rulers, by lies, by false promises, based on false premises. And when those among them who have brought this trouble on the world are eradicated, the people themselves must be permitted to know the fuller, better life that is our aim for all the world."*

---

* "When Radio Writes for War," O.W.I., Domestic Radio Bureau, 1943, p. 3.

# Appendix III

# PRUSSIANS AND GERMANS

THE Germans have been the object of all sorts of astounding analyses. Starting with Julius Caesar and Tacitus, and all through the ages to Madame de Staël and Carlyle, the German people — just as other people — have been scrutinized with real understanding as well as with prejudice. Although they belong basically to the same racial stock as most of their critics, as a rule they seem to have puzzled them no end. Emotion frequently gains the upper hand in these discussions, and many use the formula of "Prussianism" to explain the negative aspects of past and present German history.

In a preliminary way, these partisans of the "prussianist" theory ought to be reminded that Italy had her Machiavelli; that Richelieu was the first to use the *raison d'état* as a convenient pretext in politics (after a Machiavelli pattern); that Paul Deroulède, the founder of the Paris "Patriots League" of 1882, proposed a military dictatorship and preached anti-semitism with the same stubborn violence as the nazis; that Carlyle, three decades before Nietzsche, glorified "the hero who must not hesitate to use force," at the same time deprecating humanitarian instincts and expressing his scorn for democracy and parliamentary government; that Sir James Stephen in his book "Liberty, Equality, Fraternity" derided the "liberal weaklings" and demanded an energetic "élite" to top all governments, a course eloquently supported by William Lecky in his two-volume work on "Democracy and Liberty"; and finally that Thomas Hobbes taught the theory of the state as the Leviathan dominating all private life.*

Were all these men in England and France "prussianized"? Of course not, but their thinking, just as the philosophic thought of congenial contemporaries in Germany and other lands reflected certain basic and multi-faceted political and economic trends of human society. These trends are potentially present everywhere, and will break forth, elementarily, whenever a mass of people is in the frame of mind in which they can take hold.

Let us remember that some of the foremost leaders of what is considered "Prussianism" were not Prussians at all, in the geographic sense of the term. Take Field Marshal Yorck von Wartenburg who was of English ancestry; or General Gerhard von Scharnhorst, who though

---

* Cf. Carlton J. H. Hayes, *A Generation of Materialism* (New York: Harper and Brothers, 1941).

he served under Prussian colors, was born in Hanover (Prussia's arch-foe); or Field Marshal August Count von Gneisenau, who was of Austrian descent (and, incidentally, fought in the war of American Independence); or General Karl von Clausewitz who was of Polish origin.

Many great minds of Prussia have stood for self-government against narrow nationalism. Immanuel Kant, for instance, who described a political society relying upon the law of the jungle as "brutal degradation of humanity," and, in his essay on "Perpetual Peace" recommended a federation of democratic free states. The Prussian poet Heinrich von Kleist was a bitter opponent of militarism and of racial intolerance while Baron Karl vom Stein, the Prussian by choice, fought all his life for constitutional principles of representative government. He succeeded in breaking down the Prussian caste system and in abolishing serfdom.

Not all the Hohenzollerns were militarists! The first German Emperor, William I, for instance, after the Franco-Prussian War, spoke in a vein which would make him suspect to Hitler, were he alive today, for this is what he said at Versailles, less than four score years ago: "May God permit us and our successors to the Imperial crown to give at all times increase to the German Empire, not by conquests of war, but by the goods and gifts of peace in the path of national prosperity, freedom and well doing . . . to rule not in the spirit of the Emperors who during the Middle Ages wasted the strength of Germany in vain attempts to extend dominion over other nations, but with the sincere desire to constitute an Empire of peace and prosperity in which the people of Germany may find and enjoy what for centuries they have fought and struggled for."

The proponents of "Prussianism" as a theory may grant all these facts, but they will insist that it is the sum total, the whole philosophy of Prussian militarism which is at the core of the German unrest. How, then, can we explain that the element which set out to undermine the democratic constitution of Weimar was pre-eminently non-Prussian, that Bavaria nurtured hitlerism and Prussia an honest democracy? Were there not numerous non-Prussians in the Hitler camp from the early days of the nazi regime? And on the other hand, were there not political, financial and cultural leaders in Prussia, and military men in high places, who opposed the Papens, the Hugenbergs, and the Schachts? The answer is that the cliché of "Prussianism" just does not work.

# Appendix IV

# PATTERN FOR TOMORROW

CLEARLY, no one motivated by truly democratic ideals (and democratic ideals must be rightly understood as intrinsically Christian ideals) can favor a peace of revenge. The leaders of the democratic nations can but be in agreement with Pope Pius XII who set forth the essentials of a durable peace in his Christmas message of 1940 when he proclaimed the "Five Points" which have since been fully adhered to by the leading Protestant bodies in England and America, and which the Pontiff himself has summed up in the sentence that the false order of the dictators must be opposed by the greater conception of the moral order. This moral order is the only one that can last.

Pius XII has left no doubt in the minds of statesmen as to how he visualizes the peace to come. "Nothing," he said in his Christmas allocution of 1943, "would be more fatal than to leave unhealed centers of infection, from which tomorrow disastrous consequences could again arise. In a new organization of peace, of law and labor, the treatment of some nations in a manner contrary to justice, equity and prudence should not give rise to new dangers which would jeopardize humanity's solidity and stability. . . .

"It is indeed a virtue characteristic of wise minds who are true friends of humanity to understand that a real peace in conformity with the dignity of man and the Christian conscience can never be a harsh imposition supported by force of arms, but rather is the result of provident justice and a responsible sense of equity toward all. . . .

"You must not tomorrow stain that peace and repay injustice with injustice, or commit an even greater injustice. . . .

"Rise above yourselves, above every narrow calculating judgment, above every boast of military superiority, above every one-sided affirmation of right and justice. Take cognizance also of the unpleasant truths and teach your peoples to look them in the face with gravity and fortitude. . . .

"Do not ask from any member of the family of peoples, however small or weak, for that renunciation of substantial rights or vital necessities which you yourselves, if it were demanded from your people, would deem impracticable. Give mankind, thirsting for it, a peace that shall reinstate the human race in its own esteem and in that of history — a peace over whose cradle the vengeful lightning of hate and the unchecked desire for vengeance do not flash, but rather the resplendent dawn of a new spirit of world union which, sustained by the indispensable, supernatural help of the Christian faith, will alone be able to preserve humanity, after this unhappy war, from the unspeakable catastrophe of a peace built on wrong foundations and therefore ephemeral and illusory."

In England, too, strong advocates of a peace not born of vengeance have raised their voices. Foremost among them was the late Archbishop of Canterbury, Dr. William Temple, who said in an article published in the November, 1941, issue of "Fortnightly" magazine, that a durable peace settlement can only be undertaken "rightly, and without creating a resentment bound to result in another outbreak, if it is undertaken in a spirit of true justice and without any exploitation of the situation to the advantage of the victorious powers."

The Archbishop continued: "We must establish order in Germany and security for Germany. The fact that we have to do this will be a bitter humiliation. Nothing must be done which has further humiliation as its object, and everything must be done to stress that for a Germany which acts as a good neighbor there is open as good a life as for any people on earth."

Two-and-one-half years later the Archbishop of Canterbury and Free Church leaders in England offered an eight-point program for peace, and a warning against "breaches of basic human rights," which culminated in this sentence: "We must not lend ourselves in a mood of vengefulness to breaches of basic human rights, or to punitive measures against the entire German people which will be repudiated as unjust by later generations or will permanently frustrate hopes of peace and unity in Europe."

Responsible Christian spokesmen in the United States have expressed themselves no less unmistakably. Dr. Harry Emerson Fosdick, Pastor of Riverside Church in New York, for instance, said in the course of a sermon on March 21, 1943: "We say that Hitler did it. Yes, he did. But in a deeper sense we all did it. We, the nations who at the close of the last war had the greatest opportunity in history and muffed it." Or, to use the words of another eminent authority in the religious field, Dr. John C. Bennett, professor at the Union Theological Seminary in New York: "Germany is guilty so far as the immediate causes of the war are concerned, but we do not have to go far back to see that the conditions out of which this war has come can be traced to the sins and follies of all the great powers."*

Replying to Lord Vansittart in England who (though himself of German descent) condemns the whole German nation and denies that there is "another Germany" Dr. Bennett says further:

"Lord Vansittart is a very one-sided historian. He is mistaken in supposing that the permanent coercion of Germany (permanent from the perspective of our world of fast-moving events) would solve the

---

* "A Righteous Faith for a Just and Durable Peace," published by the Commission to study the bases of such a peace which was instituted by the Federal Council of the Churches of Christ in America in the Fall of 1942.

problem of European security. His plan would leave Germany in the end a center of resentment which could not but explode in the form of a third World War which it is his object to prevent. He does call attention to the fact, admitted by many Germans, that there are tendencies in German culture which are peculiarly favorable to the development of militarism and tyranny. But he sees these tendencies without observing either the strength of contrary tendencies or the factors in Germany's historical situation for which other nations share responsibility which made them the raw material of hitlerism.

"It is easy to blacken Germany the more by forgetting all that we have learned about the last war during our years of relative sanity. The present war has led many politicians and publicists to go back to the old idea that Germany was solely responsible for the last war. It would be wiser to recall the sober judgment of the British historian, G. P. Gooch, in 1925: 'The gradual recognition by informed opinion all over the world that the responsibility for the war was divided, and that the struggle was disgraced by atrocities on both sides, destroys the illusion that either the German or any other nation is afflicted with a double dose of original sin and is so far outside the pale of civilization that it must be treated as a pariah in the human family.' "*

Dr. Walter W. Van Kirk, Secretary of the Department of International Justice and Good Will of the Federal Council of the Churches of Christ in America is in full agreement with these views. In discussing what he terms "the corporate moral responsibility of all nations for the crisis in which we now find ourselves," he writes:

"It is downright pharisaism to charge one man or one group of men with the responsibility for this war or for any other war. . . . The moral guilt for the ghastly mess in which we find ourselves is a guilt shared by the leaders and the peoples of many nations. . . . If the World of Tomorrow is not to be a madhouse, there must be no peace of revenge. . . . The idea of crushing nations must be repudiated. The plain people of these countries, like ourselves, desire peace and justice. . . . There is not a people on the face of the earth possessed of a congenital lust for blood. . . . To make the acts of the psychopathic dictators the occasion for practicing vengeance upon the people who are themselves the victims of these same dictators is to cut ourselves loose from the mercy of God without Whose mercy all of us are undone. . . . This is not a war in which all the wrong is on one side and all the right is on the other side."†

Similar thoughts animated Madame Chiang-Kai-shek when she said, in addressing Congress in Washington on February 18, 1943, that "there must be no bitterness in the reconstructed world. No matter what we have undergone and suffered, we must try to forgive those who injured us and remember only the lesson gained thereby."

If any group of people might be justified in preaching vengeance it

---

* G. P. Gooch, *Germany* (New York: Charles Scribner's Sons, 1925), p. 353.
† *Religion and the World of Tomorrow* (Chicago and New York: Willett, Clark & Co., 1941), pp. 114, 121, 125 and 140.

is the Jews who have suffered so immeasurably at the hands of the criminal madmen immediately responsible for this war. Yet, the Central Conference of American Rabbis adopted a resolution on June 25, 1944 voicing the hope that the "victorious Allies will be guided by justice rather than by vengeance" in dealing with the defeated powers. These words reflect nobly the sentiment of the pledge offered with reference to the anti-semitic prejudice earlier in the year by Judge Joseph M. Proskauer, president of the American Jewish Committee, not "to indict a whole people by reason of the delinquency of any member."

It was a sentiment conveyed no less eloquently in the Memorial Day address of 1943, of the then Under Secretary of State Sumner Welles, in these words:

"I believe," said Mr. Welles, "That . . . justice (will) be done, inexorably and swiftly, to those individuals, groups or peoples, as the case may be, that can truly be held accountable for the stupendous catastrophe into which they have plunged the human race. But I believe that . . . no element in any nation shall be forced to atone vicariously for crimes for which it is not responsible, and that no people shall be forced to look forward to endless years of want and of starvation."

President Roosevelt himself underscored these views when he declared in his Lend-Lease Report of August 25, 1943 that "except for the responsible leaders . . . the people of the axis-controlled areas may be assured that when they agree on unconditional surrender they will not be trading axis despotism for ruin under the United Nations."

British political opinion, too, has been forcefully voiced in favor of peace terms that will stand the scrutiny of later generations. The notable editorial of the London *Times,* of February 29, 1944 is a good example. Opposing the dismemberment of Germany, this most influential British newspaper had this to say:

"Unless shattered and dismembered Europe can find some new vision that looks forward rather than back, some leadership bold enough to survey her needs and problems as a whole, her civilization will surely perish. . . . Germany cannot be allowed to become a cancer at the heart of the European organism. . . . After all that Europe has suffered in loss and devastation, there will be no room in the terms of peace for further policies of mere destruction."

The editor of the London monthly *Nineteenth Century and After,* in its June issue of the same year, was the spokesman of similar views when he advocated "occupying not as much, but as little, of Germany, and for as short a time as possible." He gave his reasons in these convincing terms:

"The occupation should be severely limited to one purpose — it should be a means (though not the only means) to secure fulfillment of the treaty of peace, especially of the terms relating to disarmament. There should be as little interference with German internal affairs as possible, least of all with education, and the Germans should be left to work out their own political system. If the National Socialist idea has no underground movement, no illegal army, no secret organization, no assassins and no martyrs, because there will be no one to murder and no one to inflict martyrdom; if it has no propaganda of its own because there will be no propaganda (masquerading as re-education) for it to counteract . . . it will be like an explosive in a vacuum — either it will, if detonated, explode harmlessly, or it will gradually decompose."

Sir Andrew McFadyean who was Secretary General of the Reparations Commission in Berlin during a five year period after the last war, and is therefore competent to discuss the subject, expounded exactly the same views in his *Atlantic Monthly* article of November, 1941: "Reform and the prevention of further crime, rather than retribution and revenge, must be our main objectives. Let us by all means exercise summary justice on the doctors and warders if their unhappy victims have not relieved us of the duty, but let our first concern be to throw open doors and windows; let us make it our painstaking object, by most skillful and scrupulously honest means, to reveal to the German people the truth about the history of Europe in the last ten years — and the unvarnished truth must include a recognition of our own shortcomings."

George Bernard Shaw spoke in a similar vein in the course of an interview with the *Associated Press,* on the occasion of his 88th birthday, July 26, 1944. "If Germany is defeated," said the playwright, "her relationship to her conquerors will be that of a wounded prisoner of war to his captors. When we take such a prisoner we give him every care and attention until he is cured, exactly as if he were one of our own soldiers. . . . That is how we shall treat Germany if we have any sense. . . . If we let loose our vilest passions and indulge in an orgy of plunder and revenge we shall pay for it and be sorry after."

All this sounds convincing enough. But will reason prevail? If it does not, the consequences will be disastrous for the whole world. William Henry Chamberlin, one of our most distinguished writers on foreign affairs, has summed up the alternative in an article for the *Christian Century* of March 29, 1944, in these words:

"Nothing permanent and positive can be built up in Germany except on the initiative and with the consent of the Germans themselves. . . . Any attempt to administer and police them as if they were a primitive savage tribe would end in a disastrous fiasco. . . . The German people must be not only permitted, but encouraged, to take responsibility for their own fate, to assume control over their own political destiny at the earliest feasible moment after the end of the war. . . . A republican regime can hope to succeed only if there is no territorial dismemberment of the country, no deliberate destruction of industry after the conclusion of hostilities, no foolish attempt to 're-educate' Germans from without, if there are no impracticable reparation schemes and if the difficult problem of 'war criminals' is handled with sanity and justice and discrimination."*

* Cf. the excellent brochure of this same author on "A Durable Peace in Europe" recently published by the Commission on a Just and Durable Peace, instituted by The Federal Council of the Churches of Christ in America.

The objective, then, is "to destroy the nazi ideology, not to be converted by it," to use a phrase of Professor John Hanna, of Columbia University. (*New York Times,* July 14, 1944.) If we fail in this, says Mr. Chamberlin, we will only sow "the seeds of a third world war," just as the seeds of the second one were sown when Lord Keyne's urgent warning was not heeded in 1919. What Keynes said then is certainly even more timely now:

"The policy of reducing Germany to servitude for a generation, of degrading the lives of millions of human beings and of depriving a whole nation of happiness, should be abhorrent and detestable even if it were possible; even if it did not sow the decay of the whole civilized life of Europe. . . . Nations are not authorized by religion or by natural morals to visit on the children of their enemies the misdoings of parents or of rulers." John Maynard Keynes, *The Economic Consequences of the Peace* (New York: Harcourt Brace and Co., 1920), p. 225.

In other words, to use a telling phrase of Father James M. Gillis, C.S.P. (Address on the *Radio Chapel* of the Mutual Broadcasting System, as reported by *Current Religious Thought,* Oberlin, Ohio, Oct., 1944), we must strive for a "victory beyond victory" — which means that we must seek not only the defeat of the enemy, but a new order that will rest on the stable foundation of justice for all mankind.

# Appendix V

# AND SO WE RESOLVE AGAIN —

### By DAVID LAWRENCE

(*Reprinted with permission, from the "United States News," Washington, D. C., October 1, 1943.*)

WE HAVE resolved through the Atlantic Charter.

We have resolved through the Mackinac Charter.

We have resolved through the Fulbright resolution.

We have resolved by presidential declaration to establish the "four freedoms" — freedom of speech, freedom of religion, freedom from fear, and freedom from want.

And we have said that there shall be no more war, that aggression shall cease and that righteous nations must band together to enforce the peace by every means at their disposal.

We have resolved again to make a "lasting peace."

But of what avail are these resolutions when the ones we made in the midst of World War I were rendered meaningless after the war?

Anybody drafting a postwar resolution or endeavoring to set up a charter for a world association or organization to maintain peace is respectfully referred to the speeches, resolutions, round-robin petitions, and pledges made by both Republican and Democratic spokesmen in and out of Congress in 1918 and 1919.

Anybody seeking to preserve American sovereignty as against a superstate is respectfully referred to the debates in the Senate preceding the vote on the League of Nations Covenant which was offered as an integral part of the Versailles Treaty.

And anybody wishing to find all the words and the phrases needed to commit the nations of the world — by national or international police force — to respect and preserve the territorial integrity and independence of every country, large and small, need only to read over again Article Ten of that same Covenant of the League of Nations.

We said all that could be said at the end of the last war. We adopted a constitution for the world which had in it every element of moral and physical obligation. The League Covenant remains today as splendid an expression of world idealism and practical collaboration as it was when President Woodrow Wilson submitted it to the Senate in 1919 only to have it rejected by a coalition of Democrats and Republicans though accepted by Britain and France, and, subsequently, by Russia and Germany.

It is not resolutions with high-sounding phrases that we lack.

We need only one word. And that word — translated into actuality — is Character.

Of what avail are resolutions, pledges, promises or virtuous expressions if our elected leaders are not ready as yet to sacrifice the customary political maneuvers of the hour, the personal ambitions, the quest for material gain and the greed for autocratic power which today as yesterday seems to dominate the governments of the principal allies in this war?

We are failing today not in the writing of general resolutions but to be frank about our postwar aims — frank with our own people or with the peoples of other countries.

Resolutions will not fool anybody — not even the American people who have learned something about foreign policy these past twenty years.

Nor should we be deceived by the cry that America has had no foreign policy for fifty or more years but that the British have had a foreign policy, and that the answer to the world's ills now is a new military and political partnership with Great Britain.

The truth rather is that the American people are not ready to accept imperialism and the British people are not yet ready to abandon imperialism.

We need no written alliance with Britain committing ourselves indefinitely to London's maneuvers in world politics.

We have given ample proof that we stand ready — as we have twice demonstrated — to give our blood to preserve the English-speaking civilization and culture as against militarism and tyranny and dictatorship.

We have gone to war twice now to try to make the world safe for democracy — safe for representative government, safe for nations to trade with one another in good neighborliness and mutual respect.

But what we have not demonstrated — neither we nor the British Governments of the past two decades — is that we have the Character to carry out our pledges, to make our words come true.

The first prerequisite to the attainment of Character is fundamental honesty. We must not only be honest with other peoples but honest with ourselves.

Why, for instance, do we persist in telling our own people that the League of Nations Covenant was a failure when it wasn't this document or its resolutions or provisions that failed, but the governments which, due to politics and pacifism at home, refused to support that League — we being the principal shirkers?

Why do we tell our own youth that the trouble last time was that we didn't march to Berlin in 1918, that we didn't drive home the lessons of defeat?

Is that honest?

For anyone who will take the trouble to go back to the files of our newspapers in 1918 will discover that the German Navy was completely defeated and what remained of it was ordered surrendered under the terms of the Armistice. It will be found, moreover, that the German Army was completely demobilized, and Germany was disarmed — forbidden to build big warships or war planes or submarines or to raise armies. A small police force of 100,000 men was all that was permitted Germany, and provision was made for an international commission — on which Britain and France were represented — to inspect and make public reports.

We also declared to the whole world the guilt of the German leaders and wrote this into the Versailles Treaty where all could read it.

These were the words. But what action did we fail to take to make the words mean what they said?

We — that is, the Allies — imposed an impossible reparations burden which the German people could not pay. France took all the raw materials she could extract from Germany as "payment in kind," and we left the struggling republic a ready victim of economic anarchy and chaos so that by 1923 Germany went through her terrible inflation — bankruptcy affecting the assets of 60,000,000 persons.

That was the year hitlerism won its first victory — not in 1933 when Hitler, as a symbol of a nation's desperate groping for economic equilibrium, assumed actual control. The German people had sunk to the lowest point in economic suffering. Any leader who promised any relief thereafter was welcomed.

And as Hitler saw that Germany needed more territory, needed areas from which raw materials could be stolen, the British and French Governments sat idly by and let him build up a war machine. From 1933 to 1939 — during six whole years of Hitler's regime — what did Britain and France and America do? What was behind the failure of Britain and France to see what was happening under their noses? They were close by — after all, we were 3,000 miles away.

Did the British and French resume the building of their own armament so as to enforce the terms of the Versailles Treaty? Did they stop Hitler when he marched into the Rhineland? Or did the British conservatives, anxious to preserve their capital and their trade, join with the British pacifists in ignoring the threat to the world of a new aggressor? Wasn't selfish materialism more important then to the British and to ourselves? Didn't we by action of both houses of Congress in 1935 pass a law, signed by President Roosevelt — just before his second election — which barred the weak democracies from getting arms from our shores? Of what avail are resolutions about world peace when, after winning a great war and disarming the enemy, the same victorious conquerors allow their military forces to disintegrate and refuse to allow their arsenals to be used to meet the threats of tyrants wherever they arise?

Was the British foreign policy in respect to Italian aggression in Ethiopia, in respect to Japanese aggression in Manchuria, in respect to the noble efforts of the loyalists in Spain, a foreign policy which thoughtful Americans approved then or now? Are we asked to accept that kind of Character-less behavior as the basis for a future alliance?

There were in Britain then, as there are today, men of Character who cried out at this chauvinism, who begged for a different distribution of economic resources in the postwar world of the '20's, for a peace built not on hate or revenge but on the Ten Commandments and the Golden Rule — based on tolerance, mutual respect, unselfishness and honesty.

We do not need more resolutions. We need humbleness, penitence, re-examination of our true motives, and the courage to rehabilitate the conquered as well as to restrain the conquerors.

We need, in brief, a dedication to spiritual values and a commitment not just to the words or rituals but to the actual practice of a Christian philosophy.

For the key to Character is to be found in confession of error and re-appraisal of our inner purposes and not in denunciations or hypocritical phrases.

We must honestly recognize that neither we nor the British nor the Russians are the sole proprietors of this world but merely temporary trustees obedient to the will of God. He created human beings everywhere equal — not to live under master rulers or a system of vested privileges. He gave to all persons irrespective of creed or color the right to enjoy freedom of opportunity — the inalienable right to life, liberty and the pursuit of happiness.

The Covenant of the League of Nations still lives. It is built into the existing treaty structure of 44 nations. Let the United States ratify that Covenant and pray God to give us the will and the courage to make it at last an effective instrument of international cooperation. For by its provisions, special alliances are expressly forbidden and, instead, the member nations are equally obligated to use all their force and resources as against aggressor states — whether members or nonmembers — to enforce and maintain the peace of the world.

# Index

Adlon Hotel, Berlin, 218, 231
Anglo-German Declaration, Munich, 226, 228
*Anschluss* (*see* Austria)
Anti-Comintern Pact, 163
Anti-religious Museum, Moscow, 247–248
"Appeasement" of dictators, in Germany, 63, 91, 113–122, 155, 157, 161–163, 164, 179 n.; at Munich, 212–225, 226–228; in Austria, 187, 190–191, 197; in Italy, 210
Armistice, 44, 281, 282, 284
Atlee, Major Clement, 223–224
Austria, vii, 4, 36, 39–41, 155, 156, 183–197, 212, 264
Austro-German customs union, 36, 39 ff.
"Axis," Berlin-Rome-Tokio, 163, 302
Bad Godesberg, conference of, 214–216
Badoglio, Marshal Pietro, 302, 325
Barth, Dr. Karl, 125
Bayreuth, 46, 117
Beck, General Ludwig, 224, 269
Belgium, vii, 155, 260, 277, 278, 287
Benedict XV, Pope, 7
Benes, Edouard, 51, 213, 217, 226
Bennett, Rev. John C., 374–375
Berchtesgaden, 187, 190, 214
*Berliner Tageblatt,* 11, 63, 109
Beuron monastery, 128–130
Blockades, of Germany, 7, 244, 250
Blomberg, General Werner von, 64
Bodelschwingh, Rev. Friedrich von, 176
Boeckmann, Dr. Kurt von, 136
Borah, Senator Wm. E., 43, 50
Bosch, Robert, 31, 259, 260
Brazil, 206, 208
Briand, Aristide, 17–18, 39, 51
Broadcasts (NBC) from overseas: Armistice Day, 292; Atom-splitting, 273; *Anschluss,* 192–194; Austrian "plebiscite," 195–196; Bethlehem bells, 360; Beuron monastery, 128; Bruening, Dr. Heinrich, 50–51; 53; Carol, King of Rumania, 46–47; Catacombs of Rome, 360–361; "City of Flint," 244, 249–251; Czech music (also Prague Ghetto), 227; Danish storks, 271–272, 274; Declaration of war, by Hitler, 233–236; Diamonds factory, Amsterdam, 276; Disarmament conference, Geneva, 50–52; Dollfuss, Chancellor Engelbert, 185; Dollfuss funeral, 185–186; Ethiopian war, 202–203; Finnish war, 257–258; Heidelberg University, 29–30; Henie, Sonja, 274; Hindenburg, President von, 59; Hitler, 69–70, 73–75, 202–204, 213, 217–218; Holland, invasion of, 278–279; Italy at war, 291–292; Juliana, Crown Princess, 276; Laval's arrest at Vichy, 305; Litvinov, two-way with Moscow, 244–246; Munich conference, 219–222; Oberammergau Passion Play, 144; Olympic Games, 164; Paderewski concert, 238–239; Paris riots, 285; Pius funeral, 206–208; Polish music (also Czestochova), 228–229; Schacht, Dr. Hjalmar, 33; Schuschnigg, Dr. Kurt, 189, 190; Siegfried Line, 252–255; "Silent Night, Holy Night," 184; Stratosphere flight, 46–48; Synagogue of Amsterdam, 276; Vatican Conclave, 208–209; Vesuvius eruption, 211; Vienna music, 184; Zeppelin flights, 75–76
Brown House, Munich, 220–222
Bruening, Dr. Heinrich, appointed Chancellor, 21; meeting with Ramsay McDonald, 38–39; struggle over reparations, 42–45, 48–49, 58, 119; at disarmament conference, 50–51; his personality, 30, 53, 88; relations with Hindenburg, 60–61, 89; resignation, 61; opinion of Hitler, 87–90, 93, 123–124, 177–178; views of church problems, 127; escape to England, 148; foresaw war, 154–155
Bullitt, William C., 280–281
Burckhardt, Dr. Karl, 230–231
Catholic Church, Germany, 12, 60–61, 76, 124–134, 225, 322; Italy, 201, 207, 291; Poland, 229
Censorship, Berlin, 233–236; Rome, 292
Chamberlain, Austin, 51, 210
Chamberlain, Neville, 191, 214, 215–219, 222–224, 236, 278
Chamberlain, William Henry, 377–378
Chiodelli, Raoul, 202–203, 205–206
Churches, under Hitler, vii, 76, 87, 109, 123–134, 146, 225, 266 n., 303–304, 316, 328, 346
Churchill, Winston, 155–156, 223, 274, 277, 278, 282, 291, 296, 298, 319
Ciano, Count Galeazzo, 203
"City of Flint," merchantman, 244, 249–251
Claudel, Paul, 284, 349
Cologne, city of, 158, 167
Columbia Broadcasting System, 45
Communism in Germany, 11, 16, 57, 63, 82–83, 117, 176
Concentration camps, nazi, viii, 77, 82, 82 n., 87, 91, 115, 117, 135, 140, 177; in Austria, 195, 314
Concordat, Vatican with Germany, 124, 126–127
Curtius, Dr. Julius, German Foreign Minister, 36
Czechoslovakia, vii, 155–156, 158, 191, 212 ff., 223 ff.; a "protectorate," 226–227

Daladier, Edouard, 219, 222, 260
Danzig, Free City of, 228, 230–231, 237
Dawes, General Chas. G., 20, 38, 43
Déat, Marcel, 231, 285
Democracy in Germany, 3–11, 13–14, 21, 64 n., 84–85, 87, 92–93, 115–117, 119, 263, 354–355, 364, 372
Denmark, invasion of, 270–274
Disarmament conference, Geneva, 49–52
Dollfuss, Dr. Engelbert, 184–186, 191, 201
Dunkerque, 280, 282

Ebert, Friedrich, President of Germany, 9–11, 58, 91
Eckener, Dr. Kurt, 75
Eden, Anthony, 260, 350
Eisenhower, General Dwight D., 329
England, 366; relations with Germany, 39, 157, 226, 236, 296, 297, 298; relations with France, 40–41
Ethiopia, ix, 157, 201–203, 206
Euthanasia under nazis, 127, 175–176

Fascism, Italian, 101, 199–201, 205, 302
Faulhaber, Michael Cardinal, 130, 133, 146, 225
Federal Council of Churches, 374–375
Finland, 239, 250, 257–258
France, vii, 4, 264, 366; relations with Germany, 16–19, 29, 43–44, 65, 155–156; reparation policies, 36, 39–40, 49, 158; relations with England, 40; nazi invasion, 279–281, 313
Franco, General Francisco, 302
Frankfort, city of, 7, 10, 158, 167, 169, 172, 254–255
Friday Circle, 31, 56–57, 84–85, 141, 151–152, 160–161, 173, 316
Fritzsch, General Werner von, 191
Funk, Walter, 56–57

Gainard, Capt. Jos. A., 250–251
Galen, Bishop Clemens von, 129, 133
Geneva, city of, 49–52, 202, 206
Genoa conference, 14, 18
Germans, air raids by enemy not resented, 256, 294–295; atrocities, reaction to, 263, 303 n., 323; cool to victories, 289–290; deserters, 319, 324; "Front of Decent People," 331 n., 335, 337, 354; Hitler's alleged fall celebrated, 325; moral sense, 328; Prussians and Germans, 371–372; President Roosevelt's view of German people, 309; unity behind Hitler doubted, 217, 219, 222–223, 225, 227–228, 233, 240–241, 262, 290, 294–295, 302–303; victimized by Hitler, 162 n., 165–168, 240–243, 263 n.; war-weariness, 217, 233, 236–237, 240, 253–255, 256, 289–290, 311–312, 332
Germany, Christmas in, 252–255, 303–304; elections in 1919 and 1920, 9; elections in 1930, 3; in 1932, 9, 60–62; in 1933, 83–85, 139–142; in 1934, 151; enslaved by Hitler, 69–180, 225, 227–228, 240–242, 262 n.; France, relations with, 16–19; monetary inflation, 19–20, 57, 263; "other, the," 17, 82 n., 99–100, 130, 132, 145, 152–153, 165–168, 177–178, 178 n., 217, 219, 222–223, 225, 227–228, 233, 236–237, 240–243, 258–261, 265, 289–290, 294–295, 301, 302–303, 306–307, 314–315, 321–324, 324 n., 327–328, 354, 367–368, 369, 370, 374; overpopulation, 18, 32, 263 n.; unemployment as cause of hitlerism, 30, 34–36, 42, 263, 263 n.; war guilt, 64 n., 375; Washington, relations with, 55; youth movement, 5–6, 8
Gestapo, viii, 82, 96, 101, 115, 120–121, 129, 131–133, 139, 148, 152–153, 165, 172, 173, 174, 175–178; in Vienna, 195, 214; in Prague, 227; in Poland, 240–241; "above the law," 242, 259, 260, 268; in occupied territories, 289, 290, 294, 295, 298–299
Gibson, Ambassador Hugh, 43, 363, 365
Glasmeier, Dr. Heinrich, 158–159
Goebbels, Dr. Josef, 12, 70, 82, 86, 96, 98, 100–101, 106, 109–111, 114, 132, 139, 141–142, 144, 150, 151, 153, 156; interview with, 159–160, 166, 168, 171, 177; at Sports Palace, 218, 233, 240, 243, 259, 264, 278, 303; puts NBC on black list, 305–306, 307
Goerdeler, Dr. Carl Friedrich, vii, viii, 258–271, 273, 275, 277, 282–283, 294, 298–302, 313, 321–324, 327–328, 334–338
Goering, Hermann, 86, 91, 95, 150, 162, 196, 213, 264, 277, 294
Greece, invasion of, vii, 302, 307
Grew, Ambassador Jos. C., 354 n.

Hackelsberger, Dr. Albert, 123–128, 146–148, 258, 269, 277
Haile Selassie, 202–203, 206
Halifax, Earl of, 163, 343–344, 345
Hammerstein, General von Equord, 142, 269
Hanffstaengel, E. F. Sedgwick, 69–70
Hard, William, 50–52, 53, 349 n.
Hassell, Ambassador Ulrich von, 336, 338
Heidelberg, 29–30, 91, 98
Heikenheimo, Dr., 257–258
Henderson, Sir Neville, 162, 233
Herman, Stewart W., 346 n., 353
Hess, Rudolf, 73, 124, 156, 213, 264, 307
Himmler, Heinrich, 91–92, 115, 117, 173, 176 n., 178, 221, 240, 242–243, 264, 266, 268, 289, 293–294, 299, 331, 350
Hindenburg, President, Paul von, appoints Bruening, 21; his presidential

terms, 58–61; his relations with Hitler, 78, 80, 83, 90, 92, 118, 148–150; his victory at Tannenberg, 233

Hitler, Adolf, Atrocities condoned by him, 241; in Austria, 188, 190–197; "Blood purges," 139, 144–145; Churches, persecution of, (see Churches under Hitler); Colonies demanded, 155; Conscription restored, 153–154; Danzig High Commissioner's interview with him, 230–231; Denmark invaded, 273; France and Belgium invaded, 279; German people conquered, 81–87, 122, 148, 165–167, 240–242, 262n., 290, 301, 315, 321–324; Holland invaded, 278; Impressions of, 74; Inaugurated chancellor, 92; Industrialists, dealings with, 63, 150–151; Monetary inflation capitalized on, 20; Munich coup, 14–16; Munich trial, 16; Relations with Mussolini, 198–199, 201; Norway invaded, 274; Nuremberg gatherings, 212–213; Reichstag intimidated, 9; Poland invaded, 238, 241; Product, not cause, 364–365, 374–375; Rhineland retaken, 155; Rise to power, 63–65, 64n., 70–75, 76–80; Rome visited, 202–205; Roots of his ideas, 264, 342–345; Shaw, G. B., sizes him up, 61; "Sports Palace" speech, 218–219; Stalin, pact with, 249, 257, 308; War declared, 234; War preparations, 155–156, 163, 178–180, 201, 224, 228, 231

Hitlerism in reverse, 318, 323, 324, 328, 341, 369

Holland, 155, 167, 188, 267, 276 f.

Hoover, Herbert, 43–45, 353, 363–365

Houghton, Alanson B., 43, 55

Hugenberg, Alfred, 10, 64, 78, 118

Hull, Cordell, 260

Ideologies, at bottom of war, 342–344

Innsbruck, 188–189

Isolationism in USA, 282–284, 301

Japan, 51, 163, 206, 284, 297, 354

Jewish Committee, American (see also, Rabbis), 376

Jews, persecution of, in Germany, VII, 71, 79–80, 86, 94, 96, 98, 105, 127, 150, 169–175, 240, 259, 263, 323, 331, 376; in Austria, 195–196; in Poland, 303n.; in France, 317

Junkers, 32, 65

Keitel, Field Marshal Erich, 337

Kellogg Pact, 49

Kunsti, Erich von, 184, 186–187, 192–193, 196

Lang, Anton, 144–146

League of Nations, 139, 201, 206, 239, 347, 379–380, 381

Leuschner, Wilhelm, 336, 338

Ley, Robert, 96–97, 151

Lithuania, 155, 228

Litvinov, Maxim, 217, 244–246

Lloyd George, David, 117, 155, 162

Locarno treaty, 17–18, 35, 39, 53

Ludendorff, General Erich, 7, 10 15–16, 58

Luxembourg, 278

MacDonald, Ramsay, 38–39, 118

Mackenzie, Philip, 209–210

Maginot and Maginot Line, 13, 39, 52, 191, 252, 284, 285

Marconi, Senator Guglielmo, 201, 207

Materialism, 345, 347

Maurin, General Louis, 156

McFadyean, Sir Andrew, 89, 364–365

Mein Kampf, 16, 101, 103, 108; in Austria, 186; on Russia, 251, 289, 319, 320

Memel, city of, 228

Molotov, 250, 257, 296, 307

Monarchy in Germany, 89

Moscow, city of, 244–251

Mowrer, Edgar A., 285

Mueller, Ludwig, "Reichs Bishop," 124, 125

Munich conference, 157, 212–225

Mussolini, Benito, 139, 143, 184, 198–211, 277, 343; interview with, 99–100; relations with Hitler, 198–199, 201, 205–206, 217, 219, 233; attacks France, 290; downfall, 325–326

Mutual Broadcasting System, 381

Nadolny, Rudolf, 137–139, 337–338

Narvik, 275, 277

National characteristics, 264–265, 332, 353, 366–370

Nazi movement, IX, 1; armed forces, control of, 87, 149–150, 153–154, 180, 190–191, 224, 242–243, 254, 259, 269, 270, 300–301, 331; art concepts, 107, 219; in Austria, 188, 192–193; "blood and soil" theories, 60–65, 70; book-burning, 98–100; cell system, 192–193; church persecution (see Churches under Hitler, also Catholic Church, Protestantism, Vatican); demogogic methods, 72, 76–77, 85; early phases, 10–11, 20, 34–36, 41, 44, 49, 54; hostage executions, 176, 242, 303n.; intellectuals antagonized, 100–109; relations with labor, 77, 96–97; press regimentation, 81, 109–111, 132; propaganda methods, 34–36, 77, 85–86, 117, 140–141, 157, 160, 168, 173, 212, 220, 237, 240, 262, 276, 307, 327, 331; radio and stage regimentation, 110; storm trooper ban, 61; youth, 98, 101–106

NBC (National Broadcasting Company, New York), 27, 29, 33, 45, 135, 164, 207, 222, 239, 245, 253, 276, 282, 285, 305, 339, 354n., 360; blacklisted

by Goebbels, 305–306
NCWC (National Catholic Welfare Conference) News Service, 299
Neurath, Konstantin von, 64, 116, 119, 138, 191, 337
Niemoeller, Rev. Martin, 125, 132, 133
Nietzsche, Friedrich, 99, 265, 343
Norway, 250, 265; invasion of, 256–275, 319
Nuremberg nazi convention, 212–213

Oberammergau, 46, 144–146
Oldenburg, state of, 131
Olympic Games, 164, 168
Oran, battle of, 296
Oumanski, Konstantin, 245

Paderewski, Ignace Ian, 238–239
Pan-Germanism, 6, 265, 266n.
Papen, Col. Franz von, 61–64, 78–79, 91, 122, 126–127, 145, 150, 173, 185, 337
Paris, city of, 284–286, 329
Peace, errors of past and plans for future, ix–xi, 49, 51, 64n., 341–362, 363–365, 373–378
Pétain, Marshal Henri Philippe, 281, 302
Piccard, Prof. Auguste, 46–48
Pilsudski, Jos., 156, 237
Pius XI, 13, 126, 128–129; relations with Hitler, 204–205; funeral, 206–208; interview with, 207–208
Pius XII, 208–209, 358, 373–374
Poincaré, Raymond, 13, 20
Poland, vii, 156, 227–232, 236–239, 240, 241, 269, 303n.
Portugal, 308
Power politics, 3–4, 64n., 156, 348–349
Preysing, Bishop Konrad von, 133
Price, G. Ward, 156, 220
Probst, Adrian, 322
Proskauer, Judge Jos. M., 376
Protestantism in Germany, 12, 124–125, 176, 346n.
Prussianism, 65, 264, 351 f., 368, 371 f.

Quisling, Vidkun, 275
Rapallo treaty, 14
Rath, Ernst vom, 170
Reichstag, elections (see Germany), fire, 82, 117, 262
Reparations and war debts, 13, 20–21, 35, 37–38, 42–45, 48–49, 55–56, 58, 62, 64n., 263
Revolution, French, 263, 264, 367; German of 1918, 7–9
Reynaud, Paul, 280
Rhineland, occupation by French, 13; by USA, 38; re-occupation by Hitler, 155, 157, 163, 190
Ribbentropp, Joachim von, 162, 191, 226, 236, 278, 297
Roehm, Ernst, 145
Rome, city of, 291, 329
Roosevelt, Franklin Delano, 84, 118, 186, 217, 219, 282, 290, 297, 305,

309, 310, 319, 352, 358, 376
Rothermere, Lord, 117, 142
Rotterdam, city of, 274, 278, 303n.
Royal, John F., 207–208, 305
Rudnicki, Edmund, 230, 238, 258
Rumania, 46–47, 307
Russia, Soviet, 14, 160, 162, 163, 228, 239, 244–251, 257, 264, 296, 300, 307–308, 311, 313, 367
Sackett, Frederick M., 43, 54–56, 89
Salzburg, city of, 183, 184, 187, 190
Sanctions, under treaty provisions, 13, 201
Sauerbruch, Prof. Ferdinand, 175–176
Schachleiter, Abbot Alban, 124, 125, 129
Schacht, Dr. Hjalmar H. G., 33, 41, 56, 73–74, 122, 151, 337
Schleicher, General Kurt von, 61–63, 145
Schmidt, Paul, 215–216
Schurman, Jacob Gould, 29, 55
Schuschnigg, Chancellor Kurt von, 184n., 186–191
Siegfried Line, 252–255, 336
Sports Palace, Berlin, 77, 217–218
Stalin, Josef, 228, 245, 246, 249, 257
Steinhardt, Lawrence A., 249
Stresemann, Dr. Gustav, 17, 18, 34, 51
Sudetenland, 212–217, 226
Sweden, 174, 250, 366
Switzerland, 5, 158, 167, 169, 171, 174, 183, 258, 277, 298–299, 301
Tardieu, André, 13, 20, 39
Thyssen, Fritz, 10, 63, 122, 151

Unconditional surrender, 319, 376
"Underground" movements, Christian, 361–362; European, VII–VIII, 331, 347; German, VII–VIII, 120–122, 134, 139, 258–271, 294, 295, 301–302, 328, 330–331, 332, 337–338, 346
Vatican, 127, 156, 206–211, 291
Versailles treaty, 4, 13, 17–18, 34–35, 61, 72, 117, 154, 284, 369, 379 f.
Vichy, 121, 305
Vienna, 183–184, 188
Vienna Congress, 352, 355
Villard, Oswald Garrison, 38–39, 41
Von Wiegand, Karl, 15, 19, 22

Wallace, Henry A., 364
Walzer, Archabbot Raphael, 129
Warsaw, city of, VIII, 228–229, 232, 238, 274, 303n.
Wellborn, Mary Moss, 202–203
Wilson, Ambassador Hugh, 26
Wilson, President Woodrow, 347, 349
Wirth, Chancellor Joseph, 9, 35, 42, 115–117, 256
Wolff, Theodor, 11, 27, 63, 109
World War I, 6–7, 57, 370, 379
Wurm, Bishop Theophilus, 131, 133
Young plan of reparations, 38
Yugoslavia, 199, 307